Transnational Democracy

'In an age of globalization and new supra-national forms of social, economic and political organization, the geographic form of democracy is a pressing issue. In this book clearly articulated, fresh, stimulating, often exciting, arguments are brought to bear on this question in a compelling manner. For all those interested in the future of democracy and of the state, this is essential reading.'

Professor Kevin Cox, *Ohio State University*

How are political communities and forms of democracy being changed and challenged by globalisation? How might they be reshaped to enhance rather than reduce the limited democracy traditionally available? What are the possibilities for extending representation across borders, and developing participatory democracy more amenable to border crossing?

Contemporary globalisation is simultaneously weakening national democracy and increasing transnational governance beyond democracy's traditional scope. However, this book, while critical of conventional state-bound representation and the present lack of transnational democracy, views globalisation as presenting new democratic opportunities as well as threats. It deals substantially with democratisation in the European Union – the world's most advanced transnational polity but well known for its 'democratic deficits' – and with institutions of global governance and the comparatively neglected question of political agency for establishing transnational democracy. It provides a radical critique of globally hegemonic liberal democracy and neo-liberal globalism. It argues that national democracy has to be strengthened, rather than bypassed, and articulated with new forms of democracy which cross national borders.

Transnational Democracy is a multi-disciplinary volume and covers a variety of perspectives including liberal internationalism and more radical approaches. It will interest students and academics across a range of disciplines, including political science, human geography, international relations, international political economy and sociology. It is grounded in studies of the USA, Canada and Eastern Europe as well as the European Union, and work on Australasia, South-East Asia and other developing regions.

James Anderson is a Co-Director of CIBR, the Centre for International Borders Research, and a Reader in Geography at Queen's University Belfast.

Transnationalism

Series editor Steven Vertovec, University of Oxford

'Transnationalism' broadly refers to multiple ties and interactions linking people or institutions across the borders of nation-states. Today, myriad systems of relationships, exchange and mobility function intensively and in real time while being spread across the world. New technologies, especially involving telecommunications, serve to connect such networks. Despite great distances and notwithstanding the presence of international borders (and all the laws, regulations and national narratives they represent), many forms of association have been globally intensified and now take place paradoxically in a planet-spanning yet common arena of activity. In some instances transnational forms and processes serve to speed up or exacerbate historical patterns of activity, in others they represent arguably new forms of human interaction. Transnational practices and their consequent configurations of power are shaping the world of the twenty-first century.

This book forms part of a series of volumes concerned with describing and analyzing a range of phenomena surrounding this field. Serving to ground theory and research on 'globalization', the Routledge book series on 'Transnationalism' offers the latest empirical studies and ground-breaking theoretical works on contemporary socio-economic, political and cultural processes which span international boundaries. Contributions to the series are drawn from Sociology, Economics, Anthropology, Politics, Geography, International Relations, Business Studies and Cultural Studies.

The series is associated with the Transnational Communities Research Programme of the Economic and Social Research Council (http://www. transcomm.ox.ac.uk).

The series consists of two strands:

Transnationalism aims to address the needs of students and teachers and these titles will be published in hardback and paperback. Titles include:

Culture and Politics in the Information Age
A New Politics?
Edited by Frank Webster

Transnational Democracy
Political Spaces and Border Crossings
Edited by James Anderson

Routledge Research in Transnationalism is a forum for innovative new research intended for a high-level specialist readership, and the titles will be available in

Transnational Democracy

Political spaces and border crossings

Edited by James Anderson

Routledge
Taylor & Francis Group

LONDON AND NEW YORK

First published 2002
by Routledge
11 New Fetter Lane, London EC4P 4EE

Simultaneously published in the USA and Canada
by Routledge
29 West 35th Street, New York, NY 10001

Routledge is an imprint of the Taylor & Francis Group

© 2002 James Anderson for selection and editorial matter; contributors
their contribution

Typeset in Baskerville by Taylor & Francis Books Ltd
Printed and bound in Great Britain by MPG Books Ltd, Bodmin

British Library Cataloguing in Publication Data
A catalogue record for this book is available from the British Library

Library of Congress Cataloging in Publication Data
A catalog record for this book has been requested

ISBN 0–415–22342–3 (hbk)
ISBN 0–415–22343–1 (pbk)

Contents

viii   *Contents*

Contributors

Professor John Agnew (Geography, University of California at Los Angeles) has written extensively on politics, geo-politics and international relations. Previously Professor of Geography at the Maxwell School of Citizenship and Public Affairs at Syracuse University, his publications include *Place and Politics*; *Mastering Space: Hegemony, Territory and International Political Economy* (co-authored with Stuart Corbridge); and more recently *Geopolitics: Re-Visioning World Politics*. He has worked on regional politics in Italy, and gave the annual Hettner lectures at the University of Heidelberg in 2000 on Europe's borders and the nature of the 'international'. One of North America's leading political geographers, his current interests include problems of political territoriality and spatial scale.

Professor James Anderson (Geography, Queen's University Belfast) was previously at the Open University and the University of Newcastle upon Tyne, where he held the Chair of International Development. He is now a Co-Director of CIBR, the Centre for International Borders Research, and a Reader in Geography at Queen's University Belfast. His research interests are in political territoriality, nationalism and transnational integration. Publications include edited collections on *The Rise of the Modern State* and (with James Goodman) *Dis/Agreeing Ireland*. He is currently working on the sectarian geography of everyday life in Belfast as part of the ESRC Violence Research Programme.

Dr James Goodman (International Relations, University of Technology Sydney) completed a doctorate and worked as a Research Fellow at the Open University on the national conflict in Ireland in the context of European integration. He has researched issues of regionalism and democracy in the European Union, and since moving to Australia he has developed his research interest in transnational social movements and international solidarity campaigns, particularly in the western 'Pacific rim'. Currently he is involved in an international collaborative research project on 'globalisation from below' which also encompasses Latin America. He is co-editor of *Dis/Agreeing Ireland*, and his other publications include *Nationalism and Transnationalism* and *Single Europe, Single Ireland?*

Dr Douglas Hamilton (Geography, University of Newcastle upon Tyne) has written on the Northern Ireland economy, strategies for industrial growth and comparative regional development in Europe. An economist, he has worked for local government in Britain and was employed by the Northern Ireland Economic Council before doing a doctorate at the University of Newcastle upon Tyne. He has done collaborative research on cross-border co-operation with the Economic and Social Research Institute in Dublin, and his thesis was on the economics and politics of cross-border development in Ireland. He also has research interests in Cuba and is active in the Cuba solidarity campaign.

Professor Joachim Hirsch (Political Science, University of Frankfurt) is one of Germany's leading political theorists. He has published extensively on social movements, regulation theory, and the state and system of states in capitalism. He has served as a board member of various international aid and human rights organisations, working in the 'Third World' as well as in Europe. His publications in English include two which deal directly with transnational democracy, international regulation and national states (*Review of International Political Economy* 2(2) 1995, and 5(4) 1998).

Professor Anthony McGrew (International Relations, Southampton University) was previously at the Open University. His research interests include the democratisation of transnational bodies, and globalisation as challenging the conception of 'society' as a bounded entity. He has written on these and related themes, and is the editor of *The Transformation of Democracy? Globalization and Territorial Democracy*, co-author of *Global Transformations: Politics, Economics and Culture* (with David Held, David Goldblatt and Jonathan Perraton), and co-editor of *The Global Transformations Reader* (with David Held). Currently he is engaged in research into the normative and institutional foundations of global governance.

Professor Michael Newman (London European Research Centre, University of North London) is Director of the Centre and has published widely on political and historical subjects, including French politics, political biographies, economic policy making and European integration. He is the author of *Harold Laski: A Political Biography*, *Socialism and European Unity* and *Democracy, Sovereignty and the European Union*; and co-editor of *Mitterrand's France* (with S. Mazey) and *Democratising the European Union: Issues for the Twenty-First Century* (with C. Hoskyns). He has researched a political biography of Ralph Miliband, and his current research interests include democratisation in Europe which goes beyond institutional politics.

Professor Liam O'Dowd (Sociology, Queen's University Belfast) is Director of CIBR, the University's Centre for International Borders Research, which was set up in 1999 and in 2000 organised a major international conference on cross-border co-operation involving policy practitioners from across Europe. He has researched the sociology of European integration, the national conflict in Ireland, and the role of intellectuals in nationalist movements. His publications include *Whither the Irish Border? Sovereignty, Democracy and Economic Integration in Ireland*; and he is co-editor of *Borders, Nations and States: Frontiers of Sovereignty in the New Europe* (with Tom Wilson), and a special issue of *Regional Studies* (with James Anderson) on 'State borders and border regions'.

Dr Joe Painter (Geography, University of Durham) has written extensively in political and cultural geography. His past research has focused particularly on the geographies of the state, regulation, and local and urban governance. He is the author of *Politics, Geography and 'Political Geography'*. He has been involved in collaborative research on the relationships between space, territory, democracy and citizenship, with particular reference to regions in the European Union and Eastern Europe, a project in the ESRC Europe Research Programme.

Professor Bhikhu Parekh (Politics, University of Hull) is a leading political theorist and authority on the politics of multiculturalism. He has been Deputy Chair of the UK's Commission for Racial Equality and was appointed to the House of Lords by the Labour Government. Lord Parekh has published widely on political philosophy, colonialism, humanitarian intervention, and national and European identities. His recent publications include *Rethinking Multiculturalism: Cultural Diversity and Political Theory*, and he is co-editor of *The Decolonization of Imagination: Culture, Knowledge and Power*. His current research interests include national identities in multicultural societies and the possibilities of separating political identity from state territory.

Professor Kees van der Pijl (International Political Economy, University of Sussex) was previously Reader in International Relations at the University of Amsterdam. He has done extensive research into the internationalisation of capital, focusing particularly on the formation of transnational social classes in Europe, their links with North America, and the role of elites in contemporary globalisation. His pioneering *The Making of an Atlantic Ruling Class* was published in 1984, and more recently he published *Transnational Classes and International Relations*. His current interests include the transformative potential of 'international cadres' in business, professional and cultural fields.

Professor Peter J. Taylor (Geography, University of Loughborough) is the founding editor of the journal *Political Geography* and one of the founding editors of the *Review of International Political Economy*. He has published widely on world system theory and the geography of politics in global, national and regional contexts. His books include *The Way the Modern World Works: World Hegemony to World Impasse*, and multiple editions (1985–2000) of the standard textbook *Political Geography: World-Economy, Nation-State and Locality*. He is currently leading a major research project on producer services and world cities.

Acknowledgements

The idea for the book was first conceived at a colloquium on 'The Possibilities of Transnational Democracy', held at the University of Newcastle upon Tyne and the founding conference of the Centre for Transnational Studies, set up jointly by the Departments of Geography and Politics. I would like to thank the University for funding and supporting the colloquium, and my former colleagues there, especially Professor Kevin Robins in Geography and Dr Barry Gills in Politics, for helping me organise it. Collective discussions in the colloquium informed the later work of rewriting some of the papers as chapters and commissioning some entirely new ones. Above all, I am very grateful to all the contributors for writing their chapters and responding positively to editorial requests. Thanks to Dr Steven Vertovec, Director of the ESRC Transnational Communities Research Programme, who supported the original proposal as general editor of Routledge's Transnationalism series; and thanks to the anonymous referees who commented creatively on the proposal; to Heidi Bagtazo and Grace McInnes at Routledge who brought production of the book to fruition; and to Róise Ní Bhaoill who had to live through it all.

James Anderson
March 2001

Introduction

Border crossings increase, old political spaces are disrupted, new spaces are created, and there are 'democratic deficits' all round. Global changes threaten conventional forms of democratic representation and accountability. They open up new needs and possibilities for democratisation beyond the territory of national states. They raise challenging questions about the future of national democracy and the need for new forms of democracy in transnational arenas. Pushed up the political agenda by the 'anti-globalisation' or 'anti-capitalism' movement, these issues span the spectrum of scales from global to local.

So how are political communities and forms of democracy being changed? And how might they be reshaped in ways which would enhance rather than reduce the limited democracy traditionally available? What are the possibilities for extending representation across borders, and developing participatory democracy more amenable to border crossing?

The issues are economic, cultural and social in the widest sense, not narrowly 'political'. And this volume is appropriately 'inter-disciplinary', the contributions covering political geography, international relations, political theory, economics, history and sociology. Their empirical groundings are also suitably wide-ranging, encompassing the USA, Canada, Australasia, South-East Asia and other parts of the 'Third World', and Eastern Europe, as well as European Union countries. Some contributions are grounded in practical experience, work in government or cross-border bodies, non-governmental organisations or transnational movements, on international aid and international solidarity campaigns. In theoretical terms, they cover a range of different perspectives from liberal internationalism to international socialism. The issues discussed are highly contested, including the very definition of democracy itself, the balance and relationships between representation and participation, between majority rule and minority rights, liberty and equality, formal institutional processes and practical democratic freedoms – of speech and information, rights to work and to organise, to food, shelter and security.

The book has three main strands:

- general, overarching questions of national and transnational democracy in the context of accelerated globalisation and the dominant neo-liberalism;

- democratisation in the European Union), perhaps the world's most politically advanced transnational entity but well known for its 'democratic deficit'; and
- institutions of global governance and the comparatively neglected question of political agency for establishing transnational democracy.

Democracy, national and transnational

Chapter 1 outlines how neo-liberal globalisation has increased the pressures for transnational democracy. It emphasises the need for a less state-centric democratic theory, and poses the question of agency. It discusses the limited nature of democracy in capitalism and its partial and contradictory separation of 'politics' and 'economics'. This is reformulated as the presence/absence of democracy and is posited as a precondition of economic globalisation, political sovereignty and the global hegemony of the liberal democratic state. The problems of creating transnational democracy are seen to be rooted in national territoriality, and it is argued that sovereignty has to be redefined in popular rather than state territorial terms.

The theme of disjuncture or contradiction between territoriality and globalisation is pursued further in Chapter 2. As Bhikhu Parekh points out, territory enjoys unprecedented importance in the modern state where there is an almost unique privileging of territorial identity over other identities. But now globalisation is also reaching unprecedented levels – at least compared to most of last century – and the resulting difficulties for the modern state suggest that it needs to be reconstituted. There is a clash between its vision of a culturally homogeneous polity made up of a single 'people' or 'demos', and the growing reality of ethnic mixing and cultural diversity. This is seen in how India and Canada deal – or fail to deal – with multiculturalism; and it exemplifies the general argument that the state itself needs to be radically rethought in order to develop political structures adequate to our times.

The national state is still the main arena for democracy and likely to remain an important one, but the limited nature of national democracy is also brought out in Chapter 3. John Agnew demolishes the idea that federalism, as in the USA, provides an appropriate model for transnational democracy (as in a 'United States of Europe'); and in doing so he also points out how liberal representative democracy is limited, and intentionally so. This is telling on two counts. First, the USA is the classic example of the dominant liberal democracy, in some respects more democratic than European liberal democracies such as the United Kingdom. Second, the chapter was drafted before George W. Bush 'won' the US presidential election when only around a quarter of the US electorate voted for him. We are talking here about the limitations of liberal democracy even if its rules were observed and before considering the illegalities of politicians or the alienation and apathy of voters.

Europe: community, regions and conflict

The next four chapters focus on the European Union (EU), a pioneering association of national states with innovative 'multi-level' and 'cross-border' forms of governance and a 'sharing' of sovereignty. Initiated after the Second World War to prevent a recurrence of national conflict in Europe, it has more recently been motivated by global economic competition, especially with the rival trading blocs centred on the USA and Japan. It can be seen as a creation of globalisation, but also – as in its 'Fortress Europe' manifestations – a bulwark against and barrier to further globalisation. Although more democratic than rival blocs, and now with its own directly elected European Parliament, its persistent 'democratic deficit' poses a threat to its legitimacy. This could seriously compromise, even reverse, its own project of 'deepening and widening' European integration, though there are of course reasons of principle as well as pragmatism in being concerned about the 'deficit'. Mike Newman in Chapter 4 gives a comprehensive overview of the issues involved. He specifies the democratic principles and priorities; the multiple problems involved in democratising the EU; and what genuine democracy would entail in substantive rather than simply formal terms.

Discussing the territorial dimension, Newman asks whether the 'nation-state' remains the *primary* location for democracy? Or is the EU a more appropriate site? Or do neither of these suppositions make sense? Another possible site, the sub-state region, is considered in Chapter 5, but Joe Painter opts for 'multi-level citizenship' which combines the different territorial levels or spatial scales, rather than choosing between them. He analyses the ambiguous link between citizenship and cultural identity; the nature of European identity and its bearing on a transnational European citizenship which would support ethnic and cultural difference; and the important but problematic implications of the regions for multi-level citizenship.

European integration means that state borders within the EU are becoming more permeable, with increasing cross-border processes, linkages and co-operation. In effect there is the growth of cross-border regions and cross-border political communities which both facilitate and require cross-border democracy. In Chapter 6, Liam O'Dowd examines the changing nature of EU borders and the emergence of cross-border regions for what they tell us about Europe's development. He identifies three overlapping moments in its recent history of transfrontier regionalism: the pioneering cross-border regions of the early post-war period; the EU's planned 'widening' to the East; and the ongoing 'deepening' of the Single Market.

In this context, Chapter 7 focuses on the creation of innovative cross-border institutions in Ireland which are in step with the 'deepening' of EU integration. But they have the additional impetus and primary objective of resolving a national territorial conflict which is unresolvable in terms of the nationalist disagreements, claims and counter-claims. James Anderson and Douglas Hamilton locate the underlying causes of such conflicts in fundamental socio-spatial problems of representative democracy (returning to some of its limitations discussed in the early chapters), as well as the more specific problems of nationalist doctrine and its overblown promises. They argue that territorial partition and internal consociationalism or 'power sharing' are generally national *non*-solutions which predictably fail. In contrast, these problems could be transcended by a transnational strategy which combines cross-border representative and participatory democracy with mobilisation around *non*-national disagreements and other more substantive issues.

Global governance and agency

Another four chapters 'go global', investigating the possibilities of democratising global institutions and assessing potential agents of democratisation. Much of the discussion about transnational democracy – or rather lack of democracy – has a global focus on the neo-liberalism of the contemporary world order. It attracts much more attention than the EU for instance (although the latter is also essentially neo-liberal), and the most dramatic attention from transnational social movements in the 'anti-globalisation' or 'anti-capitalist' alliance. This is partly because of the substantive issues of inequality and poverty in the 'Third World', global problems of the environment, arms sales, the nuclear threat and so forth, as much as the lack of formal democratic channels for addressing these problems in global arenas (and here the EU is sometimes dismissed as another 'rich man's club', as the phrase goes). In Chapter 8, Tony McGrew sets the wider scene, discussing how issues of democracy are being posed anew by contemporary globalisation, and outlining some of the basic arguments for and *against* the possibility of transnational democracy. He discusses whether or not it is feasible or desirable, and the alternative normative foundations for it in democratic intergovernmentalism, in republicanism and in cosmopolitanism. The World Trade Organisation (WTO) is taken to exemplify the normative foundations and current limits of global democratisation and what it could mean for the institutions of global governance.

Turning directly to the question of agency, Chapter 9 discusses how the '*cadres of capitalism*', the managers of the system, contribute to or impede democratisation when influenced by opposing social forces. Chapter 10 analyses the democratic potential of non-governmental organisations (NGOs) which are sometimes seen as the organisational backbone of transnational social movements. Chapter 11 analyses the different political strategies of these movements for reforming or rejecting neo-liberal globalism.

For Kees van der Pijl, the new middle class of technical and managerial cadre 'holds the middle ground' in the transnationalisation of capital and society. Structurally it is open to conservative and radical influences and can move in either direction depending on the prevailing 'balance of forces' in society. He sets the question of agency in historical context by discussing how the mass radicalism of the '1968 generation' led in the 1970s to the cadre getting caught up in reformist movements to deepen national democracy and reduce international inequalities. These are still live issues but the contemporary relevance of this analysis may lie in the fact that 'anti-globalisation/anti-capitalism' constitutes the most widespread and substantial mass radicalism since '1968'. It remains to be seen whether it will have a similarly important impact in different circumstances. In the 1980s, cadre were involved in reversing the previous reformist movements and reimposing capitalist ('market') disciplines (including on the cadre themselves) under the banner of neo-liberal globalism. Three new 'transnational' fractions of the cadre are identified in Chapter 9 – in business services, in the 'internationalising of the state', and in transnational NGOs – and their democratic potential and the prospects for transnational democracy are briefly assessed in terms of 'Third Way' social democracy.

In Chapter 10, Joachim Hirsch shows that the increased importance of NGOs stems from weaknesses in regulation and legitimation at national and international levels in the 'grey area' between states and the private economy. This 'grey area' has substantially expanded with neo-liberal globalisation, and he relates it to theoretical debates about 'civil society'. He questions the fashionable conception of an 'international or world civil society' in the absence of a 'world state'; and argues that 'state' and 'civil society' have to be re-theorised in contemporary transnational conditions, in order to assess the potential of NGOs for democratic and emancipatory politics. He concludes that at present their democratic potential is generally exaggerated.

How democratising agents and strategies are assessed depends on different interpretations of the dominant sources of global power and the available channels for democratisation. In Chapter 11, James Goodman categorises the forces currently opposing 'corporate globalism' in terms of three broad strategies: *globalist adaptation*, *localist confrontation* and *transnational resistance*. He argues that they interpret the main sources of global power as institutional cultural and material, respectively, and he associates them with liberal internationalism, post-Marxism, and Marxism or neo-Marxism. Their democratic potential is assessed in terms of how each approaches transnational corporations, intergovernmental institutions and global norms; and whether their different methods and objectives conflict with or complement one another.

The concluding Chapter 12 returns to some of the general, overarching questions of the early chapters and rephrases them in terms of reconstituting and relocating the demos. Who can or should constitute a demos; and what alternative political spaces are available? Cities as places in transnational networks are one answer. But can people really belong effectively to several demos(es) simultaneously, as suggested by the advocates of 'multi-layered' democracy; and who are the preferred agents of relocation?

1 Questions of democracy, territoriality and globalisation

James Anderson

Globalisation is putting democracy in question and is itself being questioned as undemocratic. Its border crossings are undermining the traditional territorial basis of democracy and creating new political spaces which need democratising. 'Global forces' are disrupting the supposedly independent, sovereign states and national communities which have provided democracy's main framework. And these 'global forces' are apparently beyond control or, more specifically, beyond democratic control. The political implications are wide reaching and far from clear.

Global changes are mainly experienced in the realms of economics, consumerism, communications and culture. Economic and cultural globalisation seem to have proceeded much further and faster than political globalisation. Democracy, largely confined to liberal representative democracy and still over-identified with the territory of the so-called 'nation-state', seems to be eroding within its traditional framework. On the other hand, liberal democracy already had its limitations and exclusions – of national and other minorities, for instance, and more generally in separating a private sphere of 'economics' from the public sphere of 'politics' and democracy. While there has been a remarkable global 'triumph of liberal democracy' in recent decades, replacing dictatorships in some cases, it is criticised as neo-liberalism which subordinates the 'state' to the 'market', now the 'world market'. It leaves democracy confined and attenuated within states and largely absent both from the transnational arenas of world politics and more localised cross-border contexts.

But perhaps globalisation should be seen positively as opening up new possibilities – new political 'spaces', both literal and figurative – for radically different conceptions of democratisation? Border-crossing transnationalism could be an escape from the confining rigidity of national frameworks and state territoriality: it might provide new opportunities for more participatory forms of democracy and augment the limited democracy traditionally on offer.

There are indeed widely differing opinions about how national territorial democracy is being affected by 'globalisation' and what should be done within and beyond states. There are disagreements about the feasibility of defending and strengthening national democracy; and about the possibilities of it being supplemented or even displaced by other territorial frameworks such as the

European Union (EU), or by the *non*-territorial politics of 'non-governmental organisations' (NGOs) and transnational social movements. The active exercise of democracy has been assumed to depend on some common 'identity' and 'community', as provided by the territorially defined national community within state borders. But how essential for democracy is such a common identity? Could it just as well be provided by non-territorial communities defined in functional terms? New information technologies, for instance, are facilitating the emergence of such transnational communities and movements, but how viable are they as a basis for democracy? And will they also lead to the creation of larger territorial communities at supra-state levels?

In fact, larger intergovernmental entities like the European Community have so far been noted for *lack* of genuine 'community', and a 'democratic deficit'. And many other multilateral associations between national governments – whether territorial trading blocs like the North American Free Trade Agreement (NAFTA) and MERCOSUR in South America, or non-territorial entities like the Group of Eight (leading industrial/military states) – are even less communal or democratic. In contrast, some of the most novel, vigorous and democratically inspired developments of recent years are to be seen in transnational movements. They point towards a more participatory and *non*-territorial future: organising functionally around a plethora of political issues – from the problems of labour, women, and refugees, to the environment, militarism and Third World debt – they herald a new transnationalism. They have added a qualitatively new dimension to world politics since they came together in the 'anti-globalisation' or 'anti-capitalism' movement which first emerged in the 'Battle of Seattle' against the World Trade Organisation (WTO) in late 1999. But in formal terms they are less 'representative'. The future of globalisation will be fought out by different kinds of self-styled democrats. Different conceptions of democracy are pivotal to the theory and practice of globalisation.

We are far from the vision of a 'borderless world': this is very much an idea whose time has not come. Indeed, not only is this neo-liberal vision highly unlikely, it is also seen as undesirable. State borders are being reconstituted rather than disappearing; and national states are still the main frameworks for the formal democratic accountability currently available, not to be given up lightly despite their limitations. While variable in accountability, they are often more democratic than some of the transnational alternatives currently on offer. But rather than simply counterposing the different forms of democracy, the key question may be how to get them working together? How to articulate participation with representation, the territorial and the non-territorial, the national and the transnational?

This chapter contextualises these questions and raises further ones.[1] First, it outlines how globalisation has put transnational democracy 'on the political agenda', then discusses how it upsets the familiar dichotomy between 'foreign' and 'domestic' affairs and calls for a less state-centric democratic theory. To know what is happening, what is desirable, what is possible, and how to get it, we need theory and, it is argued, a critical political economy approach. The third section discusses the nature of democracy in capitalism, its representative and participatory forms, and liberalism's partial separation of 'politics' and 'economics'. This contradictory and contested separation is reformulated in terms of the presence/absence of democracy, and in the fourth section it is related back to globalisation and the global hegemony of the liberal democratic state. The separation is central to the problematic relationship between the transnational and the national, a precondition both of economic globalisation and of the state's political claim to absolute territorial sovereignty. The ensuing problems for transnational democracy are seen as rooted in territoriality, and the fifth section argues for redefining sovereignty in popular rather than state territorial terms. The chapter ends by discussing the relatively neglected question of agency for bringing about transnational democracy, focusing on the 'polar opposites' of liberal cosmopolitanism and 'anti-globalisation/anti-capitalism' which frame the range of approaches discussed in this volume.

Globalisation and politics

The return of capitalist crises in the 1970s with the ending of the post-war boom, and the subsequent growth of foreign investment, transnational consumerism and other border-crossing innovations, come together in the term 'globalisation'. Together they have disrupted the familiar state-centric definitions of community, identity and politics on which democracy has depended. The term 'globalisation' is however an ideological construct which should perhaps be permanently quarantined in inverted commas – a hold-all category credited or blamed for all sorts of things, many of them long established. In fact, the general phenomenon was not new in the 1970s, and some apparently 'new' things were simply existing features now more exposed or obvious. 'Globalisation' can be seen as simply a euphemism for 'capitalism' in its contemporary phase (as 'Seattle's' interchangeable 'anti-globalisation/anti-capitalism' label suggests, the latter term indicating that the target is not so much globalisation *per se* as the particular form it is currently taking).

But the concept of globalisation does highlight some genuinely new features which put transnational democracy 'on the agenda'. Besides, it comes in many different versions, usefully classified by David Held *et al.* (1999: 2–10) as 'hyper-globalist' and 'sceptical', with their own version occupying the in-between 'transformationalist' category. We can dispense immediately with 'hyper' versions. The notion of 'some massive and absolute shift, from a *space of places* to a *space of flows* 'makes incorrect assumptions', as Doreen Massey (1999: 22–3) argues;[2] and Ohmae's (1991) neo-liberal vision of a 'borderless world' is a gross exaggeration which mistakenly implies 'the death of the nation-state' (Anderson 1995). On the contrary, transnational democracy can be expected to co-exist and interact with national democracy, rather than replacing it. But that still means some fundamental changes even in the weaker, more 'sceptical' versions of globalisation (for example, Hirst and Thompson 1996), and rather than opting in advance for the 'transformationalist' or 'sceptical' category, it is better to keep both options open. The choice can vary depending on the context and process, recognising that globalisation is inherently uneven. As already suggested, political globalisation lags behind economic and cultural globalisation, though even (?) in the political sphere there have been some fundamental transformations.

Four interrelated developments have put transnational democracy on the political agenda:

- the weakening of democracy at national state level
- the growth of transnational governance with 'democratic deficits'
- the global hegemony and spread of the liberal democratic state
- the growing demands for democracy in transnational arenas

The weakening of national democracy

National democracy's problems are experienced most immediately in perceptions that the national state is losing its sovereignty to 'outside' bodies and is being infiltrated by them. Actions taken in or by other states are having increasing impact on supposedly 'sovereign' neighbours. State electorates are more directly affected by decisions made in other jurisdictions, including supra-state bodies like the EU. Private multinational corporations have become more powerful, and foreign-owned ones may determine the success or otherwise of national economies. States are losing some of their autonomy, as power 'goes upwards' to other, supra-state, political institutions, 'sideways' to privatised operations, or in some respects 'goes nowhere' or just 'evaporates', as economics outruns politics and political control is simply lost to the global market (Strange 1994a). With democracy conventionally seen as virtually synonymous with electoral representation on the basis of state territory and territorial constituencies, the erosion of *state* sovereignty quickly translates into the loss of 'our' *popular* sovereignty and the whole basis of our democratic mechanisms, obligations and rights.

Furthermore, while state sovereignty is being eroded by globalisation, a gap is seen to be opening up between state and popular sovereignty with the latter doubly disadvantaged. Popular decision making is losing out not only to 'global' forces but more immediately to 'its own' state as well. As Robert Cox has pointed out, states are being 'internationalised' unevenly but to the general detriment of popular sovereignty:

> The state becomes a transmission belt from the global to the national economy, where heretofore it had acted as a bulwark defending domestic welfare from external disturbances…Power within the state becomes concentrated in those agencies in closest touch with the global economy – the offices of presidents and prime ministers, treasuries, central banks. The agencies that are more closely identified with domestic clients…become subordinated.

(Cox 1992: 30–1)

The more powerful sections of the state and their respective elites tend to monopolise participation in the growing field of transnational governance, trans-mitting 'top down' from 'the global' rather than 'bottom up' from the 'domestic clients' (the electorate they supposedly represent). The latter suffer a loss of power simultaneously to 'the global' and to the parts of the state most remote from popular involvement. As these state elites have become more important, and more involved in the secret decision-making of transnational institutions, the lack of democratic input and accountability has become more pronounced. There has been a widely perceived transfer of power to government depart-ments and ministers from legislative assemblies and 'ordinary elected representatives', and the electorate at large is even more excluded.

Thus globalisation is posing very serious political questions even within the limited terms of reference of conventional liberal democracy. It challenges taken-for-granted assumptions that there is a sharp dichotomy between 'domestic' and 'foreign' politics, that 'political community' is co-terminous with state territory (seen most obviously in the conflation of 'nation' and 'state' in the 'nation-state'), and the idea that these are the necessary and sufficient frame-works for democracy. These now outdated assumptions are a legacy of what was clearly in retrospect a relatively short and *un*typical period in the history of states, and mainly western European states at that. From the late nineteenth century, and especially in the more 'state interventionist' middle decades of the twentieth century – in the protectionist inter-war period and the post-war boom years of the 'welfare-warfare' state up to the 1970s – such assumptions had considerable plausibility (even if always questionable). It could be assumed that the state constituted and represented an independent, sovereign political community; and that its elected representatives formed governments which represented and protected its interests. But contemporary globalisation casts grave doubts on this simple story, presenting a major challenge to liberal democ-racy and its hold on legitimacy.

This is a challenge which liberal democracy is peculiarly ill-equipped to resist because of its 'minimalist' commitment to 'limited government' (see the chapter by Parekh in this volume). Indeed its whole point may be to *not* resist globalisa-tion. As we shall see, that is precisely why liberal democracy is central to the neo-liberal globalist strategy of leading powers such as the Group of Eight. That is why the liberal democratic state has recently achieved 'global hegemony'. On such criteria it is of course responding to globalisation with great success, but they are liberal *rather than* democratic criteria. They leave out of account the chal-lenge to democratic legitimacy among electorates led to expect not only a democratic say in decisions affecting them, but also effective state protection of their interests whether from internal or external threats. Despite considerable efforts to 'dumb down' such expectations (for example, the ideology of the 'over-loaded state'), the question of legitimacy is surfacing in the growing concerns about the low turnout in elections, and the lack of effective democracy in national as well as transnational arenas. At best, liberal democracy evades rather than meets this democratic challenge,[3] and ironically the liberal democratic state

is achieving 'global hegemony' just the point when world conditions for its existence are beginning to disappear.

Moving beyond liberalism, we shall see that the 'crisis' of democratic legitimacy is crucially conditioned by an economic dimension which liberal
democracy engages with in contradictory ways. Globalisation is often experienced as foreign direct investment (FDI), bringing jobs and wealth, or,
alternatively, responsible for the loss of jobs, taxes and state subsidies on departure, but always foreign-owned capital managed from elsewhere. Given the
prevalence of nationalism, this highlights the fact that it is not amenable to
democratic control over investment and what and where to produce/not
produce. In this lack of democracy it is of course exactly the same as indigenously owned private capital which in liberal regimes is not subject to
democratic control either. But there is the political difference that 'foreign' decision making highlights the relative helplessness of national decision makers. The
government is more likely to be put in the position of protecting explicitly
'national' interests, but if its aptitude and appetite for intervention have been
weakened by neo-liberalism, it fights with its hands tied and 'globalisation' typically becomes an excuse for ineffectiveness. In a contradictory relationship,
liberalism will triumph at the expense of national legitimacy, or vice versa.

Transnational governance and its 'democratic deficits'

The second factor putting transnational democracy on the political agenda has
been the spectacular increase in transnational governance, with its equally spectacular 'democratic deficits'. Contemporary globalisation is being accompanied
by huge growth in a range of new, or newly powerful, non-state actors. They
include multinational corporations; supra-state regional trading blocs; sub-state
regions and transnational associations of regions; multilateral economic institutions of global governance such as the WTO, World Bank and International
Monetary Fund (IMF); and NGOs and transnational social movements.[4]

This transnationalisation can be seen negatively as national states increasingly
having to share 'their' traditional power and a shrinking world stage with these
'non-state actors'. But in fact some of them are better seen as supporting or
strengthening rather than weakening state power – an important reason for
being sceptical about the 'decline', never mind 'death' of the state. However, as
we saw with states being 'internationalised' unevenly, such strengthening of the
state does not necessarily mean a strengthening of democracy. On the contrary,
it can mean the reverse if the 'external supports' are less democratic, which
some clearly are.

Looked at positively, on the other hand, there are compensations such as the
growing vigour of sub-state regionalism with local authorities now becoming
'international actors' on their own behalf rather than working through their
respective national states (Anderson 2001b). The growth of other territorial entities, such as regional blocs, and of IGOs and INGOs, provides an institutional
framework for developing a 'transnational (or global) civil society', a prerequisite

for a more developed transnational democracy. Furthermore, while many of the IGOs are more noted for their 'democratic deficits', this very fact is a stimulus for transnational movements calling for democratisation (for example, of the WTO; see McGrew in this volume). The EU, for instance, already has its European Parliament, state-like central institutions and well-developed sub-state regionalisms; but its 'democratic deficit' makes it a key test case for transnational democracy, including local democracy in 'cross-border regions' (see the chapters by Newman, Painter and O'Dowd in this volume).

Liberal democracy's global hegemony and 'anti-globalisation'

Our third and fourth developments putting democracy on the agenda show, in their very different and opposing ways, that democratisation is an integral part of globalisation. The remarkable geographical diffusion of the liberal democratic state (or approximations) in the so-called 'third wave of democratisation' from the mid-1970s to the 1990s – replacing dictatorships in southern Europe, 'Second World' centrally planned economies, and military regimes in 'Third World' countries – has been energetically encouraged by the USA and its European allies. Democratic elections have become globalised as the test of legitimacy (Arblaster 1994: 52–4). However, as explained later, this global hegemony of the liberal democratic state has mainly been propagated in the self-interest of the world's leading powers rather than in the interests of the countries themselves. The 'victory' has been at the expense of more interventionist social democratic regimes as well as dictatorships. The democratisation is limited and applies to individual states, rather than to the transnational arena in which the process was propagated; and it is part of the western neo-liberal agenda which is opposed on democratic grounds by the 'anti-globalisation' movement.

This movement, the most widespread radicalism since the '1968' upsurge thirty years earlier, does focus on the transnational arena, its undemocratic nature and western domination of it. Like the earlier movement which radicalised a generation of 'capitalist cadre' in the 1970s, the current movement could have a similar impact on these key personnel of the transnationalisation process (see van der Pijl in this volume, as well as the chapters by Hirsch and Goodman). The institutions of global governance, and liberal democracy in general, are seen as preserving the interests of the rich and powerful in a world of grotesque and widening divisions between rich and poor – a world where according to the United Nations *1996 Development Report*, the richest 358 people owned as much wealth as the poorest two and a half billion (Taylor and Flint 2000: 2).

We have here two conflicting conceptions of 'democracy': firstly ,the mainly national, formal representative democracy of the elected world leaders who would like to dismiss the 'anti-globalisation' protesters as an unrepresentative, unelected and violent rabble with confused ideas about an amorphous mass of different problems and causes; and secondly, the largely transnational, informal, participatory democracy of the protesters who are coming to see the capitalist world system as the common denominator and root cause of the different problems.

Their conflict makes democratisation the key issue of globalisation, but arguably both have a questionable hold on democracy. Formal representation increasingly lacks inclusivity and legitimacy, particularly in global arenas. For instance, the Group of Eight leaders represent less than 15 per cent of the world's people and stand accused of doing violence to the rest of the world (and some to their own electorates). On the other hand, informal participation lacks representative mechanisms and the means to do more than sporadically influence the political agenda. But might these matching weaknesses provide a basis for democratic complementarity and progress?

Globalisation and theory

> IBM is Japan's largest computer exporter, and Sony is the largest exporter of television sets from the United States…a Japanese concern assembling typewriters in Tennessee, brings an antidumping case before the U.S. International Trade Commission…against an American firm that imports typewriters into the United States from its offshore facilities in Singapore and Indonesia.
>
> (Ruggie 1993: 172)

A world turned inside out

If you find these facts rather odd, even unsettling, it is because they go against our usual political assumptions about 'domestic' and 'foreign', the internal and the external, belonging and not belonging. The facts flout the familiar inside/outside dichotomy and the traditional assumptions of democratic theory and international relations. Conventional theory cannot cope with a world at least partly turned 'inside out and outside in', if not (yet?) upside down. It was already impoverished by its acceptance of the dichotomy, and now globalisation and the increasing overlaps and ambiguities between the 'internal' and the 'external' are making a nonsense of what was always to some extent a misleading separation.

The dichotomy gave rise to an academic division of labour between Political Science, focused on the internal study of 'the state' in the singular (Barker, n.d.), including democracy, and a separate field of international relations between many states (Walker 1993). Both have suffered from a somewhat paradoxical 'state centrism'. Democratic theory focused almost entirely on the territorially delimited state 'community', effectively in isolation from other communities and states. The state is the analytical starting point, and democracy in liberal theory has been almost completely confined to relations inside the state territory, ignoring international relations (with the significant exception of David Held's cosmopolitan democratic theory; see below). States are also the starting point in the (generally separate) field of international (i.e., inter-state) relations; and it was widely assumed that states are the most, indeed sometimes the only, important 'international' actors. But paradoxically, this analytically crucial 'state' was largely unexamined particularly with respect to international relations. Here states were often seen as 'black boxes' or treated as self-sufficient, internally motivated institutions, as if they were autonomous 'individuals', and the typical categories of social science such as social classes and interest groups generally got a 'back seat', and sometimes no seat at all.

State-centrism collapsed most issues to the one level of the state, and when other alternatives were considered – as in debates about 'the death of the state' – they were almost invariably state-like bodies at other levels 'above and below'. The assumption was that any serious threat or replacement could only come from state equivalents – the state 'writ large', as in a federal 'United States of Europe' for example (see Agnew in this volume), or 'writ small', as in separate 'regional governments' and a utopian 'Europe of the Regions' (Anderson 2001b). Here the only real changes are of geographical scale or territorial extent (bigger or smaller), with no recognition that political processes and institutions at different scales are likely to be qualitatively (not just quantitatively) different in their character and interrelationships: the 'Gulliver fallacy' named after the societies Gulliver met in his 'travels': one a society of giants, the other of midgets, but both exact replicas of human society.

Moreover, the notion of separate 'levels' is itself questionable. Formal government may be based on discrete territories at different 'levels', but actual social processes span different 'levels' and their political regulation – and its democratisation – need to do likewise. The 'levels' perspective hardly captures this 'vertical' dimension of connection, or the more informal, participatory and *non*-territorial aspects of democracy which may be crucial in linking the 'levels' or in their own right. The perspective needs to be reformulated in terms of '*multi*-level' governance (see Painter in this volume). Furthermore, while the state is increasingly having to share the stage with other 'actors' (and not just other state-like 'levels'), it is not simply the 'cast' which is changing but the 'stage' as well. The ground is shifting under established institutions and assumptions as different forms of authority grow, overlap and inter-penetrate, developments imperfectly captured in the idea of 'neo-medieval' territorialities (Anderson 1996). As far as democratisation is concerned, the 'medieval model' is to say the least unhelpful, except perhaps in the negative sense of warning that democracy is under serious threat.

In this context, and with the 'inside/outside' dichotomy becoming untenable, theory as usual has to 'catch up' with reality. Globalisation has thrown the shortcomings of theory into sharp relief, and particularly in the dichotomised disciplines of political science and international relations (more affected by the dichotomy than studies of political geography, sociology or anthropology for instance). But it is also in the former two disciplines that the weaknesses and appropriate remedial actions have been most forcefully discussed, by for example William Connolly (1991), Rob Walker (1993), Justin Rosenberg (1994), Ellen Wood (1995), David Held (1995), John Hoffman (1998) and Hazel Smith (2000). We need a theory appropriate to a world turning 'inside out'. As Susan Strange (1994b) put it in the marvellously haughty title of an article criticising a realist theorist of international relations: 'Wake up, Krasner! The world *has* changed'.[5] We need a less state-centric theory; and given the importance of economic globalisation, we need to see the 'international realm' in a broader political economy perspective.

Conceptions of space and politics beyond the state

This means finding alternatives to the state as the analytical starting point; and a less dichotomised, limited and limiting conception of political space. On political space, some of the options (and some of the problems) can be summed up in six terms commonly used (or misused) to refer to 'society', or social relations including democracy, beyond the state. They are *global, cosmopolitan, supra-state* or *supranational, international* and *transnational,* and here the latter is the preferred choice. The other alternatives are too specific, too sweeping, or both.

Global is clearly too extensive in that some of the border-crossing processes which raise questions of democracy are not global at all. They are spatially limited to particular parts of the world, such as the EU, or smaller cross-border regions. Even if our ultimate interest is global democracy, we would not want to exclude these more limited phenomena, and not least because they may provide pointers to global democracy. Besides, ideas of 'global society' (or 'global civil society') can conceal the huge discrepancies and growing gap between rich and poor countries, and the rich and poor people within them. The poorest are being excluded from 'global society' by, ironically enough, globalisation, which is not only extremely uneven but also contradictory in its effects.

Cosmopolitan, implying a worldwide political community and shared, universal political values, has some of the same problems as *global,* implying both too much and too little. There are many interesting developments in cross-border democracy with an actual scope well short of cosmopolitan and not motivated by any cosmopolitan ideal of humanity as a whole. Moreover, given the uneven-ness of globalisation and the neo-liberal agenda, the reality may well be Western, hegemonic or imperialist values masquerading as a fake universalism.

Supranational or *supra-state* (effectively the same, as in English 'nation' and 'state' are linguistically conflated) do not have the same universalist aspirations or pretensions and can refer to more ideologically modest and spatially limited cases. But they directly suffer from the problems of the 'levels' perspective already outlined. They counterpose supra-state to state and sub-state levels; and at least implicitly reinforce state-centrism. Similarly, whereas a lot of border crossing is by other 'non-state actors', the more traditional term *international* is loaded with connotations of relations between states, and it also reinforces the 'domestic/foreign' or 'national/international' dichotomy.

Transnational can of course also be given such connotations, but in general it is more inclusive and for our purposes more accurate than the other terms. It comes with less historical 'baggage' than *international,* and it can in principle include all of the other options. It does not prejudge geographical scope like *global,* nor does it have the universalist pretensions of *cosmopolitan,* but both these terms can be subsumed under *transnational*. With its prefix *trans*, meaning 'across', it has less of a 'levels' flavour than *supra-state*. Instead of implying a counterposing of different territorial levels, it arguably gives more sense of including state, supra-state and sub-state in a multi-level conception which can also accommodate *non*-territorial phenomena. Thus transnational democracy can be seen as involving state and non-state actors operating across different territorial levels, rather than as something separate from 'national' democracy. The term implies including and *trans*cending 'the national' – a crossing of borders and a bridging of dichotomies. That at least is the way it is being used here.

Finding an alternative to states as the analytical starting point is to treat them as a 'second order' category which needs explaining, rather than taking states as 'pre-existing givens'. It means seeing them as continually contested historical constructions rather than timeless essences; and as Hazel Smith (2000: 4) argues, 'a serious problematisation of the state [offers] ways into understanding the pursuit of democratisation in post-Cold War international politics'. For this we need to get beyond Weber's political conception of the state as an administrative-coercive apparatus which claims a monopoly of the legitimate use of violence within its sovereign territory. As already implied, the states' relations with private sector production and the world market are of key importance as well. And here the Marxist conception of states as a 'second order' category set within a mode or system of production is particularly appropriate. For this conception is firstly 'internationalist' (or in our terminology 'transnationalist') rather than 'nationalist'. States are primarily seen as nodes within complex social relations of production, shaped by, as well as shaping, the 'forces and relations of production', the outcome and the site of an ongoing history of class struggles between different groups within and without the state territory (Smith 2000: 23–6). These conflicts between different social classes (and fractions of classes) are the primary analytic focus.

States as 'second order' categories can be explained in these terms, and that includes their territorial configurations. The conflicts take place within, between and across territorial borders. The borders themselves are a product of past class struggles, and they are used to further the interests of dominant classes as the winners of the struggle (albeit usually 'on points' with the result contested). They are a means of class control – used for instance to control international flows of labour – and giving up this control for a 'borderless' (i.e., stateless or single state) world is entirely implausible (Anderson 2001a). This is especially so because structural conflict in capitalism is not only between classes, it is also between different capitalists who are in competition with each other for raw materials, labour and markets, and this competition is spatialised in terms of particular capitalist interests being located in different places or countries. This was even more clearly the case when 'national economies' were the 'building blocks' of the world economy, and with globalisation is now less obvious. But there is still a very strong geographical dimension to capitalism's highly uneven development – a lot of 'fixed' as well as 'footloose' capital – and this feeds into the continued reproduction both of nationalist sentiment and state territoriality.

With (inter- and intra-) class conflict the primary analytical category, there is no longer any reason to always or necessarily privilege the state over other 'second order' sites. As we shall see, explaining the global hegemony of liberal democracy requires an understanding of how other sites of struggle as well as states are being (re)constituted in the context of globalisation, something which state-centric international relations cannot explain (Smith 2000). Such an understanding is likewise required for redefining sovereignty in popular democratic rather than state territorial terms (Hoffman 1998). But first we need to problematise the concept of democracy in a capitalist context.

Democracy and capitalism

The strengths and weaknesses of democracy in capitalism can be outlined in terms of the dominant liberal representative tradition and alternative participatory or direct forms. Liberal democracy has been confined to a 'public' realm of politics from which the 'private' spheres of personal life and of economic production were largely excluded. There is a partial and contested separation or 'contradictory unity' of 'politics' and 'economics' in capitalism, and this can more accurately be reformulated in terms of the presence/absence of democracy.

Liberal and participatory democracy

Democracy literally means 'rule by the people', the demos, but what it actually means in practice is highly debatable. The problems arise as soon as we ask 'what people', 'who decides', 'what sort of rule', and 'over what'? Is it rule by the people themselves, or their representatives, or a majority of their representatives, or a majority of those who bother to vote, and what rights do minorities have, however defined? But despite its problems, the alternatives to democracy are worse. Democracy, however imperfect, can allow the ruled to put some constraints on their rulers; it may allow the rulers to know what the ruled want. It allows more collective and equitable decision making, more people have a say in setting agendas, and their social cohesion and overall effectiveness may be increased. Power rests with the people as 'popular power', 'popular sovereignty', 'the people' as the final political authority.

This is undoubtedly to be preferred to non-democratic decision making. Yet up to the nineteenth century the rich and powerful openly opposed it as 'rule by the mob' (and no doubt many of them still think that way even if they do not admit it). Anthony Arblaster (1994: 8) suggests that democracy lost its 'mob' image because it was modified to accommodate the earlier suspicions and hostility. In the seventeenth century democracy was associated with participation in public meetings of some of the citizens, but by the nineteenth century it meant meetings of elected representatives which could encompass larger, including national, communities, albeit indirectly.

Direct participation within and against undemocratic social structures, including political agitation for democracy by the so-called 'mob', was an essential, if not *the* essential element in the origins of modern representative democracy. Yet decision making was effectively distanced from 'the people' in various elitist ways. Direct participation was seen as less practical, especially with the advent of full 'mass democracy' for adult men and women by the early twentieth century. Liberal government meant government limited in relation to basic individual rights, particularly economic property rights and 'market freedoms' guaranteed by state law. In the USA, for example, an elaborate division of powers between different parts of the federal system was designed to restrain popularly elected assemblies (see the chapter by Agnew in this book); while for J.S. Mill, representative democracy provided safeguards against the dangers inherent in more direct forms (Arblaster 1994: 38–9). Clearly safeguards are needed against a 'dictatorship of the majority' (as Northern Ireland demonstrates; see Anderson and Hamilton in this volume). But it does seem that as democracy was widened to include more people it became shallower in content; and now it seems that the 'global hegemony' of liberal democracy comes just when national democracy is losing more of its content.

This suggests that there is considerable scope for deepening it. Writing in the 1990s, Arblaster (1994: 103) found that he could not improve on E.H. Carr's 1951 conclusion:

> Mass democracy is a difficult and hitherto largely uncharted territory; and we should be nearer the mark, and should have a far more convincing slogan, if we spoke of the need, not to defend democracy, but to create it.

These conclusions referred to national democracy and are given added weight when the focus is widened to transnational democracy. Conventional liberal democracy mainly relies on the infrequent election of representatives for fixed, contiguous and bounded territories and their enclosed 'communities'. In contrast to more participatory democracy, it tends to encourage a passive individualism, rather than active or collective citizenship, and a negative conception of freedom *from* government interference, rather than freedom *to* achieve various objectives with help from an enabling state. But the democratic process can and sometimes does involve much more than the formalities of territorially based voting. It can also involve the shaping of political agendas – deciding what issues get considered – not just voting once some other people have decided the question. It can be expressed through various forms of participatory democracy, involving, for instance, social movements, political campaigns, NGOs, local community groups, associative democracy and work-based organisations including trade unions (see for example Held 1993). Rather than relying on party politicians elected every four or five years, participatory democracy can involve a wide variety of organisations and associations in civil society, some of which are responsive to continuous internal democratic pressures from their own members. Many people, and perhaps especially women and younger people, are excluded or alienated from conventional 'party politics', but are nevertheless active in the 'small p politics' of civil society. And their participatory democracy with its more varied, flexible and often non-territorial, functional social basis is inherently better suited than conventional representative democracy for crossing territorial borders. Yet territorially based liberal democracy retains its dominance, often to the point of monopoly, and therein lies much of the problem.

The partial separation of 'economics' and 'politics'

Liberal democracy's biggest exclusion is of economic production and decisions on what needs to be produced, where to invest, buy, sell and so forth. This exclusion underpins 'production for profit rather than need' and is based on the partial separation of 'economics' and 'politics', or their 'contradictory unity' in capitalism (Wood 1995; Amin 1996). This has profound implications for democracy, allowing formal political equality to co-exist with, and to some extent cover up, gross material inequalities, exploitation and oppression, while also effectively putting the latter outside the scope of democracy.

The partial separation is a central theoretical and practical issue in the functioning of capitalist society, fought over for instance in issues of state ownership and privatisation. It underpins and partly overlaps the related and more familiar distinctions between 'state' and 'market', 'state' and 'civil society', the 'public' and 'private' spheres or sectors. At the simplest level, the separation involves a 'public sphere' of 'politics' and the state, which is territorially delimited, and a 'private' sphere of economic production, distribution and exchange which can straddle state borders. As such, it has direct implications for democracy, territoriality and globalisation.

However, we have to re-cast this separation as not so much between 'politics' and 'economics', or 'state' and 'civil society', but more precisely as the exclusion of democracy from the realm of economic production whether privately owned or state operated. Democracy tends to stop at the gates of workplaces in both sectors.

The separation is structural to capitalism and is materialised in separate 'political' and 'economic' institutions and arenas, rather than being simply ideological. In capitalism, unlike other social systems, production and the allocation of labour and resources are generally separated off from the arena of 'politics' and displaced to a separate 'non-political' sphere of 'economics'. This uniquely capitalist separation, rather than being contingent, is structurally rooted in the capitalist mode of production where surplus is extracted from the direct producers by the 'apolitical' mechanisms of 'the free market', rather than by political force or other non-economic means. This contrasts with pre-capitalist modes where surplus was extracted from generally 'unfree' producers by political or 'non-economic' methods – by military force, whether wielded by individual slave-owners, feudal lords, or tribute-taking centralised administrations, and/or through religious obligation or other traditional ideological processes. Similarly, resources in capitalism are not generally allocated by political direction, but by anonymous and democratically unaccountable 'market forces'. Thus political issues of exploitation, domination and resource allocation, which in non-capitalist modes of production were clearly bound up with political power, are in capitalism at least partially de-politicised and transformed into distinctively 'economic' issues; perhaps, as Ellen Wood (1995: 20) remarks, 'the most effective defence mechanism available to capital'.

In the abstract capitalist mode of production, labour is legally 'free' and 'freely exchanged' as a market transaction for wages or salaries; but the monetary value of wages is less than the value of what is produced, the difference equating to 'surplus value' (appropriated as profits, interest or rent). What 'enforces' this surplus transfer from wage or salary worker to capitalist employer is not directly 'political' but the economic needs of the worker her/himself. Workers generally have little or no means of production (farmland, factories, raw materials, etc.) of their own; these are privately owned as capital by the capitalist class; and hence workers have no option but to work for wages or salary. Thus the threat of economic sanctions against workers, individually and collectively – for example, being refused a pay rise or promotion, or worse, being made unemployed – can discipline the workforce despite it being 'free' in political and legal terms.

This process of surplus extraction and capital accumulation happens in capitalism's separate 'private' sphere of 'economics'. However, despite appearances to the contrary, this sphere does not operate on its own or in isolation from 'politics'. On the contrary, it depends on the latter: hence the need to specify 'politics/economics' as a 'contradictory unity' (or only partial separation), rather than accepting the conventional false dichotomy of them as separate 'independent' factors which may or may not be brought together in an external relationship with each other. The supposedly 'non-political' sphere of 'economics' is in fact bound up with 'politics' in two senses. Firstly, the power relations between capitalist and worker in the 'private' sphere depend on the state maintaining 'private property' and the capitalist class monopoly of the means of production on which the capitalist exploitation of 'free' labour depends. Coercive force, not wielded directly by the economic appropriator (as it was by feudal lords) but by the state separately from civil society, is ultimately necessary to sustain private property and expropriation (Wood 1995: 28–9). Secondly, the crucially important 'private' sphere domination via 'economic' sanctions (promotion refusal, unemployment, etc.) is a form of coercive *class politics* rather than simply a technical 'economic' matter, notwithstanding the dominant ideology of legal equality and 'freedom' of labour and the fact that *political* inequality is not officially recognised (as it usually was in pre-capitalist contexts). Politics operates but in different ways in the 'private' sphere of 'economics' and the market, as well as in the 'public' sphere of 'politics' and the state.

But modern states clearly do much more than ensure the necessary political and legal conditions for 'private' capital accumulation. Despite or contrary to neo-liberal anti-state propaganda, they generally combine these 'purely political' functions with substantial direct and indirect involvement in the 'economic' sphere, including through the state capitalist production of 'nationalised industries'. This is why we have to reformulate the separation as not so much between 'politics' and 'economics', or 'state' and 'civil society', but more precisely as the exclusion of democracy from the realm of economic production. Politics operates but in different – non-democratic – ways in the sphere of 'economics', whether in the private or state-owned sectors. State enterprises generally have little 'worker democracy', or democratic decision making over what to produce. Publicly owned companies often operate in just the same democratically unaccountable fashion as private firms.

Thus our reformulation specifies democracy as the key differentiator rather than 'politics' in general. The 'economic' sphere is not necessarily 'private', but it is separated off from the public sphere where democracy operates; and its internal politics are different in that democracy is excluded from production whether privately or state owned. The separation is really the exclusion, not of 'politics' or the state, but of democracy from economic production. This presence/absence of democracy is the basis of territorial sovereignty and the inside/outside dichotomy in politics. Conversely, it facilitates economic processes which transcend territoriality.

Democracy and globalisation

Democracy tends to stop at the borders of the state as well as at the gates of the workplace. The more abstract or aspatial presence/absence of democracy in the capitalist mode of production becomes more concretely a *double* presence /absence in the spatial system of states. Concretised in space, the partial separation or 'contradictory unity' of 'politics' and 'economic' can be seen as a precondition of economic globalisation and of political claims to absolute territorial sovereignty. It seems that 'undemocratic economics' can straddle state borders, whereas 'democratic politics' are generally confined within them. This points us more clearly to the economic reasons why the liberal democratic state became globally hegemonic.

The double 'contradictory unity'

The separation of the 'political' and the 'economic' in capitalism is structural both to the globalisation of economic production (unconfined by territorial 'politics' and state borders), and to territorially delimited political sovereignty (untrammelled by 'economics'). Claims to 'absolute sovereignty', otherwise unbelievable (and whatever the material actuality), gain plausibility from the exclusion of 'economics' (or the 'private' sector) from their 'political' remit (Rosenberg 1994: 128, 172). Liberalism's formal equality of 'free' individuals in capitalist democracy has its international counterpart in the sovereign equality of independent states, and both only make sense in 'purely political' terms with 'economics' excluded. The separation is the essential basis of the formal equality of all sovereign spaces, and what would otherwise be a totally implausible fiction when set against the huge variation in the size of states and the polarisation between rich and poor in the global system. The principle of 'absolute' state sovereignty was rendered practical through the differentiation of a supposedly 'non-political' economic sphere in civil society where the principle did not apply, or at least not with the same force or comprehensiveness. The separation of 'economics' from 'politics' underpinned the political dichotomy between internal and external affairs.

At the same time, and conversely, the separation facilitated the external expansion of economic production across the political dichotomy. The global expansion of capital – 'the empire of civil society' – has increasingly rested on the partial separation of the 'economic' sphere from the political sphere of sovereign independent states. Constituting capitalist relations of surplus extraction as 'non-political' in a separate sphere of 'economics' encouraged their increasing extension beyond the borders of a given state, and allowed the exploitation of productive labour within the supportive 'political' sphere of other, foreign states. Economic interests and actors, not defined in territorial terms (though they may pose as 'patriots'), could thus cross state borders and get the political protection (at least in principle) of whatever state they happened to be operating in (for example, the case, above, of the Japanese-owned typewriter firm in Tennessee bringing an anti-dumping case before the US state authorities, against a US firm importing typewriters into the US from its factories in Asia). Rosenberg (1994: 87) suggests that uniquely under capitalism the extra-territorial extension of 'political' power is not essential for economic expansion beyond borders. While this will need qualifying, it is generally true that the 'politics/economics' separation has enabled modern capitalism, and more specifically production as distinct from simply trade, to expand transnationally much more freely than under earlier systems of production. Its reaches its apogee with 'third wave democratisation' and the global hegemony of the liberal democratic state.

Towards the hegemony of liberal democracy

This can be seen from the overall historical progression of political regimes as capitalism developed. It helps explain the dynamism of capitalist globalisation and why liberal democracy has become its preferred political form. When absolute territorial sovereignty was first introduced in sixteenth-century Europe, it really was 'absolute' in that newly sovereign states wanted to control everything, which not surprisingly led to various interesting problems and threatened to seriously impede all sorts of international exchange. For instance, should the Catholic ambassador of a Catholic country worship as a Protestant when resident in a Protestant state? This 'embassy chapel controversy' was solved by treating the embassy premises as 'extra-territorial' and in effect part of the territory of the ambassador's own country. In general, absolute sovereignty was tempered by such territorial devices, including international fairs and customs-free zones. But in time the general reliance on such devices was replaced by more fundamental changes in the nature of the states system, the forms of imperialism and how surplus was extracted from foreign labour.

The early empires of still-feudal Portugal and Spain, for example, relied mainly on slave labour in overseas mines and plantations; and these were politically managed from Lisbon and Castile in a direct territorial extension of their political and military power: the colonies were considered an integral part of the 'home country' on the model of the Roman Empire. By contrast, the later British Empire was a looser, more politically varied entity where slave labour became less important, and semi-free indentured labour and eventually free labour predominated with slavery finally outlawed. Furthermore, Britain's 'informal empire' (for example, in Latin America) did not involve direct British political rule (apart from the occasional 'gunboat'). In the twentieth century, US imperialism has continued this trend, its 'empire' almost all 'informal': the internationalisation of its production has depended mostly on private US corporations with 'free labour forces and private property rights upheld by alien state authorities' (Rosenberg 1994: 169, 171). As contemporary hegemon, the USA has actively promoted the separation of 'private economic' and 'public political' spheres across the world (for example, through privatisation programmes). Generally it has supported sovereign state independence (whether or not democratic) against (other imperialisms') formal empires, and it has opposed post-colonial radical nationalist regimes and centrally planned economies whose statism would exclude American private capital.

The global development of 'free' labour and of 'free' states are indeed opposite sides of the same coin, both dependent on the 'economics/politics' separation, and a necessary (though not sufficient) condition for liberal democracy. The transnational global economy and the system of sovereign national states have common origins and are structurally interdependent. As with the 'economics/politics' divide in the abstract, their separation is only partial and they constitute a 'contradictory unity' (with, for instance, private firms still dependent on state help despite neo-liberal rhetoric). Indeed the 'economics/politics' separation is crucial for circumventing the main contradiction in the global system, namely the trend towards a world market but with the stubborn persistence of a multiplicity of states.

Political power continues to extend across borders, but it now does so predominantly in the 'non-political' economic sphere (Rosenberg 1994: 172). However, while in capitalism the extra-territorial extension of 'political' power may not be *essential* for cross-border economic expansion (Rosenberg's (1994: 87) suggestion above, my emphasis), or necessary in all cases, it still occurs on a very substantial scale, and several important qualifications are in order. Firstly, while border-crossing economic expansion has depended less on direct political control, there has been a general counter-tendency in leading powers having progressively larger bounded territories as their 'home base' (for example, the historical sequence of hegemonic powers from the city state of Genoa, through the Dutch United Provinces and Britain, to the continental-scale USA). And recently this historic tendency has been boosted by the creation of regional economic blocs involving direct political control, most notably NAFTA and the EU. It raises the question of whether or not the tendency is towards a single 'world state' – the traditional ideal for transnational democracy? But the answer is likely to be negative (see also Hirsch in this volume), partly because, as already mentioned, spatialised capitalist competition and the highly uneven development of 'fixed' capital help reproduce nationalism and state territoriality.[6] Secondly, political agencies of transnational governance such as the World Bank, the IMF and the WTO, all dominated by the hegemonic USA and its allies, exercise political leverage on individual states, leverage related to the 'economic' sphere but not reducible to it. Thirdly, there is still substantial direct 'political' control in the conventional sense of political or military intervention, whether used as a threat or actually carried out by client states, or as an 'action of last resort' by leading powers themselves (such as the high altitude bombing of Iraq; or US helicopter gunships as the equivalent of nineteenth-century British gunboats).

With these qualifications, the overall historical tendency for economic globalisation to depend less on direct political control has culminated in the contemporary hegemony of liberal democracy. For economic expansionists, liberal democratic states are clearly preferable to more interventionist ones, whether or not democratic, and especially to nationalistic states (including many military dictatorships) which prioritised the interests of indigenously owned and state capital (for example, Brazil). There was also the added bonus that privatisation programmes, to make such states more liberal, offered state-owned assets at bargain prices. But 'third wave democratisation' is not dismissable as mere ideological window-dressing (though it can be that as well). As Hazel Smith (2000: 28) points out with respect to the EU's encouragement of democracy abroad, there is a real commitment to democracy (albeit liberal and limited) in line with its own economic interests, and 'not merely a superficial or hypocritical gloss designed to mask...old-fashioned imperialism'. Leading powers want to ensure a stable and secure political environment for their own business interests abroad; to ensure that foreign states where they invest will uphold the rule of law, particularly private property rights and contracts; and also individual rights for workers and voters in the interests of political stability – emphasising, in short, the liberal aspects of liberal democracy as opposed to notions of collective democratic participation. Indeed, the latter may well be diminished as the 'sovereignty of alienated individual Rights displaces the sovereignty of local community loyalties...and notions of...human emancipation' (Smith 2000: 28–9). By no means all the states transformed were dictatorships; and some of 'the people' may have had more say *before* liberal democratisation became the global norm, not least because the neo-liberal agenda involves a more thoroughgoing exclusion of 'economics' from 'politics'. The neo-liberal commitment is thus to a very particular – and from a local viewpoint, not necessarily appropriate – form of individualised democracy. As Bell and Staeheli (2001: 191) conclude, it emphasises formal institutions and procedures rather than substantive outcomes and political identities. Rather than democratisation fitting specific geographical-historical contexts, societies are forced to adapt to 'universal' (i.e., Western) norms.

The US-led global hegemony of liberal democracy is part of the '*new-fashioned imperialism*'. It once was said that 'What's good for General Motors is good for America', but now – like it or not – it is deemed good for the world. The dominant sections of capital worldwide have found that a system of liberal democratic states, with individual states kept on track where necessary by *il*liberal intervention from the leading powers, provides the 'best shell' for corporate globalism. Given its minimalism, 'shell' is perhaps the operative word, for it is limited and limiting democracy in three senses. Firstly, it is shallow where applied within the territory of individual states, emphasising *negative* freedom from minimal government, rather than the *positive* freedoms from an enabling state which might be more helpful to the world's poor majority. Secondly, it has served to exclude economic issues (such as growing world inequalities) from the public realm of 'politics' and effective political debate (de-politicising them being perhaps capitalism's 'most effective defence mechanism'). And thirdly, neo-liberal democratisation does not apply to the global system as a whole where it might well conflict with the minority interests of the world's elite. Hence the 'anti-globalisation' opposition in the name of democracy.

Territory and sovereignty

Globalisation is challenging the traditional territorial basis of democracy and exposing its limitations. The state's claim to a monopoly of legitimate force is incompatible with the cross-border sharing of authority and 'multi-level' democracy. Sovereignty needs to be democratised in terms of popular rather than state sovereignty. But the problems are easier to specify than rectify. We need to see the advantages of territoriality as well as its disadvantages in (re)defining 'political community' or the demos of democracy: its advantages create problems of inertia in replacing existing territorialities. The problems in reconstituting political communities – whether in territorial or non-territorial, functional terms – are highlighted by the paradox that national democracy generally had undemocratic origins (Kratochwil 1986) and this may be repeated with transnational democracy.

Repeating democracy's undemocratic origins?

The paradox, as William Connolly (1991: 464–6) argues, is that democratic polities require democratic institutions for the ongoing functioning of democracy, but democracy is generally absent until the institutions are established, and undemocratic origins must be 'forgotten' if democracy is to be accepted as legitimate. As already suggested, establishing democratic institutions required action – including action by 'the mob' – within and against undemocratic social structures, and inevitably the democracy which emerges is at least partly shaped by non- or even anti-democratic forces. This initial absence of democracy applies to the delimitation and institutionalisation of democracy's territorial framework – whether this involves accepting existing borders or creating or imposing new ones. Typically it is violence or the threat of force, rather than democracy, which is embodied in state borders whether established before or after the advent of mass democracy. But the legacy of undemocratic and often violent origins –

whether in national conflict, political revolution or the slaughter of native populations – needs to be concealed for territorial democracy to perform its
legitimising functions. The contemporary relevance of these origins has to be
officially denied by the hegemonic interests in what Connolly (1991: 465) calls 'a
politics of forgetting'.

The problem surfaces most clearly where people cannot or will not 'forget'
and the legitimising 'forgetting' does not (yet) operate. This is quintessentially the
case in national conflicts where territories and borders are contested; their
origins, however ancient, are not 'forgotten' (or they are re-invented, which
amounts to the same thing). They are a contemporary not simply an historical
problem. Their stories or conflicting stories are daily retold. A new, more appropriate territorial framework for democracy which might resolve the conflict
cannot be agreed because the framework bears directly on the conflict (for
example, determining the outcome of conventional majority decision making),
which of course is usually why there was conflict over territory and borders in
the first place (see the chapter by Anderson and Hamilton in this book).

The same problem (albeit less charged) applies in principle to the framing of
any new territorial configuration, decision-making community or constituency.
The paradox is repeated. The decision on the new institutional framework for
democracy – deciding who should decide – is not itself amenable to democracy
(or involves a regress to undemocratic beginnings); the framework's origins, being
new or in the process of creation, clearly cannot be forgotten; and thus it may
lack legitimacy or general acceptance. For instance, a new community, territorial
or functional, might be more appropriate than the pre-given framework of the
state, or its existing territorial sub-divisions, for taking substantive decisions on a
particular issue (for example, an environmental matter affecting only some parts
of a state and/or only particular functional interests such as agriculture, but also
affecting adjacent parts of a neighbouring state or states). But how, or by whom,
would a more appropriate community be delimited? Creating a new decision-
making framework may increase legitimacy problems and add a prior dispute
about the framework (as in national conflicts where the all-consuming disagree-
ment about borders takes over and energies are deflected from other substantive
issues). Where generally accepted, pre-given frameworks while in theory less
appropriate may in practice be better: their origins are probably already
'forgotten', and, even if not, they gain legitimacy precisely because they were *not*
created specially to decide the particular issue.

For transnational democracy, however, there generally are no 'pre-given
frameworks'. Again, the new ones may have unforgotten origins and lack legitimacy, with substantive decisions more likely to be disputed. It seems that in some
senses Connolly's paradox of undemocratic origins has to be repeated in implementing transnational democracy – the existing territorial frameworks for
democratic representation are inadequate, the controlling powers are unwilling,
and the participatory oppositional agents of democratisation (some again seen as
'the mob') have not been constituted democratically. But the criteria of
'undemocratic origins' refer more to the absence of formal representation than

to the presence of informal participation. Maybe we should concentrate on the destination rather than origins, with the agents defined as 'democratic' by virtue of their objectives and participation, rather than where they are coming from or who they 'represent'.

Territoriality and community

Territoriality's advantages and disadvantages for democracy can be briefly outlined.[7] Territoriality is a mode of social organisation which operates by delimiting geographical 'territories' and controlling movements between them (see Sack 1986: 21–34). It is a 'spatial strategy' which uses territory and borders to control, classify and communicate – to express and implement relationships of power, whether benign or malign, peaceful or violent (for example, locking people in, or out; or giving voting or other rights to people in specified areas but not others).

Its advantages include simplifying issues of control, giving relationships of power a greater tangibility, and providing easily understood symbolic markers 'on the ground' – to denote possession, rights to privacy, inclusion, exclusion. Interestingly, its main modern manifestations are the territorial state and 'private property', corresponding to our two main realms of democracy's presence/absence. It provides representative democracy with a pre-given, 'all-purpose' territorial community whose adults have voting rights on a whole range of issues deemed to effect the territory, rather than the constituency of voters having to be decided issue by issue according to the people actually affected. As we have seen, the need to delimit the 'relevant political constituency' each time – difficult, time-consuming and perhaps impossible to achieve by purely democratic means – is obviated by having the standard 'pre-given framework'; and it gains legitimacy from being created before and independently of particular contemporary issues. It is further distanced from particular issues through having a more abstract or general spatial basis in territory rather than in social attributes. It avoids a recurring 'problem of origins' and the regress of 'who decides the decision makers'.

But territoriality's strengths are also its weaknesses. While simplifying control, territoriality over-simplifies and distorts social realities, and it arbitrarily divides and disrupts social processes, its barrier effects at borders often indiscriminate or unintended in their consequences. While giving greater tangibility to power relationships, it de-personalises and reifies them, obscuring the sources and relations of power. It sharpens conflict and generates further conflict as its assertion encourages rival territorialities in a 'space-filling process'.

Territoriality defines 'political community' by area, on the assumption that people who share contiguous physical space also interact socially and share common benefits, problems and interests. But this means that strangers with nothing in common except a location inside particular borders are allocated to the same 'community'. Conversely, *non*-territorially defined communities, based on shared functions or interests irrespective of geographical location, and those who do interact but across the borders, are disadvantaged or excluded. Territoriality can be crudely inefficient in delimiting communities.

These weaknesses or limitations are increasing with globalisation. While the 'all-purpose' territorial community obviously still has its uses, it makes even less sense than previously to see 'politics' or 'political communities' as stopping at state borders. With intensified though uneven transnational integration, people sharing the same *physical* pieces of territory are, in at least some respects, becoming less likely to share the same *social* spaces. With huge advances in space-spanning technologies for moving people and information, but with continuing unequal access to them, people's actual social communities are more likely to be spatially *dis*continuous, less territorially delimited, or defined by function rather than territory; and their communities are also increasingly likely to vary, or vary more widely, for different functions or purposes. People are increasingly likely to have as much in common with individuals and groups living in another part of their city or country, or across the border in another country, than with their next-door neighbours. In consequence, as the traditional territorially based 'all purpose' social community weakens, the social base for territorially defined democracy becomes less coherent.

These increasing problems are cause for thought in considering alternative and particularly other territorial bases for political community. With social space becoming more 'relativised', and the territorial state's monopoly on democracy becoming increasingly problematic, other territorial bases are thought more appropriate, including the EU, or its constituent sub-state regions. But is this perhaps to fall for the 'Gulliver fallacy', if problems of state territory are replicated in other territories? Indeed, in some respects they may be worse. Some sub-state regions do retain more coherence than states, but in general they are weaker, highly varied and even more problematic (Anderson 2001b). Larger blocs are the more common alternative, but re-creating a coherent community may be even more difficult in new, larger territories which lack the degree of common history, language and political culture of the traditional state, and in fact the EU lacks its own public sphere separate from the national arenas of the member states (Buchmann 1995). And this is despite the space-spanning technologies which make transnational communication much easier. Indeed these same technologies and the other forces which are disrupting traditional territorial communities also disrupt at the larger scale.

Democracy will not be found by choosing some other territorial 'level' to replace the state as the basis of political community (Anderson and Goodman 1997). As 'places' go, the state may be 'as good as it gets'. Looking for a new 'place' in which to invest political loyalty is to look in the wrong direction. As William Connolly (1991: 480–1) concludes, 'there is no such place – at least if "place" is...defined through...nostalgia'. Nostalgia for 'local communities' developed on 'the assumption that isomorphism between culture and place was "natural" ' (Massey 1999: 22), and Connolly argues that in constituting a barrier to transnational currents, and having a near monopoly on existing democratic accountability, the territorial state encourages nostalgia for a time when a coherent politics of 'place' could be imagined as a real possibility for the future...[It] liberates because it organises democratic accountability through electoral institutions. It imprisons because it confines and conceals democratic energies flowing over and through its dikes....

(Connolly 1991: 463–4)

If it is accepted that globalisation has made 'a coherent politics of place' irretrievable, it follows that territorial representative democracy needs to be complemented by other types of border-crossing, participatory democracy, including transnational movements representing non-territorial political communities (for example, particular interest groups and classes, as in 'anti-capitalism'). The state's monopoly on democracy also needs to be replaced by including (rather than choosing) different 'levels', and other 'places' such as city networks (see Taylor in this volume) which differ in character from the state-like 'levels'. But while such a 'multi-level' and multidimensional democracy may be a preferable and ultimately more realistic goal, the problem remains that it is not compatible with territorial sovereignty and the state's continuing claim to a monopoly of legitimate force.

Democratising sovereignty

For a genuine sharing of authority and democracy in 'multi-level arrangements', sovereignty would need to be democratised in terms of popular sovereignty rather than state territoriality. The temptation is to dispense with this elusive and contentious concept, made even more controversial by globalisation, but 'sovereignty' refers to issues in the real world which cannot be defined away (Hoffman 1998: 11–20). It links democracy and state territory, underpinning electoral representation. As already mentioned, there is a widening gap between state sovereignty and popular sovereignty; and rather than ignoring the concept, it may be preferable to redefine it in less state-centric and more democratic terms. This confronts the assumption that the state is the only framework, and it is compatible with taking class struggle rather than the state as our primary category. Conversely, it needs to be recognised that the state, because of its unique claim to sovereignty and a monopoly of legitimate force, is not just another 'level' among others, much as we might wish it. States as presently constituted have an irreducible element of absolutism in their assertion of 'sovereignty'. 'Monopoly' does not easily square with border crossings and multi-level sharing.

This issue has been addressed by John Hoffman partly through a critique of David Held's model of cosmopolitan democracy, widely regarded (by, for example, Falk 1995; Hoffman 1998; Smith 2000) as a major contribution by one of the few democratic theorists who have taken international relations seriously. Held (1995) persuasively argues for a complex set of new transnational institutional structures for cross-border democracy at various different levels. Drawing mainly on liberalism, he emphasises the extension of 'cosmopolitan democratic law', not as the law of states, or between one state and another, but to all in the 'universal community', in 'an expanding institutional framework for the democratic regulation of states and societies' (Held 1995: 232):

> some of the duties and functions of the state are and must be performed at and across different political levels – local, national, regional, and international...the idea of the modern state...[must] be adapted to stretch across borders...Cosmopolitan law demands the subordination of regional, national and local 'sovereignties' to an overarching legal framework, but within this framework associations may be self-governing at diverse levels.
>
> (Held 1995: 234)

In this model the state itself is not 'wholly defunct', but sovereignty is to be 'stripped away from the idea of fixed borders and territories'; cosmopolitan democratic law is 'to provide shape and limits to political decision-making'; specific innovations include various supra-state assemblies such as continental-scale parliaments and a more representative United Nations assembly; and intensive and participatory democracy at local levels complements the deliberative and representative assemblies of the wider global order (Held 1995: 234, 272, 278)

This impressive architecture can be taken as one benchmark for transnational democracy and Hoffman's critique is not of the model overall, but of its treatment of sovereignty in relation to cross-border, multi-level democracy. He suggests that Held does not follow through the radical implications of his own model. Although essentially a transnational extension of liberal democracy, the model is not intentionally state-centric, but Hoffman (1998: 61–4) argues that Held is unwilling to conceptualise sovereignty in a 'post-statist' manner, and there is an unresolved dualism or contradiction between this state-centrism and his cosmopolitanism. On the one hand, states must 'stretch across borders', and he wants the concept of sovereignty to be 'stripped away from the idea of fixed borders and territories' and broadened to embrace different supra- and sub-state levels as well as states. On the other hand, however, he continues to identify it with the state, retaining the conventional statist definition of sovereignty and the state in terms of 'a monopoly of legitimate force'. He is reluctant to define sovereignty in a way which would challenge the centrality of the state; and according to Hoffman (1998: 5, 61–2), his statist 'confusion' leads Held to argue that cosmopolitan democracy has to limit popular sovereignty, and that supranational decision making 'erodes' sovereignty.

For democracy to become a reality at different levels and across borders, the absolutist, monopolistic aspirations of the state have to be confronted. Sovereignty's indivisible character of final decision making has to apply to political communities in which different territorial levels, border-crossing institutions and non-territorial associations and movements can all participate. Popular rule has to be detached from its subservience to hierarchical and repressive state institutions; sovereignty has to be freed from the monopolistic embrace of the state to become compatible with democracy (Hoffman 1998: 62–4). But it will not be easy to escape what John Agnew (1994) described as 'the territorial trap' – the geographical assumptions of international relations, the inside/outside dichotomising which obscures cross-border processes, and the ahistorical reification of states as fixed units of sovereign territory. Despite its advantages, territoriality *per se* is partly the problem. But because of its advantages, it has a firmly entrenched dominance which will not easily be displaced.

Transnationalism and agency

This, finally, brings us to the crucial question of agency. Who is going to deliver transnational democracy and by what means? Possible agents range from established political forces (though we saw the more powerful have a very limited vision of, or commitment to, democracy), to NGOs and more oppositional transnational social movements. The choice of agents is also a choice of what sort of democracy is desired, and here the range of alternatives to the status quo is framed by the 'polar opposites' of transnational democracy: liberal cosmopolitanism and the 'anti-globalisation' movement, particularly its 'anti-capitalism' manifestations. They present conflicting visions and mutual criticisms, but might their respective and complementary strengths be articulated together? Could 'anti-globalisation' provide cosmopolitan democracy with more critical, participatory 'teeth' and the political agency which it currently seems to lack, while the cosmopolitan model provides some permanent structures of transnational decision making and accountability? One is relatively strong on 'structure' and weak on 'agency', the other vice versa. And in between there are large 'grey areas' where agents might be seen as working within the structures to change them, or alternatively as being co-opted and disempowered.

From liberal cosmopolitanism to 'anti-capitalism'

The architectural plans for cosmopolitan democracy are impressive but who or where are the builders? As Hazel Smith (2000: 18–20) points out, the cosmopolitan model concentrates on the 'ought' at the expense of the 'is'. It has relatively little to say on how to get from the latter to the former. David Held (1995: 237) allows that the impetus for cosmopolitan democracy includes 'grassroots movements' with a transnational focus (on, for example, environmental and human rights issues), and that 'a political basis exists on which to build a more systematic democratic future', but it is unclear who will do his building. Indeed the attention paid to the question of agency in an otherwise very detailed account is minimalist; and the discussion of some potential agents seems to be about what they might do once the 'model' is in operation, rather than how to actually establish it.

Perhaps not surprisingly given his liberal perspective and emphasis on institutional structures, Held seems to put his faith in state elites and is rather dismissive of social movements as having only a marginal and generally more local potential (but see Goodman in this volume). They are seen as diffuse and problematic, and he cautions against romanticising grass-roots movements, some of which have reactionary, chauvinistic agendas rather than progressive, transnational ones. He wants 'intensive and participatory democracy at local levels as a complement to the deliberative and representative assemblies of the wider global order' (Held 1995: 278–86). But in actuality, 'intensive and participatory' agitation for transnational democracy has been most prominent in the 'wider global' arena thanks to 'anti-globalisation' (and comparatively absent at more 'local' EU levels for instance). It may also be the case that the movement's participants would not accept the 'local/global' dichotomy, seeing themselves as having to be active at both levels and some intermediate ones as well; the language of 'levels', appropriate to territorial representative democracy, is less useful for participatory politics.

Held argues that global governance cannot be delivered through an extension of grass-roots democracy alone; and he is understandably opposed to a simple counterposing of grass-roots associations 'from below' against global governance 'from above'; or of participatory, direct democracy against liberal representative democracy (Held 1995: 283–5). However, the impression given is that cosmopolitanism will mainly come 'from above'. For instance, he argues the need to co-ordinate the fragmentary policies of the IMF, the World Bank and the WTO (Held 1995: 259), but to the 'anti-globalisation' forces from below this might seem like a call to co-ordinate the main anti-democratic forces of neo-liberalism which they are contesting. As Richard Falk (1995: 7) rather acidly observes, 'The only elites…likely to contemplate world government favourably in the foreseeable future are those that currently seem responsible for the most acute forms of human suffering.' He comments that while the cosmopolitan approach is informed in general terms by

> participation, accountability, lawmaking, and agenda-setting by the peoples of the world, through their representatives…it doesn't carry us very far. It doesn't tell us whether and in what circumstances governments are representatives of peoples, thereby satisfying democratic requirements, and when they are not.
>
> (Falk 1995: 119–20)

Falk and others put their faith in the participatory democracy of those transnational movements 'from below' which are 'animated by a vision of humane governance', rather than simply extending liberal representative democracy and the institutional networks of established power beyond state borders. And of course there already were many such autonomous or self-organising movements with an established record of transnational action (Hirsch 1995), as the 'anti-globalisation' alliance now clearly demonstrates. It was these movements which had already begun to organise the transnational consciousness from which the alliance emerged in 1999. As Falk argues, the new institutional arrangements needed for a humane cosmopolitan democracy will only be created, not through the self-motivated agency of established elites who are often part of the problem, but through transnational mobilisation 'from below' involving a wide variety of non-governmental institutions and social (i.e., political) movements (Falk 1995: 7, 119–20). He goes on to make the more general point that

> the necessary enlargements of democratization will occur, if at all, only through pressure and struggle. Economic and political elites will not protect the general human interest on the basis of their own values or even through…enlightened self-interest…Only a transnational social movement animated by a vision of humane governance can offer any hope of extending the domain of democracy.
>
> (Falk 1995: 120)

Since that was written, just such a movement emerged and grew with 'Battle of Seattle' against the WTO in 1999, the protest against the World Bank and IMF in Prague 2000, and later demonstrations about global governance. Its significance lies not only in being the most widespread mass radicalism since 1968, but in identifying the capitalist world order as the common cause of global/local problems and a basis for unifying previously separate campaigns and movements. The battle lines are now more clearly drawn, though violence at the demonstrations has 'muddied the waters'.[8]

The difficulties facing democratisation have also been clarified. Research into relations between 'multilateral economic institutions' (MEIs: the World Bank, IMF and WTO) and 'global social movements' (GSMs: the environmental, women's and labour movements) has shown that while the institutions want reforms in order better to achieve their neo-liberal agenda, the movements generally want to radically change the agenda or get more transparency and accountability in their implementation (O'Brien *et al.* 2000: 5–17). But the study's not very optimistic conclusion was that

> global governance is inching towards a more democratic form. However, the degree of responsiveness on the part of MEIs is limited [and] reflects a narrow base in developed countries. Our conclusion is that there has been a very slight move to democratise MEIs, but the emphasis must be on its incremental and tentative nature.
>
> (O'Brien *et al.* 2000: 231–2)

The member states oppose participation by social movements in a more complex 'multilateralism', actively seeking to monopolise transnational arenas themselves and split the transnational opposition along national lines.[9] And the opposition is further divided on political strategy and what the articulation of institutions and movements can mean:

> For those who see moderate social movements as the hope for increasing global democracy, complex multilateralism needs to be strengthened and

supported. People with a more radical agenda seeking greater transformation away from the liberal programme may view complex multilateralism as
a threat because of its ability to co-opt parts of the social movement
community and deradicalise their project.

(O'Brien et al. 2000: 5–6, 231–2)

Conclusions

The future of globalisation is being contested through rival conceptions of
democracy. We have seen that the leading state powers adhere to the limited and
limiting form of liberal democracy. This peculiarly shallow form of national,
territorial representation, and the almost non-existent democratisation of inter-
state and transnational relations, suits their neo-liberal and profoundly
undemocratic economic globalism. The emphasis is very much on democracy as
representation rather than participation, though even in its own terms its repre-
sentativeness is being seriously compromised by globalisation. As we saw,
globalisation is simultaneously weakening the base of national democracy and
extending the transnational scope of decision making beyond democracy's
existing range. Elevation of the liberal democratic state to hegemonic world
norm is part of the 'new imperialism'. It is greatly facilitated by the partial separation of 'economics' and 'politics' in capitalism, a precondition of territorial
sovereignty and of economic globalisation, and one which we reformulated in
terms of the presence/absence of democracy. Democracy generally stops both
at the gates of the workplace and the borders of the state.

On the other hand, the democratic opposition to neo-liberal forces, which by
definition lacks the transnational representative institutions it wants to see established, necessarily emphasises participatory democracy. Ideally complementing
representation, participatory forms are more amenable to border crossing,
escaping the limitations and problems of territoriality and state sovereignty, and
'oiling the wheels' of 'multi-level governance'. However, we saw that state
sovereignty with its monopolistic claim to legitimate force, or 'the final say', is
ultimately incompatible with a 'multi-level' or, better, a multidimensional sharing
of authority across borders and between different territorial and non-territorial
entities. It was argued that a less state-centric democratic theory is required.
Globalisation has called into question the familiar 'inside/outside' dichotomy
and further debilitated the respective fields of liberal democratic theory and
international relations to which it gave rise. Rather than being 'prime movers'
which can be taken as given, states should be seen as a 'second order' category
set within a system of production and relations of social power; and sovereignty
needs to be democratised in terms of popular social relations rather than state
territoriality.

The democratic opposition which would change politics in this general direction is, however, divided on various lines. Most obviously, the reformists of liberal
cosmopolitanism (and many NGOs) try to work within the system to change it,
while the radicals of 'anti-capitalism' reject an accommodation with neo-liberal

globalism and seek to build transnational resistance to it; and there are of course other divisions.[10] These differences militate against any easy or automatic articulation of democratising forces. Nevertheless, our 'polar opposites' of radicalism and reform are both working for transnational democracy; and both, albeit to varying degrees, reject or qualify the dominant state-centrism and monopolistic notions of state power and sovereignty. We saw that they have complementary strengths and weaknesses – with respect both to 'agency/structure' and to 'participation/representation'. And the extent to which they combine forces will depend very much on the unpredictable course and levels of future struggles.[11] But just as the international movement of 1968 radicalised a previous generation including key 'capitalist cadres', so the 'anti-capitalist' movement, if it develops, has the potential to re-politicise or subvert a new and more transnational generation, including key cadres within the structures of the transnationalisation process. Like the earlier movement, it will gain 'teeth' when its still largely rhetorical 'anti-capitalism' more centrally involves the power of organised labour, taking democracy through the workplace gates as well as across state borders. Here its potential is significantly greater, not only because transnationalism has grown apace since 1968 but because the contemporary movement is much more 'economic' in its concerns. That helps explain why elected world leaders are so keen to dismiss the radicals of 'anti-capitalism' as an unelected, unrepresentative and violent rabble – 'the mob' of earlier democratic agitations reborn.

Democracy is not a zero-sum game. It is not a matter of choosing 'participation' rather than 'representation', or transnational as against national arenas, the global or the local. An increase in one form of democracy, or in one arena, is likely to stimulate growth in the others, rather than subtract from them. To succeed, transnational democracy must embrace all of them. However, participatory democracy is especially important – indeed essential – for creating new forms and institutions of representation. If agitating for transnational democracy by participation is deemed undemocratic in representative terms, it is only and necessarily repeating the paradox of national democracy's undemocratic origins. And if the rich and powerful see the participants as 'the mob', that on historical precedent is only to be expected.

Notes

1 My thanks to Liam O'Dowd and Ian Shuttleworth who commented on an earlier draft of this chapter, and to the participants in the Newcastle Colloquium where some of these ideas were discussed.
2 It is misleading to imagine space in the past as already divided up into bounded 'places' as if these had always existed in isolated self-sufficiency, rather than being social constructions. Conversely, bounded 'places' are still being constructed, and contemporary globalisation is far from its popular image of unfettered mobility in unbounded space (Massey 1999: 11–15, 23). If true for relatively 'footloose' capital or fluid identity or cultural processes, this is even more true for some political phenomena, such as territorial constituencies or absolutist claims to sovereignty, where borders continue to be of paramount concern.

3 In the 1990s there was some rolling back from the highpoint of neo-liberal ideology in the 'Reagan–Thatcher' 1980s to the 'Third Way' neo-liberalism of the 'Clinton–Blair' era.

4 This 'internationalisation and transnationalisation' can be traced in the growth of intergovernmental organisations (IGOs) – created by two or more governments – and international non-governmental organisations (INGOs). IGOs approximately tripled in number over the second half of the twentieth century (123 in 1955, 337 in 1986; only 37 in 1909), while there was an even more remarkable fivefold increase in INGOs (from around 1,000 in 1950 to 5,500 in the 1990s; 176 in 1909) (McGrew 1995: 29–36; Held *et al.* 1999: 53–4).

5 In homage I started writing an article, 'Slow down Susan, not everything's changed', but unfortunately – or fortunately – I never got beyond the title.

6 Regional economic blocs such as the EU are clearly a response to globalisation, but they may well prove obstacles rather than staging posts to further globalisation. In attempting to theorise state borders (Anderson 2001a), I have further discussed the generally decreasing dependence on direct political control, and the increasing territorial extent of hegemonic states.

7 Wider questions of territoriality are also discussed further in relation to borders in Anderson 2001a.

8 This seems to be intentional, both to scare off some of the protestors and give the others a bad name. Some of the violence has clearly been the work of police *agents provocateurs*, some is blamed on an 'anarchist' group, and there is considerable overlap between the two.

9 For example, member states in the WTO opposed increased participation by NGOs partly by trying to confine their involvement within national frameworks on traditional state sovereignty grounds: groups attempting to lobby the WTO should lobby in their own countries (O'Brien *et al.* 2000: 150).

10 Goodman (in this volume) indicates the heterogeneous nature of the opposition to western 'corporate globalism', distinguishing democratic movements and strategies which seek to build transnational alliances of resistance, and those which confront it on a local and particularistic (or literally 'anti-global') basis. Furthermore, the latter also include some very reactionary, *anti*-democratic movements, such as Afghanistan's Taliban and fundamentalist sects and survivalists in the USA.

11 In the light of this unpredictability, it can be argued that what is needed now are some broad guiding principles for transnational democracy rather than detailed architectural plans. Elitist model-building may provide a sense of direction, but democracy will only be increased by the struggle of others, we/they have to be open to the future, and who knows what wonderful and (to present eyes) weird political forms may be developed in the course of the struggle.

References

Agnew, J. (1994) 'The territorial trap: the geographic assumptions of international relations theory', *Review of International Political Economy* 1(1): 53–80.

Amin, S. (1996) 'The challenge of globalisation', *Review of International Political Economy* 3(2): 216–59.

Anderson, J. (1995) 'The exaggerated death of the nationstate', in J. Anderson, C. Brook and A. Cochrane (eds.), *A Global World? Re-ordering Political Space*, Oxford: Oxford University Press, 65–112.

—— (2001a) *Theorizing State Borders: 'Politics/Economics' and Democracy in Capitalism*, Electronic Working Paper Series, WP 01, Centre for International Borders Research (CIBR), Queen's University Belfast (*www.qub.ac.uk/cibr*).

—— (2001b) 'The rise of regions and regionalism in Western Europe', Chapter 2 in M. Guibernau (ed.), *Governing European Diversity*, London: Sage 35–64.

Anderson, J. and Goodman, J. (1995) 'Regions, states and the European Union: modernist reaction or postmodernist adaptation?', *Review of International Political Economy* 2(4): 600–32; reprinted in R. Higgott and A. Payne (eds) (2001) *The New Political Economy of Globalisation*, Cheltenham: Edward Elgar.

—— (1997) 'The European Union: remaking democracy beyond the nation-state', Third Conference of the European Sociological Association, University of Essex, August 1997.

Anderson, J. and O'Dowd, L. (1999) 'Borders, border regions and territoriality: contradictory meanings, changing significance', *Regional Studies*, Special Issue on State Borders and Border Regions, 33(7): 593–604.

Anderson J., Brook C. and Cochrane A. (eds) (1995) *A Global World? Re-ordering Political Space*, Oxford: Oxford University Press.

Arblaster, A. (1994) *Democracy*, Buckingham: Open University Press.

Archibugi, D. and Held, D. (eds) (1995) *Cosmopolitan Democracy*, Cambridge: Polity Press.

Barker, C. (n.d.) 'A note on the state', *Capital and Class*.

Bell, J.E. and Staeheli, L.A. (2001) 'Discourses of diffusion and democratization', *Political Geography* 20: 175–95.

Buchmann, M. (1995) 'European integration: disparate dynamics of bureaucratic control and communicative participation', Second Conference of the European Sociological Association, Budapest, August 1995.

Connolly, W. (1991) 'Democracy and territoriality', *Millennium* 20(3): 463–84.

Cox, R.W. (1992) 'Global perestroika', in R. Miliband and L. Panitch (eds), *Socialist Register*, London: Merlin Press, 26–44.

Falk, R. (1995) *On Humane Governance: Towards a New Global Politics – A Report of the World Order Models Project*, Cambridge: Polity Press.

Held, D. (1993) *Models of Democracy*, Cambridge: Polity Press.

—— (1995) *Democracy and the Global Order: From the Modern State to Cosmopolitan Governance*, Cambridge: Polity Press.

Held, D., McGrew, A., Goldblatt, D. and Perraton, J. (1999) *Global Transformations: Politics, Economics and Culture*, Cambridge: Polity Press.

Hirsch, J. (1995) 'Nation-state, international regulation and the question of democracy', *Review of International Political Economy* 2(2): 267–84.

Hirst, P. and Thompson, G. (1996) *Globalization in Question*, Cambridge: Polity Press.

Hoffman, J. (1998) *Sovereignty*, Buckingham: Open University Press.

Kratochwil, F. (1986) 'Of systems, boundaries, and territoriality: an inquiry into the formation of the state system', *World Politics* 39(1): 27–52.

Massey, D. (1999) 'Imagining globalisation: power-geometries of time-space', in *Power-Geometries and the Politics of Space-Time*, Heidelberg: University of Heidelberg, Department of Geography.

McGrew, A. (1995) 'World order and political space', in J. Anderson, C. Brook and A. Cochrane (eds), *A Global World? Re-ordering Political Space*, Oxford: Oxford University Press.

O'Brien, R., Goetz, A.M., Scholte, J.A. and Williams, M. (2000) *Contesting Global Governance: Multilateral Economic Institutions and Global Social Movements*, Cambridge: Cambridge University Press.

Ohmae, K. (1991) *The Borderless World*, London: Collins.

Rosenberg, J. (1994) *The Empire of Civil Society*, London: Verso.

Ruggie, J. (1993) 'Territoriality and beyond: problematizing modernity in international relations', *International Organisation* 47(1): 139–74.

Sack, R. (1986) *Human Territoriality: Its Theory and History*, Cambridge: Cambridge University Press.

Smith, H. (2000) 'Why is there no international democratic theory?', in H. Smith (ed.), *Democracy and International Relations: Critical Theories/Problematic Practices*, Basingstoke: Macmillan.

Strange, S. (1994a) 'The power gap: member states and the world economy', in F. Brouwer, V. Lintner and M. Newman (eds), *Economic Policy Making and the European Union*, conference proceedings, London European Research Centre, University of North London, 14 April, Federal Trust.

—— (1994b) 'Wake up, Krasner! The world *has* changed', *Review of International Political Economy* 1.

Taylor, P. and Flint, C. (2000) *Political Geography: World-Economy, Nation-State and Locality*, London: Prentice Hall.

Walker, R.B.J. (1993) *Inside/Outside: International Relations as Political Theory*, Cambridge: Cambridge University Press.

Wood, E.M. (1995) 'The separation of the "economic" and the "political" in capitalism', in E.M. Wood *Democracy Against Capitalism: Renewing Historical Materialism*, Cambridge: Cambridge University Press.

2 Reconstituting the modern state

Bhikhu Parekh

In this chapter I examine the difficulties faced by the modern state in coping with the problems thrown up by such factors as the ethnic and cultural diversities, globalisation and transnational communities that are characteristic of our age. I argue that the modern state is not the culturally neutral instrument of order that it is often assumed to be, but is committed to the vision of a homogeneous and self-contained polity made up of a single demos; that this vision acquires a particularly disturbing orientation when the state takes the form of a nation-state; and that not only the idea of the nation-state but that of the state itself needs to be radically rethought in order to develop political structures adequate to our times.

Characteristics of modern states

Every polity has four constitutive features. It has a territory; a group of people who inhabit that territory; a way of life or a body of beliefs and practices in terms of which members of that group are united and distinguish themselves from others; and a structure of authority to take collectively binding decisions. Different polities, such as the Greek *polis*, the Roman *civis* and medieval kingdoms, define and relate these four features differently, and represent distinct political formations or structures. This is just as true of the modern state, a historically unique form of polity that began to emerge in some parts of Europe during the late fifteenth and sixteenth centuries and in others a little later, and that acquired a distinct and unmistakable identity by the late eighteenth century. Since the state is a uniquely modern institution, the term 'modern state' is no doubt a tautology, but a useful one as it highlights the state's historical specificity and guards us against the tendency to universalise it.[1]

In pre-modern Western and non-Western polities, territory played a largely instrumental role, and the way of life and not the territory was the locus of identity and primary object of loyalty. Territory mattered because the community concerned had, among other things, enacted its history, buried its ancestors and built its temples there, and thereby made it its own. The community gave its identity to the territory, not the other way round. Many an African tribe defined their collective identity in terms of their traditional ways of life, moving to new places with their gods and totems to recreate the community and ensure their sense of continuity. Traditional Muslim societies also defined themselves in terms of their shared body of personal laws and practices, and carried these with them when their members migrated elsewhere. That is why Muslim kingdoms and the Ottoman rulers left such minorities as Jews and Christians free to lead their traditional ways of life, and believed that their authority did not extend over the latter. The Greek *polis* defined and distinguished itself as a people sharing a common way of life, and the territory it occupied had only a limited political, moral and legal significance. Athenians were not those who lived in Athens; rather Athens was where the Athenians lived and it was recreated wherever two or more Athenians met. This was also broadly the case in traditional Hindu societies and, with some variations, in medieval Europe. In all these polities territorial boundaries, although reasonably clear, were relatively porous whereas social boundaries were rigid and zealously guarded.

In contrast, and broadly parallel to the individual's changing relation to his body, territory enjoys unprecedented importance in the modern state. It is the material basis or the body of the state and is unambiguously marked off from others, lest there should be any doubt in the minds of its members and outsiders where it begins and ends. Its territorial boundary encloses its members and gives them a distinct geographical and political identity including a collective name. To enter the territory of the state is to enter its jurisdiction and be subject to its authority. Unlike almost all the earlier polities, the modern state offers protection to everyone who happens to be within its territorial boundaries, irrespective of whether or not they are its full members. In Athens, such protection was a political privilege available only to its citizens, and the outsider required a citizen patron to qualify for it. In the feudal polity the protection and the right to claim indemnity against attack or harm were limited to those owing fealty to the lord. Unlike most pre-modern polities, which were socially exclusive and denied citizenship to those who did not share their ways of life, the modern state can accommodate total strangers and might even be composed of them.

In many earlier polities, individuals had multiple identities such as the ethnic, the religious, the social and the territorial, and the last was not privileged. The various identities and the concomitant loyalties were accepted as an inescapable feature of social life, and were regarded as independent sources of rights and duties that limited the government's authority. The modern state is almost unique in privileging the territorial identity. Its members do, of course, have multiple identities, affiliations and allegiances, but the territorial identity is overarching and dominant. When a state is at war with another, all ties between their citizens are suspended. Their citizens are not at liberty to claim that since they share social and cultural ties with, and are not at war with, the citizens (as distinct from the state) of the enemy country, they should remain free to travel there unhindered. Unlike earlier political formations, the modern state territorialises and totalises human relations and activities, and gives them a wholly new dimension.[2]

The modern state also represents a historically unique mode of defining and relating its members. Unlike pre-modern polities which were embedded in and composed of such communities as castes, clans, tribes and ethnic groups, the modern state is abstracted from society and forms an autonomous realm of its own. It abstracts away its citizens' class, ethnicity, religion, social status, etc., and unites them in terms of their subscription to a common system of authority, which is similarly abstracted from the wider structure of social and economic relations. To be a citizen is to transcend one's ethnic, religious and other particularities, and to think and act as a member of a particular territorially bounded political community.[3] Since their socially generated differences are abstracted away, citizens are homogenised and related to the state in an identical manner, enjoying formally equal status, possessing identical rights, and bearing identical obligations. The state and the citizen represent two interdependent polarities of the political relationship, each defined in formal and abstract terms. Since the two are directly related, the modern state is suspicious of and feels threatened by well-organised ethnic, religious, national and other communities lest they should mediate its relations with its citizens and set up rival foci of loyalty. Unlike pre-modern polities, the modern state does not generally grant these communities legal recognition and political status, invest them with rights, or allow its citizens' loyalty to them to be on a par with their loyalty to itself.

The authority of the modern state is not a collection of discrete rights and prerogatives; rather these are all aspects or attributes of a unitary, basic and overarching power called 'sovereignty'. Almost all earlier polities were characterised by plural systems of authority, each derived from a different source and functioning autonomously. And often they all had to agree before the ruler's decision became binding. As for the specifically legal authority, it too was plural, consisting of different and mutually irreducible powers, each valid within a specific area. By contrast, in the modern state different systems of authority are replaced by sovereignty, the unitary, supreme and legally unlimited power to take collectively binding decisions concerning all areas of communal life. Sovereignty is deemed to be inalienable in the sense that if a state parts with its sovereignty, it ceases to be a state. States cannot therefore share or pool their sovereignty without compromising their independence. Unlike pre-modern polities in which civil authority was inherently limited and did not extend to certain areas of individual and collective life, the authority of the modern state extends to all human activities and relationships. In principle the state is at liberty to regulate any of these, and only prudence and good sense dictate its self-restraint. All authority within its boundary is either explicitly or implicitly conferred by it or exists because of its silence.

The modern state, then, is constituted in terms of, and is expected to meet, the following six characteristic requirements. First, it should be territorially distinct, possess a single source of sovereignty, and enjoy legally unlimited authority within its boundary. Second, it should rest on a single set of constitutional principles and exhibit a singular and unambiguous identity. A state whose constitution enshrines a mixed body of principles, or applies them differently to different parts of the country or different sections of citizens, is supposed to possess a hybrid or confused identity and to form what Pufendorf called *corpus irregulare monseto simile* (an irregular body, like that of a monster).[4]

Third, citizens of the state should enjoy equal rights. And since their social, cultural and other differences are abstracted away, equal rights generally mean identical or uniform rights. The state represents a homogeneous legal space within which its members move about freely, carrying with them a more or less identical basket of rights and obligations. Fourth, citizenship is a unitary, unmediated and homogeneous relationship between the individual and the state. Since it involves abstracting away cultural, ethnic and other identities and seeing oneself solely as a member of the state, all citizens are directly and identically related to the state, not differentially or through their membership of intermediate communities.

Fifth, members of the state are deemed to constitute a single and united people. They might be divided along ethnic, cultural and other lines, but these are politically irrelevant and do not detract from the fact that they are 'one people' and that the majority of them is entitled to speak and act in the name of all of them. Sixth and finally, if the state is federally constituted, its component units should all enjoy the same rights and powers. If their rights and powers were to differ, citizens in different parts of the country would possess different rights, thereby detracting from the principles of equal citizenship and homogeneous legal space.

Since this is how the modern state is constituted, it expects its citizens to privilege their territorial identity over all others, to abstract away their religious, cultural, ethnic and other identities when conducting themselves as citizens, to consider what they share as citizens more important than what they share with other members of their religious, ethnic and other communities, to define themselves and to relate to the state in an identical manner, and to ask for and enjoy an identical basket of rights and obligations. This common self-understanding is the necessary cultural basis of the modern state, and it predictably uses the educational, cultural, coercive and other means at its disposal to ensure that all its citizens share this understanding. In this important sense, the modern state is a homogenising institution.

As a unique historical formation, the modern state raised several questions, of which two were most important. First, what kind of entity is it and what is its place in social life? Second, how should it unite its members and create a stable and cohesive polity capable of surviving among other such units? The two questions, one about its nature and purpose, the other about the conditions of its unity and stability, are closely connected, and so are the answers given to them.

Broadly, and at the risk of considerable oversimplification, the questions received two different answers and gave rise to two different theories of the state.[5] For some writers such as Hobbes, Locke, Bentham, Mill and Kant, the state was basically a voluntary and consensual association of free and self-determining individuals, and was expected to provide a framework of order and civility and protect their basic rights. It was limited in nature, was concerned

only with the formal aspects of interpersonal relations, and pursued no independent goals of its own. It made minimal moral demands on its citizens, and
required of them nothing more than that they respect its authority, show it a
basic sense of loyalty, and practice such largely formal virtues as civility, mutual
respect and toleration. For the advocates of this view, the state was best understood as civil society, the term they preferred, or civil association, the term
preferred by such recent writers as Michael Oakeshott.

Other writers such as Rousseau, Hegel and Herder took the opposite view
that the state was or should become a close-knit cultural community sharing a
substantive vision of the good life. It represented not a mere community of interests or even a formal convergence of wills, but a unity of moral beliefs and
sentiments. The state was not made up of individuals for that implied that they
were ontologically prior and morally superior to the state; rather individuals
were embedded in and were an integral part of the state and derived their identity from their membership of it. In other words, for the advocates of this view
the state was or should become a nation-state, a body of people morally and
culturally united on the basis of a shared vision of the good life, possessing a
strong consciousness of collective identity, and bonded to each other and to the
state by the ties of affection and love that are characteristic of the family. The
nation-state was not a formal and limited association pursuing the limited goals
of maintaining order and protecting rights, but a comprehensive cultural
community shaping the moral identity of its members.

Theorists of the nation-state disagreed among themselves about its nature and
basis. For some of them, such as Herder and other German nationalists, the
nation, consisting of an ethnically and culturally homogeneous people, preceded
the state and formed its basis. The nation was not a conscious product of human
efforts but primordial and historically given. The task of the state was to give political expression to the nation, ensure its self-reproduction, and create conditions in
which its members can live out their shared vision of the good life. For convenience we shall call it *an ethnic nation-state*, and its inspiring ideology *ethnic nationalism*.

Other theorists of the nation-state such as Rousseau and Hegel took the
opposite view that the state preceded and created the nation. Thanks to migra-
tions of people, territorial conquests, etc., that had characterised much of
human history, ethnically homogeneous nations were rare. And in any case such
nations were closed, intolerant of legitimate dissent, severely restricted individual
liberties, and were for these and related reasons undesirable. According to these
writers cultural unity was, of course, essential, but it had to be achieved independently of, and even in opposition to, ethnic unity. Only the state was capable of
such a task, especially in a secular society in which religion had lost its culturally
unifying role. For these theorists, the state was to foster a shared national culture
including a substantive vision of the good life and a strong sense of national
identity, embody it in its educational, legal, political and other institutions, and
create a community based on the ties of familial attachments and love. For
convenience I shall call it a politically constituted or *civic nation-state*, and its
underlying ideology political or *civic nationalism*.

The *ethnic* and *civic* nation-states differ in significant respects. In general, the former is closed to outsiders, subordinates the state to the nation, relies on the largely unconscious role of the family, language and customs to reproduce itself, and privileges folk culture over the more articulate elite culture. By contrast, the civic nation-state is in principle open to outsiders, assigns the state an active role in creating the nation, relies on education, legal and political institutions, etc., to reproduce itself, and privileges and expects the elite culture to shape popular consciousness. However, while these and other differences should not be under-estimated, they should not blind us to the basic fact that they are both forms of the nation-state as defined earlier and are subject to its inescapable logic. Both alike are based on a collectively shared substantive vision of the good life, expect the state to embody and reproduce it, view the state as a cohesive and tightly knit cultural community, invest it with familial sentiments, and view the national identity as a central component and even a determinant of personal identity.

The state conceived as civil society or civil association is different from both the ethnic and civic nation-states. For it the individual, and not the nation or the state, is the fundamental unit of moral life and is ontologically prior to both. It sees the state as a partial and largely formal association, and either takes no interest in the idea of national identity or treats it as marginal to the citizen's sense of personal identity. These and other crucial differences, however, do not detract from the fact that the civil association is a form of state in just the same way as the nation-state of either variety, and possesses all the essential features of the state mentioned earlier. It is territorially articulated, cherishes its sovereignty, and is separated from society even more than the nation-state is. More impor-tantly, it has a deeply homogenising tendency. It expects its citizens to define themselves as individuals, relate to the state in the same way, make identical demands on it, share the same view of public reason, to debate public affairs in an identical manner, and so on. The civil association escapes the logic of the nation but not that of the state. Although not a nation-state, it has the state's homogenising thrust, and is halfway towards the nation-state.

Although the modern state need not be constituted as a nation-state, it encourages a tendency in that direction because of its insistence on a common self-understanding and common political culture of the kind referred to earlier. It is because the state requires homogeneity at this basic level that it creates both the temptation and the political possibility to reproduce it at other levels as well. The state simply could not be constituted as a nation-state if the nation and the state did not share a common nature. It is often argued that the nation-state is a result of the unfortunate nationalist hijacking of the state. This does not explain why the nationalists were able to do so, why state after state actively sought to become a nation, and why this did not happen to pre-modern polities. It is striking that almost all the major theories of the state such as the liberal, the communitarian and the nationalist take it for granted that it should be uniformly and homogeneously constituted, and differ only in the kind and degree of homogeneity they prefer. Liberals insist that all citizens should define themselves in individualist terms, communitarians that they should all subscribe to common substantive goals, and nationalists want them to share a common national identity and culture. Many writers rightly criticise nationalism and the nation-state, but fail to appreciate that their criticisms remain relatively shallow and their proposed alternatives infected with the same virus unless they undertake a deeper critique of the state itself.

The modern state is a remarkable and truly original European achievement. It raises the individual above religious, ethnic and other forms of communal consciousness, and creates an unprecedented regime of individual liberties and rights. It eliminates personalised rule and replaces it with an impersonal system of government in which the citizen is subject only to the authority of the law. It establishes legal and political equality between its members, bypasses the social hierarchies of status, caste and class, and nurtures their sense of individual dignity. It also provides them with an impersonal and enduring object of allegiance and loyalty, widens their moral sympathies, creates shared citizenship and the possibility of concerted action, and represents the triumph of human will over natural and social circumstances. Not being based on the unity of race, ethnicity, religion or substantive moral beliefs, it is able to provide space for personal autonomy and cultural and religious freedom. It fosters a sense of community among its otherwise unrelated members, institutionalises their sense of mutual concern, and gives their collective life both a public focus and a historical continuity. By interposing itself between society and government, it protects each from the unrestrained domination of the other, and creates conditions for a relatively inviolate private realm, a thriving civil society, and an autonomous public realm governed by publicly articulated and debated norms of rationality.

The modern state, however, also suffers from several limitations, such as its homogenising thrust, obsession with sovereignty, monopoly of political power, claim to be the sole spokesman of the society as a whole, and its tendency to privilege the national over wider human interests. Since its first limitation severely affects its ability to cope with ethnic and cultural diversity, my main concern in this chapter, I shall concentrate on it and make only a few general remarks about the rest.

The modern state makes good sense in a society that is either culturally homogeneous in the manner required by it or is willing to become one. However, in multi-ethnic, multinational and multicultural societies – whose constituent communities hold different ideas about the nature, powers and goals of the state, have different histories and needs, and who cannot therefore be treated in an identical manner – the modern state can easily become an instrument of injustice and oppression. It can even precipitate the very instability and secession it seeks to prevent. Many contemporary societies are of this kind; and those that are not are becoming so as a result of globalisation, immigration on which some of them depend more and more for their economic well-being, the easy movement of cultural products, and the demands of long-suppressed groups for greater autonomy and cultural self-expression. The homogenising thrust of the modern state renders it unable to cope with the problems thrown up by these societies. I shall take the case of Canada to illustrate the point, and also look more briefly at the debate in India before drawing some general conclusions.

The Canadian debate

For over a quarter of a century the French-speaking majority in Quebec has insisted that it constitutes a distinct cultural community with its own history, language, legal system, values, conception of its place in the world, collective consciousness of being a distinct people, and so forth. In its view its cultural identity is increasingly being eroded by the combined pressures of Canada's federal government and the economically and linguistically dominant Anglophones in Quebec, and it believes that the only way to preserve Quebec's identity is to secure greater political autonomy by suitably restructuring the Canadian state. For the Quebecois, Quebec is not just a province of Canada like any other, but is a co-founder of the Canadian federation and is entitled to full equality with the rest of English-speaking Canada, as guaranteed by the Quebec Act of 1774, the Constitution Act of 1791 and the British North America Act of 1867. Indeed it had entered the Canadian federation 'on the faith of promise of equality and of respect for our authority in certain matters that to us are vital', and had expected Canada to be a binational state. The Quebecois consider it an act of betrayal that with the exception of Ontario and New Brunswick, the French-speaking people in the rest of Canada were pressurised to abandon their language and culture, and they are themselves determined to avoid that fate at all cost.

With that objective in mind, Quebec has made two sets of demands.[6] It wants the Canadian state to recognise Quebec as a 'distinct society', enshrine this in its Charter, and define itself as a binational country committed to nurturing its dual identity. This would confirm Quebec's status as a Francophone homeland, mark it out from other provinces and ethnic groups, and require the Supreme Court of Canada to take its cultural requirements into account when adjudicating on the constitutionality of its laws. Quebec's other demands are more specific and relate to the powers it thinks it needs to preserve its identity. It wants the right to control immigration into Quebec and to require immigrant children to go to French language schools. It also wants the right to do all that is necessary to make French its dominant *lingua commune* and give Quebec a 'French visage', including the right to require that all commercial signs should be in French, all products sold in Quebec should have French labels, all work places of a certain size should conduct their business in French, and so on. Quebec also demands that the Canadian Charter and all future constitutional amendments should apply to it only with its consent, and that at least three justices of the Supreme Court should be Quebecois.

After considerable resistance and protracted negotiations, the rest of Canada has met many of Quebec's demands. Quebec now has some control over immigration, most though not all the powers it needs to promote French language, its own pension plan, and a right to diplomatic representation abroad. Economically and politically it has not done badly either. It annually receives more Canadian dollars ($3.1 billion) from the federal government than it pays in taxes, and during most of the past thirty years Canadian prime ministers have come from Quebec. But all this falls short of Quebec's demands in two important respects. The Meech Lake Accord of 1987, which recognised it as a 'distinct' society and the Francophone presence as a 'fundamental characteristic' of Canada, was not ratified by all the provincial legislatures in time, and it only got the support of just over 20 per cent of Canadians outside Quebec. Quebec is also bound by the Canadian Charter, some of whose provisions prevent it from pursuing the cultural language policies it wishes to pursue, and which it would be able to pursue if it were an independent country. Since most of the Quebecois remain dissatisfied, the threat of Quebec's secession is real, as confirmed by a referendum in 1999.

As in all such cases, the reasons for the rest of Canada's reluctance to meet Quebec's basic demands are mixed. Some think that it is determined to secede anyway and that no amount of accommodation would stop that. For some others, Canada would be a more cohesive society without Quebec and should let it go. Some would like to accommodate Quebec, but fear that that would provoke similar demands in other provinces and render Canada so messy, weak and asymmetrical that it would not last long, or be a country to which they would be proud to belong. Yet others simply cannot make sense of Quebec's conceptualisation of the Canadian political reality. For them Canada is not a binational country, for such a description takes no account of the aboriginal peoples, homogenises highly varied English-speaking Canada, and ignores Quebec's own minorities. It is not a bicultural country either but multicultural, made up of several old and new communities of which the Quebecois are only one. While agreeing that Quebec is a distinct society, they insist that its distinctiveness has declined after the 'silent revolution' of the 1960s and that other provinces are just as distinct.

It is not my concern to analyse the politics of Canada or arbitrate between competing conceptualisations of its history and origins. I intend instead to explore the reasons why a large number of Canadians, who otherwise sympathise with Quebec's aspirations and delight in their country's bicultural ethos, feel that the Quebec demand for an asymmetrical federation goes against their deeply held beliefs about how a state should be constituted. Their arguments, and they all echo the dominant theory of the state discussed earlier, are broadly as follows:[7]

Argument 1: Every state should be based on a single set of legal and political principles to which all its citizens owe their allegiance and which form the basis of their patriotism and collective identity. The Canadian Charter of Rights and Freedoms lays down such principles, which all Canadians including the Quebecois should accept. Quebec's demand to interpret and apply these principles differently in the name of an asymmetrical federation makes Canada a messy, incoherent and ill-shaped polity.

Argument 2: Quebec's demand for a privileged status and the asymmetrical federation that this creates violates the principle of the equality of provinces that should characterise a just and well-constituted federal state.

Argument 3: All Canadians are 'above all' Canadians and only secondarily and derivatively Quebecois, Ontarians or anything else. Quebec's view that its citizens are Quebecois first and only secondarily Canadians privileges their Quebecois identity, dilutes the significance of Canadian citizenship, and weakens the unity of the Canadian state. Quebec is a part of Canada and cannot be allowed to claim moral and political equality with it.

Argument 4: As its Charter shows, Canada is a liberal state committed to upholding the fundamental rights of its individual citizens. Quebec's wish to restrict these rights in the name of preserving its French identity has a collectivist thrust and cannot be allowed. When it is pointed out that Quebec's respect for fundamental rights is just as great as that of the rest of Canada, that it has its own *Charter des Droits* which in some respects is more liberal than its national counterpart, and that it generally seeks to restrict only the relatively unimportant rights, critics rejoin that all parts of Canada should subscribe to the same basic rights, define and prioritise them in the same way, and should be liberal in a more or less identical manner. Quebec's proposal to create a differential system of rights amounts to creating a state within a state and undermines the unity and cohesion of the Canadian state.

Argument 5: Citizens of a state should enjoy equal rights and freedoms regardless of where they live. The restrictions Quebec intends to impose on individual rights do not obtain in other parts of the country, and offend against the principle of equal citizenship.

Argument 6: The Canadian state represents a single and united people, and majority decisions bind all its citizens. Since the Quebecois are a minority within Canada, they are wrong to dictate its constitutional arrangements and should have the democratic grace to accept the system of rights agreed upon by the majority of their fellow countrymen.

All of these six arguments presuppose the dominant theory of the state sketched earlier and highlight its inability to cope with deep diversity. We can see this by taking each argument in turn.

As for *Argument 1* – that every state should be based on a single set of legal and political principles – although it is not always necessary for a country to have a constitutionally enshrined bill of rights, a good case can be made out for one in a multicultural society, provided that the rights enjoy broad support among its constituent communities, do not enshrine the domination of one culture, and, subject to certain constraints, allow these communities the freedom to interpret and prioritise these rights to suit their culture, traditions and aspirations. The Canadian Charter fails all three tests. It was adopted in the teeth of Quebec's opposition. It enshrines the liberal-individualist view of human rights and frustrates, and according to some commentators was designed to frustrate, Quebec's cultural aspirations. And it does not give Quebec sufficient power to reinterpret its provisions. Some of these difficulties could be overcome by recognising it as a distinct society with all that it entails, which is why Quebec is right to press for it.

Argument 2 against asymmetrical federation is mistaken because it fails to appreciate that when provinces are different in their history, background and needs, to treat them as if they were the same is to treat them unequally. Indeed to call them all provinces is to impose a uniform identity on what are otherwise very different collectivities. Quebec is not so much a province as a national society or a territorially concentrated cultural community, and is qualitatively different from most of the rest of the country. Furthermore, like other federal states, Canada acknowledges that since different provinces are unequally endowed in their natural and human resources, the poorer ones should be given additional resources to equalise them with the rest. This is why it follows the policy of equalisation of payments, enacted the Canadian Constitution Act 1982 which allows provinces with higher than average unemployment to prefer their own residents to migrants from others, and allows common law in English-speaking Canada but the Napoleonic code in Quebec. Since the Canadian state rightly takes account of the economic and legal differences between its provinces, there is no obvious reason why it should not take account of their cultural differences as well.

Argument 3 about the primacy of the Canadian identity makes an important point but exaggerates and misunderstands it. No political community can last long, let alone remain cohesive, unless its citizens identify with it and develop a common sense of belonging. Since some Quebecois see Canada as a necessary nuisance or merely a source of financial benefits, they need to be reminded that they are political free-riders and cannot claim equal rights and benefits of citizenship without acknowledging the corresponding obligations and loyalties. As we saw earlier, they also need to define their Quebecois identity in such a manner that it does not exclude or undermine their Canadian identity. However, this is very different from saying that the two are inherently incompatible, that one cannot be equally loyal to both Quebec and Canada, or that one might not relate to the latter through one's mediating membership of the former. For centuries, European states insisted that their members should share a common religion and doubted the loyalty of those who did not. Over time and after much bloodshed they realised that this was counterproductive, and that the best way to win over their members' loyalty was to respect their religious differences within a suitably broadened theory of citizenship. They now need to learn a similar lesson in relation to ethnic and especially national differences. The lesson is harder to learn because unlike religious groups, territorially concentrated national minorities compete with the state on its own terrain and demand a share in the exercise of its authority over their territory which the state finds deeply threatening. Unless the state finds ways of accommodating the demand, and that involves an appropriate redefinition of its relation to its territory, it runs the risk of provoking a cycle of violence from which no one benefits.

Arguments 4 and 5 about the equality of individual rights rest on a common fallacy. Whether or not Canada should be a liberal state needs to be decided by all its major communities and not by one of them alone. And when they do so decide, there is no reason why they should all be required to subscribe to an uniform version of liberalism. There is no single and universally valid way to be a liberal any more than there is to be a Christian or a Hindu. The American Bill of Rights does not include rights to culture and language whereas its Indian and Canadian counterparts do; the United States builds a wall of separation between state and religion, whereas England has an established church and Sweden recognises two state religions. It would be wrong to say that only one of these countries is 'truly' liberal. Quebec should be at liberty to define and apply liberal principles in a manner that best suits its cultural goals, and develop either its own distinct form of liberalism or evolve a kind of good society which, while incorporating essential liberal values, rests on different foundations. There is also nothing wrong or even unusual about having somewhat different rights in different parts of the country. In many federal polities laws, and therefore citizens' rights and obligations, vary from state to state. In the United States some states ban hard pornography but others do not, and some give greater welfare rights to their citizens than do others.

Finally, *Argument 6* makes a valid point but fails to appreciate its limits. The principle of majority rule presupposes a single and homogeneous people who see themselves and behave as one. Just because a group of men and women share a common state, they do not constitute a single people. They might over time become one but they might not, and until they do they are clearly not one. Quebec is obviously not a foreign country in Canada and is bound to the latter by close political, economic, historical, emotional and other ties. However, since the Quebecois also have a distinct history, culture, traditions, etc., and constitute a more or less distinct people, they both are and are not a part of the Canadian people. Peoplehood is not a closed and exclusive category such that one cannot belong to more than one people. Since Quebec is a distinct society, it cannot be bound without its consent by the majority of the rest of Canada in matters that are central to its identity and in which it is not a part of the Canadian people.

In the light of our discussion, the resistance to Quebec's demand for greater cultural autonomy and an asymmetrical federation is unjustified. This is not to say that Quebec has pursued its demands with requisite sensitivity to the deepest fears and anxieties of the rest of Canada. Some of its nationalist spokesmen have so heavily privileged their Quebecois identity over the Canadian, and taken such pleasure in mocking Canada or reducing it to a weak, amorphous and largely instrumental federation, that the rest of the country has sometimes rightly wondered if it should reconstitute the state to accommodate Quebec. Our concern, however, is not to judge the political wisdom of the parties involved, but to highlight the ways in which the dominant theory of the state has muddled the situation and rendered the question of accommodating cultural diversity intractable.

The Indian debate

The kind of debate taking place in Canada is also to be found in many other countries, and sometimes involves both territorially concentrated and territorially dispersed minorities. Take the case of India. Recognising that the state of Kashmir is culturally distinct and anxious to preserve its identity, Article 370 of the Indian Constitution gave it powers and protections not available to other Indian states, and subsequent legislation barred citizens of the rest of the country from settling and buying land in Kashmir. A few years ago the Indian Constitution extended many of these provisions to the newly created states in the north-eastern-regions, where the culturally distinct and economically backward tribes were anxious to preserve their ways of life and maintain control over their lands.

Partly out of respect for their religious and cultural identities, and partly to assuage their fears of Hindu rule, the Constitution of India undertook to respect the separate customary or personal laws of its religious minorities and not to change these without their consent. India has a common criminal law but not a common civil law, and the Constitution hoped that the latter would be developed over time. It remained vague on whether the minority personal laws were subject to the constitutionally enshrined set of fundamental rights, and the Supreme Court subsequently ruled that they were not. The Constitution also exempted minority educational institutions from the policy of affirmative action, and unlike their majority counterparts they do not have to set aside a proportion of seats for the ex-untouchables and backward tribes. It did so partly to preserve the distinct cultural character of minority institutions, and partly because the beneficiaries of affirmative action are all Hindu and their current predicament is largely a result of Hindu high-caste oppression or neglect. The Indian parliament and state legislatures have passed laws banning bigamy among Hindus but not other religious communities, exercising greater control over Hindu religious institutions than over the non-Hindu, regulating the activities of criminals masquerading as Hindu holy men but not their counterparts in other communities, and so on. Reasons for differences are complex. Most Hindus trust the state and are prepared to use it or at least to allow it to act as their reformist arm. Since Hindus form a vast majority, their scale of religious corruption in absolute terms is also greater. And the state hopes that by starting with them, it will set an appropriate example for minority communities.

All this has aroused considerable opposition among many militant Hindus as well as some liberals.[8] Invoking the dominant theory of the state outlined earlier and using many of the arguments made by the rest of Canada against Quebec, they argue that the state should be based on a single and uniform set of fundamental principles; that it should have a common and uniform legal system; that the principle of equal citizenship requires all citizens to have exactly the same body of rights and obligations; that allowing minority personal laws and giving the communities concerned a veto over changes compromises the sovereignty of the state; that the state should take no cognisance of religious, ethnic and other identities; that all its constitutive units should have identical powers; and so on. Since the Indian state 'deviates' from the model of a 'properly constituted' state, and has both liberal and non-liberal elements which give it what Pufendorf called an 'irregular shape, like that of a monster', critics argue it should radically be rationalised. The implications of this are clear. Kashmir should lose its special status, minority religious, educational and other institutions should be treated equally with and subjected to the same requirements as their Hindu counterparts, minority personal laws should not be recognised, India should enact a single civil code, and the state should in general stop 'privileging' and 'pampering' its minorities.

The Indian case illustrates once again the difficulties of applying the dominant theory of the state to societies characterised by deep diversities. Its minorities have reacted most strongly against the proposed rationalisation of the state, and the predominantly Hindu Bharatiya Janata Party, which is currently in power, had to tone down or shelve its proposals. The proposals are not only politically unworkable but have no basis in justice. When different communities have different needs and are not alike in relevant respects, it is unjust to insist on treating them alike. Like Quebec, Kashmir has a distinct history, identity, tradition and so on, and needs powers not demanded or required by other Indian states. This is equally true of the Punjab with its distinct Sikh identity, and the north-eastern states with their tribal identities. Muslims, Christians, Parsis and other national minorities too have their distinct ways of life, and a common civil code either cannot be easily evolved out of their different systems of personal laws, or runs the risk of enshrining the views of the powerful Hindu majority. Since the state cannot remain indifferent to the iniquities of some of these laws, the only just and practicable course of action is to aim at what the Catholic Bishops' conference in India called a unified rather than a uniform civil code. Such a code would lay down collectively binding principles of gender equality, individual liberty and social justice, and leave the minorities free to follow their suitably revised personal laws. Since most Indians define themselves as both individuals and members of particular cultural communities, and demand both individual and collective rights, justice, democracy and political prudence dictate that the Indian state should respect their dual political identity and concede the demand. If as a result it acquires both liberal and non-liberal features and an asymmetrical character, there is no reason why they should be viewed with unease.

Conclusions

Like other human institutions, the modern state as we have hitherto known it is undergoing profound changes. It still has an important historical role to play and is neither withering away nor becoming absolete. It alone is currently able to provide a stable system of order, sustain a democratic structure of authority, ensure justice to its citizens, and give them a collective sense of agency. However many of its traditional functions have either lost their relevance and value, or can no longer be discharged by it on its own. The dream of a happy unity of territory, people, sovereignty, culture and identity that has lain at its basis and legitimised many of its aggressively homogenising activities is now patently unrealistic.[9]

The state today is too plural and diverse to consist of a single people. Since it is constantly exposed to external influences and its members do not share a moral and cultural consensus, it cannot aspire to be a single cultural unit and base its unity on the cultural homogeneity of its citizens. It cannot claim to embody and legitimate itself in terms of their sense of collective identity either, both because many of them no longer place much emphasis on their national identity or privilege it over their other identities, and because some of them increasingly have and cherish transnational ties and identities. The state cannot defend its territory on its own and is not a self-contained military and territorial unit. It is not fully sovereign over its own territory and is subject to the constraints of supranational agencies. And conversely, its power is not limited to its territory and might extend outside it, as when a state uses its fellow ethnics in another state to shape the latter's policies. Thanks to the growing spirit of global citizenship, and the need to tackle global poverty and the common problems of an interdependent world by ensuring co-operation between governmental and non-governmental organisations, a globally articulated politics is increasingly shadowing, and in some cases replacing, the more familiar territorially based and state-centred politics, and thus weakening the emotional hold of the territorial boundary.

We can then neither write off the modern state nor continue with it in its current form. We need to explore either new ways of reconstituting it, or perhaps altogether new types of political structures that are better able to cope with contemporary challenges. This involves rethinking the nature and traditional interrelationships of territory, people, sovereignty, culture and national identity. Since human interests the world over are interdependent, and people frequently move across states, territorial boundaries have less and less political, moral and emotional significance. The state often consists not of a single people but several, and is more like a community of regional, cultural, ethnic and other communities. The state does not constitute a homogeneous legal space either, for its territorially concentrated communities with their different histories and needs might justly ask for different powers within an asymmetrical political structure. And when its cultural communities are not territorially concentrated but scattered, accommodating their legitimate demands calls for an even more complex system of rights and an even more asymmetrical federal structure. There is no reason either why the state should have a uniform system of laws in all areas: its different communities, be they indigenous peoples, subnational groups or national communities, might not be able to agree on these laws, or they might legitimately demand the right to adapt the laws to their different circumstances and needs.

The doctrine of state sovereignty also needs to be radically redefined. All states today are enmeshed in a complex system of interdependences. Their internal affairs are so profoundly affected by external forces and agencies that the traditional distinction between the internal and external aspects of the state, and the corresponding distinction between political theory and the theory of international relations, makes limited sense. A country's currency is often at the mercy of international speculators with the power to destabilise its economy. One country's interest rates affect another's ability to attract foreign investment and manage its fiscal affairs. No country can ensure internal order and protect its borders on its own against internationally linked terrorist movements. Nor can it deal on its own with the problems of pollution, climate change or global warming.

Every state therefore is faced with two choices. Either it avoids joining international organisations for collective action that restrict its capacity for unrestrained self-determination, or it joins them as an equal, subjects external forces to collective human control and compromises its independence. In the first case, it retains its formal sovereignty but remains helplessly subject to the constraints of external forces and the consequences of others' decisions. In the second case it compromises its formal sovereignty but acquires the power to participate in determining other countries' actions, controlling external forces, and thus enjoys greater effective autonomy. On any rational calculation, the latter represents a better trade-off. Contrary to what the traditional theory of the state asserts, sovereignty can be pooled and shared, admits of degrees, and can increase at one level while diminishing at another. As states become part of regional, continental and global systems of interdependence, they need to develop increasingly wider units through which to exercise their shared and institutionally co-ordinated sovereignty. And these units must be constituted and run democratically, if they are not to become remote and oppressive. Although the state remains an important unit of government, political power today stretches from the local to the global, from the smallest to the widest possible unit of government, with the national government playing an important co-ordinating role in the process.

There is also the further question as to whose interests are served by the doctrine of sovereignty. The sovereignty of the state does not amount to the sovereignty of its people unless the state is democratically constituted. When a state denies its citizens basic rights, or declares a war on some of them and claims immunity to external pressure or intervention in the name of sovereignty, the latter is clearly of no benefit to its citizens. Indeed the sovereignty of the state is here usurped by the executive and undermines the sovereignty of the people. Even in a liberal democracy, the sovereignty of the state is not an unmixed blessing. A state's membership of a regional organisation might restrict its sovereignty but might confer rights on its citizens that they would otherwise not enjoy. When, for example, the European Union requires its member states to ensure equality of the sexes in the work place, enact stronger anti-racist legislation and provide training and time-off to part-time workers, some of its members or powerful vested interests in them complain of the 'loss' of state sovereignty, but many of their citizens are only too happy to see it restricted. In short, we should not fetishise sovereignty but look behind and beyond it to see if it serves worthwhile goals, we should not take a quasi-theological view of it but realistically locate it in a wider political context and accept its limits.

The modern state needs to be radically rethought if it is to meet the pluralistic, democratic and global challenges of our times.[10] While exploring new ways of reconstituting it, or altogether new types of political structure, we should avoid the traditional mistake of thinking that one model suits all societies.

Different societies face different problems, are at different stages of historical development, and are heirs to different traditions. Each of them needs to evolve its own appropriate political structures, and that requires both the courage to do its own thinking for itself and the wisdom to recognise the limits of the possibilities open to it.

Notes

1 For an excellent account, see Quentin Skinner, *The Foundations of Modern Political Thought* (Cambridge University Press, 1978), vols 1 and 2, especially vol. 2, Conclusion.
2 Although all writers on the state mention territory, hardly any of them appreciates and analyses its unique moral and emotional importance. See, for example, G. Poggie, *The Development of the Modern State* (Cambridge University Press, 1990), and Andrew Vincent, *Theories of the State* (Oxford University Press, 1987). For parts of the following discussion, rely on my *Rethinking Multiculturelism* (Macmillan, 2000).
3 Several writers such as Gierke, Figgis and Lord Acton saw the state as a community of communities, but they were largely outside the mainstream tradition.
4 For a valuable discussion of this as well as a good critique of the dominant theory of the state, see James Tully, *Strange Multiplicity* (Cambridge University Press, 1995), Chaps 2 and 4.
5 For a fuller discussion of these theories, see my 'Ethnocentricity of the nationalist discourse', *Nations and Nationalism*, March 1995, and 'The incoherence of Nationalism', in Beiner Ronald (ed.), *Theorising Nationalism* (State University of New York Press, 1999).
6 For a good discussion, see Jeremy Webber, *Reimagining Canada* (McGill-Queen's University Press, 1994), Chaps 5 and 7.
7 See Webber, and also Charles Taylor, *Reconciling the Solitudes* (McGill-Queen's University Press, 1993), Chaps 7 and 8.
8 For a good discussion, see Christopher Jaffrelot, *The Hindu Nationalist Movement and Indian Politics, 1925 to 1990s* (Hurst & Co., 1996), and Thomas Blom Hansen, *The Saffron Wave: Democracy and Hindu Nationalism in Modern India* (Oxford University Press, 1999).
9 Many of the things we find unthinkable in the modern state were widely accepted in earlier polities or in the earlier stages of the modern state. These included ethnically mixed juries and the right to be tried by those sharing one's cultural customs.
10 For the critiques of the state from different philosophical and political perspectives, see Poggie, *The Development of the Modern State*; N. Elis, *The Civilising Process: State Formation and Civilisation*, trans. E. Jephcott (Oxford University Press, 1982); David Held (ed.), *Political Theory Today* (Polity Press, 1991), and John Hoffman, *Beyond the State* (Polity Press, 1995).

3 The limits of federalism in transnational democracy

Beyond the hegemony of the US model

John Agnew

In the historical context of 'globalisation', in which territorial boundaries no longer offer even the promise of popular, democratic control over a wide range of policy-areas, one seemingly more attractive strategy is to seek a solution in available models of multi-level governance. Given the dominant role of the United States in world politics, and of North Americans in contemporary political theory, it is not surprising that the US federal system has become a model for debating transnational democracy. In the case of the European Union, for example, the US federal system is both an implicit and an explicit model. The best-selling book by Larry Siedentop (2000), *Democracy in Europe*, for example, explicitly uses the American federal model as the datum for discussing proposals for European governance. Siedentop (2000: 231) concludes that 'Federalism is the right goal for Europe. But Europe is not yet ready for federalism.'

The American model has a number of attractive qualities, not the least of which are its 'pure territoriality', or clear hierarchy of territories with functions allocated to levels on the basis of the best geographical scale for their administration, its separation of powers among different 'branches' of government to reduce the concentration of public power, and its application to a very large land area. Other federal systems, such as the German, Canadian, Indian and Brazilian, bear similarities to the American in terms of the geographical division of powers but have had either a shorter existence or a history of instability. Furthermore, as in the case of Switzerland, these divisions are often seen as peculiar and archaic. These systems and others like them also offer less of a match than the American to the transnational liberal consensus underpinning contemporary economic globalisation, resulting as it does from a projection of US experience onto the world at large (Agnew and Corbridge 1995).

In the context of contemporary globalisation, however, the strengths of the US model of federalism turn to weaknesses. The main burden of this chapter is to offer some arguments as to why the US federal model fails to suffice both as a general model of transnational democratic governance and as a satisfactory response to globalisation.

Of course, thinking about federalism need not necessarily be restricted to the US case. Recent advocates of a 'federal Europe', in particular, have drawn attention to seventeenth-and eighteenth-century ideas for loose confederation within which greater powers are allocated to units at a lower level than those allowed by strict adherence to the US and other federal models. Nevertheless, the long-term persistence of the US as a large-scale *working example* of federalism allied to the power of US governments and intellectuals within the post-Cold War world makes US federalism an attractive model to those searching for a political response to the contemporary crisis in global governance.

The chapter is divided into five sections. The first section addresses the issue of the *democratic deficit*: why existing governmental arrangements under globalisation fail the test of popular influence and accountability. The second part identifies the main features of the US federal model that lead to its proposal as a suitable approach to transnational democracy. A third section briefly suggests why the US federal model has such a hold over discussions of transnational democracy notwithstanding its possible drawbacks. Fourth, I outline the main problems of the US federal model in practice and how the model fails to address the main features of globalisation. Finally, a concluding section summarises the limitations of federalism as a model of transnational democracy and suggests that we need to look elsewhere for political inspiration.

Democracy beyond the national state?

The contemporary democratic deficit can be considered under three headings: sovereignty, flows versus territories and non-territorial identities. As various forms of democracy developed in the nineteenth and twentieth centuries they all tended to be associated with either capturing or influencing national-state governments because the lot of populations was seen as largely bound up with the economic growth and cultural autonomy of the territories those governments controlled. Globalisation calls each of these associations into question.

Sovereignty

Modern state sovereignty is strongly interwoven with modern democratic theory and its claims. Democracy in large part is about controlling or leveraging states in the interest of this or that *domestic* group. The geographical boundaries of the state define the boundaries of the 'social contract' upon which modern citizenship rests. Thus, claims about political and social rights are bounded by the sovereignty of particular states. The state itself is thereby understood as a sovereign agent 'located at the centre of the body politic wielding absolute power and authority. Explicitly or implicitly, the sovereign is endowed with a distinctive, identifiable will and a capacity for rational decision-making' (Camilleri and Falk 1992: 238). The contemporary dilemma is that the successes in the struggle for democracy have been largely confined to the democratisation of the national state and its extension of social and political rights (including those of the 'welfare state') to its own citizens. Yet, the trend towards the globalisation of markets and finance opens up the territories of the state to substantially increased international competition and can lead to the rolling back of the state in precisely those areas of greatest democratic achievement, for example in welfare rights, unemployment benefits, public health and the regulation of conditions of work (despite these being areas which largely remain the preserve of national states in formal terms). Such rights are considered as financially untenable, once minimalist norms of labour regulation follow the opening up of domestic markets (Rodrik 1997). As states begin to enforce the new standards, state sovereignty appears increasingly as a barrier more than a stimulus to the deepening of democracy. Rather than being the instrument for an infrastructural power that states alone can provide to bounded territories (as described in Mann 1984), sovereignty in a deterritorialising world becomes the instrument for a hollowing out of states to the benefit of those businesses, social groups and markets that are best able to exploit the new technologies, financial and production arrangements, and security agreements.

Flows versus territories

Democratic theory and practice are predominantly organised by reference to discrete territorial blocs of terrestrial space. Most representative governments are based upon territorial constituencies, and their administrative agencies organise themselves into hierarchical service areas with smaller units aggregated into progressively larger ones. Territoriality has been a vital means of organising governance (Sack 1986). Democratic struggles, from those governing working hours in the nineteenth century to the civil rights movements in the twentieth century, have generally focused on achieving changes in laws and rules that have well-defined spatial jurisdictions. Increasingly, however, if as a trend more than an accomplished 'fact', localities and city-regions find themselves differentially incorporated into the emerging global economy. (For a view sceptical of overestimating the current extent of this trend, see Görg and Hirsch 1998; and Hirsch, this volume). Worldwide commodity and financial chains now stretch across the globe drawing small areas and metropolitan areas into webs of flows of capital, goods, messages and people that are not primarily organised territorially but as nodes in networks. Somewhat paradoxically, globalisation relies on localised processes of growth and development because of the lowering of barriers to the movement of capital, goods and technology, and the increased importance in many dynamic sectors of localised external economies of production (specialised labour forces, supportive industries and institutions, etc.) (Scott 1998). This evolving world of flows is not well served by territorial models of governance in which localities and city-regions are subordinated to national states which may sometimes belong to world-regional higher order organisations such as the European Union, and global ones such as the World Trade Organisation, the International Monetary Fund and the World Bank. There is a growing mismatch between the geographical anatomy of the emerging world economy and the territorial basis to democratic governance (Parekh, this volume).

Non-territorial identities

Democratic politics has long been underwritten by the assumption that national political identities are superordinate in the minds and behaviour of citizens. Indeed, democratic politics and nationalism grew up together. Not only did the extension of democratic politics often occur as a 'reward' for services to the nation (for example, in the widening of the franchise in many countries after the First World War, or the construction of the national health service in Britain after the Second World War), but struggles for democracy and national independence often went hand-in-hand (as in the post-colonial independence movements in India and Africa). Although national and ethnic identities associated with discrete territories retain considerable attractive power, they must today share the political arena with a much more complex set of identities only some of which have an explicit territorial dimension. Some identities involve a direct shift in economic interests and political allegiances to levels other than the national, such as the regional, or world-spanning class identities (such as with employees of global companies). Others involve new sources of identity, such as gender, sexual orientation and other 'social movement' identities, that have risen in importance at the very moment when national identities have ceased to have the *inclusive* hold over large populations that they once had (Young 1989; Phillips 1993; Beiner 1995; on this literature, see for example Deitz 1998). The new sources of identity are probably the result of cultural globalisation, the increase in shared media images and the choice of identities available from a marketable stock. But they also result from the declining efficacy of singular national identities in a world in which national membership no longer guarantees the status and rewards that it once could (see Parekh this volume). From this perspective, heretical identities can flourish when powerful pressures towards conforming to singular national identities are reduced. To the extent that national identities reflect the power of states to channel or command other identities into a chosen path, the decreased power of states in the realms of communication, education and adult socialisation (as in military conscription) allows for a greater variety and combination of identities. The 'communitarian' current in contemporary political theory is largely devoted to trying to re-establish the ground for a stable, inclusive territorial-political identity upon which an inclusive democratic politics can be based. The likelihood *and desirability* of doing so under conditions of globalisation is akin to the fabulist's attempt at getting the escaped genie back into the bottle from which it had escaped (Linklater 1998).

US federalism

The American political scientist Samuel Huntington (1968: 93) once referred to the United States as a 'Tudor polity'. By this he meant that the US Constitution was not so much a product of the eighteenth-century America in which it was written, as a formal restatement of principles of national government that had arisen during the reign of the Tudors in sixteenth-century England. Unlike France, where power was concentrated in the hands of the absolutist monarch, in Tudor England power was dispersed across a wide range of institutions: the monarchy, the two houses of Parliament, the Church of England, and a host of lesser bodies such as the municipal corporations and the Inns of Court. A web of customs and traditions held the whole fabric in place; the Ancient Constitution it was called, though it was neither old nor formally written down in a single document. Likewise in the United States, under the Constitution power was dispersed and decentralised, only now it was formalised in a written constitution. As in Tudor England, but without the decisive role of the monarch, power in America was divided both horizontally, between the branches of central government, and vertically between the constituent units, in this case the states, which, in coming together following American independence, had created the larger nation-state itself.

The main architect of the codification of the system of divided public power, James Madison, saw particular virtue in the tension between the executive branch and the legislature. He represented that ideology within the Anglo-American world of the eighteenth century which saw politics eternally poised between law and public virtue, on the one hand, and tyranny, on the other, with the advantage in recent years clearly going to the latter. The question of sovereignty was central to this worldview. Rather than resting with the monarch or with the population through representative institutions, it was seen as resting *in* the law. This was the basis to constitutionalism, the idea that the basic law had to be codified and placed more or less beyond the reach of the institutions it brought into existence. 'Madisonian' federalism, therefore, starts with a formal constitution in which the distribution of powers between branches and levels of government is formally codified and with little possibility, save through judicial review and a cumbersome process of amendment, of adapting the Constitution in response to political and economic change. Its basis in law leads to textual exegesis as a permanent part of the political process. In other words politics in considerable part is reduced to disputes over the meaning and scope of the various sections of the Constitution and the Amendments to it (including the so-called Bill of Rights) (see, for example, Lynch (1999) for a cogent examination of interpretive disputes over the US Constitution in the early years of US independence and their continuing importance down to the present).

American 'centralizing federalism', to use Riker's (1993: 509) turn of phrase, came into existence in the historical context of a colonial war of independence and was a compromise between 'nationalists' and 'provincials' once the war was under way. The former stood for a powerful central government; the latter represented the view that more powers should be vested in the states than at the centre. Only the pressure to aggregate resources and co-ordinate rebellion led to the adoption of the US Constitution. In the absence of something as equally compelling as a colonial rebellion, Riker sees little incentive for existing territorial units, such as national states, to throw in their lot with a federal supranational authority. Many of the federal schemes invented and imposed around the world over the past century without some local or world-regional military pressure to counteract disorder and dissatisfaction have either not lasted or been wracked by instability. New Zealand, Yugoslavia, the West Indies, Czechoslovakia and Nigeria come to mind.

Federal constitutionalism, however, has had a number of advantages for a geographically large, culturally diverse and conflict-ridden polity such as the United States. First, it provided a political means of overcoming fundamental economic differences, particularly those over slavery, by imposing a 'pure' territorialism in which each state, irrespective of area or population size, had equal representation in the Senate and representatives to the House were drawn from single-member districts whose territorial interests they were to represent at the federal level. This provided a second advantage: different governmental functions could be allocated at different levels – federal, state and municipal – depending upon the match between the spatial scope or necessary size of the territory of a given function and the level of government that seemed most appropriate to it. Vesting directional authority at the federal level was a particularly important feature of the Constitution in contradistinction to the weak central government of the Confederation it replaced in 1789, and notwithstanding the popular contemporary folklore that the Founders saw the federal government as only a 'necessary evil' (Wills 1999).

Third, territorial representation served to entrench the idea of individual representation as the basis for representative democracy. The legal focus on the aggregation of individual voters into single-member districts that elect *local* representatives obscured the possibility of group rights and ideological politics (more generally, see Parekh 1993). In this way the American conception of the 'collective' has been defined territorially in terms of the formal aggregation of individual votes, rather than socially with respect to distinctive group identities and interests. Fourth, constitutionalism institutionalised a mechanical balance of powers between the various branches of government. Indeed, deadlock between the executive (President) and legislative (Congress) branches was written into the system. American constitutionalism, therefore, is more about limited and limiting government than about balancing the concentration of power and personal liberty (Preuss 1996). It has become popular to criticise the 'deadlock' in Washington (Phillips 1994), but this was in fact part of what Madison had in mind. He feared concentrated public power and its threat to private property from the property-less more than he feared deadlock within the federal government (Nedelsky 1990).

Fifth, and finally, the focus on a founding document encourages a scripture-like attitude towards it. This is a very important part of socialisation into American citizenship. The US Constitution is a key element in the 'Americanism' or civic nationalism by means of which diverse peoples have been inducted into a common identity as 'Americans', notwithstanding the claim to the label from the other inhabitants of the 'Western hemisphere'. Along with the flag and the national anthem, it constitutes a firm datum for 'naturalising' people into belonging to a national enterprise that has sacred more than secular roots. It also provides the foundation for a national political consensus within narrow ideological limits that Tocqueville contrasted to the vibrant oppositionalism which characterised the European politics of his day (Gauchet 1994). Americanism based on constitutionalism begets the 'Un-Americanism' around which so much American politics has been organised in this century. Every political position outside of the 'mainstream' is thereby made potentially subversive of the Constitution itself.

Still the 'American century'

Of course, the idea that US federalism might have relevance to a globalising world is not merely an intellectual one. Although its constitutionalism and emphasis on balance between levels of government offer obvious attractions as ways of moving beyond national state boundaries towards transnational democracy, it is the role of the US as a global geopolitical force that pushes the American model to the fore without regard to its particular relevance. From at least the turn of the twentieth century, if not before, many influential Americans and others have offered the American experience as a relevant one for the rest of the world. The original design for the United Nations (UN) system, and the discussions within the European Union over the institutional form that a more politically integrated Europe might take, are examples of the extent to which the logic of American federalism has entered into 'common sense' thinking about democracy beyond national-state boundaries. Some assorted examples are worthy of attention.

For example, the influential arguments of the Italian exponents of European federalism, Altiero Spinelli and Ernesto Rossi, and those of British federalists, from Lionel Robbins to John Pinder, are based on explicit borrowing from the American Founding Fathers (Pinder 1998). Paul Piccone (1991) detected in the early 1990s the beginning of a trend across North America and Europe towards the emergence of a 'federal populism' in which the pure territorialism of the original American federation (before it degenerated into just another massive welfare-state bureaucracy) would combine with popular outrage against current state-based liberalism to revitalise political community. Recent polemics in Italy pro and con a federalism based on subnational regions rather than existing states likewise look to the American model as both backdrop and inspiration (see, for example, Chiti-Batelli 1999; Luverà 1999).

In a different vein, David Marquand (1994: 25) also looks to the American federal model for inspiration in creating a European Union that would balance competing tendencies within economic unification to concentrate wealth in some places and remove it from elsewhere. It would benefit both the 'core' states (the original six members) and the needs of the periphery with a 'significant redistribution of functions between the regional, national, and supranational tiers'. The extra tier he has added to a two-tier model elicits no comment; the model's longevity and openness to subsidiary units varying widely in economic success and public sector activity serve to legitimise his own quite distinctive scheme. The content and goals of specific policies and how they are reached are occluded by the rush to an institutional 'fix' based, albeit loosely, on a vision of American federalism (see Newman in this volume). Finally, Larry Siedentop (2000) takes off from the American experience to identify the barriers that currently exist in Europe to the successful implementation of American-style federalism. His hope is that a constitutional debate similar to that which seized the American Founders will erupt in Europe and use as its basis the old debate over American federalism. The New World will return to educate the Old.

Of course, thinking about federalism in a global context has older roots than the American one. Johannes Althusius (1557–1638) attacked the doctrine of undivided territorial sovereignty emerging in his time in Europe. Althusius attributed the ownership of sovereignty to an ascending order of autonomous yet interconnected communities, from families and guilds to cities, provinces and, finally, to the 'universal commonwealth'. Althusius's *Politica* was the first modern theory of federalism, one that Hüglin (1990) sees as seeking to square the democratic virtues of the Athenian *polis* with the size and strategic stability of the Roman Empire. Recent advocates of a 'federal Europe', such as Jacques Delors, have traced back the principle of subsidiarity to the thinking of Althusius. Their thinking is anchored to that of Althusius in the Maastricht Treaty of 1992, which asserts that policies should always be made at the lowest possible level. Althusius's lack of enthusiasm for either what later became market liberalism or notions of individual political rights (as opposed to those of factions or groups) suggest the difficulty in turning the hitherto obscure German theorist into an intellectual source of legitimacy for a federal European Union.

Jean-Jacques Rousseau, in his *The Social Contract*, and Immanuel Kant, in the *Idea for a Universal History with a Cosmopolitan Perspective* (in Reiss 1970), however, also suggested confederation and a 'federal covenant', respectively, as solutions to the dilemma of combining active local democracy with a sufficient population base to secure the peace and justice under which local democracy could best flourish (Friedrich 1955: 513). But it was not until the drafting of the US Constitution in 1787 that an actual example of a federal system was first realised (Chryssochoou 1998). This experience has unavoidably had a major impact on subsequent debates about federalism *sui generis*.

The existence of a large-scale working example in a country that has also been economically successful down the years, however, has been a necessary but insufficient condition in driving its centrality to the debate over the applicability of the American federal model to transnational democracy. To this has been allied an impressive American capacity to influence public and intellectual opinion all over the world. The first of these two elements has been termed Wilsonian internationalism after the president, Woodrow Wilson, who did most to articulate it. The second can be termed American hegemony.

Wilsonian internationalism

From the time of its initiation, American federalism has been touted as a model for the formation of new combinations of nations on the path towards more complete union. Tom Paine's *The Rights of Man*, published in 1791, was perhaps the first text to make this claim (Kuehl 1969). But it was not until the time of American intervention in the First World War that such an ideal began to serve as a guide to policy. During the latter part of his term of office from 1913 to 1921, President Woodrow Wilson provided the best 'packaged' version of a vision of the United States in relation to the rest of the world that had inspired the leaders of the country from the outset of American independence. This was the idea of the United States as an 'exceptional' state which provided an example to the rest of the world. Although challenged by the more conventional *realpolitik* espoused by Theodore Roosevelt and certain other American presidents, such as Truman, Kennedy and Nixon, it has been Wilson's image of American exceptionalism that has dominated down the years, even after its temporary defeat by proponents of a stay-at-home isolationism in the 1920s (Perlmutter 1997: 20–59). The idea of American exceptionalism as expressed by Wilson and his heirs, such as Franklin Roosevelt, Jimmy Carter, Ronald Reagan and Bill Clinton, is based on the uniqueness of the American experience. As Gordon Levin (1968: 3) writes of Wilson:

> America was for Wilson the incarnation of the progressive future of European politics and diplomacy, after Europe had cast off the burdens of its militant pre-bourgeois past and in favor of more rational, liberal-capitalist development. The President never doubted that American liberal values were the wave of the future in world politics. Soon the whole world would follow the lead of the United States to the establishment of an international system of peaceful commercial and political order.

This projection of American experience onto the rest of the world involved recourse to such phrases as 'a world safe for democracy', 'open borders', 'open diplomacy', 'free trade' and 'collective security'. These have been routinely recycled in American political rhetoric to the extent that they have become clichés. The subtext running through them is that the more like America the world becomes the safer the world is for America. Wilson wanted to abandon balance-of-power politics in favour of global institutionalism based on such entities as the League of Nations which expressed a 'new world order' that would organise the world benignly in America's image. The idea of a 'new world order' has been a persisting theme in American foreign policy (Perlmutter 1997) and in American political theory (see, for example, Calabresi 1998; Pogge 1992, 1997), long before President George Bush Sr's invocation of it at the time of the Gulf War. Rhetorically, it represents an alternative to the cynical realism of practitioners of *realpolitik*, on the one hand, and, on the other, to more participatory visions of transnational democracy, which focus either on democratising existing international institutions (see McGrew in this volume) or opening up 'discursive contests' about global issues to non-state actors such as social movements (Linklater 1998; Dryzek 1999; Bohman 1999; also see Goodman in this volume).

American hegemony

The irony is that it was when the United States effectively turned itself into a superpower, with the military and political assets to coerce other states, that it was able to sell its model abroad. This happened in the years after the Second World War when the USA combined the vision of itself as a political-economic model with the will and capacity to pursue hegemony that had been lacking previously. This meant that American power now flowed much more effectively beyond its territorial boundaries. It did so because of the perceived threat to the American model at home that was seen as emanating from the Soviet Union.

American hegemony came to have a number of key elements, several of which not only brought about an internationalisation of American experience but also the very economic globalisation that now poses a crisis for all national states (including the United States itself) (Agnew 1993). The major elements have been: (1) stimulus to economic growth through indirect fiscal and monetary policies; (2) commitment to a unitary global market based on producing the greatest volume of goods at the lowest cost in the widest possible market through a global division of labour; (3) establishing the US dollar as the world's major reserve currency and the Federal Reserve Bank as the overseer of the world economy; (4) unremitting hostility to communism or any other political-economic ideology that could be associated with the Soviet Union; and (5) assumption of the burden of military intervention whenever changes in government or insurgencies seemed to threaten the political status quo.

The spread and acceptance of American hegemony have been uneven and subject to frequent challenge. Nevertheless, despite the ups and downs of the Cold War and US involvement in it, the American model of liberal capitalism and the federal system of governance associated with it have emerged as the dominant ideological elements in the hegemony that now governs the world after the Cold War. This is not to say that the Wilsonian model of a world order built upon the American example has been realised. Indeed, in practice American foreign policy has tended to favour the defence and extension of liberal capitalism over the spread of any sort of democratic ethos (Robinson 1996). In other words, it has encouraged economic globalisation over Madisonian federalism, notwithstanding the rhetorical support given to the latter.

Federal sclerosis

Yet, even if American foreign policy had more consistently pursued the path of Madisonian federalism beyond American shores, the American federal model is not necessarily appropriate for democratising the emerging global economy. It is also difficult to see that other federal models might have any greater appropriateness, even if they had equally powerful sponsorship. There are at least four major problems with the US model of federalism that deserve wider discussion. The first is the inflexibility of the division of powers and the difficulty of revising it within a rigid constitutionalism. The second is its reliance on consensus more than oppositional politics. The third is its hierarchical territorialism. Fourth is its reliance on folk beliefs about historical chosenness. In combination, these are very serious limitations to Madisonian federalism as a model for transnational democracy.

Inflexibility

The United States is in many ways a 'frozen republic' (Lazare 1996) in which political change is held hostage to a system designed in the late eighteenth century to bind together in a limited way a set of distinctive and often hostile sub-units, the states. The vaunted 'checks and balances' between the branches and levels of government serve to frustrate collective adjustment to changing times. Unlike, for example, the more flexible British system of government which slowly emerged in the eighteenth and nineteenth centuries in response to changing material conditions, the American one was designed to restrain institutional change in the face of new conditions of life.

Inflexibility has several problematic consequences today. One is that the system is only partially democratic. Though open to public gaze, institutions such as the US Senate and the judiciary are essentially elite-based, the result of attempts at democratising pre-democratic institutions but still based largely on appointment and privilege. The Senate represents the equality of the states, not the equality of citizens. Election to it also requires resources that tend to restrict membership to wealthy individuals capable of financing statewide campaigns. The appointed federal judiciary has powers of legislative review that involve constant reference back to the founding document and subsequent amendments. It is a fundamentally conservative institution. Amending the Constitution is also next to impossible without a very large nationwide majority of support. It requires a two-thirds vote of both Houses of Congress and three-quarters of the states by simple majority.

Finally, and more controversially, incomplete power such as is built into the US separation of powers can potentially reduce both public accountability and the possibility of co-ordinated policy making. Tocqueville, often quoted to justify the separation of powers and a high degree of decentralisation as universal norms, in fact thought of American federalism as suitable only in social conditions such as those he saw on his American travels (Gauchet 1994; Siedentop 1994). He also was a powerful advocate of a strong national government with 'its own fiscal basis and capacity to act upon individual citizens directly (by force if necessary) independent of its member-states' (Schmitter 2000: 41; Siedentop 1994 might differ here). Using a *Titanic* analogy, however, Lazare (1996: 145–6) makes the point both colourfully and with a degree of exaggeration, that Tocqueville's expectation has not been realised: 'Rather than placing the navigator in one part of the ship, the captain in a second, the helmsman in a third and seeing to it that they all worked at cross-purposes, modern democratic theory [from the nineteenth and twentieth centuries] called for them to be placed in a single room so they could coordinate their actions in case an iceberg loomed suddenly ahead'. Some sort of 'constrained parliamentarianism' may provide a better model for the separation of powers than the US one with the law-making powers of a parliament 'constrained by other institutions of democratic self-government, including popular referenda on the national level and the representation of provincial governments in federal systems' (Ackerman 2000: 641).

In actuality, the separation of powers is hardly as immobilising as Lazare contends (Zvesper 1999). There is considerable co-operation between the various branches and, if anything, US history suggests that the system, contrary to Woodrow Wilson's (1885) opinion, as founder of American political science rather than as president of the United States, has been to the net benefit of the presidency and to central direction, particularly from the Depression of the 1930s until the end of the Cold War. It is the control of the two different branches by different political parties that has tended to produce the greater immobility of the federal government in recent years. Be that as it may, many commentators and reformers see the US separation of powers in a largely negative light: as frustrating decisive government and protecting vested interests.

Consensus politics

Tocqueville in his writings on American democracy and the impact of the French Revolution plausibly claimed that the blessing of the United States and the misfortune of Europe lay in the 'living intellectual unity' (Gauchet 1994: 98) of the United States. This gave American politics a set of shared presuppositions that was, and if Siedentop (2000) is correct, is still lacking in Europe. Above all, however, Americans shared an intellectual constraint, furnished, Tocqueville thought, by a widely shared faith in the divine, which limited the questioning of and opposition to institutions that he associated with the excesses of the French Revolution. Yet, one critical test of modern democracy is the extent to which opposition is not only allowed but nurtured within institutions. If the century after Tocqueville established anything at all, therefore,

> it is that we must reverse Tocqueville's terms and take as essential traits of democracy what he imputed to the consequences of the revolutionary accident – whether with regard to internal discord concerning the forms of government or to debates over the fundamental issues. Since the day in which Tocqueville wrote, neither intellectual unity nor constraints on intelligence have appeared as irreducibly original contributions to the democratic universe. To hold men [sic] together by means of their opposition, to engage in endless appraisal of the signification uniting them in society: in the final analysis, these are the crucial properties of democracy in the Old World...Contrary to Tocqueville's earliest American vision, democracy is not the profound agreement of minds; it is the merciless dissolution of meaning and antagonism of ideas.
>
> (Gauchet 1994: 101–2)

The historic basis of the American model in widespread social consensus over values, even though today that consensus has long since receded, nevertheless sets limits to the export of a constitutional model that requires identification with a set of beliefs associated with a particular set of institutions. At a global scale, an oppositional model of democracy in which everything is in question, including the institutions themselves, seems more appropriate. Within the European Union, for example, an argument could be made that what is required to reduce the current 'democratic deficit' is not a formal federal structure so much as openings for systematic access to and opposition within existing institutions, in order to work towards a common good through contest and critique (Neunreither 1998; Newman, this volume).

Hierarchical territorialism

Madisonian federalism rests on a fervent commitment to territoriality as a spatial organising principle. Two tiers of government, one nested within the other, provide the public goods and services demanded by a citizenry in conformity with the most efficient mode of administration. Historically, as demands on government changed, the balance shifted from the states to the federal government, although recent attacks on the power of the federal government have led towards some devolution of power to the states. In a globalising world, however, the pattern of private *and* governmental externalities is less territorial than formerly. Transnational forces create communities of interest and defence that are not well accounted for within a territorial conception of the public realm. In this setting, the possibility of neatly allocating different regulatory, distributory and allocative functions to different territorial units is much reduced. As the span of control governing various economic and cultural activities conforms more to webs of interconnections between regional nodes widely scattered in space, the territorial structure of American federalism offers less and less purchase on the 'real world' to which it needs must adjust. Finally, beyond the American context, construction of a federal model of transnational democracy would require centralised action for it to occur and the danger is that it would create an even greater 'top-down' flow of power than that which characterises the American system today.

Historical chosenness

The term 'manifest destiny' was coined in the 1840s to refer to the civilising/constitutionalising mission inherent in the progressive expansion of the United States from its eastern origins to the Pacific Ocean. This reflected an older sense of providential mission that inspired early European settlers and their descendants, the Founding Fathers. But it also had its origins in the defence of colonialism offered by the seventeenth-century political theorist John Locke to the effect that those who used land productively (i.e., in systematic agriculture) were those who had the right to own it. Settlers could thus claim land if the natives were defined as *un*engaged in its productive agrarian use (Arneil 1996).

Manifest destiny had two contradictory impulses. One was to point to the uniqueness of America and, in particular, its Constitution, the other was to suggest its universal appeal. Either way, US federalism has always had a set of cultural loadings that differentiate it from a merely technical or instrumental 'solution' to the 'problem' of governance. These came out of the American experience.

In the first place, balance between the states (and, thus, within the system) depended historically on the expansion of the whole. Madison believed that expansion by addition of new states was the secret to preventing any one region, faction, or interest from dominating and subverting the whole. In practice, this is not how it worked, since the conditions for inclusion of new states, particularly whether slavery would be allowed or not, provided a major impetus for the crisis that gave rise to the Civil War and the subsequent enlargement of the powers of the federal government relative to the states. Second, the Constitution quickly established itself as the key to American identity. This was a political identity that rested on belief in and subscription to the Constitution. Third, there was a racial element in the continuities that were drawn between American expansion and the civilising proclivities of English forebears. Anders Stephanson (1995: 18–20) nicely, if somewhat too caustically, captures the mutual dependence of American constitutionalism and American colonial expansion into the interior of North America:

> There was a huge and empty land here to be transformed. The new nation was a condensation of all that was good in the hitherto most advanced and westward of civilizations, namely the British…A set of simple symbols was required that would distill the past and at the same time proclaim the future. The extraordinary rapidity with which the Revolution was *monumentalized* actually showed the urgency: the revolutionary avant-garde turned into the Founding Fathers, biblical patriarchs, Washington presiding as a near-deity, all evoked with ritual solemnity every July 4.

Finally, the US model of federalism has relied on a fusion of two distinctive understandings of political community that is neither readily transferable else-where nor expresses a coherent definition of political community suitable for global adoption. On the one hand, the division of national space into purely territorial units rests on a Cartesian rendering of terrestrial space as an abstract surface upon which political representation can be inscribed. On the other hand, this division is justified on Aristotelian grounds as a world of particular places in which different modes of political attachment and contrasting ideals of justice, equality and liberty can be pursued within the broad confines of a wider consti-tutional framework (Entrikin 1999: 274). The tension between these two conceptions of political space has long riven American political life, from conflict over slavery to contemporary disputes over state-level boycotts of trade with and investment in specific foreign countries. Yet, the 'pure' territorialism of the US model relies for political justification in large part not so much on its aggregation of individual voices as on an appeal to different political traditions associated with different places (regions and localities). In any number of respects, there-fore, US federalism is not easily disentangled from its particular roots.

Conclusions

The US model of federalism has a number of features that might suggest it as a model in contemporary debates over transnational democracy. Of course, it also has a powerful material and rhetorical sponsor in the United States government itself. Its advantages would seem to be its conception of two territorial levels matching different levels of functions, the division of public power to prevent absolutism, and its capacity to draw together a diverse population within a large area. On critical examination, however, none turns out to be so advantageous. Not only is the world to which transnational democracy is a reaction one in which territorial conceptions of government may be increasingly limited or inad-equate, but in addition the division of powers rests on a number of assumptions, particularly those of consensus and suspicion of centralised government that reflect American history more than contemporary global needs. Transnational democracy is not best formulated in terms of a single territorial model. The proliferation of 'power sources' without a territorial form mandates that we look towards a proliferation of democratic control mechanisms rather than to a single system of government reproducing globally a single national experience. We might look instead to functional and community-of-interest models, such as those of Burnheim (1985) and Walker (1988) (see McGrew 1997, and in this volume), for better ways of thinking about and organising transnational democracy. As James Goodman suggests, democratisation is best thought of as a matter of *process* rather than of *scale*, so inquiry should focus on 'how to harness transna-tional forces – be they economic, social or political – in the name of democracy' (Goodman 1997: 182, and also Goodman in this volume). This is precisely the opposite of trying to squeeze the emerging global configurations of power into the eighteenth-century territorial categories and institutions of US federalism.

Note

I wish to acknowledge the help in writing this chapter of James Anderson and Felicity Nussbaum.

References

Ackerman, B. (2000) 'The new separation of powers', *Harvard Law Review* 113: 634–729.
Agnew, J.A. (1993) 'The United States and American hegemony', in P.J. Taylor (ed.), *The Political Geography of the Twentieth Century*, London: Belhaven Press.
Agnew, J.A. and Corbridge, S. (1995) *Mastering Space: Hegemony, Territory and International Political Economy*, London: Routledge.
Arneil, B. (1996) *The Defence of English Colonialism*, New York: Oxford University Press.

Beiner, R. (ed.) (1995) *Theorizing Citizenship*, Albany, NY: State University of New York Press.

Bohman, J. (1999) 'Citizenship and norms of publicity: wide public reason in cosmopolitan societies', *Political Theory* 27: 176–202.

Burnheim, J. (1985) *Is Democracy Possible?*, Cambridge: Cambridge University Press.

Calabresi, S.G. (1998) 'An agenda for constitutional reform', in W.N. Eskridge Jr and S. Levinson (eds), *Constitutional Stupidities, Constitutional Tragedies*, Cambridge, MA: Harvard University Press.

Camilleri, J.A. and Falk, J. (1992) *The End of Sovereignty? The Politics of a Shrinking and Fragmenting World*, Aldershot: Edward Elgar.

Chiti-Batelli, A. (1999) 'Un'Europa federata al di là degli Stati?', *Nord e Sud* 45: 45–67.

Chryssochoou, D.N. (1998) 'Federalism and democracy reconsidered', *Regional and Federal Studies* 8: 1–20.

Deitz, M. (1998) 'Merely combating the phrases of this world: recent democratic theory', *Political Theory* 26: 112–39.

Dryzek, J.S. (1999) 'Transnational democracy', *Journal of Political Philosophy* 7: 30–51.

Entrikin, J.N. (1999) 'Political community, identity and the cosmopolitan place', *International Sociology* 14: 269–82.

Friedrich, C.J. (1955) 'Federal constitutional theory and emergent proposals', in A.W. MacMahon (ed.), *Federalism: Mature and Emergent*, New York: Doubleday.

Gauchet, M. (1994) 'Tocqueville', in M. Lilla (ed.), *New French Thought: Political Philosophy*, Princeton, NJ: Princeton University Press.

Goodman, J. (1997) 'The European Union: reconstituting democracy beyond the nation-state', in A. McGrew (ed.), *The Transformation of Democracy?* Cambridge: Polity Press.

Görg, C. and Hirsch, J. (1998) 'Is international democracy possible?', *Review of International Political Economy* 5: 585–615.

Hüglin, T.O. (1990) *Sozietaler Föderalismus*, Berlin: De Gruyter.

Huntington, S.P. (1968) *Political Order in Changing Societies*, New Haven, CT: Yale University Press.

Kuehl, W. (1969) *Seeking World Order*, Nashville, TN: Vanderbilt University Press.

Lazare, D. (1996) *The Frozen Republic: How the Constitution is Paralyzing Democracy*, New York: Harcourt Brace.

Levin, N.G., Jr (1968) *Woodrow Wilson and World Politics*, New York: Oxford University Press.

Linklater, A. (1998) *The Transformation of Political Community*, Cambridge: Polity Press.

Luverà, B. (1999) *I confini dell'odio. Il nazionalismo etnico e la nuova destra europea*, Rome: Riuniti.

Lynch, J.M. (1999) *Negotiating the Constitution: The Earliest Debates over Original Intent*, Ithaca, NY: Cornell University Press.

Mann, M. (1984) 'The autonomous power of the state: its origins, mechanisms and results', *European Journal of Sociology* 25: 185–213.

Marquand, D. (1994) 'Reinventing federalism: Europe and the Left', *New Left Review* 203: 17–25.

McGrew, A. (1997) 'Democracy beyond borders? Globalization and the reconstruction of democratic theory and practice', in A. McGrew (ed.), *The Transformation of Democracy?* Cambridge: Polity Press.

Nedelsky, J. (1990) *Private Property and the Limits of American Constitutionalism: The Madisonian Framework and its Legacy*, Chicago: University of Chicago Press.

Neunreither, K. (1998) 'Governance without opposition: the case of the European Union', *Government and Opposition* 33: 419–41.

Parekh, B. (1993) 'The cultural particularity of liberal democracy', in D. Held (ed.), *Prospects for Democracy: North, South, East, West*, Stanford, CA: Stanford University Press.

Perlmutter, A. (1997) *Making the World Safe for Democracy: A Century of Wilsonianism and its Totalitarian Challengers*, Chapel Hill, NC: University of North Carolina Press.

Phillips, A. (1993) *Democracy and Difference*, University Park, PA: Penn State University Press.

Phillips, K.P. (1994) *Arrogant Capital: Washington, Wall Street, and the Frustration of American Politics*, Boston: Little, Brown.

Piccone, P. (1991) 'The crisis of liberalism and the emergence of federal populism', *Telos* 89: 7–44.

Pinder, J. (1998) *Altiero Spinelli and the British Federalists: Writings by Beveridge, Robbins and Spinelli 1937–1943*, London: Federal Trust.

Pogge, T.H. (1992) 'Cosmopolitanism and sovereignty', *Ethics* 103: 48–75.

—— (1997) 'How to create supra-national institutions democratically: some reflections on the European Union's democratic deficit', *Journal of Political Philosophy* 5: 163–82.

Preuss, U.K. (1996) 'The political meaning of constitutionalism', in R. Bellamy (ed.), *Constitutionalism, Democracy and Sovereignty: American and European Perspectives*, Aldershot: Avebury.

Reiss, H. (ed.) (1970) *Kant's Political Writings*, Cambridge: Cambridge University Press.

Riker, W.H. (1993) 'Federalism', in R.E. Goodin and P. Pettit (eds), *A Companion to Political Philosophy*, Oxford: Blackwell.

Robinson, W.I. (1996) *Promoting Polyarchy: Globalization, US Intervention, and Hegemony*, Cambridge: Cambridge University Press.

Rodrik, D. (1997) *Has Globalization Gone Too Far?*, Washington DC: Institute for International Economics.

Rousseau, J-J. (1968) *The Social Contract*, London: Penguin.

Sack, R.D. (1986) *Human Territoriality: Its Theory and History*, Cambridge: Cambridge University Press.

Schmitter, P. (2000) 'Federalism and the Euro-polity', *Journal of Democracy* 11: 40–7.

Scott, A.J. (1998) *Regions and the World Economy: The Coming Shape of Global Production, Competition, and Political Order*, Oxford: Oxford University Press.

Siedentop, L. (1994) *Tocqueville*, Oxford: Oxford University Press.

—— (2000) *Democracy in Europe*, London: Allen Lane.

Stephanson, A. (1995) *Manifest Destiny: American Expansion and the Empire of Right*, New York: Hill and Wang.

Walker, R.B.J. (1988) *One World, Many Worlds: Struggles for a Just World Peace*, Boulder, CO: Lynne Reinner.

Wills, G. (1999) *A Necessary Evil: A History of American Distrust of Government*, New York: Simon and Schuster.

Wilson, W. (1885) *Congressional Government: A Study in American Politics*, Boston: Houghton Mifflin.

Young, I.M. (1989) 'Polity and group difference: a critique of the ideal of universal citizenship', *Ethics* 99: 250–74.

Zvesper, J. (1999) 'The separation of powers in American politics: why we fail to accentuate the positive', *Government and Opposition* 34: 3–23.

4 Reconceptualising democracy in the European Union

Michael Newman

If democracy needs to move beyond its territorial basis in the 'nation-state', the European Union (EU) has an obvious relevance. It is already the most complex transnational political and economic structure in the contemporary world: it has an established policy-making system, and it includes both a democratically elected supra-state parliament and informal networks and pressure groups which span state borders. It is therefore tempting to believe that the task is 'simply' to democratise the existing set of interactions that constitute the Union. On the other hand, there is now widespread agreement that earlier proposals for overcoming the EU's so-called 'democratic deficit' tended to be over-optimistic and that the problems are deeply embedded in the process of European integration. A variety of solutions are now advocated, including consultative referenda, the elaboration of constitutions, and direct elections of the Commission.[1] However, the underlying assumptions about democracy are often taken for granted when such proposals are canvassed, and this is not an adequate basis for advancing either its theory or practice. For democracy is obviously a contested concept and proposals for its enhancement within the EU will be dependent upon the priorities and principles assumed by the theorist – whether or not these are avowed. There is also a second and equally difficult issue involved in thinking about democracy in relation to the EU: the spatial or territorial dimension. Does the 'nation-state' remain the *primary* location for democracy or is the EU a more appropriate site? Or do neither of these suppositions make sense? This chapter begins by exploring these conceptual questions. After clarifying the underlying assumptions about democracy and drawing some conclusions about the territorial issue, it offers suggestions for addressing the multiple problems involved in democratising the EU.

Democracy

How many people can really conceptualise democracy? When the Soviet bloc collapsed, neo-liberals assumed that this meant the introduction of free elections and the establishment of a competitive market system. Now that they have seen the results in Russia, even some of the proponents of marketisation are having second thoughts and realising that matters are a little more complicated. This is hardly a surprise for those who never identified the 'free market' with freedom, or for those who saw capitalism as the antithesis of democracy. But this does not necessarily mean that the critics of capitalist democracy had a very clear conception of the alternatives. It is not difficult to produce a definition of democracy, but the problems begin as soon as one considers the relative weighting attached to the component elements in 'rule by the people'. What is the balance between participation and representation, between liberty and equality, between majority rule and the rights of minorities? How important are institutions, constitutions and formal procedures? None of these are straightforward questions, even for those who are working within the same general ideological framework. Yet variations in the relative weighting attached to different elements in the constellation of values and procedures associated with democracy will result in very different policy prescriptions for the EU. For example, those whose conception rests primarily on institutional factors may attach great importance to the relative weakness of the European Parliament, while those who perceive greater social equality as a precondition for democracy may be more concerned about the way in which neo-liberalism is embedded in the Treaties. It is therefore necessary to outline the assumptions and priorities underlying the approach in this chapter.

I take as the starting point acceptance of some key features of the current dominant model of democracy: free speech, a free flow of information, freedom to organise, universal suffrage, a separation of powers, representation, and a choice of parties.[2] This is normally regarded as 'liberal democracy' and this term is acceptable with two provisos. First, it needs to be recalled that many of the elements did not emerge from the liberal tradition at all but were forced on it by pressures from below and from working-class and socialist movements. This, for example, was generally the case with the extension of suffrage and the recognition of trade union rights. Secondly, use of the term does *not* mean acceptance of the necessity for the so-called economic freedoms which are conventionally seen as the concomitant of such political freedoms. It may be valid to argue that, historically, liberal democracy has developed on the basis of a capitalist economy, but I do not accept the argument that there is a *necessary* connection between the political and economic aspects of the system. While there is compelling evidence that an economy controlled by a bureaucratic central planning system is incompatible with the requisite dispersal of power for liberal democracy, it is not self-evident that this would be true of a decentralised socialist economy with a variety of different forms of ownership.[3]

If the dominant model (thus refined) is accepted, the key questions concern the relative priorities within the general constellation of values that the term implies. For example, is a democracy of this kind to be regarded as a set of procedures (voting systems, choice of parties, institutional structures)? Or is it also concerned with the promotion of substantive values: securing freedom, rights, justice, equality and so on? My answer would be that it cannot just be about procedures, but must also incorporate values. But this means that there will sometimes be clashes between procedures and values; and, when making judgements about the ways in which democratisation might be enhanced, we must also have regard to possible outcomes and the relationship between these and the key values. This point may be illustrated with a simple example.

The British 'first past the post' electoral system is currently under review and, on procedural democratic grounds, it is difficult to justify a system in which there is such a poor relationship between the number of votes cast and the number of candidates elected in each party. For this reason, there seems to be a very good procedural case for changing to one of the systems of proportional representation. But just suppose that there was really strong evidence to suggest that the most significant immediate result of this change would be the break-up of the Conservative Party, and the development of an extreme Right racist party with similar power to that of the *Front National* in France. Let us also suppose that, in the longer term, it could be predicted that other political parties (as in France) would seek to reduce the appeal of this new force by emulating some of its policies, perhaps diluting race relations legislation and instituting still harsher immigration and asylum policies.[4] Now, if these were the most probable outcomes, would it still be so obvious on democratic grounds that the electoral system should be changed? Surely there would then be a clash between procedural concerns (a fair electoral system) and substantive values (protection of human rights, and equality of peoples). Which would be the priority? Of course, this is an illegitimate example because there is no reliable evidence that a change in the electoral system would have these results. However, the attempt to predict the probable outcomes of changes in procedure in relation to substantive values is surely necessary. Otherwise, the implication would be that each element in the constellation of democratic values and procedures should be considered in isolation from all the rest. Yet if this point is accepted, there is a further difficulty, for there may also be clashes between the values themselves. It is necessary to indicate my general position on three key tensions.

One obvious potential tension within the cluster of values is between *liberty* and *equality*. For many conservatives and liberals the clash between the two is almost total. Thus any increase in state intervention so as to enhance equality *ipso facto* constitutes a reduction in liberty. I would reject this on a number of grounds. First, there is no justification for distributing life-chances on the basis of accidents of birth: much of what passes for liberty is therefore more often a defence of privilege. Secondly, since social and economic inequalities lead to political inequality – in the sense that deprived groups participate less in the political system and wield less power when they do participate – it follows that substantial social inequality can negate other democratic values. This means that 'libertarian' definitions of liberty, which uphold the notion of a minimal state, are in fact little more than rationalisations for the defence of those who already hold decisive power. Since the capitalist system inevitably rewards these interests, democratisation must involve, at the very least, a constant intervention in the market for redistributive purposes through the provision of public goods, progressive fiscal policies, inheritance taxes and so on.[5] Yet although the socialist critique of capitalism remains as valid as ever, it also seems evident that the problem of liberty remains. If equality is elevated to become the *sole* value – on the dubious assumption that there is no clash between equality and liberty – this can lead to the elimination of fundamental liberties. This suggests that democracy implies some compromise between the goals of liberty and equality. The emphasis here is on egalitarianism since socio-economic inequalities are endemic within capitalism and have been growing in many countries during the neo-liberal era. Such inequalities are both unjust and politically unacceptable.

A second tension is between different types of democracy, particularly representative and participatory forms, the former emphasising the leadership of elites and parties, the latter stressing popular involvement and pressure from below.[6] The assumption in this chapter is that both are necessary. In large modern *polities*, institutions and systems of representation are indispensable. Similarly, political parties are necessary for articulating and implementing policies, and leadership involves highlighting goals and values rather than simply responding to the preferences of focus groups. At the same time protest movements and direct participation must be regarded as of fundamental importance, and democratisation involves the nurturing of organisations and channels through which popular demands are expressed and mobilised, thus leading to empowerment.

A third tension concerns the question of *exclusiveness* and *inclusiveness*. Some political traditions stress the interests of the 'insider' against the 'outsider', the dominant nation against the minority nation, and traditional roles and values against ideas that challenge the existing norms. Such ideas are constantly mobilised by right-wing populist movements. The model on which this chapter is based is in complete opposition to this approach: it holds that the political system should be as *inclusive* as possible in relation, for instance, to gender, sexuality and ethnicity (see also Parekh in this volume).[7]

These, then, are the general values and priorities which underlie my approach to democratisation. The next difficulty concerns that of 'location'.

Territory and polity

It is difficult to conceive of democracy without primary reference to a territorially defined *polity*. There are, of course, ways in which we do think of democracy – or, more often, its absence – in other contexts, such as work-based organisations, pressure groups and parties. However, when the public sphere of politics is the focus, territory becomes dominant (see Anderson in this volume). Since the rise of the modern 'nation-state', the political system *in* a particular territorially bounded state is the conventional reference point. As the development of modern notions of democracy has followed the establishment of the 'nation-state', the task of democratisation has been seen to lie within the borders of such states. Of course, there have been proponents of democratisation both 'below' and 'above' the state throughout the twentieth century but, until recently, these have not disturbed the dominant conception.[8] The prevalence of the state-centred approach has an obvious relevance for the EU.

The state-centred approach and the European Union

Those who are most attached to the idea of the 'nation-state' as the obvious territorial location for democracy may regard the EU as a threat and argue that the best way to enhance democratisation is to resist further integration. Currently such attitudes are most commonly associated with the 'Eurosceptic' Right, and the 'Thatcherite' argument in Britain, for example, has been that the parliamentary system constitutes British democracy and that EU encroachment in the domestic sphere should be resisted or rolled back. The general approach to the EU then involves an insistence on inter-governmentalism, protected by veto power in the Council, a strict limitation on Community competences, control over the Commission, and contempt for the democratic pretensions of the European Parliament. However, in this form, the argument contradicts the normative principles of democracy outlined above in at least three respects. First, the British Conservative argument against the EU has been conducted in the name of neo-liberal economic principles and has involved opposition to European social policies which offer even minimal protection against the rigours of the free market. This contradicts equality as a primary goal. Secondly, Britain's Eurosceptic Right has insisted that the Westminster parliamentary system is a sufficient form of democracy. In fact, this has always been a system of democratic elitism and the centralisation of the Thatcher and Major governments weakened all alternative centres of power. This view therefore also contravenes the goal of participation. Thirdly, the opposition has been conducted in a highly xenophobic way with a stress on the threat to British (and particularly English) life from mainland Europe, a tendency which was exacerbated under William Hague's leadership in the campaign for the 1999 Euro-elections. This is incompatible with the goal of inclusion. Yet refutation of the right-wing Eurosceptic position does not, in itself, end the argument.

In recent years the growth of opposition to the EU from the Right has become so marked that it is easy to forget that, historically, the state-centred arguments against European integration have at least as often been associated with the Left, and not only in Britain. Of course, in some cases, these have also taken a strongly nationalistic form, as, for example, with much of the anti-integrationist rhetoric of the French Communist Party (PCF).[9] Such approaches are also unacceptable on the normative ground that they contravene the goal of inclusion. However, there have been left-wing arguments against the EU which have not been conducted in this way.

Ralph Miliband's last book, *Socialism for a Sceptical Age* (1994), attempted to reaffirm the case for his version of Marxism, and one of its key characteristics was his insistence that democracy was a fundamental part of socialism. He made it absolutely clear that this involved the pluralist tradition more normally associated with liberal democracy. The work was thus a refutation of a strand in Marxist thought which had implied that political questions of this kind could be postponed until after a seizure of power: for Miliband it was now self-evident that a commitment to so-called 'bourgeois' freedoms must be an integral part of the socialist project at every stage in its development. He was also a committed internationalist without any party attachment who could not be accused of exploiting nationalist prejudices in arguments against the EU. He was nevertheless adamant in his avowal of a state-centred view:

> The fact of class struggle on an international scale inexorably points to the need for a socialist government to preserve as large a measure of independence as is possible. Notwithstanding the globalisation of capital and the ever greater interdependence of nations, the nation-state must remain for the foreseeable future the crucial point of reference for the Left. This is not a matter of clinging to an 'obsolete' notion of sovereignty but simply to assert the right of a government seeking to carry out a programme of radical social renewal not to be stopped from doing so by external forces. Such a government would clearly need to impose various measures, including exchange and carefully selected import controls, to protect its economy; and it would need to reject the constraints which the General Agreement on Tariffs and Trade seeks to impose upon governments.

However, after arguing against the project for a monetary union, and expressing scepticism about the arguments of 'Left integrationists', he concluded:

> Left parties cannot retreat into a national bunker; and a socialist government would not leave the Union of its own volition, but would rather seek to find allies in its attempts to overcome unacceptable constraints. Its general aim would be to loosen integration in favour, at most, of arrangements which would leave a socialist government with the greatest possible degree of autonomous decision-making in economic and all other fields of policy. There are conservatives who advocate loose arrangements on narrow nationalist grounds. Socialists should advocate such arrangements on very different grounds, and should be committed to an internationalism based on solidarity with all left forces in the world. It will be time enough to consider closer connections when socialist governments exist in many countries: until this happens, the Left cannot accept integration into a 'union' whose members are actively opposed to the kind of fundamental transformation which it is the purpose of a left government to achieve.[10]

Is this argument tenable? And is it acceptable in relation to the goals and principles outlined above?

In effect, Miliband was suggesting that the 'nation-state' could still be regarded as a *polity* which is sufficiently discrete to effect fundamental change within its own frontiers. Clearly the constraints were already formidable at the time he was writing (1994). Since the establishment of the EEC, very considerable economic integration had progressively been created, with a new legal and political framework to enforce it. The implementation of the Treaty of Rome (from 1958) reinforced by the Single European Act (implemented from 1987) proscribed a vast number of measures deemed to conflict with the requirements of economic competition. Community law superseded domestic law in cases of dispute, with the European Court of Justice as the highest court, and much Community law took direct effect without substantial involvement by domestic parliaments. At the administrative level there was a very high degree of inter-penetration between domestic civil servants and both the Commission and the Council and, since the Maastricht Treaty (implemented since 1993), majority voting had become the most common decision-making procedure in the Council. Since Miliband's death in 1994, the establishment of Economic and Monetary Union (EMU) by eleven countries in January 1999, with the use of the euro as a common currency since January 2002, proscribes a further series of measures which were possible at the level of the nation-state. To recapitulate these points is *not* to suggest that they are fixed for eternity: after the collapse of the Soviet bloc and the disintegration of Yugoslavia, it would be folly to imply the immutability of any supranational structures. It is rather to suggest that any individual government which attempted to emancipate itself from the EU in the way that Miliband envisaged would require formidable political determination. In which, if any, of the current member states is this likely?

It would seem almost inconceivable that Luxembourg, as the smallest state, or Greece, as the poorest, would be able to adopt such a stance. Despite the apparent universality of his argument, Miliband was almost certainly thinking of the larger, more advanced capitalist states when he suggested the possibility of an autonomous democratic transformation. Germany is the country which, in theory, has the greatest potential for such a development because it possesses easily the most powerful economy in the Union. However, it is highly improbable that any such political will would emerge in the Federal Republic. It is true that there is less popular enthusiasm for the EU than in the past, but the belief that European integration is an integral part of the new Germany has been a central element in its political culture since 1949. Furthermore, the Federal Republic *is* now the most important state within the Union with a decisive role in shaping its agenda, and this makes it unlikely that even a Left-inclined political movement would perceive the conversion of the EU into a loose confederation as a desirable goal.[11]

If Germany's post-war development makes it a highly unlikely candidate for an autonomous strategy, this is still more true of one of the other 'big four', Italy. Ever since the transformation of attitudes towards the EEC by the Socialist Party (PSI) in the 1950s and the Communist Party (PCI) in the early 1960s, Italy has been a country in which 'Europeanism' has been virtually unquestioned.[12] Given the widespread cynicism about domestic politics and the Italian state itself, the EU has been perceived as a force for 'good government' and, still more, for economic stability. The preparation for membership of EMU may be taken as an illustration of this point. Since the convergence criteria for membership imposed sharp deflationary pressures on the Italian economy – and may even have been partially designed to keep Italy out – it might have been expected that they would provoke an outcry. Quite the contrary. The dominant Italian view was that these external requirements were necessary for reforming the domestic economy and were justified because of past malpractices within the state.[13] And, more positively, the majority of the Italian Left have long believed that the future lies in democratising the EU rather than in thinking of a separate Italian road to socialism.

France and Britain have stronger traditions of left-wing opposition to European integration. Does Miliband's state-centred position have more relevance in these countries?

Even if sometimes vitiated by populist nationalism, the French Communist Party (PCF) has presented a state-centred view throughout the post-war period and, until the early 1980s, the perspective of the left-wing of the Socialist Party (PS) on the EU was quite similar to that suggested by Miliband. However, the PCF has now dwindled in power and popular support (securing only 6.8 per cent of the vote in the Euro-elections of 1999) and the PS seeks to enhance the social policy and 'economic governance' of the EU rather than to pursue an autonomous strategy. Certainly, 'Euroscepticism' has developed in France, as was manifest in the narrowness of the victory in the referendum in 1992 on the Maastricht Treaty. It is also true that those involved in the industrial unrest that paved the way for the surprise electoral victory of the PS in 1997 perceived the link between the austerity measures and the EMU. However, it is equally clear that anti-EU sentiments are now mobilised more by the extreme Right in French politics than by the Left.[14] This, of course, is still more the case in Britain, where the years of 'Thatcherism' led to a transformation of attitudes to the EU by the major political movements, with the Right ever more closely associated with 'Europhobic' positions. Meanwhile, two significant factors affected the Left. First, the combination of neo-liberalism and centralisation in Thatcher's Britain led to a reappraisal of the EU by many of its erstwhile opponents. The notion of withdrawal was abandoned, with some now viewing the Community as a moderate centrist force which might counteract the excesses of the British government, and others positively embracing it as their vision of the future. Secondly, the election of Blair to the leadership of the Labour Party in 1994 and to the premiership in 1997 completed the routing of the traditional Labour Left, which now occupies a marginal position in Britain. The combination of these two processes means that those who oppose the EU from a specifically left-wing perspective have become a rather elderly minority of a minority. Tony Benn's passion on the subject has not diminished, but his message no longer has the resonance that it did in the 1970s.

If Miliband's version of state-centrism is considered in the context of current European politics, rather than in his abstract universalist terms, it appears much less persuasive. There is no serious likelihood of left-wing forces mobilising in this way in Germany or Italy because of the role of the EU in the political culture of these countries, and in France and Britain 'Euroscepticism' has become a phenomenon of the Right rather than the Left. Because of popular attitudes, Britain remains the country in which anti-EU mobilisation has the most potential.[15] But, with the weakness of socialism and the Europhobic form in which anti-EU attitudes are currently expressed, any such campaign is far more likely to take place on populist-nationalist grounds than on the basis of democracy and socialism. If so, this would violate Miliband's own principles and the goal of inclusiveness.

There is one final problem with the state-centred approach, which Miliband acknowledged, and then 'ducked'. Having stressed the importance of maintaining autonomy from the Union for the purposes of domestic transformation, he continued:

> This is not to under-estimate in any way the importance of the globalisation of capital or the internationalisation of economic life. It is simply to say that socialists cannot accept a parallel political internationalisation which, for the present and the immediate future, is bound to place intolerable constraints on the purposes they seek to advance.[16]

But the key question, which he did not attempt to answer, was the extent to which those constraints operated *whether or not the political internationalisation took place*. Clearly, there are persuasive arguments against the view that globalisation is an uncontrollable force against which all governments are powerless and that the only option is to submit to the pressures and dismantle all forms of social protection. The extent of globalisation has been exaggerated, the neo-liberal option has been *chosen* by many governments rather than being forced upon them, and some states – particularly the USA – may have secured *greater* relative external power through the process.[17] But even if a medium-sized European state has some room for manoeuvre, left-wing state-centrists need to demonstrate its extent if they suggest that autonomous social transformation is possible.

The EU as a territorial polity

If the European 'nation-state' can no longer be regarded as a polity in which autonomous radical democratic transformation is easy to envisage, there is a temptation to accept an argument at the other extreme. Because the identification between a *polity* and a territory is taken for granted, once the claim that the 'nation-state' is an autonomous 'location' for democracy is rejected, the alternative may be to regard the EU as a kind of replacement.[18] For those who have followed the federalist tradition, this has also been a normative preference, with the argument that 'nation-states' are, in any case, inherently aggressive and nationalist. Others may simply argue that the development of globalisation and European integration mean that the nation-state is obsolescent and that it is now time to transform the EU into a federal state. On this view, the new territorial polity in which to construct a democracy is defined by the external frontiers of the fifteen members – or wherever these frontiers lie after future enlargements. Various institutional versions of such a *polity* are possible but there are, I believe, objections to all of them.

The most fundamental problem is that it is surely clear that the EU does not really resemble a federal state (see Agnew in this volume).[19] The governments, particularly of the larger and more powerful states, retain primacy in the decision-making process and exercise a range of powers in domestic and external policy which differ very considerably from those of regional governments within a federal state. It is true that there is considerable variation in the relationships between the state and sub-state tiers of government in federations and that some sub-state tiers exercise very considerable powers.[20] Nevertheless, federal systems retain a hierarchical structure with the central state at the summit. In the EU, however, countries such as Germany, France and the UK not only retain a vast array of domestic powers but, of perhaps still greater significance in comparison with the federal model, they remain important international actors. Despite the aspirations of the Common Foreign and Security Policy, the bilateral relationships of individual states, particularly with the United States, are often of greater significance than those between the member states. Thus major international events, such as the Kosovo crisis in 1999, demonstrate the leadership of the USA and the way it operates on a state-to-state basis with its junior partners in Europe. It is true that in economic terms and in 'normal' times the interactions within the EU are of far greater significance than during US-led international crises, and it is also true that some states are more willing to cede new powers to the EU than others. However, it is evident that the member states would be totally opposed to the wholesale transformation of the Community and that they retain sufficient power to prevent this happening. Indeed the 'three pillar' structure of the Union, erected in the Maastricht Treaty and confirmed in the Treaties of Amsterdam and Nice, appears to consolidate the power of the governments.[21]

The fact that the EU is quite distinct from a federal state is not a normative argument against trying to transform it in this direction. However, there are also some major problems with this aspiration. First, given that democratisation is the fundamental goal, the construction of a federal Europe would itself need to be democratic. But at present popular attitudes to the EU are lukewarm or even hostile in the majority of states and would provide no legitimacy for a total transformation in its nature. On normative grounds, the establishment of a federation should follow from popular demands, rather than being effected from above. At present the evidence suggests that the people who are the most concerned about the 'democratic deficit' tend to be among those who are highly informed about the EU, while its democratic weaknesses are not perceived as a problem by the mass of the population.[22] Secondly, since inclusiveness is a democratic value, any attempt to re-create the model of a 'nation-state' at EU level would, in any case, be undesirable. Democratisation should involve a greater respect for existing identities rather than seeking to suppress or submerge them in an EU identity.[23] Emulation of 'nation-statism' at an EU level would also carry the dangers of reinforcing European exclusiveness in relation to peoples from other parts of the world, including ethnic minorities, who might be excluded from the dominant definition of 'Europeanism'. Thirdly (as John Agnew warns from the US example in this volume), federations tend to freeze the distribution of constitutional authority in accordance with the prevailing power relations at the time of their establishment. They then become extremely difficult to change. Applied to the current EU, this could mean that a capitalist free market, reinforced by a Central Bank committed to orthodox deflationary monetary policies, would be underwritten constitutionally with lower-level governments unable ever to introduce different forms of economic governance. It is difficult to reconcile this with the goal of *equality*, since redistributive measures would be greatly hampered.[24]

States and the EU: a complex, multi-level site for democratic politics

If neither the state-centred view nor the doctrine which perceives the EU as a would-be federation is tenable, the alternative is to move away from a territorial definition of politics. Some would adopt an extremely radical version of this approach, arguing that the whole notion of states as distinct territories has been superseded through the process of globalisation and new forms of communication.[25] The development of the Internet, making worldwide communication so easy, epitomises this new situation. My position is much more conservative than this, on the grounds that territorially bounded states continue to be major actors and that power remains concentrated in rather traditional forms. Nevertheless, it seems that the current situation in the EU is most helpfully represented as one in which there are complex interactions between a variety of actors and interests. Some of these take place within each state, some between states, some within EU institutions, and some are functionally rather than territorially based – for example in transnational networks and pressure groups. Furthermore, while no political framework has ever been static, the current configuration is particularly fluid and unclear. This is an important reason for the difficulty that analysts have found in characterising the EU: is it an international organisation, a confederation, or some kind of *sui generis* entity? Whatever term is used, it seems that the processes of integration and interdependence have created a mixed and ever changing set of relationships. But this makes the notion of democratisation still more complex.

One approach to the problem might be termed that of 'new democratic politics'.[26] Drawing on both earlier traditions and post-modernism, this tends to emphasise the efforts of both individuals and new social movements to gain greater control over their lives locally, regionally, nationally and transnationally, and to suggest that new forms of citizenship and democracy will emerge from these efforts. These may be embodied in new structures and networks, formal and informal, which will help to 'deconstruct' the existing dominant institutions: above all, the state. From this perspective, it may be argued that the EU is a valuable arena for the establishment of new forms of governance of different kinds and at a variety of levels. Indeed the EU may be seen as an embryonic framework for this approach, but one which is currently stultified by bureaucracy and the dominance of the states.

This multi-centred perspective appears to have much validity both as a representation of the current situation and as an attractive vision, which may incorporate all the values of democracy outlined at the beginning of the chapter. It also transcends the notion of a discrete polity – either at state or EU level – and therefore reconceptualises the task of democratisation. Yet there are major obstacles in the EU which need to be taken into account.

The first is that the 'democratic deficit' is not an incidental or contingent feature of the Community: it is structurally embedded in its development. The political and economic elites of the original 'six' constructed the European Coal and Steel Community and the EEC in the 1950s on the basis of the so-called 'permissive consensus'. They wanted to overcome the historic conflicts in the region and to create economic interdependence as a basis for growth, and the new institutional structures reflected these priorities. The parliamentary assemblies paid no more than lip service to democratic principles – particularly as their members were nominated by the governments – and could safely be ignored. It was only after the policy-making system had been well established that the accession of new and less *communautaire* member states (for example, the UK and Denmark), the downturn in the economy, and the rise of populist nationalism, progressively undermined the tacit support for the integration process. And even then the first reaction by the Community was to attempt to counter the growth of indifference and hostility by a search for legitimacy through symbols rather than democratic processes: a logo, a flag, a passport and an anthem.

This is not to deny that some significant changes have occurred. The European Parliament (EP) has been directly elected since 1979 and has gained in legislative power, and in relation to the Commission; there has been a stronger commitment to transparency in decision making; the introduction of EU citizenship under the Maastricht Treaty has potential importance; and the introduction of new articles concerning human rights and democracy in the Amsterdam Treaty is also an encouraging development. However, all these are belated attempts to inject some democratic elements into a decision-making system, which is still characterised by its non-democratic features.

First, at root, policy making is based on secretive intergovernmental bargaining, with a high degree of inter-penetration between national and EU civil servants. In general, this has enhanced the power of governments and bureaucracies over members of the national parliaments and parties and, while powerful financial and industrial interests have good access to the policy makers at national and European levels, non-governmental organisations (NGOs) and poorer groups do not. The EU has thus reinforced the existing trend in which executives have become stronger in relation to the bodies to which they are theoretically accountable. Viewed in one way, the EU might appear a rather weak and immobile policy-making system. But from the perspective of those seeking radical change it is a formidable coalition of established interests. It is therefore a barrier to the goals of participation and empowerment, which has in some respects *reduced* the democratic possibilities which existed within the member states.

The second important non-democratic feature of the EU system is the array of repressive measures, particularly against immigrants and asylum seekers, which have been agreed since the mid-1970s. This apparatus, including police co-operation, common data systems, and moves to standardise visa policies, has been of crucial importance in the construction of 'Fortress Europe' and, until Maastricht, it took place entirely on an informal intergovernmental basis. While it was then regularised in the so-called three pillar structure, it remained outside normal Community procedures, depriving both the EP and the Court of Justice of any genuine involvement. And although some elements were brought into the first pillar in the Amsterdam Treaty, the most crucial aspects remain entirely intergovernmental.[27] This means that the most repressive aspect of EU power remains one in which there is close and secretive co-operation between the states without any substantial possibility of scrutiny or accountability at national or EU levels.[28] This is another aspect of the power of the EU, which is clearly incompatible, both with the liberal principles of freedom of information, scrutiny and accountability, and with the goal of inclusiveness.

The third key feature of the EU is that its primary task has been the construction of a Single Market on capitalist principles. Ever since the Treaty of Rome, the removal of barriers to competition has been the primary principle, while the agricultural, social and regional policies have, in effect, been side payments to compensate particular states, regions and sectional interests which may be negatively affected by the competitive pressures. Furthermore, it is this principle which has mainly been embodied in legislation. This is not to say that the Community has been confined to the task of establishing a free market economy: bargains, pressures and lobbying have, for example, caused it to go further in gender equality policies, environmental protection and anti-poverty programmes than some of the individual states would otherwise have chosen. But the embedded economic project of the competitive Single Market is its most fundamental feature. Moreover, the EMU probably constitutes the most significant step in the process of European integration since the establishment of the EEC itself and, whatever its ultimate economic effects, this has further negative implications for democracy.

Any monetary union is likely to threaten the most vulnerable economies. Because a country can no longer devalue when suffering from competitive pressures, a recession means that people in the relatively weaker regions and states will face the prospect of either accepting a decline in living standards or, in theory, moving to the more dynamic areas. These tendencies could be counteracted by monetary policies which included employment and social protection as goals, and by significant fiscal transfers from the richer to the poorer countries and regions. But such policies would depend upon a significant EU budget and the retention of a considerable degree of political control over macroeconomic strategy.[29] However, the Maastricht convergence criteria for EMU were deflationary and an orthodox monetary framework has been built into the system.[30] The primary considerations have been currency stability and international competitiveness, despite the inherent probability that these will exacerbate existing social and regional inequalities. Moreover, because the guidelines for the European Central Bank are based on the Maastricht principles, this tendency is perpetuated. The current system of EMU seeks to minimise political intervention, and in 1997 French attempts to counter this were resisted.[31] Furthermore, the notion that Central Banks should be politically independent – on the grounds that governments have often abused their power for electoral purposes – has become a new conventional wisdom.[32] The

Amsterdam Treaty did little to redress the balance, since its Employment Chapter has no teeth,[33] and there is no move to increase the budget so as to make fiscal transfers possible: indeed the current emphasis is on budget stability. All this means that the Community's embedded economic system and the EMU represent further negative elements in relation to the goal of equality.[34]

While the EU's role in bringing about a partial deconstruction of the state may therefore appear positive in some ways, it has also established new concentrations of power. Enhanced democratisation therefore depends on changing the nature of the Community in fundamental ways. But how is this to be achieved?

Towards democratising the EU

Some of the underlying assumptions about democracy on which the analysis in this chapter is based were outlined in the first section. In particular, it was argued that it was insufficient to concentrate on procedures without reference to substantive values; that both representative and participatory forms of democracy were necessary; and that greater inclusiveness and equality were the most important current goals. If these are now applied to the EU and to conventional proposals for reform, some conclusions about the path to greater democratisation become apparent.

Much of the conventional discussion about democratising the EU has emphasised procedural reform, whether by enhancing the power of the European Parliament (EP), electing the Commission, or instituting a greater use of majority voting in the Council. However, it is not evident that any of these reforms will have any major impact on the fundamental problems in the foreseeable future. Some of the EP's work – particularly in the committees – has been important and many of its critics have ulterior (for example, 'Eurosceptic') motives for denigrating it. Yet it is clear that neither direct elections since 1979 nor the enhanced powers that the parliament has had since 1987 have done much to embed it in popular or political consciousness within the member states.[35] Furthermore, the EP itself has generally been more concerned to strengthen its own position within the institutional and policy-making system than to secure wider support, partly because there is no obvious way in which it can achieve this latter goal. Further increases in EP power will no doubt be necessary at some stage in the future, but I would suggest that these would have little impact on the primary goals at present. Similarly, direct election of the Commission would appear a false route for democratisation. It would add a third element of electoral legitimation into the system – rivalling both the governments and the EP – which would further complicate matters without enhancing popular control over the decision-making system. And indirect election by the EP would be unhelpful, given the weak electoral legitimation of the parliament itself.

It is often claimed that further increasing the use of majority voting in the Council is necessary in order to speed up the policy-making process, and further reforms of this kind may be anticipated.[36] However, this is normally suggested as an argument for *efficiency* rather than democracy. Similarly, the rebalancing of voting in the Council (in favour of the larger states) may be expected in the near future, but this raises problematic issues about the role of smaller states in the Union. For the real motivation for the change is the concern of the major states to maintain or enhance their own power. But any move towards a Concert of Great Powers model would hardly constitute a democratic reform.[37]

In my view, the weakness of the above proposals for reform is that they separate *procedures* from the pursuit of the key *values* assumed in this chapter. Some of them may be justified in terms of an institutional model of representative democracy, but they are much closer to the concerns of elites than to the goals of participation, inclusiveness and equality.

At the other end of the scale are those who simply advocate the goals of participation and direct democracy without any specific consideration of the EU. From this perspective, the main concern is that political and social movements should operate at all levels to press for alternative policies. This approach does not begin with a blueprint for the EU, but assumes that its institutions and policies will be shaped by the interactions between movements and by continuing conflicts over the distribution of power. Those who adopt this as their starting point may happily accept the likelihood that the EU will remain an inchoate, untidy and fluid entity which will be pushed and pulled in different directions as a result of the contradictory pressures upon it. However, while this perspective on democratisaton is essential, it also appears insufficient. The EU is now a system of power which structures and constrains social and political movements within the member states. It cannot therefore be assumed that its shape and direction will simply emerge from disparate campaigns at lower levels. Advocates of participatory democracy therefore also need to consider ways of changing the policy-making process of the Union itself.

The goal in relation to procedures is therefore to seek a synthesis between direct and representational forms of democracy by proposing reforms which could enhance participation and empowerment.[38] A basis for such an approach is suggested by the concept of 'deliberative democracy' which elaborates an ideal in which all those affected by decisions should be able to participate in the deliberative process by which policy outcomes are determined.[39] One obvious reform of this kind would require the EU to introduce greater transparency and freedom of information. A prerequisite for active campaigning for new policies is the greatest possible openness about the policy-making process and, as *Statewatch* has documented, the EU has resorted to a variety of stratagems to impede access to information on key issues, despite its commitments to greater transparency.[40] Secondly, channels could easily be created for greater participation in each stage of the legislative process. At present, although the Commission may be informal and relatively easy to approach, the procedures through which proposals are initiated and turned into legislation are opaque. A forum for social movements to present their views without the Commission setting the agenda or controlling the discussion could be established, and the subsequent legislative process could also be opened up to participation by groups affected by the proposed measures.[41]

Neither of these changes would mean any fundamental transformation in the EU's institutional structure, but they would provide some possibility for non-elite interests to have an input into the policy-making processes.

The goal of inclusion is also inherent in deliberative democracy since this seeks to accommodate difference and diversity. However, this would also require extensive changes in the EU's procedures and policies on human rights and citizenship. It is true that the Amsterdam Treaty introduced some relevant new articles. It provided for sanctions (ultimately including a suspension of membership) against member states violating the principles of democracy and human rights, and the Court of Justice was also granted jurisdiction to ensure that the Community institutions respected fundamental rights as guaranteed by the European Court of Human Rights. Furthermore, provisions for legislation against racism (and other forms of discrimination) were included in the Treaty. These represent some advance, and the response of the EU governments to the inclusion of the Far Right in the Austrian government in February 2000 offers some encouragement that human rights issues are being taken seriously. However, the clauses in the Amsterdam Treaty are vitiated by evident weaknesses. For example, it will be extremely difficult to secure a Council decision in favour of sanctions for human rights abuses; and the implementation of effective anti-discrimination legislation will depend upon governments demonstrating a political will which is not currently in evidence. Nor is there any sign that they are willing to provide full rights of movement to legal residents who do not have citizenship in any of the member states or to implement a humane, transparent and accountable policy on asylum and immigration.[42] Such aims might be advanced by the incorporation of the charter on fundamental human rights agreed at Nice into the Treaty, and this step will be considered in the intergovernmental conference in 2004. However, it is necessary to remain sceptical about the extent to which the governments have really embraced the value of inclusion.[43]

Progress towards the goal of equality will be still difficult to achieve, for this would require a fundamental change in the economics of the EU, the foundation on which it has been established. Social and regional policies would need to be evaluated in their own right, rather than as compensations to balance the negative impact of competition, and both new economic guidelines and forms of political control would have to be devised for the European Central Bank.[44] Because the establishment of a competitive Single Market and, more recently, a single currency based on orthodox monetary policy, have been integral to the development of the European capitalist economy, it will be extremely difficult to reverse EU priorities, particularly in view of the extent to which European Social Democracy currently embraces the market. What does seem clear, however, is that an alternative approach would have a greater possibility of success if undertaken by the EU as a whole, or at least by a group of states, than by an individual government.[45] For the Union would be more able to withstand external competitive pressures, and a co-operative initiative would reduce the probability of sanctions by other member states.

It is therefore possible to envisage some ways in which the EU could be democratised. Yet it is evident that fundamental problems remain. Some of the above changes would require treaty amendments necessitating unanimity by the governments, and all would require a general consensus within the European Council. It is difficult to imagine this transformation unless pressures were being exerted both territorially through the member states and functionally across them. But this would also require the development of a far stronger sense of transnational European solidarity in the pursuit of democratic goals. It is difficult to reconceptualise a theory of democracy in the EU without this kind of change in consciousness. Of far greater significance, this is also a prerequisite for real progress in practice.

Notes

1 For a variety of views on ways of reducing the democratic deficit, see David Beetham and Christopher Lord, *Legitimacy and the European Union* (Routledge, 1998); Christopher Lord, *Democracy in the European Union* (Sheffield Academic Press, 1998); Heidrun Abromeit, *Democracy in Europe: Legitimising Politics in a Non-State Polity* (Berghahn, 1998); D.N. Chryssochoou, *Democracy in the European Union* (Taurus, 1998); Catherine Hoskyns and Michael Newman (eds.), *Democratising the European Union: Issues for the Twenty-First Century* (Manchester University Press, 2000).

2 For a more sustained analysis, see M. Newman, *Democracy, Sovereignty and the European Union* (Hurst, 1996); also, M. Newman, 'Democracy and the European Union' in V. Symes, C. Levy and J. Littlewood, *The Future of Europe: Problems and Issues for the Twenty-First Century* (Macmillan, 1997). For useful recent analyses of concepts of democracy, see Anthony Arblaster, *Democracy* (Open University Press, 1987); John Dunn (ed.), *Democracy: The Unfinished Journey* (Oxford University Press, 1992); David Held (ed.), *Prospects for Democracy* (Polity Press, 1993); James L. Hyland, *Democratic Theory: The Philosophical Foundations* (Manchester University Press, 1995).

3 For a sophisticated statement of the alternative view stressing the need for a market economy, see David Beetham, 'Liberal democracy and the limits of democratization' in David Held (ed.), *Prospects for Democracy* (Polity Press, 1993)

4 The dynamics of French racist politics are analysed by Peter Fysh and Jim Wolfreys, *The Politics of Racism in France* (Macmillan, 1998); and Jonathan Marcus, *The National Front and French Politics: The Resistible Rise of Jean-Marie Le Pen* (Macmillan, 1995).

5 For the most influential modern view of this kind, see John Rawls, *A Theory of Justice* (Oxford University Press, 1972). For an earlier version, see Harold Laski, *A Grammar of Politics* (Allen & Unwin, 4th edition, 1938). For the libertarian notion, see R. Nozick, *Anarchy, State and Utopia* (Basil Blackwell, 1974). For a recent critique of libertarian views, see Alan Haworth, *Anti-Libertarianism: Markets, Philosophy and Myth* (Routledge, 1994).

6 J.A. Schumpeter, *Capitalism, Socialism and Democracy* (Allen and Unwin, 1976), is the classic defence of the elitist view, while participation is stressed in Carole Pateman, *Participation and Democratic Theory* (Cambridge University Press, 1970).

7 In other words, my approach is much closer to the 'cosmopolitan' than to the 'communitarian' position: see Janna Thompson, *Justice and World Order: A Philosophical Inquiry* (Routledge, 1992).

8 Recent examples include David Held and Daniele Archibugi (eds), *Cosmopolitan Democracy* (Polity Press, 1995); Paul Hirst, *Associative Democracy* (Polity Press, 1994); and Anthony McGrew (ed.), *The Transformation of Democracy? Globalization and Territorial Democracy* (Polity Press, 1997).

9 The tone of much of the PCF rhetoric was set before the liberation of France when it denounced a socialist proposal for a United States of Europe as follows: 'For all thinking patriots, the essential problem after the liberation is the maintenance of the unity of France and the restoration of its grandeur.' 'Observations du Parti communiste sur le projet de Programme commun presenté par le Parti socialiste', Paris, 25 April 1944, in H. Michel and B. Mirkine-Guetzevitch (eds), *Les idées politiques et sociales de la Résistance* (PUF, 1954), pp. 218–238, quoted in Michael Newman, *Socialism and European Unity: The Dilemma of the Left in Britain and France* (Hurst, 1983), p. 38. This was to lead to stridently anti-German propaganda, particularly in the campaigns against the Coal and Steel Community and European Defence Community in the 1950s.

10 Despite qualifications, he effectively ties socialist democracy to the 'nation-state': see Ralph Miliband, *Socialism for a Sceptical Age* (Polity Press, 1994), pp.179–80.

11 For supporting evidence, see Peter J. Katzenstein (ed.), *Tamed Power: Germany in Europe* (Cornell University Press, 1997).

12 Italy's 'Europeanisation' is discussed in detail by Vassilis Fouskas, *Italy, Europe, the Left: The Transformation of Italian Communism and the European Imperative* (Ashgate, 1999).

13 This view was not taken by the Rifondazione Comunista (Party of Communist Refoundation), which was deeply critical of the austerity programme. See Fausto Bertinotti, 'Report to the 1996 Congress of Rifondazione Comunista', in *Labour Focus on Eastern Europe* 57, 1997. Yet even this party, which secured only 4.3 per cent of the vote in the 1999 Euro-elections, supports the notion of a European road to socialism.

14 The different political attitudes to the EU are discussed by Alain Guyomarch, Howard Machin and Ella Ritchie, *France in the European Union* (Macmillan, 1998).

15 In the UK electoral participation in European elections has declined from a peak of only 36.4 per cent in 1994. In 1999 the turnout was the lowest ever at 24 per cent.

16 Miliband elaborates this point in *Socialism for a Sceptical Age*, p. 180.

17 For a sceptical view of globalisation, see Paul Hirst and Grahame Thompson, *Globalization in Question: The International Economy and the Possibilities* (Polity Press, 1996).

18 This is often accompanied by a simultaneous movement down the scale, with the argument that sub-state regions have become more important.

19 There are, of course, many theorists who disagree with this view. Some of the most persuasive arguments have been put by Joseph Weiler, who argues that there is, in effect, a constitution which makes the Community a federal system, but that this has taken place without any explicit authorisation from any demos (J.H.H.Weiler, *The Constitution of Europe*, Cambridge University Press, 1999). However, I do not believe that Weiler's legal and philosophical arguments contradict the view expressed here that, in terms of power and political reality, the federal analogy is unhelpful.

20 Belgium is particularly complex in this respect: see J. Fitzmaurice, *The Politics of Belgium: A Unique Federalism* (Hurst, 1996). For an extensive discussion of federalist theories, see Preston King, *Federalism and Federation* (Croom Helm, 1982).

21 The Treaty of Maastricht maintained the existing European Community as the first pillar, while creating a second and third pillar (respectively, Common Foreign and Security Policy and Justice and Home Affairs), which were fundamentally intergovernmental in character.

22 This is the view of Jean Blondel, Richard Sinnott and Palle Svensson, *People and Parliament in the European Union: Participation, Democracy and Legitimacy* (Clarendon Press, 1998).

23 For a debate on this point, see Thedora Kostakopoulou, 'Why a "community of Europeans" could be a community of exclusion', and Paul Howe, 'Insiders and outsiders in a community of Europeans: a reply to Kostakopoulou', *Journal of Common Market Studies* 35, 1997. Also Karlheinz Reif, 'Cultural convergence and cultural diversity as factors in European identity', in Soledad García (ed.), *European Identity and the Search for Legitimacy* (Pinter, 1993).

24 The current EMU is also difficult to reconcile with this goal and difficult to change since it would require unanimity to amend the treaty (see below).

25 For a discussion of a whole range of such theories, see Steve Barrett, 'International relations theories, the state and representations of a changing Europe', M. Phil. thesis, University of North London, 1999.

26 There is no such agreed category. The discussion here draws on a variety of theorists, including David Held, 'Democracy: from city states to a cosmopolitan order?', in David Held (ed.), *Prospects for Democracy* (Polity Press, 1993); David Held and Daniele Archibugi (eds), *Cosmopolitan Democracy* (Polity Press, 1995); Paul Hirst, *Associative Democracy* (Polity Press, 1994); James Goodman, 'The European Union: towards a transnational politics of "movement"', *Via Europa*, Summer 1995; and Elizabeth Meehan, *Citizenship and the European Community* (Sage, 1993).

27 The Treaty of Amsterdam transferred immigration, asylum and border controls to the first pillar, but with restrictions in the Court of Justice's role. It also allows for further transfers to this pillar to take place later. Police and judicial co-operation remain in the third pillar, with the Schengen system divided between the two pillars. The role of the Court remains weak on these issues.

28 This case is strongly made by Tony Bunyan, *Secrecy and Openness in the European Union* (European Dossier Series, Kogan Page, 1999).

29 This argument is substantiated by Valerio Lintner, 'Controlling EMU', in C. Hoskyns and M. Newman (eds), *Democratising the European Union: Issues for the Twenty-First Century* (Manchester University Press, 2000).

30 The Maastricht convergence criteria were a maximum annual budget deficit of 3 per cent of GDP; a maximum total public sector debt of 60 per cent of GDP; no realignments within the ERM; a sustainable rate of inflation of not more than 1.5 per cent above the average of the three lowest inflation countries in the year before decision; and long-term government bond interest rates to be no more than 2 per cent above the average of those in the three lowest rate countries. These conditions were supplemented by the stability pact agreed at the Dublin summit of December 1996 which was incorporated in the Amsterdam Treaty. This limits government borrowing to the Maastricht criteria and imposes fines for those who deviate from this position. Countries may spend more by raising taxes, but the free movement of capital is likely to inhibit wide variations in taxation. For an extensive discussion of these issues, see Lintner, 'Controlling EMU'.

31 The Luxembourg jobs summit, following pressure from the French, did not lead to any major changes in policy. Valerie Symes, *Unemployment and Employment Policies in the EU* (European Dossier Series, Kogan Page, 1998), pp. 35–6.

32 Some analysts are also now arguing in favour of a similar regulation by 'independent' non-elected experts over a whole range of policy making in the EU to insulate it from political and electoral pressures: see G. Majone, 'A European regulatory state?', in Jeremy Richardson (ed.), *European Union: Power and Policy Making* (Routledge, 1996).

33 The main changes (in Article 109 of the Treaty) are to allow the development of a co-ordinated strategy, but there is no enforcement mechanism (in contrast to the convergence criteria and stability pact associated with EMU). An employment committee was also established, but this has only advisory status.

34 Sverker Gustavsson, 'Monetary union without fiscal union: a politically sustainable asymmetry?', paper presented at the American ECSA International Conference, 2–5 June 1999, Pittsburgh.

35 Overall participation in the European elections has actually declined: 63 per cent in 1979; 61 per cent in 1984; 58.5 per cent in 1989; 56 per cent in 1994; 49.4 per cent in 1999 (Eurostat).

36 Majority voting is now the normal procedure for a very wide range of issues in any case, although in practice votes are comparatively rare and decision making is normally by consensus.

37 However, the movement is towards one commissioner per country, with the larger states securing the most important responsibilities.

38 Heiden Abromeit argues very forcefully, and with considerable empirical and theoretical substantiation, that the injection of direct democracy through the use of referenda would be the most effective way of enhancing democracy: see H. Abromeit, *Democracy in Europe: Legitimising Politics in a Non-State Polity* (Berghahn, 1998). I would argue that such referenda may be an adjunct to participation rather than the primary approach.

39 For deliberative democracy, see O. Gerstenberg, 'Law's polyarchy: a comment on Cohen and Sabel', *European Law Journal* 3, 1997; J. Bohman and W. Rehg (eds), *Deliberative Democracy. Essays on Reason and Politics* (MIT Press, 1997); and Catherine Hoskyns, 'Democratising the EU: evidence and argument', in C. Hoskyns and M. Newman (eds), *Democratising the European Union: Issues for the Twenty-First Century* (Manchester University Press, 2000).

40 For further details, see Tony Bunyan, *Secrecy and Openness in the European Union* (European Dossier Series, Kogan Page, 1999).

41 For the argument that the existing channels for participation are 'managed' by the Commission, see Sue Cohen, 'Barriers to participation', in C. Hoskyns and M. Newman (eds), *Democratising the European Union: Issues for the Twenty-First Century* (Manchester University Press, 2000).

42 For details of discrimination, see John Wrench, *Migrants, Ethnic Minorities and Discrimination in EU Labour Markets* (European Dossier Series, Kogan Page, 1998).

43 A number of proposals have been made for a human rights charter and an *ad hoc* committee, chaired by the former German president, was established with the aim of reporting to the European Council on the subject by the end of 2000. However, many of the governments are reluctant to accept a definition which might imply a strengthening of rights. For a comprehensive overview, see P. Alston and J.H.H. Weiler, 'An "ever closer Union" in need of a human rights policy: the European Union and human rights', in P. Alston *et al.* (eds), *The EU and Human Rights* (Oxford University Press, 1999).

44 This is argued by Valerio Lintner, 'Controlling EMU', in C. Hoskyns and M. Newman (eds), *Democratising the European Union: Issues for the Twenty-First Century* (Manchester University Press, 2000).

45 The case for an alternative approach is made by J. Michie and J.A. Grieve-Smith (eds), *Unemployment in Europe* (Academic Press, 1994); Stuart Holland, *The European Imperative: Economic and Social Cohesion in the 1990s* (Spokesman, 1993); Ken Coates and Stuart Holland, *Full Employment for Europe* (Spokesman, 1995); and 'Put Europe to work', Report of the Parliamentary Group of the Party of European Socialists (Brussels: 1993).

5 Multi-level citizenship, identity and regions in contemporary Europe

Joe Painter

The European Union (EU) is the most developed set of transnational political institutions anywhere in the world. Europe is therefore a logical place to search for signs of transnational democratisation. There has been much debate about Europe's 'democratic deficit', but most discussion has focused on the institutions of the EU, such as the European Parliament, rather than considering the complex European political system as a whole, including areas outside the EU, as a potential medium for the development of transnational democracy.

Most democratic forms of governance have a concept of citizenship at their core, and this chapter is concerned with the nature of, and prospects for, transnational citizenship in Europe. In common with other recent commentators, I shall argue that Europe's emerging transnational citizenship should not (and probably cannot) be based on the conventional 'nation-state' model (where 'nation' and 'state' are assumed to be congruent: see also Parekh and Newman in this volume). Instead it should be a 'multi-level citizenship' reflecting individuals' simultaneous membership of political communities at a variety of spatial scales (local, regional, national and European) and perhaps of various *non*-territorial social groups, such as religions, sexual minorities or ethnic diasporas.

The chapter is organised in three main sections. In the first I examine the ambiguous link between citizenship and identity, arguing that while citizenship and democratic rights should not be based on cultural identities, identity does affect the acquisition and practice of citizenship. The second section focuses on debates about the existence and nature of a specifically European identity and their influence on proposals for the development of transnational European citizenship. I suggest that since citizenship cannot be wholly divorced from identity, care needs to be taken to ensure that any definition of European identity is inclusive and supportive of ethnic and cultural difference. One way to do this is through the relatively new concept of multi-level citizenship. In the third section I consider the implications of 'new regionalism' (Keating 1998) for multi-level citizenship in Europe and suggest that while the regional scale is central to the definition of multi-level citizenship in theory, it is likely to make aspects of it highly problematic in practice, not least because of the ambiguous relationship between citizenship and identity.

Citizenship and cultural identity

In recent years there has been a remarkable growth of academic interest in citizen-ship, reflecting some urgent practical political problems in the (re)constitution of political communities and the preconditions of democracy. This growth has been marked by the establishment of a new journal, *Citizenship Studies*, in 1997 and by numerous books, articles and collections of essays (for example, Beiner 1995; Brown 1997; Dauenhauer 1996; Holston and Appadurai 1999; Kymlicka 1995). Globalisation, the development of supranational polities, ethnic tensions, demands for group recognition and group rights, and the restructuring or retrenchment of the welfare state have all contributed to pressure for a rethinking of the concept of citizenship, and in some cases to a questioning of its continuing relevance. As Michael Ignatieff notes, there is a 'tension between the republican discourse on citizenship and the liberal political theory of market man [sic]' (Ignatieff 1995). Currently, this tension has been particularly acute in the context of the apparent hegemony of neo-liberal market economics.

Since the abandonment in 1954 of the proposed European Political Community, the development of the European Community (now the European Union) has placed more weight on economic integration and the development of the Common Market, and subsequently the Single European Market, than on building a political community based on the principle of citizenship. It is thus somewhat ironic that the EU should explicitly create a formal concept of European Citizenship (in the 1991 Maastricht Treaty) just at the time when the very idea of citizenship is increasingly seen as problematic.

Citizenship is commonly defined as 'membership of a political community', but the *basis* of that membership is a matter of considerable debate (Beiner 1995; Dauenhauer 1996; Kymlicka 1995). The difficulties begin with the very constitu-tion of the community. Where do its boundaries lie? Who may belong and who is excluded and by what criteria? Most conceptions of citizenship work with territo-rial definitions of community. While these may have the merit of simplicity and can provide the basis for efficient practical administration and institution building, they do not necessarily reflect the complex geographies of the actual social and political relations that are in other circumstances thought of as constitutive of community. Moreover, as the spatial structures of politics and governance become increasingly elaborate, the merits of simplicity and seeming practicality no longer always apply, as we shall see.

Demarcating the political community in question is by no means the only problem facing the analyst of citizenship. There is also much debate over the nature of the relationship between the citizen and society; over the *terms* of membership, in other words. In the literature at least two major themes can be identified. The first is the idea of citizenship as a formal relationship between an individual and a polity. Here the emphasis is on citizenship rights and duties and the procedures for defining these. The second is the idea of citizenship as a cultural identity involving a feeling of belonging to an 'imagined community' (Painter and Philo 1995). Liberal political theory typically emphasises the former theme, while communitarian writers emphasise the latter.

For many years work on citizenship was framed by the work of Marshall (Marshall 1950), who argued that the development of citizenship since the eighteenth century had involved the successive acquisition of civil rights, political rights and social rights. Civil rights include such innovations as the right to a fair trial, freedom from arbitrary detention and violence, freedom of speech, the right to hold property, and rights of contract. The emergence of these rights was particularly associated with the development of the institutions of the judicial system and a free press. Political rights include the right to vote and to stand for election. These are associated with the development of institutions such as an elected parliament and payment for parliamentary representatives. Social rights include rights to health care, education and a subsistence income, and arise with the development of the institutions of the welfare state. Marshall regarded social rights as of vital importance (indeed, his work was partly aimed at promoting the development of the welfare state). He insisted that citizenship that was limited to civil and political rights would exclude many from full membership of society, because people who were struggling with poverty or disease, or who were poorly educated, would not have the time, resources or capacity to exercise their citizenship rights in practice. The Marshallian model has been widely criticised on a variety of accounts (Turner 1989), but it still remains an important reference point for rights-based approaches to citizenship.

The concept of the 'imagined community' is usually associated with work on national identity and nationalism and particularly the writings of Benedict Anderson (Anderson 1983). However, it has important implications for theories of citizenship too. As Kofman (1995) points out, the ability to exercise one's *de jure* citizenship rights depends in part on being recognised as a citizen in daily life by other members of society, which often in practice seems to mean sharing some of the same cultural values or identity. Those whose faces do not fit with the majority collective perception of the 'imagined community' may find that they are excluded *de facto* from full participation in social life. Institutionalised racism in the welfare state, for example, means that members of minority cultural and ethnic groups have worse access to health care, education and welfare benefits than others despite equal citizenship status in law (see also Parekh in this volume). Citizenship laws can also be framed explicitly or implicitly along cultural or ethnic lines, such that those who do not belong to the imagined (ethnic) community are excluded from citizenship altogether. Even where citizenship laws are framed along civic, rather than ethnic lines (as in the United States, for example), it is still possible for them to be applied in discriminatory ways.

The affective, or identity, aspect of citizenship is both about feeling part of society and about being accepted as a member of society, though this does not necessarily require ethnic homogeneity. Individuals who lack one or both of these elements are likely to find it difficult to gain the full benefits of formal citizenship rights. Legal rights, in other words, while essential, are not sufficient. Identification with an imagined community also underwrites a further aspect of citizenship, namely citizenship as active participation in society. Citizens will be more likely to contribute to society in a variety of ways and to participate in its political processes if they have an emotional identification with the wider community, developed through cultural affiliation. Finally, theories of citizenship commonly refer to the obligations of membership as well as its rights. Again, those with an affective attachment are more likely willingly to undertake these obligations.

Some seek to divorce the formal rights of citizenship from issues of identity for the good reason that legal rights should not be made dependent on adopting a particular cultural identity. If that path were followed, it is argued, citizenship could be denied to all kinds of groups on highly discriminatory or even fascist lines. Such concerns are understandable and justified, but the argument here is not that formal rights should be dependent on acceptance of a particular ethnic, national or other identity. Rather, I am suggesting that in practice the capacity to take advantage of formal rights already allocated is influenced positively or negatively by cultural factors. The relationships that underpin citizenship are not only legal but also inevitably social and cultural.

Until recently it was simply taken for granted by most writers that the political community of which citizens are members is the national state. The nineteenth century saw the consolidation of the sovereign, territorially bounded national state as the pre-eminent political institution (Giddens 1985). This seemed to offer the prospect of territorial congruence between the imagined community of the nation and the institutions of the state so that citizenship in the sense of formal rights would coincide with citizenship as a cultural identity and feeling of belonging. In practice, the neatness of this fit was always limited. Formal rights were distributed unequally (for example, women often acquired the right to vote much later than men), state borders have always split some national groups into two and there are many multi-national states. Nevertheless, the model provided by the nineteenth-century ideal of the 'nation-state' had enormous power, both because it defined the terms of debate and because the states involved were what, in another context, Brubaker has labelled 'nationalizing states' (Brubaker 1996). Nationalising states are states engaged in the propagation of nationalism in order to generate a sense of belonging and collective identity; in short, they are nation-building states.

At the turn of the twenty-first century, the idea that there is or should be a congruence between national identity, territoriality, statehood and citizenship is being challenged and undermined in three related ways. First, the pre-eminence of 'nation-states' as institutions of governance is being eroded (Camilleri and Falk 1992), although at present they are still the most important sources of political authority. According to Bob Jessop (1994), the 'nation-state' has been 'hollowed out' with power moving 'up' to the European Union, 'down' to the local and regional level and 'out' to inter-regional networks. Governance in Europe is increasingly polycentric and multi-layered. For James Anderson (1996), this involves the emergence of overlapping spheres of political authority at several spatial scales (local, regional, national and European). Anderson's argument develops that of Hedley Bull (1977), who suggested that one alternative to the contemporary states system was a 'new medievalism' in which sovereign states might disappear and be replaced not by a world government but by a modern and secular equivalent of the kind of universal political organization that existed in Western Christendom in the Middle Ages. In that system no ruler or state was sovereign in the sense of being supreme over a given segment of the Christian population; each had to share authority with vassals beneath, and with the Pope and (in Germany and Italy) the Holy Roman Emperor above.

(Bull 1977: 254)

Commenting on Bull's prescience, Held *et al.* note that

the existence in medieval times of an array of authority structures from the local to the transnational and supranational, coexisting with an evolving system of territorially defined political units, has similarities to the contemporary period. This is not to argue that nothing has fundamentally changed. Rather, it is to suggest that a 'new medievalism' may be a useful metaphor for thinking about the present era.

(Held *et al.* 1999: 85)

This restructuring of governance, with its multiple, overlapping and sometimes conflicting and competing extra-territorial and intra-territorial flows of political authority, has considerable implications for citizenship. It challenges the assumption that the 'political community' of which citizens are members is the 'nation-state', and raises the intriguing possibility of multi-layered citizenship. To add to this complexity, in post-communist central Europe several newly independent nationalising states appear to aspire to precisely the form of statehood that is declining elsewhere (Brubaker 1996). In some cases this involves forms of citizenship that link territory, state and identity tightly together again.

Second, in many parts of Europe state-based national identities are challenged by regionalist or minority nationalist identities. These challenges undermine the fit between identity and would-be 'nation-state'. In addition, successful mobilisation behind regionalist goals can lead to increased political autonomy or secession, intensifying the restructuring of governance and potentially reconfiguring both the rights-based and the identity-based aspects of citizenship. Prominent examples include demands for Catalan, Basque and Galician autonomy or independence in Spain, while in the United Kingdom, Scottish, Welsh and Irish identities have provided the basis for nationalist challenges to a unitary United Kingdom state. In both Spain and the United Kingdom, a degree of devolution and decentralisation has been effected in response.

Third, international migration has increased cultural diversity. In some cases members of diasporas form distinct regional populations, such as the Russians in north-east Estonia (Smith and Wilson 1997). In other cases they may be dispersed more evenly. Both situations undermine the link between citizenship and national identity. In Estonia, Russians have found it difficult to acquire formal Estonian citizenship. In other cases the attribution of citizenship to ethnic minorities weakens the link between identity and *de jure* citizenship, though minority groups may still be subject to *de facto* discrimination.

These processes are producing a geography of citizenship that marks a break with the nineteenth-century ideal of territorial congruence. The twenty-first century seems to be ushering in a phase of territorial dislocation.

European citizenship

Nowhere is the complexity of twenty-first century citizenship revealed more clearly than in the European Union. Europe was the cradle of modern ideas of citizenship, and it is in Europe that we can see most clearly the simultaneous effects of polycentric governance, regionalism, national separatism, migration and cultural diversity. In the face of this complexity, the European Union has inaugurated the concept of European citizenship, and it can be related to both the aspects of citizenship outlined above: formal rights and cultural identities (Delanty 1997). The European Union's publicity material describes formal EU citizenship as 'the most important innovation of the [Maastricht] Treaty' (Fontaine 1993). By establishing a transnational citizenship in this way the EU has arguably made an essential first step towards transnational democracy.

Formal EU citizenship consists of a package of rights. The *Treaty on European Union* was agreed at a meeting of the European Council in Maastricht in 1991. It was signed in Maastricht in February 1992 and came into force in November 1993. While the proposals for Economic and Monetary Union form its centre-piece, the Maastricht Treaty is wide ranging, and one of its innovations was the formal introduction of European citizenship, by an amendment to the Treaty of Rome. Article 8 of the amended Treaty states that 'every person holding the nationality of a Member State shall be a citizen of the Union', and goes on to set out the rights of citizenship. These are the rights to move and reside freely within the territory of the member states; to vote and stand for election in municipal and European elections in the member state in which the citizen is resident; to receive protection from the diplomatic and consular authorities of any member state in any country where the citizen's own state is not represented; and to petition the European Parliament and refer matters to the Ombudsman. Article 8e allows these rights to be strengthened by unanimous agreement among the member states of the EU. Indeed, the Treaty of Amsterdam of June 1997 did add the further right of citizens to bring cases in the European Court of Justice against EU institutions.

As Shaw points out in her comprehensive discussion of EU citizenship:

> It will quickly be seen that this catalogue of citizenship rights is exceedingly limited and rather specific, and hardly comparable with domestic (generic) conceptions of citizenship. In fact, one of the key concessions made to Danish sensibilities after the first referendum, which narrowly rejected the Treaty of Maastricht, was a declaratory confirmation by the European

Council that nothing in the provisions of the Treaty of Maastricht in any way displaces national citizenship. Furthermore, it is not an 'independent' status of membership: EU citizenship attaches to those with the nationality of the Member States, and it is *prima facie* the Member States who determine – as sovereign states under international law – who are their nationals.

(Shaw 1998: 246)

Thus formal EU citizenship is *supplementary* to citizenship of a member state; to be a citizen of the EU one must first be a citizen of a member state. Notwithstanding this proviso, or the rather 'thin' conception of citizenship involved, EU citizenship is an important development, because of the open-ended nature of EU constitutional policy making. The EU is a work in progress and the concept of EU citizenship is likely to evolve further.

Citizenship and European identity

The treaties say almost nothing about the affective aspect of citizenship; that is citizenship as membership of an imagined political community and as a subjective political identity. This dimension of citizenship is often regarded as a *sine qua non* of durable legitimacy for political institutions and of meaningful democratic participation, and can therefore be seen as a crucial step towards transnational democratisation. Furthermore, despite the neglect of the issue in the treaties, the development of a common European identity has long been a goal of those steering the processes of European integration, dating back to the vision and idealism of Monnet and Schuman who saw that a sense of shared values and cultural norms (rather than a stress on national differences) might contribute to the aim of bringing peace to a war-torn continent. Moreover, it has been argued that the future sustainability and development of the European project will depend in part on the legitimacy provided to EU institutions by a popular sense of European identity (Garcia 1993; Leonard 1998a, 1998b).

Today, the importance of this affective dimension is recognised in principle by the EU. According to EU publicity, 'common citizenship is forged over time, through shared experience and the *affectio societatis* which unites individuals and gives them a sense of belonging to a collectivity. Until people have a clearer idea of the real issues in the political debate at the European level, there is bound to be a lack of information and civic commitment which has to be overcome' (Fontaine 1993). In one speech, Marcelino Oreja, then European Commissioner with responsibility for culture, declared that 'our aim is to bring to the fore the cultural features shared by Europeans, which are to be found in the fundamental values adhered to by the vast majority…[and] to show Europeans what unites them, and to show them the strength of their common cultural roots, despite the wide variety of cultures that Europe has produced' (Oreja 1997). To date, however, practical steps to develop European identity have been limited. The 1973 Copenhagen Declaration on European Identity referred to shared values of representative democracy, civil rights and the rule of law. In the mid-1980s the

Adonino Committee proposed a range of initiatives to give a European identity concrete form, including a common television area, European sports teams, greater co-operation and interchange in education, and a flag and anthem. However, 'the implementation of these measures has been patchy' (Leonard 1998b: 36).

For Delanty (1997) and Leonard (1998a), these attempts to develop both the rights and identity aspects of European citizenship are deeply flawed. The formal citizenship provided by the treaties is both limited and subordinate to national citizenship: 'a second-order citizenship' (Delanty 1997: 296). In addition, it has been introduced at a time when the rights model has itself been criticised for its concern with procedures rather than outcomes, for its individualism and for its exclusionary character: 'European citizenship is in danger of becoming an even more formalised kind of citizenship than national citizenship currently is and, moreover, is pointing in the direction of becoming an exclusionary supranationality defining Europe by reference to the non-Europeans' (Delanty 1997: 296–7). At the same time, the idea of European identity fostered by the EU is based on the essentialist model provided by the nineteenth-century 'nation-state'. The development of the modern 'nation-state', especially in the 'long nineteenth century' (1789–1914), saw the mutual constitution of sovereign, territorially centralised states (Mann 1984) and national political identities through mechanisms such as the education system, the suppression of minority cultures and languages and preparation for and prosecution of warfare. Although the end of the twentieth century saw this close tie between state formation and the development of national identities break down, the framework it provides seems to continue to set the agenda for the EU.

Moves to promote European identity have tended to focus on high culture (classical music, fine art, theatre, philosophy) and on Renaissance and Enlightenment thought and values:

> Europeans are defined…by reference to a cultural discourse whose reference points are: the geopolitical framework of the European continent, the cultural heritage of Europe, and a strong sense of the uniqueness of Europe…Europeanness is constructed in opposition with the non-European, in particular Islam'.
> (Delanty 1997: 297–8; see also Morley and Robins 1995: 43–69; Tassin 1992)

There are several difficulties with this approach. First, by combining an 'abstract and heavily political conception of European identity' (Leonard 1998b: 35) with the cultural forms of the European social elite, this model of identity is likely to alienate the majority of Europeans rather than unite them. By contrast, current work in cultural studies emphasises the significance of everyday and popular culture in constructing identity (Billig 1995). Second, it excludes (by definition) non-Western (and to some extent non-Judaeo-Christian) cultural and political traditions which are now firmly part of a multicultural, multi-ethnic and multi-faith Europe. Third, despite a heightened emphasis on respecting cultural diversity (Oreja 1997), this approach still tends to imply the construction of a shared, universal and unitary identity. The nineteenth-century nation-state depended on an essentialist conception of political communities (nations) coterminous with and grounded in homogeneous and spatially contiguous cultural communities. By contrast, much contemporary work in political theory and cultural studies emphasises the theoretical and political problems with this perspective. In its place recent approaches stress pluralism, multiculturalism, ethnic and cultural hybridity, multiple and fragmented identities and spatial complexity and transnationalism (Benhabib 1996; Kymlicka 1995; Morley and Robins 1995; Mouffe 1993). The cultural diversity within Europe is such that it is highly unlikely that a single, homogeneous European identity could be a lived reality for more than a small minority of European citizens, unless it was so thinly developed as to be an ineffective basis for the development of citizenship. As Leonard puts it:

> Too often European leaders seem to be trying to construct a European identity on the nation-state model...In fact, any European identity that does emerge will have to be radically different...It must take its place in the multiple identities and social roles...that most Europeans recognise as central to their lives.
>
> (Leonard 1998a: 23–4)

The power of the 'nation-state' model may also explain why the EU also seems to see *national* identity (defined as identification with one of the fifteen member states) as offering the only other possible claim on citizens' loyalties in addition to 'feeling European'. For example, the regular *Eurobarometer* opinion polls ask respondents to measure their sense of European identity only against their sense of national identity. Yet, in many parts of Europe, minority national, regional and local affiliations are as, or more, important than state-national ones.

Multi-level citizenship

In the light of these difficulties with the idea of a unitary European identity, its use as the foundation for European citizenship has been greeted sceptically by many academics. For Tassin, there can be no common supranational European identity. He proposes instead the development of a 'European fellow-citizenship' that 'requires citizenship to be broken away from nationality' in contrast with the 'nation-state principle of citizenship...based on an amalgamation of nationality and citizenship' (Tassin 1992: 189). Kofman (1995) suggests that rights could in future be accorded on the basis of 'denizenship' (residence), rather than (identity-based) citizenship. Delanty (1997: 299) argues that 'something like a multileveled framework of citizenship will emerge, incorporating the subnational, the national and the supranational'. For Leonard, 'if there is to be a true Euro-identity, it will be a supplement to national identity, and other regional, local and associational affiliations, not a replacement for them' (Leonard 1998b: 38).

Morley and Robins (1995) identify three scales of identity and claim that 'to be European now is to be implicated in all three – continental, national and regional – and being European is about managing some amalgam of these' (1995: 20). Finally Meehan (1993) and Gamberale (1997) suggest the idea of multiple citizenship. As Meehan argues:

> a new kind of citizenship is emerging that is neither national nor cosmopolitan but that is multiple in the sense that the identities, rights and obligations associated...with citizenship, are expressed through an increasingly complex configuration of common Community institutions, states, national and transnational voluntary associations, regions and alliances of regions.
>
> (Meehan 1993: 1)

In different ways all these proposals represent attempts to break with the assumption that citizenship, national identity and the national state territory are, or should be, congruent. Instead they attempt to fashion and theory of citizenship that is more complex, less exclusionary and better suited to an era of polycentric, multi-level governance and increasing cultural pluralism.

Regions and multi-level citizenship

There is thus an emerging consensus that multi-layered governance and multiple and overlapping political communities in Europe will both enable and require the development of multi-layered identities and forms of citizenship. However, to date there has been little research on whether such complex, multi-layered identities are in fact emerging, what form they might take, what processes generate or undermine them, how they relate to the restructuring of governance and institutions and how they vary across Europe. Multi-layered governance will hardly deserve the name if it involves only the two layers of the European Union and the member states, and most writers on the subject give a significant role to the subnational scales of the region and the locality.

The emergence of new regionalism

Regions have featured in the rhetoric of advocates of European integration since the Second World War and for many years the EU's structural funds have placed considerable emphasis on assisting the development of less prosperous regions. However, it was not until the Treaty of Maastricht, which entered into force in November 1993, that regions gained formal representation. The Maastricht Treaty made two innovations on the regional front. First, it allowed representatives of regional governments, such as Germany's *Länder*, occasionally to take the place of national ministers in the Council of Ministers. Second it set up the Committee of the Regions (CoR). The CoR, established in 1994, is an advisory body made up of representatives of the regions and localities of the EU who are nominated by their respective member states. The establishment of the CoR gave some encouragement to proponents of a 'Europe of the Regions', a sugges-tive but vague term favoured by those regionalists who look forward to a Europe consisting of a federation of autonomous regions. However, the CoR is in many ways an example of 'top-down' rather than 'bottom-up' regionalism. (Some writers such as Loughlin – Committee of the Regions (1999) – reserve the latter term 'regionalism' for popular 'bottom-up' mobilisation within regions for greater autonomy and use the label 'regionalisation' for 'top-down' measures, but others – such as Keating (1998) – use 'regionalism' to refer both to popular mobilisation and to 'top-down' national and EU policies to promote regional development and representation.)

Keating (1998) distinguishes between 'old' and 'new' regionalism in Europe. As the modern national state emerged in Europe from the seventeenth to nine-teenth centuries, it did so in the context of a much older and more complex pattern of territorial politics, in which regional identities, interregional differ-ences and decentralised authority played important roles. This pattern had developed haphazardly and largely without central co-ordination over centuries. It left a legacy of regional variation that partly limited the integrating tendencies in the process of state formation, but was also reworked by it (Keating 1998: 29). In addition, there are important differences between states in their degree of integration and centralisation.

The development of the welfare state during the twentieth century saw the extension of social citizenship and a growing reliance on planning and techno-cratic approaches to social and economic management. In many cases this modernisation led to attempts to downgrade regions, though in the new post-war democracies of Germany and Italy, 'regional decentralization was associated with democratization, pluralism and stability, and was written into their new constitutions' (Keating 1998: 39). Regionalism in the heyday of the welfare state often took the 'top-down' form (sometimes labelled 'regionalisation'), as regional development policies were introduced in an effort to ensure balanced economic progress across regions. They were thus clearly an instrument of central policy, and by the early 1970s this centralisation increasingly came to be challenged by 'bottom-up' regionalist movements (Keating 1998: 49–50).

In the late 1980s a new form of regionalist politics emerged in the context of globalisation and European integration, and the concomitant erosion of the power of the state:

> This has produced a new regionalism marked by two linked features: it is not contained within the framework of the 'nation-state'; and it pits regions against each other in a competitive mode, rather than providing comple-mentary roles for them in a national division of labour. The new regionalism is modernizing and forward-looking, in contrast to an older provincialism, which represented resistance to change and defence of tradi-tion. Yet both old and new regionalism continue to coexist in uneasy partnership, seeking a new synthesis of the universal and the particular.
>
> (Keating 1998: 73)

Many of the practices of the new regionalism, and much of the academic commentary on it, have been couched in resolutely economic terms. The 'competitive mode' referred to by Keating is above all an economic competition and 'regional economic competitiveness' has become a shibboleth of policy makers throughout Europe. This economic emphasis has gained impetus from developments during the 1980s and 1990s in regional economic theory and economic geography that stressed the importance of intra-regional networks, regionalised production systems, local milieu and regional cultural assets in the development of globally competitive regional economies (Putnam 1993; Scott 1996; Storper 1995). One influential interpretation of these arguments is that the goal of regional public policy should be to foster the 'soft assets' of regions (social networks, institutional relationships, skills and knowledge, cultural vibrancy) on the contestable assumptions that such assets are now the necessary (perhaps even the sufficient) condition of regional prosperity and that because there appears to be a link between 'soft assets' and prosperity in some well-known 'successful' regions, such as Italy's Emilia-Romagna, this link can be replicated through deliberate action in Europe's presently impoverished areas.

This thinking forms the current regional policy orthodoxy. Politically it suggests that regions can (and perhaps should) increasingly influence their own economic destinies; that regions' economies are now linked more directly to the European and global scales and that decision making about the nature of those links will be most effective if decentralised to the regional level. This is the economic argument for devolution. However, it does not necessarily follow from this economic argument that devolved governance will be democratic or accountable or that devolution itself is inherently more democratic than more centralised forms of authority. To address these issues we must consider the politics, as well as the economics, of the new regionalism.

Regionalism and citizenship

Regionalism and regional governance in contemporary Europe take many political forms. Some nationalist movements seek secession and the establishment of the region as an independent nation-state. Such nationalisms can take an atavistic, ethnic form, or a more inclusive civic form. In other cases regionalism is limited to regional autonomy within an existing European state. Yet other regions are principally administrative or planning units without decision-making roles, and some polities have no political structures at the regional scale at all, but may have regionally distinct cultures or communities.

Given this patchy picture, there is no immediate prospect that the regional scale of politics will form the basis of some new Europe-wide transnational democracy, whether along the lines of the federation of regions associated with the 'Europe of the Regions' concept or in some other way. What is clear, though, is that regions will certainly play an important role in Europe's developing multi-level polity ('Europe with regions'). Furthermore, if that polity is to be democratic and accountable it will in principle need to be associated with a multi-level form of citizenship which will stretch at least from the EU level down to the region.

In comparison with the welter of writing on the economics of regionalism discussed above, relatively little attention has been paid to regions as democratic spaces, or arenas for the practice of citizenship. The idea of 'regional citizenship', for example, has no real currency in either the academic or policy literatures, and while regional cultures have long been the focus of ethnographic and geographical research, more sociological notions such as 'regional civil society' receive less attention that 'regional economy'. Part of the reason for this may be the emphasis placed by EU institutions on the supposedly 'neutral' terrain of economic competitiveness at the expense of more politically sensitive issues such as the relative powers of the EU, the nation-state and the region. Whatever the explanation, the elaboration of a model of multi-level citizenship requires that the relative neglect of the relationship between regions and citizenship needs to be remedied.

One exception to the general inattention paid to the issue is the recent survey of *Regional and Local Democracy in the European Union* prepared for the Committee of the Regions by John Loughlin and others (Committee of the Regions 1999). Most of the text consists of chapters outlining the condition of local and regional democracy in each of the member states (with the exception of Luxembourg). The introductory chapter, though, does cover more general issues of regional democracy. Loughlin argues, for example, that 'the Committee of the Regions is...an important factor for the strengthening of democracy in the EU, as it has the potential to bring the processes of European decision-making closer to the ordinary citizen', and that 'many of the regional and local authorities surveyed in this report are experimenting with different methods of bringing citizens more into the political system at this level' (Committee of the Regions 1999: 10–11). These comments are echoed by the political commentator Jonathan Freedland, writing about the UK:

> Putting the people in charge will require one enormous change in our political culture: a vast switch of emphasis from central to local government... genuine popular sovereignty means placing power with the people – in their own backyard. Moves towards self-rule in Scotland and Wales and a mayoralty in London represent a good start. The US, with its mini-parliaments in each of the fifty states, is a useful guide to how the distribution of power could go further...the idea of democratic assemblies for each nation or region in Britain – with one or two chambers, it is up to them – is hard to oppose.
>
> (Freedland 1998: 214–15)

The argument that devolved decision making is somehow intrinsically more democratic than more centralised forms because it is 'closer to the people' is long standing, albeit contestable (see Agnew in this volume). While it may be true that people are more immediately concerned and thus more likely to be politically active about issues that affect them directly, not all such issues are local or regional in character. There is also a tension between universal democratic rights and devolution which may result in a greater emphasis on ethnic, national or regional particularism. Freedland's proposal must therefore be balanced by the other elements of a multi-level model, in which the democratising gains of decentralisation are additional to, and not a replacement for, citizenship rights and participation at the EU and member state levels.

If fully developed, multi-level citizenship will have a 'variable geometry' with citizens in some regions having different sets of rights than those in others. This is already apparent to some extent, with specific cultural and language rights often limited to one part of a current member state (official support for the Welsh language in Wales but not in England is a good example). Multi-level citizenship will thus be unevenly developed across Europe as a result of the uneven development of new regionalism, though it is possible that interregional links, alliances and competition will tend to even things out.

I argued above that there was an important relationship between citizenship and identity. Citizenship is not only about rights and duties but also concerns membership, belonging and mutual recognition; formal rights are of little use in practice if the citizen who possesses them is not accepted as a full member of the community. Effective multi-level citizenship will thus involve more complex and multiple identities in which citizens may feel a part of several political communities operating at a variety of spatial scales, from the local to the global. Despite the importance of the regional scale in this mix, links between regional identity and European citizenship are routinely ignored in official policy making (as shown, for example, in the absence of questions on regional identity in the *Eurobarometer* polls), and bear further investigation.

Regional and minority national identities are not pre-given cultural phenomena, but are constituted through, in and against, cultural and political institutions, social movements and processes of governance, and evolve in relation to patterns of socio-economic development. Hechter (1975), Lijphart (1977) and Nairn (1981) emphasise in different ways the relationship between regionalism and uneven development. However, for Smith (1981), these 'uneven development' arguments neglect the cultural basis of regional identities. Similarly, according to Keating (1988: 17), 'a sense of history does appear as an important element in many cases of regional mobilisation, with the sense of identity rooted in an independent past – but it does not have to be accurate history'. This view emphasises the discursive construction of identities. However, discourses are not free-floating but are embedded in institutions, and Keating stresses the role of institutions, such as the distinctive Scottish legal and educational systems, in the formation and shaping of regional identities.

Regional institutions are thus important to both identity and citizenship, but the relationship between citizenship and regional identity remains ambiguous. While strong regional identities may enhance the sense of belonging and participation that effective citizenship and legitimate governance requires, they may also become exclusive. They may work to exclude other ethnic or national minorities producing a regional polity in which 'regional citizenship' is denied to those whose faces do not fit. They may also exclude multi-level citizenship by becoming the singular focus of belonging to the neglect of the other levels in the system.

Conclusions

Ideas about multi-level citizenship are increasingly well developed as abstract concepts in the political philosophy and political theory literatures. In addition, it has obvious attractions as a normative ideal in conditions of post-modernity. However, as I have suggested, there are a number of major difficulties to be addressed before multi-level citizenship can be adopted as a description of an emerging political reality, or developed further as a practical political project.

First, regionalism and regional identities vary widely in intensity around Europe. This suggests that the complexity of multi-levelled citizenship (crudely, the number of levels) will vary widely too, which is likely to lead to markedly uneven development in the package of rights and affiliations across Europe.

Second, regional identities take many forms, ranging from very mild or weak identification to rationalist civic nationalism or to the barbarism of ethnic cleansing. Clearly not all types are equally compatible with the vision of multi-level citizenship. Indeed, rationalist civic nationalisms as well as reactionary ethnic essentialism sit uneasily with the multi-level model. Ethnic nationalism is too particularist, denying the rights associated with other 'levels' of identity, or even the very existence of such other levels. Civic nationalism appeals to 'universal' values, but is in practice also particularistic, denying membership to those who do not share the civic values concerned, and being predicated on the idea of a single public sphere, rather than the complex overlapping and inter-locking forums of debate and contestation implied by the multi-level idea.

Third, regional identities are themselves often complex, contested and inter-nally heterogeneous, though the degree of such complexity varies greatly. Among other things, this means that there will be conflicting understandings within regions of the potential for articulating regional and other identities, and competing visions of what such articulation might involve. An important element of the complexity of regional identities is their intersection with a range of other social cleavages and their associated identity, such as social class, gender, ethnicity, religion and so on. This raises the possibility that specific interest groups, such as elite class fractions with hegemonic aspirations, will seek to undermine, or in other cases to promulgate, multi-level citizenship.

Fourth, while there is a close relationship between the emerging pattern of multi-tiered governance and the proposals for multi-level citizenship, the patterns of institution formation that constitute the developing map of European gover-nance also vary widely from region to region. Some regions have strong and strongly autonomous regional government, others are mere statistical units. Some regions are under the 'top level umbrella' of the European Union, others are located outside the EU with presently much looser supranational or interna-tional governance structures. Some national states are authoritarian in character, and unwilling to countenance the development of regional government, or even the expression of regional cultural identities; conversely others are already federal, or consociational in form. This diversity adds to the likely unevenness in any future development of multi-level citizenship as an expression of both rights and identities.

Finally, very little is known at present about the views of citizens themselves. What is the appetite for multi-level citizenship? Does the idea of multiplex identities linked to more variegated and fluid governance structures have any significant popular appeal? How does its appeal vary from region to region, particularly along the various axes of differentiation between regions mentioned above? Are strong regional identities mainly associated with ethnic regionalism of an essentialist or primordial type, largely incompatible with the multi-level model? Answers to these questions are urgently required if the development of multi-level citizenship in Europe is to progress as a political project.

The European Union is the foremost and best-developed example of a transnational structure of political authority. To be a vehicle for transnational democracy, however, it will need to develop greater legitimacy, accountability and transparency. It will also need to promote a sense of affinity among its citizens both with each other and with the EU itself. European citizenship appears to offer the prospect of this in theory. However, full citizenship involves a sense of identity as well as legal and political rights. The challenge for policy makers and Europeans is to develop both the rights and the identity aspects of citizenship, and to do so in ways that are sensitive to the emerging complexities of governance in Europe and to the multiple identities now evident in Europe's nations and regions.

References

Anderson, B. (1983) *Imagined Communities: Reflections on the Origins and Spread of Nationalism*, London: Verso.

Anderson, J. (1996) 'The shifting stage of politics: new medieval and postmodern territorialities', *Environment and Planning D: Society and Space* 14: 133–53.

Beiner, R. (1995) *Theorizing Citizenship*, Albany, NY: State University of New York Press.

Benhabib, S. (1996) *Democracy and Difference: Contesting the Boundaries of the Political*, Princeton, NJ: Princeton University Press.

Billig, M. (1995) *Banal Nationalism*, London: Sage.

Brown, M.P. (1997) *Replacing Citizenship: AIDS activism and Radical Democracy*, New York: The Guilford Press.

Brubaker, R. (1996) *Nationalism Reframed: Nationhood and the National Question in the New Europe*, Cambridge: Cambridge University Press.

Bull, H. (1977) *The Anarchical Society*, London: Macmillan.

Camilleri, J. and Falk, J. (1992) *The End of Sovereignty?*, Aldershot: Edward Elgar.

Committee of the Regions (1999) *Regional and Local Democracy in the European Union*, Luxembourg: Office for Official Publications of the European Communities.

Dauenhauer, B.P. (1996) *Citizenship in a Fragile World*, Lanham, MD: Rowman and Littlefield.

Delanty, G. (1997) 'Models of citizenship: defining European identity and citizenship', *Citizenship Studies* 1: 285–303.

Fontaine, P. (1993) *A Citizen's Europe*, Luxembourg: European Commission.

Freedland, J. (1998) *Bring Home the Revolution: The Case for a British Republic*, London: Fourth Estate.

Gamberale, C. (1997) 'European citizenship and political identity', *Space and Polity* 1: 37–59.

Garcia, S. (1993) *European Identity and the Search for Legitimacy*, London: Pinter.

Giddens, A. (1985) *The Nation-State and Violence*, Cambridge: Polity Press.

Hechter, M. (1975) *Internal Colonialism*, London: Routledge.

Held, D., McGrew, A., Goldblatt, D. and Perraton, J. (1999) *Global Transformations: Politics, Economics and Culture*, Cambridge: Polity Press.

Holston, J. and Appadurai, A. (1999) 'Cities and citizenship', in J. Holston (ed.), *Cities and Citizenship* , Durham, NC: Duke University Press, 1–18.

Ignatieff, M. (1995) 'The myth of citizenship', in R. Beiner (ed.), *Theorizing Citizenship*, Albany, NY: State University of New York Press, 53–77.

Jessop, B. (1994) 'Post-Fordism and the state', in A. Amin (ed.), *Post-Fordism: A Reader*, Oxford: Blackwell, 251–79.

Keating, M. (1988) *The State and Regional Nationalism*, Hemel Hempstead: Harvester Wheatsheaf.

—— (1998) *The New Regionalism in Western Europe: Territorial Restructuring and Political Change*, Cheltenham: Edward Elgar.

Kofman, E. (1995) 'Citizenship for some, but not for others: spaces of citizenship in contemporary Europe', *Political Geography* 14: 121–37.

Kymlicka, W. (1995) *Multicultural Citizenship*, Oxford: Oxford University Press.

Leonard, M. (1998a) *Making Europe Popular: The Search for European Identity*, London: Demos.

—— (1998b) *Rediscovering Europe*, London: Demos.

Lijphart, A. (1977) 'Political theories and the explanation of ethnic conflict in the western world: falsified predictions and plausible postdictions', in M.J. Esman (ed.), *Ethnic Conflict in the Western World*, Ithaca, NY: Cornell University Press.

Mann, M. (1984) 'The autonomous power of the state: its origins, mechanisms and results', *European Journal of Sociology* 25: 185–213.

Marshall, T.H. (1950) *Citizenship and Social Class*, Cambridge: Cambridge University Press.

Meehan, E. (1993) *Citizenship and the European Community*, London: Sage.

Morley, D. and Robins, K. (1995) *Spaces of Identity: Global Media, Electronic Landscape and Cultural Boundaries*, London: Routledge.

Mouffe, C. (1993) *The Return of the Political*, London: Verso.

Nairn, T. (1981) *The Break-up of Britain*, London: Verso.

Oreja, M. (1997) *Culture and European Integration*, Vienna.

Painter, J. and Philo, C. (1995) 'Spaces of citizenship: an introduction', *Political Geography* 14: 107–20.

Putnam, R.D. (1993) *Making Democracy Work: Civic Traditions in Modern Italy*, Princeton, NJ: Princeton University Press.

Scott, A.J. (1996) 'Regional motors of the global economy', *Futures* 28: 391–411.

Shaw, J. (1998) 'Citizenship of the Union: towards post-national membership', in Academy of European Law (ed.), *Collected Courses of the Academy of European Law*, Volume VI, Book 1, The Hague: Kluwer Law International, 237–347.

Smith, A. (1981) *The Ethnic Revival*, Cambridge: Cambridge University Press.

Smith, G. and Wilson, A. (1997) 'Rethinking Russia's post-Soviet diaspora', *Europe-Asia Studies* 49: 845–64.

Storper, M. (1995) 'The resurgence of regional economies, ten years later: the region as a nexus of untraded interdependencies', *European Urban and Regional Studies* 2: 191–221.

Tassin, E. (1992) 'Europe: a political community?', in C. Mouffe (ed.), *Dimensions of Radical Democracy*, London: Verso, 169–92.

Turner, B. (1989) 'Outline of a theory of citizenship', *Sociology* 24: 189–217.

6 Transnational integration and cross-border regions in the European Union

Liam O'Dowd

Transnational (or more accurately trans-state) integration necessarily involves changes in the functions, meanings, and sometimes the location of state borders. Accordingly, no account of transnational integration is adequate without an analysis of what is happening to, and at, national borders. Yet, with the exception of sub-disciplines such as political geography, mainstream analysts have been slow to problematise borders. They have tended to emphasise the 'universal' forces that transcend borders, such as capitalism, industrialism and globalisation, consigning borders to the realm of the contingent, the particular or the peripheral. It may also be significant that the major institutional growth of social science in Europe and North America coincided with a period of remarkable border stability between 1950 and the late 1980s. This led to a tendency to equate state and society and to take borders for granted rather than as objects of analysis.

In recent decades, the accelerating globalisation of economic and cultural life, and the growing density of international and supranational institutions, have led many to assume the decreasing significance, even redundancy, of state borders. However, these borders have not disappeared, and indeed in Eastern Europe they have proliferated in the wake of the disintegration of the Soviet bloc. Within the European Union (EU), border zones have become significantly more salient as sites where a multiplicity of local governmental and non-governmental agencies promote a great variety of cross-border links in conjunction with their national states and the European Commission. It appears that state borders are being reconfigured as their functions and meanings change. These developments have encouraged a limited but widespread revitalisation of research on borders across a range of social science disciplines.[1] It can provide clues to the nature and direction of transnational integration and the needs and implications of transnational democracy.

In this chapter, 'cross-border' or 'trans-frontier regions' are examined as a means of elucidating some key aspects of transnationalism. The *raison d'être* of these 'regions' is based on the national borders which divide them, in the sense that they have come into existence to overcome the disadvantages posed by the existence of state borders. Unlike typical sub-state regions, they are constructed around a central and constant territorial divide while their own boundaries are often imprecise and elastic. The critical factors in transfrontier regionalism are cross-border institutional links. These links have some of the characteristics of networks, generally lacking constant boundaries and operating as open structures mainly definable through their functions and communication flows (Eger 1996: 23).

Another way of conceptualising 'cross-border regions' is to see them as a form of 'border regime' defined as 'networks of rules, norms and procedures that regularize behaviour at borders and controls its effects' (Langer 1996: 62–3). These regimes are the outcome of complex interactions between broad geo-political forces, national states and the populations residing in borderlands or crossing the national border.[2]

The various stages of European integration have been characterised by changes in border regimes. In the main, there are two separate, if related, means of reconfiguring borders and advancing transnational integration. The first is war, coercion and conquest, long integral to the process of state formation in Europe as well as European expansion overseas. The second is largely functional and economic: it involves creating and building on interdependencies, most obviously but not exclusively, associated with the globalisation of trade and production.

What follows falls into three main sections. The first comprises brief theoretical and historical comments on the study of state borders in Europe. The second discusses three overlapping moments of transfrontier regionalism: pioneering cross-border regions in the early post-war period; the initiation of the Single Market; and the collapse of state socialism and EU enlargement to the East. The final section consists of a summary of the evolution of transfrontier regionalism and advances tentative conclusions on how it illuminates key characteristics of transnational integration in the EU.

Theoretical and historical comments

Border ambiguities

To grasp the social import of state borders we must recognise that boundary creation, maintenance and transcendence are integral features of human behaviour, including the organisation of political communities.[3] Malcolm Anderson (1996: 189) points out that all major political projects have included images of frontiers and conceptions of territorial organisation. In the past, boundaries have appeared at times to be fluid while at other times they have appeared as fixed and immutable; as part of a deep-rooted divine or natural pattern. Today, boundaries are much more likely to appear as social constructions vulnerable to change. As William Connolly (1994: 19) notes, 'more boundaries now appear to be less natural to more people'.

But this realisation makes us more sharply aware of the abiding ambiguity, or contradictory nature, of borders:

- they may be seen as protections against violation and violence but also as enshrining considerable coercion and violence in their construction;
- they provide the conditions for social identity, for individual and collective action, but they also close off possibilities which might otherwise flourish.

Nowhere are these ambiguities more apparent than with respect to state borders. The creation of territorial state borders has seldom been a product of democratic consensus or plebiscite. As Malcolm Anderson (1996: 37) notes in a recent book on borders, 'the great majority of the world's frontiers have been established by force and intimidation', but they are deemed sustainable in the long term because *ex post facto*, they rest on self-determination and consent. Of course, struggles continue over 'whose self-determination' and 'whose consent' should be institutionalised in state borders. Indeed, such struggles have been at the root of the endemic conflicts over state formation in Europe for several centuries.

The drawing of state borders has been largely if not exclusively a preserve of powerful elites. Once established, state borders have included and excluded many people against their will. The territorial state has generated projects of social and cultural homogenisation while sustaining hierarchies based on class, ethnicity, gender and religion. At the same time, in Western Europe, it has created a rule of law tied to territory rather than people, in order to regulate these inequalities and the dissent they produce. Borders have facilitated the creation of democracies based on the rule of law, but they are also a reminder of the coercive, often violent and non-democratic roots of contemporary democratic states (see Anderson in this volume) and of the difficulties of constructing transnational democracy within the state system.

Borders, wars and state formation

The history of state borders in Europe is the history of the formation of sovereign states from the hundreds of diverse political units which characterised medieval Europe. Inter-state war to acquire and defend territory has been a central theme of this history. The several paths to state formation identified by Tilly (1990) have involved mass mobilisation for war, the development of taxation systems to support wars, and subsequent processes of civilianisation (including democratization). In other words, wars have made states as much as states have made wars. Inter-state war not only created borders, it also shaped border regimes and the nature of the political community within the fixed territorial limits. Internal pacification within these limits became the *sine qua non* of the effective mobilisation for war against other states, but is also became the basis for a functioning state-centred political system.

Indeed, modern warfare, particularly the Second World War, laid the basis for a vast expansion of what Michael Mann (1993) has termed the infrastructural power of the state. By this he means the capacity of the state to monopolise the legal means of coercion, surveillance, taxation and welfare distribution within fixed territorial boundaries. The remarkable density of state institutions, and the unprecedented complexity of their relationship to citizens, greatly increased the practical importance of belonging to one state rather than another, thus increasing the 'territorial boundedness' of existing states. This was the case in both Western and Eastern Europe despite their post-1945 ideological division over the forms of economic and state organisation. Systems of health, education, welfare and civil administration generally constituted distinctive, territorially exclusive, national citizenship regimes, stimulated by the experience of wartime mobilisation but with deep historical roots. Not surprisingly, it is precisely these areas that have proved most resistant to supranational integration and control.

Nationalism, long the most potent ideology of the territorial state, emerged from the Second World War with its ambiguities enhanced. Its fascist and Nazi manifestations were discredited and defeated. But their victorious opponents had also drawn heavily on their own nationalisms, particularly in Britain, Russia, the USA and the French Resistance. In Europe, nationalism had involved two broad processes: states seeking nations and nations seeking states. The more states can identify themselves with a shared homeland and national solidarity against outsiders, the more they can manage internal divisions and enhance their own legitimacy. The growth in the infrastructural power of the post-war welfare states deepened this state nationalism. Moreover, appeals to nationhood helped conceal the arbitrary nature of established state borders (Habermas 1996: 288).

Nations seeking states, on the other hand, continued to expose the arbitrariness and injustice of existing borders, in order to improve their version of the fit between nation and territorial state. But in Europe, the process of matching nation and state has been doomed never to reach finality: many stateless nations remain, and few, if any, genuine nation-states exist where the state territorially incorporates all the members of a single nation and no significant others. This ideological struggle to identify state with nation has interacted with the frequent inter-state conflicts over territory and state borders (see Anderson and Hamilton in this volume). Thus there were three major waves in the geographical reconstruction of state borders in Europe last century, associated with the two world wars and the post-1989 upheaval in Eastern Europe respectively. Apart from a period of relative stability between the 1950s and 1980s, European borders have been fluid rather than fixed, demonstrably arbitrary rather than natural, but this has sustained rather than undermined the appeal of the nationalist search for a political homeland.

Borders, however, are not merely a product of war and inter-state conflict. As political geographers remind us, boundaries and border zones perform dual functions, as barriers or buffers on the one hand, and as gateways, bridges and zones of interaction on the other. They are manifestations of power, conquest and conflict but they are also sites of voluntary, productive and enriching exchange and identification with others. They are both enabling and disabling, standing for opportunity as well as denial, inclusion as well as exclusion, for voluntary affiliation as well as coercive power. Transnational integration that involves the reconstruction of existing borders and the creation of new ones inevitably shares these same contradictory characteristics. The contradictions involved also shape the prospects for transnational democracy.

European integration: a new departure?

The process of integration in what is now the EU ostensibly marks a historic departure in that it has sought to break the link between inter-state war and borders. For both federalists and intergovernmentalists, the Second World War had finally shown the impracticality and folly of modern inter-state warfare. Even if war mobilisation helped to build nations, the price of assured devastation was too high given the impossibility of defending borders and national populations. Inter-state war as a means of state formation or enforced transnational integration seemed self-defeating. The alternative proposed was the ending of territorial wars, the acceptance of the state boundaries produced by the post-war balance of coercion, and the development of economic and political interdependence across frontiers in order to advance European integration.

From the outset, the European Economic Community (EEC) was based on a form of compartmentalisation. It accepted the geo-political division of Eastern and Western Europe and sought transnational integration under the shadow of two huge military alliances led by the USA and the USSR respectively. The responsibility for overall defence and war-making was effectively located outside the EEC while the latter concentrated on transnational economic integration within its own borders. Transfrontier regionalism was one of the means of advancing and deepening this integration. Although relatively weak initially, it became more important as the process of integration advanced.

A leading role for transfrontier regions?

For their most enthusiastic advocates, transfrontier 'regions' are central to European integration, an alternative to a Europe of sovereign states. Ricq argues, for example:

> Unlike the closed system of nation-states…the transfrontier regions, transforming themselves from regions of confrontation to regions of concentration, will see the first real signs of the surrender of sovereignty – Europe of the future will have to base itself on these regions in order to redesign itself and produce a better structure.
>
> (cited in Duchacek 1986: 25)

In the early 1990s, in the wake of the Single Market Programme, a Council of Europe report envisaged a new alliance between an EU, with new competencies to integrate European economic space, and regional and local bodies with a long-standing interest in transfrontier co-operation. It went on to argue that this alliance will reduce the national states' monopoly of control in border regions: 'transfrontier co-operation constitutes in this light, the first step towards political union and possibly even represents the cornerstone of the future European political Community' (Mestre 1992: 14).

In theory at least, transfrontier regions could be seen as involving a redesign of territorial governance and a blurring of state boundaries. They promised a challenge to the principles of state sovereignty, exclusivity and territoriality which hindered closer European unity. At the very least they might serve as experimental laboratories for generating better insights into transnational integration and EU policy (van der Veen and Boot 1995: 90).

Even if the political and theoretical claims for transfrontier regions seemed exaggerated, they did appear to promise a more practical and democratic grass-roots form of European integration than the rather secretive bargaining between elites at intergovernmental level in Brussels. Given their practical agenda and illustrative value, a closer examination of the history and characteristics of transfrontier regions seems appropriate.

Moments of transfrontier regionalism

Three overlapping moments of transfrontier regionalism may be identified following the trajectory of European integration overall:

1   the pioneering post-war transfrontier developments mainly in the Rhine Basin;
2   the stimulus to transfrontier regionalism provided by the Single European Market and the direct EC/EU funding of cross-border projects;
3   the impact of the EU's expansion eastwards following the end of the Cold War and the upheavals in Eastern Europe.

The main thrust of cross-border regionalism has remained functional and mainly economic throughout. However, it has been shaped at each moment by the interaction between the existing geo-political framework, the bordering states, the role of borderland residents and organisations, and by cultural factors such as language.

Early transfrontier regionalism

After 1945 there was a period of adjustment and stabilisation of state borders, influenced by NATO and the Warsaw Pact at continental level, and by the activities of organisations such as the Council of Europe and the EEC. In border regions, states were preoccupied at the outset with their political, military and historical dimensions borders rather than with questions of economic rationality and development (Hansen 1983: 256).

In the immediate aftermath of the Second World War, the most pressing issue was the designation and management of new German borders in the wake of the Nazis' failed attempt at uniting Europe under their leadership. The war and its aftermath had involved not only the slaughter but also the physical displacement of millions of people, particularly in the USSR, Poland and Germany. The major issue was the role of a defeated Germany in the new post-war European order. The outcome reflected the post-war balance of coercion in Europe. The pre-war German border was moved westwards to the Oder–Neisse line and the country was partitioned. East Germany became a member of the Soviet bloc while the French, British and American zones of occupation were merged into a reconstructed polity, the Federal Republic of Germany. A series of agreements under the aegis of the Western powers also stabilised the Italian borders with France, Austria and Yugoslavia (Lill 1982).

Perhaps the greatest boost for post-war cross-border co-operation was the resolution of the Saarland question with the full re-incorporation of the province into Germany in 1959 after a prolonged territorial dispute between France and Germany. The site of major coalfields, it became an associate member of the Council of Europe in 1950 while economically integrated into France. Unusually, this border problem was solved by a series of plebiscites and these were crucially facilitated by the internationalisation of its coalfields under the European Coal and Steel Community, an organisation that was subsequently to prove a model for the EEC.

However, it was the relatively powerless and consultative Council of Europe rather than the EEC which first became involved in promoting transfrontier regionalism. It sought to facilitate it by developing new legal instruments and by identifying frontier regions as illustrative laboratories for the problems and potentialities of European integration. It was the Council rather than the European Community that helped systematise, legitimise and publicise early efforts at cross-border co-operation by local and regional authorities (Dupuy 1982: 59). It sought to develop triangular relationships between European institutions, national states and local institutions within border regions (Strassoldo and Delli Zotti 1982; Anderson 1982).

From the 1950s onwards, a tradition of regional cross-border co-operation had developed in the Rhineland involving Dutch, German, Belgian, Swiss and French border areas (Strassoldo and Gubert 1973: 12). In the 1960s, a tri-national, three-way co-operation between southern Alsace, Baden-Wurttemberg and Basel developed under the aegis of Regio Basiliensis (1962) dealing with land-use planning and labour market requirements (Maillat 1990: 47). Indeed, the upper Rhine marked the area of most intense transborder co-operation involving municipalities, universities, private sector interests and consultative committees of central and local government officials.

Just as Franco-German and Benelux co-operation was the engine for European economic integration at intergovernmental level, Rhine basin regions and local authorities were the pioneers of cross-border regions. Much of the collaboration was project-specific, focusing particularly on problems of industrial decline, pollution, transfrontier workers and land-use planning (Anderson 1996: 123; Mestre 1992: 13). However, some of the more ambitious attempts involved the creation of more permanent and inclusive institutions such as Euregio on the Dutch–German border and Regio Basiliensis. The former consisted of a board, working party and secretariat. Gabbe (1987: 127) notes that its board was the first transfrontier, regional, parliamentary and local authority assembly in Europe.

Significantly, the Regio Basiliensis border region was not merely based on instrumental links. It shared cultural and economic ties long before France, Germany and Switzerland were created. Central to the economy of Europe, its inhabitants shared a common German, Alemannic dialect. The wider project of European integration provided an opportunity for the reforging of cross-border links in a transborder region equally divided between the three states (Briner 1986: 46).

The Rhine Basin had particular advantages that facilitated cross-border co-operation. As well as serving as the focus of Franco-German rapprochement, it constituted the dynamic economic core of the EEC. There were compelling practical reasons for establishing cross-frontier links in an area of dense settlement and intense economic activity. Hansen (1983) suggests that here economic rationality took precedence over political factors such as the preservation of national sovereignty (in contrast to other border regions). The involvement of Swiss cantons external to the European Community underlines this point. Moreover, the nature of the existing regional institutions also facilitated cross-border co-operation. Many local authorities in Germany, Switzerland, and the Benelux countries had substantial devolved powers. In addition, local corporatism, involving chambers of commerce, trade unions, banks and universities, provided a flexible institutional framework for regional cross-border initiatives.

While the density of cross-border networking in the Rhine Basin has not been replicated elsewhere, it has been influential in the wider EU context. The term 'Euroregion' was coined here as referring to both a spatial and institutionalised entity. The Association of European Border Regions (AEBR) also originated in the Rhineland and now plays a wider advisory and consultancy role on border regions within the EU.

The Single Market

Until the mid-1980s, the European Community confined its borders policy to the 'negative integration' policy of gradually removing barriers to inter-state trade. Since 1975, limited EC regional funds had been directed towards selected cities and regions suffering from economic peripherality and industrial decline and, although some happened to be involved in cross-border networks (Mestre 1992: 13; Williams 1996), there was no targeting of border regions as such. The Council of Europe continued its attempts to construct a viable legal framework of cross-border 'regions' in the face of some indifference and resistance from national states. In 1981, it finally promulgated a Framework Convention on Transfrontier Cooperation (the Madrid Convention). This Convention advanced new models and juridical principles for cross-border links but had limited practical effect. At this time, the EC was undergoing a period of stagnation due to economic recession and stalemate over the precise nature of the links between economic integration and national sovereignty.

The initiation of the Single Market Programme involved a much more radical version of the 'negative integration' approach by attempting to abolish all internal controls on the cross-border movement of capital, commodities, services and labour. The packages of Structural Funds (Delors I and II) associated with the Single European Act (1986) and the Maastricht Agreement (1992) attempted to shift the emphasis to 'positive integration' measures. A new INTERREG (International Regions) programme was set up by the EC Commission on its own initiative as part of the Structural Operations budget to help border regions specifically. INTERREG had a dual purpose: firstly to integrate the economic space of the EU as a whole, and secondly to address the negative legacy of border areas such as the isolation of many from the main centres of economic activity and decision making, the separation of commercial centres from natural hinterlands, generally inferior infrastructure, often poor natural resources, and the specific difficulties arising from having different legal, administrative and social welfare systems, and frequently different languages and cultural traditions in contiguous regions across the border (Commission of the European Communities 1991: 169).

Those areas where cross-border co-operation was already institutionalised were well placed to benefit from the new funds and their relative accessibility to the core centres of EC economic activity promised immediate benefits. The AEBR helped monitor and advise on the INTERREG programme. It was able to claim that by the mid-1990s there were nearly 100 examples of cross-border networking involving regional and local authorities across EU state borders (AEBR 1996). However, it was also clear that the existence of a single EU programme for border areas also helped expose the great variety of border regions within the EU and how little they had in common. These regions varied in terms of their origins, longevity and prosperity, the permeability of their national boundaries and their historical legacy of cross-border contacts, both formal and informal.

The difficulty of designing one borders policy for the EU became apparent. In the event, what emerged was a wide variety of different organisational and practical arrangements, what Scott (1998) has termed 'multilevel institutionalisation' (see Painter in this volume). These strategies were influenced by the more established examples of transfrontier co-operation and typically linked three institutional levels:

1   intergovernmental planning commissions in border regions;
2   locally based structures such as the 'Euroregions';
3   co-ordinating structures associated with INTERREG.

Just as the Single Market and INTERREG were being introduced, however, the wider context of cross-border networking was being altered dramatically by the collapse of the post-war geo-political framework in Europe after 1989 and the often violent proliferation of new state borders in Eastern Europe.

Eastern European disintegration and EU enlargement

The early pioneers of transfrontier regionalism had been able to compartmentalise functional, socio-economic issues from high politics insofar as they were working within a framework of stabilised borders set by the geo-politics of the Cold War (Anderson 1982; Mestre 1992). The Single Market programme further enhanced and extended transfrontier regionalism with the EU Commission becoming a major actor through its INTERREG programme.

After 1989, however, the collapse of the post-war geo-political framework in Europe, the disintegration of Yugoslavia and the Soviet Union and the break-up of Czechoslovakia made it increasingly difficult to see regional transfrontier co-operation simply as instrumental, functional and economic in nature. The political, military and cultural dimensions of borders and their coercive and non-democratic characteristics now came to the fore. EU-sponsored cross-border economic co-operation continued but in a new relationship to the other dimensions of borders.

The coercive dimension of state borders was refurbished as the Single Market came into force (O'Dowd *et al.* 1995). The Maastricht Treaty confirmed a renewed concern with borders as instruments of exclusion and control in 'Fortress Europe', in part linked to the abolition of controls along *internal* EU borders and in part in response to the upheavals in Eastern Europe. The Treaty established the 'K4 Coordinating Committee', building on the work of the preceding 'Trevi group', with a remit to deal with immigration and asylum, police and customs co-operation and judicial co-operation. This represented a form of transnational integration aimed at creating a common borders policy. The Committee, however, was not accountable to either the European Parliament or the Commission and reported directly to the Council of Ministers. The lack of democracy in the historical creation and reconstruction of European borders now seemed to be repeating itself. Some libertarians discerned the formation of an embryonic, unaccountable and repressive European state apparatus behind the formal institutions of the EU (Bunyan 1993). Somewhat ironically, the relaxation of border controls in ex-socialist states was accompanied by their enhancement in Western European states as the latter sought to limit the flow of criminals, drug trafficking and illegal immigrants across the southern and eastern borders of the EU.

Central Europe or *Mitteleuropa* had been re-emerging as a factor in European integration in political and cultural discourses for over a decade prior to the implosion of the state-socialist bloc. Changes in Eastern Europe increased the influence of Germany on EU borders policy. In contrast to the Nazis strategy of moving borders, post-war German policy had been to minimise geographical alterations to state borders (exceptions being German reunification and support for Croatian and Slovenian secession). Committed to working through the EU, Germany sought to allay any suspicions its neighbours might have over territorial expansionism.

The German influence on the EU opposed state-centrism while encouraging regionalisation and the recognition of the rights of national minorities. As

Waever (1993: 183) observes, 'Federal Germany remains passive and a German Mitteleuropa is constructed by firms, Lander and individuals linking up in a tight pattern of interaction'.[4] One consequence of this policy was the creation of four Euroregions along the German–Polish border while others spanned the German–Czech border, the Baltic Sea region and the Italo–Austrian borders. While these cross-border regions vary in terms of their degree of institutionalisation, they all adopt a networking approach linking non-governmental bodies with each other and with the participating states and the EU Commission.

This 'German' form of transfrontier regionalism is also firmly embedded in the wider EU policy of gradated enlargement eastwards and is seen as a form of practical preparation for it. The promise of accession is linked to a set of political and economic criteria with direct implications for border regimes and regional cross-border relationships. In preparation for EU membership, candidate countries, as well as accepting existing EU rules and regulations, must have 'achieved a stability of institutions guaranteeing democracy, the rule of law, human rights and respect for and protection of minorities' (Commission of the European Communities 1997: 42). Similarly, they have to possess a 'functioning market economy' and be able to 'withstand competitive pressure and market forces within the Union' (1997: 46–7). Significantly, the EU also stressed that enlargement should not mean importing border conflicts and it has developed a pre-accession strategy which pressurises applicants to submit any territorial disputes to the International Court of Justice (1997: 59).

The huge socio-economic disparities between EU and non-EU countries created highly asymmetric border regions, making cross-border economic co-operation more difficult than along internal borders (Kratke 1997; Paasi 1996). These disparities have encouraged a more complex approach to cross-border integration. As in the case of the US–Mexican border, there is a renewed EU emphasis on the external border as permeable for certain forms of capitalist activity and as exclusionary in the face of flows of immigrants, refugees and criminal activities across it.

EU states have made separate agreements with sending countries by swapping economic aid for a willingness to take back illegal immigrants. Alternatively, such agreements allow temporary, licensed access to the labour markets of receiving countries. Asylum seekers can be returned to the first country of transit deemed to be 'safe', although what is deemed safe is highly contestable (Morris 1997: 200). Carriers, such as airlines and taxis, are being fined for carrying illegals. EU funds are being used to subsidise prospective member states to fortify their eastern borders with much poorer countries like Belarus, Romania and Russia that have little immediate prospect of entry into the EU. Stemming the flows of illegal immigrants, drugs and criminals is part of the process of strengthening the external borders of the EU while stabilising countries like Poland, Hungary and the Czech Republic which have been selected for early entry. In fact, a migrant buffer zone has been created on the eastern side of the EU's external borders where settled populations coexist with a mobile population comprising refugees, traders, criminals and a migrant young population

(Wallace 1999). This has led to an increase in xenophobia and racist crimes in parts of Poland, the Czech Republic and Hungary.

Transfrontier regionalism: summary and conclusions

Moments in a shared trajectory

As can be seen from the preceding discussion, the natural history of transfrontier regionalism in many respects mirrors that of the European Union as a whole. Like the EU, its origins centred on the Rhineland and it developed against a background of the stabilisation of western European state borders, and the creation of the European Coal and Steel Community and the Council of Europe. From the outset, the EEC prioritised functional forms of cross-border co-operation in terms of promoting economic and infrastructural development. As such, it has influenced all subsequent forms of EU sponsored cross-border development. However, the reluctance to develop specific programmes for cross-border regions until 1989 reflected the political sensitivity of borders and state sovereignty and the extent to which economic integration was ostensibly insulated from 'politics' (see Newman in this volume).

The second phase of transfrontier regionalism was initiated by the Single European Market programme and the introduction, for the first time, of European Community initiatives specifically targeted at internal and external border regions. With the INTERREG initiative, the European Commission became a major actor in cross-border regions. A triangular strategy, long advocated by the Council of Europe, could now be implemented involving European organisations, participating governments and regional and local authorities in border zones. INTERREG enabled the spread of transfrontier regionalism to peripheral and 'external' borders of the EU with little tradition of regional cross-border co-operation, where 'political sovereignty' and 'security' had long taken precedence over issues of economic interdependence and development in border regions.

Finally, the changes in Eastern Europe and the proposed enlargement of the EU have re-problematised the links between economic and political integration. The extension of the market economy to the post-state-socialist countries highlights the huge structural disparities on either side of the external border and provides a dynamic for a multifaceted reconstitution of the boundary. The vehicles of this reconstitution include various forms of capitalism, from the use of cheap Polish labour, to the creation of huge border bazaars, to smuggling and other criminal activities (Kratke 1997; Stryjakiewicz and Kaczmarek 1997). In the face of these developments and the fall of the 'Iron Curtain', the EU and its member states seek to police the border more closely and to control border regions more thoroughly in order to restrict illegal immigration, crime and potential for ethno-national conflict. The rush to establish Euroregions is part of the unfinished business of constructing the external border of the EU, but it is only one part of a wider reconstruction.

Changing the symbolic meaning of borders

From the Rhineland pioneers to the Eastern Euroregions of the 1990s, there has been a dramatic increase in the number of regional, local and non-governmental bodies engaged in cross-border co-operation. Perhaps their most striking impact has been symbolic. They have challenged the existing symbolic association of state borders with exclusive state sovereignty over sharply delineated territories.

In generating new relationships between supranational, national and local level institutions they seem to represent one possible future for the EU as a multi-level system of governance where authority is diffused among agencies of different sizes, scope and function (Risse-Kappen 1996: 68). They seem to symbolise what many observers have termed the emergence of a neo-medieval Europe where the old hierarchical order of sovereign states is giving way to 'much more flexible, overlapping, intersecting and cross-cutting networks of social interaction that do not (necessarily) form a totality and whose sociospatial dimensions are not (necessarily) territorially fixed through state boundaries' (Mlinar 1995: 161). Transfrontier networks seem to reflect what James Anderson (1996: 149) sees as an emergent 'mixture of old, new, and hybrid forms – territorial, trans-territorial and functional forms of association and authority coexisting and interacting'.

Although most transfrontier or cross-border regions are created for pragmatic or instrumental reasons to access EU funding as a means of addressing shared environmental, planning or economic development problems, it may be argued that their real significance lies elsewhere. They may be seen as harbingers of what Risse-Kappen (1996: 70–1) calls cross-national policy communities, advocacy and discourse coalitions, and epistemic communities where the logic of communicative action, discourse and consensus creation may be just as important as the logic of instrumental action. Here the state is seen as 'one sub-system among many' (Mlinar 1995: 162) sharing power with transnational coalitions including regional and local bodies, non-governmental agencies and capitalist firms. Certainly, the *modus operandi* of transfrontier regions is predicated on communication, negotiation and consensus. In this sense, they sustain and build on the traditional role of border regions as sites of interaction and exchange. Their structure is potentially conducive to the development of participatory rather than exclusively representative forms of democracy.

Structural weaknesses of transfrontier regions

While cross-border regions may symbolise a more consensual and peaceful form of transnational integration, it is easy to exaggerate their structural importance. They fall far short of the expectations of their most enthusiastic advocates that they might constitute key territorial building blocks of European political union. Despite their profusion, they control remarkably few resources. They comprise shifting and skeletal networks covering territorial areas with rather vague and elastic boundaries. Within these areas, the hierarchy of state institutions wields far more influence on daily life. The 'infrastructural power' of national states, especially in its coercive and redistributive aspects, remains paramount. INTERREG, the main EU initiative for border areas, constitutes less than 1 per cent of EU Structural Fund expenditure (1994–9) (Williams 1996) and the Structural Funds themselves account for less than half of the EU budget which itself is frozen at a level not above 1.3 per cent of the GDP of member states.

The financial management and implementation of EU-sponsored cross-border initiatives underpin rather than challenge the territorial state system. All monies are channelled through national governments which provide matching funds or oversee the provision of such funds by bodies outside of central governments. States develop single 'operational programmes' on their own side of the border, bringing forward projects themselves and eliciting proposals from local governments and non-governmental organisations.

Inter-governmental steering committees retain responsibility for co-ordinating and monitoring cross-border projects although applications are encouraged from bodies which have already forged cross-border links and which propose integrated cross-border projects. In many border regions, particularly those that are economically peripheral and part of centralised states, the states loom very large in a landscape characterised by a multiplicity of small and fragmented agencies. While there is much multi-level consultation with the EU and sub-state and non-governmental bodies, the states take the critical decisions in the allocation of limited resources involved. There are exceptions where, as in Germany, regional authorities can act in lieu of the state but with its authorisation. In general, transfrontier regions are stronger in federal systems and where there is greater regional devolution as in Germany, Austria, Belgium and Switzerland.

Cross-border secretariats consisting of administrative and technical personnel may be set up to propose or implement particular projects. Their territorial remits span the border and are more precise than those of cross-border institutional networks. Yet their existence is dependent on programme funding and accordingly they are unable to provide continuity. Their importance, however, illustrates the bias towards bureaucracy and technocracy in transfrontier regions. Electoral constituencies do not span borders and this limits democratic involvement of elected representatives in cross-border networks. Instead, cross-border regions involve a series of flexible strategic alliances between local political, administrative and business elites. To this extent they are forums for limited forms of participatory democracy. The availability of funding brings into being new voluntary bodies and activates established bodies, including municipal and regional authorities. It provides opportunities for such bodies to influence regional developments in border zones where historically the priorities of national governments have minimised local influence on cross-border regimes.

Transfrontier regionalism and the coercive dimensions of borders

Like the EU generally, transfrontier regionalism has had some effect in enhancing the consensual and negotiated aspects of borders at the expense of their coercive dimensions. For example, Mlinar (1996: 10) argues plausibly that 'it has become practically impossible today for an EU member to exercise its superiority to forcibly change borders at the expense of another country'.

Transfrontier regionalism, again like the EU generally, has been premised on stabilising existing state borders while modifying their functions and meanings. However, cross-border regions in conjunction with other challenges to exclusive state sovereignty are also potentially destabilising. In highlighting border regions they expose the chronic lack of fit between nations and states and the arbitrary and coercive basis of many borders. They provide a glimpse of alternatives to existing states in reforging links across historical, national, ethnic, religious and linguistic entities ruptured by the violent process of state formation. Cross-border regions on Germany's eastern frontier, and those involving the South Tyrol, the Irish, and Basque border regions provide examples of cross-border regions seeking to reforge old territorial links.

While transfrontier regions pose a very modest challenge to existing state sovereignty, their significance is enhanced as part of wider processes of fragmentation connected with the dilution of the states' capacity to control economic, political and cultural activity within their territorial limits. Against this background the existing (imperfect) fit between nations and states is under further threat (Baumann 1992). As Rupnik (1994) suggests, 'balkanisation' tendencies are present in Western Europe also. These trends involve the reconstruction of state borders as all manner of intra-state tensions emerge based on growing ethnic and cultural diversity, and nationalist, secessionist and regionalist pressures interacting with social inequalities. The resulting *intra*-state conflicts are becoming far more common globally than traditional *inter*-state wars (Tilly 1990) and are much more significant for the future of state borders.

The revitalisation of state nationalisms, partly in response to globalisation and European integration, and the emergence of strong 'security' states, coexist with trends towards more consensual networking across state boundaries. The old ambiguities inherent in territorial boundaries are emerging in new forms. Transfrontier regions symbolise how these ambiguities might be restructured to make the management of borders more consensual, and they also suggest that negotiation might replace coercion as the medium of contemporary border change. Although their limited control over resources and their structural weaknesses inhibit their potential, cross-border regions provide a glimpse of how transnational integration might be rendered more democratic.

Notes

1   The long-standing concerns of political geographers (for example, Prescott 1987; Paasi 1996) with the topic have now been supplemented by contributions from political science (M. Anderson 1982, 1996), economics (Hansen 1981, 1983), economic geography (Ratti 1993; van der Velde and van Houtum 2000), sociology (Eger and Langer 1996; O'Dowd and Wilson 1996), cultural anthropology (Wilson and Donnan 1998), historical anthropology (Sahlins 1989), international relations and geopolitics (Rupnik 1994; Sparke 1998), and multi-disciplinary approaches (Anderson and O'Dowd 1999). Although points of departure and conventional concerns vary

according to discipline, all are responding to the renewed salience of border changes in Europe linked to the evolution of European integration and to the post-1989 upheavals in Eastern Europe.

2   The capacity of borderland residents to shape the course and nature of state borders varies considerably. For example, it was very substantial on the French–Spanish border in the eastern Pyrenees (Sahlins 1989), while very limited on the Finnish–Russian border (Paasi 1996).

3   Not all political boundaries, however, have been as sharply delimited, or as territorially fixed, as those associated with state sovereignty in the West. Nomadic cultures and traditional Arab lands had more flexible concepts of territory and territorial boundaries, although they have become increasingly influenced by Western conceptions (Mendelson 1998).

4   Waever distinguishes German-style border policies from those of the British and French within the EU. The British prioritise intergovernmental cross-border relationships, while a 'French Europe' emphasises the need for the EU to exercise 'a state-like role in as many areas as possible – to operate as a political actor with a defence identity and a cultural mission'. In French thinking, this means clearly demarcated borders (Waever 1993: 184).

References

AEBR (Association of European Border Regions) (1996) *An Introduction to the Association of European Border Regions*, Gronau: AEBR.

Anderson, J. (1996) 'The shifting stage of the political: new medieval and postmodern territorialities?', *Society and Space: Environment and Planning D* 14(2): 133–53.

Anderson, J. and O'Dowd, L. (eds) (1999) 'State borders and border regions', special issue, *Regional Studies* 33(7).

Anderson, M. (1996) *Frontiers: Territory and State Formation in the Modern World*, Oxford: Polity Press.

—— (ed.) (1982) 'Frontier regions in Western Europe', special issue, *West European Politics* 5(4).

Baumann, Z. (1992) 'Soil, blood and identity', *Sociological Review* 40(4): 675–701.

Briner, H.J. (1986) 'Regional planning and transfrontier cooperation: the Regio Basiliensis', in O.J. Martinez (ed.), *Across Boundaries: Transborder Interaction in Comparative Perspective*, El Paso, TX: Texas Western Press, 45–56.

Bunyan, T. (1993) 'Trevi, Europol and the European state', in T .Bunyan (ed.), *Statewatching the New Europe: A Handbook on the European State*, London: Statewatch.

Commission of the European Communities (1991) *Europe 2000: Outlook for the Development of the Community's Territory*, Brussels: CEC.

—— (1997) *Agenda 2000: For a Stronger and Wider Union*, Brussels, CEC.

Connolly, W. (1994) 'Tocqueville, territory and violence', *Theory, Culture and Society* 11: 19–40.

Duchacek, I.D. (1986) 'International competence of subnational governments: borderlands and beyond', in O.J. Martinez (ed.), *Across Boundaries: Transborder Interaction in Comparative Perspective*, El Paso, TX: Texas Western Press, 11–30.

Dupuy, P.-M. (1982) 'Legal aspects of transfrontier regional cooperation', *West European Politics* 5(4): 50–63.

Eger, G. (1996) 'Region, border and periphery', in G. Eger and J. Langer (eds), *Border, Region and Ethnicity in Central Europe*, Klagenfurt: Norea Verlag, 15–30.

Eger, G. and Langer, J. (eds) (1996) *Border, Region and Ethnicity in Central Europe*, Klagenfurt: Norea Verlag.

Gabbe, J. (1987) 'Euregio': Symposium on Transfrontier Cooperation in Europe – Reports of a Colloquy, Strasbourg: Council of Europe.

Habermas, J. (1996) 'The European nation-state – its achievements and its limits. On the past and future of sovereignty and citizenship', in G. Balakrishnan (ed.), *Mapping the Nation*, London: Verso, 281–94.

Hansen, N. (1981) *The Border Economy: Regional Development in the Southwest*, Austin, TX: University of Texas Press.

—— (1983) 'International cooperation in border regions: an overview and research agenda', *International Regional Science Review* 8(3): 255–70.

Kratke, S. (1997) 'Regional integration or fragmentation: the German-Polish border region in a new Europe', paper presented to EURRN Conference on Regional Frontiers, Frankfurt/Oder.

Langer, J. (1996) 'The new meanings of the border in Central Europe', in G. Eger and J. Langer (eds), *Border, Region and Ethnicity in Central Europe*, Klagenfurt: Norea Verlag, 49–67.

Lill, R. (1982) 'The historical evolution of the Italian frontier regions', *West European Politics* 5(4): 109–22.

Maillat, D. (1990) 'Transborder regions between members of the EC and non-member countries', *The Built Environment* 16(1): 38–51.

Mann, M. (1993) 'Nation-states in Europe and other continents: diversifying, developing, not dying', *Daedalus* 122: 115–40.

Mendelson, M.H. (1998) 'The application of international legal concepts of sovereignty in the Arabian context', *Geopolitics* 3(2): 133–8.

Mestre, C. (1992) *The Implications for Frontier Regions of the Completion of the Single Market*, Strasbourg: Council of Europe.

Mlinar, Z. (1995) 'Territorial dehierarchization in the emerging new Europe', in J. Langer and W. Pollauer (eds), *Small States in the Emerging New Europe*, Klagenfurt: Verlag fur Soziologie und Humanethologie Eisenstadt, 161–79.

—— (1996) 'Managing the openness of border regions in the context of European integration', paper to the European Regional Science Association, 36th European Congress, Zurich, August.

Morris, L. (1997) 'Globalization, migration and the nation-state', *British Journal of Sociology* 48(2): 192–209.

O'Dowd, L., Corrigan, J. and Moore, T. (1995) 'Borders, national sovereignty and European integration', *International Journal of Urban and Regional Research* 19(2): 272–85.

O'Dowd, L. and Wilson, T. (eds) (1996) *Borders, Nations and States, Frontiers of Sovereignty in the New Europe*, Aldershot: Avebury.

Paasi, A. (1996) *Territories, Boundaries and Consciousness: The Changing Geographies of the Finnish-Russian Border*, New York: John Wiley and Sons.

Prescott, J.R.V. (1987) *Political Frontiers and Boundaries*, London: Allen and Unwin.

Ratti, R. (1993) 'Spatial and economic effects of frontiers', in R. Ratti and S. Reichman (eds), *Theory and Practice of Transborder Cooperation*, Basle: Helbing and Lichtenhahn.

Risse-Kappen, T. (1996) 'Exploring the nature of the beast: international relations theory and comparative policy analysis meet the European Union', *Journal of Common Market Studies* 34(1): 53–80.

Rupnik, J. (1994) 'Europe's new frontiers: remapping Europe', *Daedalus* 123(3): 91–114.

Sahlins, P. (1989) *Boundaries: The Making of France and Spain in the Pyrenees*, Berkeley, CA: University of California Press.

Scott, J. (1998) 'European and North American contexts for transboundary regionalism', mimeo Institute for Regional Development and Structural Planning, Berlin.

Sparke, M. (1998) 'From geopolitics to geoeconomics: transnational state effects in the borderlands', *Geopolitics* 3(2): 62–98.

Strassoldo, R. and Delli Zotti, G. (eds) (1982) *Cooperation and Conflict in Border Areas*, Milan: Franco Angeli Editore.

Strassoldo, R. and Gubert, R. (eds) (1973) *Boundaries and Regions*, Trieste: Edizioni.

Stryjakiewicz, T. and Kaczmarek, T. (1997) 'Transborder cooperation and development in the conditions of great socio-economic disparities: the case of the Polish-German border region', paper presented to the EURRN Conference on Regional Frontiers, Frankfurt/Oder.

Tilly, C. (1990) *Coercion, Capital and European states AD 990–1990*, Oxford: Basil Blackwell.

van der Veen, A. and Boot, D-J. (1995) 'Cross-border cooperation and European regional policy', in H. Eskelinen and F. Snickars (eds), *Competitive European Peripheries*, Berlin: Springer, 75–94.

van der Velde, M. and van Houtum, H. (2000) *Borders, Regions and People*, London: Pion.

Waever, O. (1993) 'Europe since 1945: crisis to renewal', in K.Wilson and J. van der Dussen (eds), *The History of the Idea of Europe*, London: Routledge, 151–214.

Wallace, C. (1999) 'Crossing borders: mobility of goods, capital and people in the Central European region', in A. Brah *et al.* (eds), *Global Futures: Migration, Environment and Globalization*, London: Macmillan, 185–209.

Williams, R.H. (1996) *European Union Spatial Policy and Planning*, London: Paul Chapman.

Wilson, T. and Donnan, H. (eds) (1998) *Border Identities: Nation and State at International Frontiers*, Cambridge: Cambridge University Press.

7 Transnational democracy versus national conflict

Border crossings in Ireland

James Anderson and Douglas Hamilton

The ideal of the 'nation-state', centrepiece of nationalist doctrine, is seriously flawed. This can be seen where reality falls short of the assumed geographical coincidence of 'nation' and 'state'. It is most obvious where attempts to make reality fit the ideal lead to serious conflicts over national identity, sovereignty and territory. Such conflicts are not amenable to 'normal' democratic resolution precisely because what is at issue is the territorial framework for the exercise of democracy as conventionally understood. Strategies to manage or resolve these conflicts have included the redrawing of external territorial borders and the partitioning or repartitioning of states, while within given state borders there have been various consociational or power-sharing arrangements which reinforce inter-communal boundaries and 'internal partitioning'. Both types of strategy may ameliorate particular conflicts at particular times, but they can be seen as 'national solutions to national problems' or contradictions in terms. Not surprisingly, they fail to deliver a solution in many cases. They 'manage' rather than 'resolve' conflict, and sometimes they fail even to 'manage' because of their built-in tendency to reproduce if not exacerbate the problems they are supposed to solve. Typically, the state powers who 'manage' share the same flawed assumptions as those they are 'managing'.

This chapter contends that in such situations transnational strategies which stress the importance of crossing the borders between states and between national communities are more appropriate. It draws on the national Irish–British conflict now centred on Northern Ireland and previous research into border crossings in both senses (for example, Anderson 1994; Anderson and Goodman, 1998; Anderson and Shuttleworth 1998; Hamilton 2001). Ireland's cross-border strategy for territorial realignment and conflict-resolution is relatively advanced, partly by virtue of the context and encouragement of the European Union. Although its success is far from assured, people involved in other national conflicts (for example, the Basque Country–Spain, and Palestine–Israel) are now being recommended to look to the Irish example for inspiration following the 'Belfast Good Friday Agreement' of 1998 (*Agreement* 1998).[1] It is just possible that Ireland, long a byword for intractable national conflict, could pioneer a new transnational approach to conflict resolution, though it will only succeed if there is a radical extension and reorientation of present developments.

Intra-state national conflicts are becoming more common and significant, while cross-border regions and institutions are showing how borders can be handled in more consensual rather than conflictual ways (see O'Dowd in this volume). These conflicts and their attempted resolution highlight the propensity of territoriality to generate or increase competitive, antagonistic relations. They demonstrate the need for transnational democracy and also the obstacles to creating it. While there are dangers in generalising from Ireland to other national conflicts – and every one is different – many of their features reoccur. As in Ireland, they are rooted in problems which are inherent to nationalism and representative democracy and their territorial basis. The same inherent limitations are found in 'solutions' to different conflicts which rely centrally on territorial (re)partition or the communal 'internal partitioning' of consociationalism. For genuine resolution of these different conflicts, there is the same need to get beyond the nationalistic preoccupations with territorial sovereignty and borders, and this will not happen through well-meaning exhortation. It will only happen through the practical encouragement of thought and action on *other* matters and *other* bases for political mobilisation. This relatively underdeveloped aspect of the Belfast Agreement needs to be strengthened if it is to succeed.

The chapter discusses national problems, national non-solutions and transnational resolutions. The first part outlines some fundamental socio-spatial problems of nationalism and representative democracy; the second focuses on the limitations of territorial partition and internal consociationalism; and the third discusses the possibilities of transcending these problems by extending representative democracy across state borders and combining it with non-territorial forms of democratic participation.

Socio-spatial problems of nationalism and democracy

Conflicts involving national movements – for example, in Sri Lanka, Kashmir, Palestine, Cyprus or Ireland – reflect particular problems of history and geography. But they stem from more general territorial and social limitations of nationalism and representative democracy, and not only within the contested regions – where in some cases democracy may be more notable for its absence – but also in the basic nature of the modern state (see Parekh in this volume). These more general limitations help explain the high failure rate of the national 'solutions' to national conflict attempted by dominant states and international institutions.

The search for resolutions is given added impetus by the recent intensification of transnational integration (McGrew 1995). Paradoxically, its disruptions can heighten nationalist conflicts, but at the same time it calls into question many of the assumptions underlying national 'solutions' and seems to offer the possibility of transcending them. While the 'death' of the nation-state is a gross and misleading exaggeration (Anderson 1995), exclusive forms of territorial sovereignty, and of democracy as tied to 'national' territory, are being at least partially transcended, particularly in the European Union (Goodman 1997, and see chapters by Newman and Painter in this volume). Liberal democracy depends on a spatial 'fix' between territory and representation, but globalisation is making it harder to contain political life within fixed territorial units. So, there are good reasons for looking to transnationalism as a means of getting above and beyond what is often seen as the petty parochialism of narrow nationalisms, to achieve emancipation from their mutually destructive animosities. There is encouragement in the growth of less territory-centred transnational social and political movements and new modes of transnational democracy emerging or becoming imaginable.

The problems of nationalism go much deeper than the historical and geographical particulars of national conflict. They go to the very nature of nationalism itself and its ideal of the 'nation-state'. Its flaws in turn reflect the limitations of representative democracy, with problems of *territoriality* a 'common denominator'.[2]

Problems of nationalism

Nationalism is a doctrine which has always 'promised to deceive'. It is simultaneously a cultural and a political phenomenon which links historically and culturally defined territorial communities, called 'nations', to political statehood, either as a reality or as an aspiration. Nations and states are specifically territorial entities: they explicitly claim and are based on particular geographical territories. Both employ territoriality: they use geographical space to control and influence social processes, as distinct from merely occupying space which is true of all social activity (Anderson 1986: 117). The ideal of nationalist doctrine is that nations and states should coincide geographically in 'nation-states'. The state territory and the nation's territory should be one and the same, each state expressing the 'general will' of a single, culturally unified nation, and each nation having its own state.

This has a very powerful democratic appeal, and especially where democracy is denied by neighbouring nations or imperialistic states. The history of nationalism is closely bound up with the history of democratisation, anti-colonialism and communal struggles against 'outside interference'. Thus, when posing transnationalism as a means of emancipation from the conflicts of nationalism, it is well to remember that others, including the protagonists, see nationalism as itself emancipatory, and sometimes with good reason. This underlines the difficulty of solving national conflicts; and those adopting a lofty moral disdain for the 'petty parochialism' of others' conflicting nationalisms frequently do so from the security of their own unstated, even unconscious, nationalism.

But nationalist theory promises more than it can ever deliver in practice. Nations and states often fail to coincide, frequently leaving sizeable 'national minorities' on the 'wrong side' of state borders. The happy spatial coincidence of a single cultural community with a single political sovereignty is rarely achieved in reality, and attempts to make reality fit the ideal have often had unhappy, indeed horrific, consequences, as in so-called 'ethnic cleansing'.

Furthermore, even where the ideal of geographical coincidence is approximated, nationalism is a contradictory and flawed phenomenon, 'two-faced' in several respects. It is 'progressive' and forward-looking in promising a better future, but typically backward-looking and often reactionary in its use of an often mythical or invented past. It is simultaneously unifying and divisive, inclusive and excluding. It brings together different groups and classes in a political-cultural community defined as 'the people' or 'nation' with a strong shared and mutually supportive sense of belonging. At the same time, however, it separates out different 'peoples', emphasising non-belonging and fuelling tensions and conflicts between nations and between states. While national conflicts reflect disagreements over the appropriate territorial framework for democracy – who is 'in' with whom, who is to be excluded from the political community, how are majorities to be achieved – democracy within the community is often sadly lacking in practice. The supposedly unifying 'national interest' is inevitably a limited, ideological or illusionary unity given that any sizeable territorial community is internally riven with different and competing interests. Rather than serving the interests of 'the whole nation', nationalism often serves the interests of dominant social groups and classes, and particularly where they have state power. And here nationalism's generation of external differences and conflicts can be a useful ideological means of covering up internal differences and asserting internal control.

Problems of democracy

The clashing rhetorics of national conflict – of 'democratic rights', 'majority wishes', 'self-determination' and so forth – indicate the close connections between nationalism and democracy (at least in theory). But they also suggest that the limitations of conventional representative democracy are a central part of the problem, and that a democratic resolution of these conflicts is impossible in terms of national territoriality.

Conventional democracy mainly relies on periodically electing representatives for fixed, contiguous and bounded territories and their enclosed 'communities'. But the democratic process can and sometimes does involve much more than the formalities of territorially based voting. It can also involve the shaping of political agendas: deciding what issues get voted on. It can be expressed through various forms of participatory democracy (see, for example, Held 1993) involving a wide variety of organisations and associations in civil society, some of which are responsive to continuous internal democratic pressures from their own members, and it can thereby include people who are excluded or alienated from conventional 'party politics'. Participatory democracy with its more varied, flexible and often non-territorial social basis is inherently better suited than conventional representative democracy for crossing territorial borders. Yet territorially based representative democracy retains its dominance often to the point of monopoly, and therein lies much of the problem.

Indeed, the problem starts with democracy's institutional basis in territory and the paradox of its generally *un*democratic origins. As William Connolly (1991: 464–6) has pointed out, democratic polities require democratic institutions for democracy to function, but democracy is generally absent until the institutions are established. This applies to the delineation and institutionalisation of the territorial base for democracy, typically established by violence or the threat of violence rather than democracy, whether 'national' territories embody borders from a predemocratic era, or new borders which have been carved out or imposed even after the advent of mass democracy. These undemocratic origins of the crucial framework of democracy have to be concealed in 'a politics of forgetting' (Connolly 1991: 465) if territorial democracy is to perform its legitimising functions.

The problem in situations of national conflict is that these 'origins' are precisely what is at issue and cannot be 'forgotten'. For example, the unionist view that the 'democratic wishes of the majority' in Northern Ireland should be decisive in choosing its constitutional future seems entirely reasonable and legitimate, but only if we forget Northern Ireland's undemocratic origins. Its territorial border was established so as to give unionists a permanent, built-in 'two to one' majority, and it was imposed unilaterally by British force in 1920 (contrary to majority wishes in Ireland, and despite the advent of mass democracy and border plebiscites).[3] The core issue is the very existence of Northern Ireland and the legitimacy of its unionist majority as the framework for democracy. If the territorial framework determines the outcome of the 'democratic majority vote', who decides the framework?

Here again there is the paradox – this time in the present. While all sides in the conflict profess democratic intent, a new territorial democracy cannot be established by conventional democratic procedures precisely because the 'territory' has not been decided: the national conflict is seen to be a conflict over who should have the vote and who should organise the election in the first place. None of the state powers involved in Ireland has fully grasped this particular nettle, or its non-territorial antidote.

Their failure is not entirely surprising. In over-identifying democracy with territory, the governments are caught in their own 'territorial trap' (Agnew 1994). They share in capitalism's partial separation of 'politics' from 'economics' and its consequently shallow conception of democracy. This tends to distance their conflict resolution from the cross-border context and the sphere of production,[4] two central components of the 'non-territorial antidote', as we shall see. In contrast, alternative socialist conceptions emphasise the need for deeper and more extensive forms of democracy which are capable of spanning both the spheres of consumption and production, within and across territorial borders (see, for example, Cowling and Sugden 1994; Miliband 1994; Archer 1995).

Problems of territoriality

A 'common denominator' of these problems of democracy and nationalism is their reliance on territoriality as a mode of social organisation. Its drawbacks help explain these problems, while its strengths and ubiquity suggest the problems will not easily be overcome. Territoriality uses geographical areas and borders to 'control, classify and communicate', by assigning things to particular territories and controlling movements between them (see Sack 1986: 21–34). For representative democracy, it designates a pre-given, 'all-purpose' area whose adult population has voting rights on a whole range of issues deemed to effect that area, rather than the constituency of voters having to be decided issue by issue (for example, according to the people actually affected by each issue, which might well be more or fewer people than the pre-given area's population). Delineating a standard 'all-purpose' area and territorial community independently of particular issues increases the legitimacy of subsequent decisions, and it avoids repeating the 'paradox of undemocratic origins' or a recurring conflict over who 'decides the decision makers'.

For 'controllers', spatial strategies of territoriality have powerful advantages, providing symbolic markers on the ground, giving power relationships a greater tangibility, and generally simplifying administration and management. But their strengths are also weaknesses or disadvantages, especially for the 'controlled'. Territoriality depersonalises social relationships and reifies and obscures the sources and relations of power. It oversimplifies and distorts social realities. 'Community' is defined by area, on the assumption that people who share contiguous physical space also interact socially and share social values. One consequence is that strangers with nothing in common except location inside particular borders are deemed to belong to the 'community', while those who do interact but from across the borders are excluded.

There is no simple, automatic or necessary relationship between the 'social' and the 'spatial', and considerable evidence that their interrelationships are becoming even more complex. The 'all-purpose' territorial community obviously has its uses, but its limitations appear to be increasing in this era of intensified 'globalisation'. With the ground shifting under traditional political conceptions and institutions (Anderson 1996), it makes even less sense than previously to see 'politics' as stopping at state borders, or cross-border economic integration as somehow 'non-political' and beyond the scope of democracy (see Anderson in this volume). With intensified though highly uneven transnational integration and space-spanning technologies, social space is becoming more 'relativised', and territoriality on its own a more inadequate mode of social organisation. The territorial state's monopoly on democracy is increasingly problematic; and cross-border institutions and movements are becoming more necessary.

This is especially the case because of territoriality's inherent propensity to generate or increase antagonisms. Territory is an obviously finite resource and assertions of territoriality generate defensive responses and rival territorialities in a 'space-filling' process. Unlike 'ordinary' or unbounded places not used for purposes of control, 'territories' and their borders need constant maintenance, itself a potential source of conflict.[5] Their role in reproducing conflict is particularly marked in the 'zero-sum games' characteristic of national conflicts where territory is materially and/or symbolically crucial. Whereas there is a fixed total amount of territory, and more for one side does indeed mean less for the other, the same zero-sum argument does not apply to the economic, social or cultural realities which are the main substance of conflict. Social life is not so simple; economic development, cultural riches, democratic responsiveness, wealth and welfare do not have static, fixed totals. The totals to be 'shared' can go up, or down (and more likely down in situations of serious conflict). More for one need not mean less for another, and it is possible for everyone in a society to be better off. But such 'positive-sum' thinking tends to be precluded by territorialist mind-sets locked into 'zero-sum' nationalism.

National 'solutions' to national conflict

The fact that the national state elites who try to contain or solve national conflicts often suffer from a similar territorialist mindset themselves – at least as far as their own territorial sovereignty is concerned – helps explain why national conflicts are reproduced rather than superseded. Their national solutions to national conflict are generally not solutions. Some are one-sidedly conde-scending, as in trying to 'buy off' nationalist opposition movements with concessions on what are seen as 'peripheral' issues.[6] They may be attempts to manage rather than resolve conflict which are in effect *mis*management (as evidenced during decades of conflict in Northern Ireland:[7] see O'Leary and McGarry (1993); Ruane and Todd (1996)). But the most obvious non-solutions are those one-sidedly brutal oppressions of 'national minorities' carried out by rival nationalists, with or without state power or state terror, and including mass murder, mass population movement, non-recognition of a minority's existence and forced cultural or national assimilation. Not only morally obnoxious, they are generally counterproductive because they generate even more opposition.[8]

However, other strategies such as the redrawing of state borders, and internal 'consociationalism' or 'power sharing' between different ethno-national groups, are less obviously non-solutions. In combination with other measures they may indeed have some ameliorative effects which prepare the ground for a resolution, but in practice they too are often counterproductive.

Partitions and 'territorial integrity'

Territorial partition is one of the standard responses to national conflict, but as in Ireland, the Indian subcontinent, Palestine, Cyprus and former Yugoslavia, it has a dismal record, often creating more problems than it solves (Fraser 1984; *Index: on Censorship* 1997). It tends to satisfy the political aspirations of some groups at the expense of others, and sometimes satisfies none of the protagonists. It is typically impossible to have a simple territorial separation of the contending ethnic or national groups because they are geographically intermingled, and the pre-partition territory of the groups is not continuous and separable. In consequence, partition processes are inherently bitter and often bloody, actively encouraging forced population movement and sometimes so-called 'ethnic cleansing', and at the very least generating further conflict.[9] Subsequent proposals for repartitioning generally add farce to tragedy.[10] Rather than being agreed democratically, partition has usually been imposed autocratically by 'outside' or imperialist powers, often (presented) as a short-term expedient which becomes a long-term source of conflict, and sometimes a logical extension of 'divide and rule' policies (or 'divide and quit' in the case of India). Indeed, in India, Palestine, Ireland and Cyprus, partition was imposed against the wishes of the majority of the population in each country. The politics of partition typically ride roughshod over economic realities, and economic arguments rarely prevail over nationalistic political appeals, though, by the same token, the continuation of these 'economic realities' may provide a material basis for ameliorative border-crossing reconciliations (see below).

There are thus many good reasons for not trying to solve national conflicts by redrawing territorial borders, as distinct from transforming or crossing them, and given its dismal record it is not surprising that partition has generally been out of favour internationally since the inter-war period. However, the main reasons for this also reflect the prevailing territorialist mindset. Redrawing borders, while perhaps quite justified in particular instances, creates 'dangerous precedents' which can be seen as threatening the 'territorial integrity' and cohesion of national states in general.[11] Thus, the principle of self-determination for 'nations', directly associated with the inter-war creation of independent 'nation-states' in Eastern Europe, has been successfully transmuted into self-determination for 'peoples' which does not have the same connotations of independent or separate statehood (Cassesse 1995). For dominant state powers, maintaining existing state borders and finding 'internal' power-sharing solutions is the preferred option.

'*Internal solutions*' and consociationalism

This alternative to redrawing borders maintains 'territorial integrity' and in some circumstances it contains and regulates conflict, but typically it does so at the expense of 'internalising', institutionalising and perpetuating division. It is based on the 'consociational model' developed primarily in Holland (Lijphart 1983). In contrast to the Westminster electoral system of 'winner-takes-all' within territorially defined entities, consociationalism offers a set of non-majoritarian devices for diffusing and sharing power between different ethnic or national groups. A power-sharing government is drawn from the different segments in the society, and elite representatives further their group's interests through (often secretive) negotiation. Minorities are given a veto to protect their particular interests, and there can be separate voting systems for each group, with political parties and sometimes individuals being classified or classifying themselves into one or other category. Thus ethnic and/or national differences are officially recognised and the associated conflict is consensually managed.

This strategy sees political identity only or mainly in terms of ethnic or national categories, and these categories as essentially fixed. It is a very influential view of nationalism, one generally shared by nationalists themselves: group identity is a universal human need, and each ethnic group has its own inherent identity. It may be activated or stimulated by external factors, such as industrialisation or the rise of capitalism, but basically it is a group inheritance (Smith 1981). Even if advocates of consociationalism deny that they follow this theory, the practical tendency of their strategy is to make reality conform to such a theory, in a sense forcing people into one or other ethnic or national 'camp'.

Rupert Taylor (1994) argues that the 'consociational model' is empiricist in failing to address the complex social dynamics of ethnic or national identity: it uncritically accepts the primacy and the permanency of ethnic divisions, and further reifies them. It simply assumes that ethnicity is the independent, pre-existing 'cause' of conflict, rather than questioning why and how ethnic divisions arose, why they are sustained, and how they might be superseded. It actively excludes other perhaps more fruitful social categories, other bases of political mobilisation such as gender and class which cross-cut ethnic divisions. Where it defines just two main 'ethnic groups', people who do not want to belong to either may be marginalised or forced to 'take sides'. The so-called 'middle ground' of compromise, or 'other grounds' for alternative politics, are actively eroded and ethnic polarisation is reinforced.[12]

As Rick Wilford (1992) has pointed out, consociationalism endorses a bleak view of humanity, with distrust seen as endemic. Rather than promoting social contact and co-operation, it effectively argues the virtues of segregation. In short, while its advocacy of 'power-sharing' appears factual, fair and liberal, the model is weak theoretically and generally reactionary in its assumptions and effects. From the viewpoint of governments trying to manage national conflict, consociationalism has the great advantage of dealing with symptoms rather than causes,[13] and therefore not requiring any fundamental restructuring of state and society (but see Douglas (1998) for a more favourable 'bottom up' view of it in a local 'politics of accommodation'). However, in pragmatically assuming that ethnic or national identities and divisions are largely fixed, consociationalism in the last analysis further entrenches the divisions and colludes in perpetuating conflict.

Academic defence and criticism

John McGarry (1998) has defended this policy in the case of Northern Ireland partly by criticising 'liberals, marxists and post-modernists' for being preoccupied, respectively, with the individual, social class and the fluidity of identities; and all failing to recognise the tenacity of 'nations' and the need to accommodate them.[14] With Brendan O'Leary, McGarry has been an enthusiastic supporter of the 1998 Belfast Agreement and appears to believe that a successful outcome is possible once the appropriate institutional arrangements are put in place to force unionists and nationalists to 'compromise' and 'moderate' their maximalist claims. But their stance is simply a 'politics of ethnic regulation' (McGarry and O'Leary 1993); and while not apologists for one or other national group in Northern Ireland,[15] they are uncritical of nationalism, the nation-state and territorial democracy in general.

Given the history of mismanagement with military containment taking precedence over political initiatives in Ireland, current policy is indeed a very definite improvement. It may succeed in transforming a military conflict into a largely non-violent political one. But that falls well short of a resolution of the conflict.[16] To the extent that internal consociationalism has a positive role, it is only as a transitional, enabling element in a much broader strategy. It is not the centre-piece of a permanent solution but rather a component which becomes increasingly counterproductive.

At root the conflict has been over the existence of Northern Ireland and its exclusively British territoriality, and here an 'internal solution' is a clear contradiction in terms, merely reproducing the British status quo. Yet the cross-border dimension has followed behind and still remains very subordinate to internal power-sharing.[17] The mindsets of the British and Irish governments, still wedded to a territorialist view of their own sovereignty, are so far incapable of the wider border-crossing vision which is needed to imagine a genuine resolution. It is not only the 'mindsets' of Northern Irish unionists and nationalists that need 'decommissioning'.

Towards transnational conflict resolution

A resolution of the Irish conflict will clearly not come from moral appeals to 'compromise' on maximalist national demands – tried, and failed, for decades – nor will it be delivered by the 1998 Belfast Agreement's clever institutional attempt (so admired by conflict 'regulators') to 'box in' the North's unionists and nationalists. Instead, their nationalistic preoccupations with the territorial framework for representative democracy will only be superseded when they themselves (or a substantial proportion of them and their supporters) mobilise around and engage democratically with other important issues which cross-cut national and state borders, including, more directly, democracy itself, as distinct from being preoccupied with its territorial shell. As already argued in more detail elsewhere (Anderson and Goodman 1998), agreement in the conflict over territorial sovereignty will, paradoxically, only come in the process of working through *other*, more substantial *dis*agreements on a non-nationalist basis.

Whatever its limitations, the Belfast Agreement begins to open the door to this possibility. Despite its strong 'internal consociational' bias and weak cross-border dimension, most of the ingredients for a pioneering transnational resolution of national conflict are present in embryo.[18] Cross-border representative institutions, albeit weakly developed, are a key element in the Agreement, and it even alludes tangentially to cross-border participatory democracy. Moreover, there is a growing material basis for such developments in the economic and social dynamics for cross-border integration. These are the specifically Irish expressions of the transnationalising tendencies of European integration and globalisation. Democratising them means extending territorially based representative democracy across the state borders, combined with the development (partly by institutional means) of participatory and non-territorial forms which deepen the meaning of democracy and can more easily straddle borders. This is what the Belfast Agreement tentatively implies, though to be effective its scenario needs to be radically augmented.

Representative democracy and cross-border institutions

It could, for instance, be argued, on grounds both of democratic principle and pragmatic politics, that all three electorates of Ireland and Britain should have a direct (but not necessarily equal) say in deciding Northern Ireland's future. But this is something precluded by nationalistic mindsets – Northern unionists and nationalists in Britain opposing 'foreign interference' by the South, Irish nationalists 'interference' from Britain (not that the unionists would trust Britain's electorate, which does not identify with them and probably favours Irish reunification). But both sets of nationalists blithely ignore the fact that all three electorates might have a democratic right to be involved in decision making on the basis that all are seriously affected by the unresolved conflict. In pragmatic terms, all three together would be more likely to forge a settlement than the North on its own.[19]

Here the Agreement's elaborate 'North–South' and cross-border institutions[20] are a significant advance, beginning to offer an alternative to the mutually exclusive and unattainable demands of traditional unionism and nationalism. A bridging of the disputed border to undercut the mutually contradictory 'zero-sum' alternatives of exclusive British or exclusive Irish sovereignty is indeed essential for a settlement. The institutions constitute some practical expression of 'parity of esteem' for Irish nationalists in Northern Ireland, which is usually how they are seen by friend and foe alike. Alike, that is, in seeing things only in terms of nationalism.

Cross-border institutions offer much more. To be fully implemented in the minimal forms officially envisaged, given unionist opposition, they need to be tied more closely to the non-nationalist dynamics for cross-border integration already evident in civil society. If developed to anything like their full potential – the big 'if' – they could conceivably bring mutually reinforcing economic, social, cultural and democratic advantages which would in turn bolster their potential for conflict resolution.

In Ireland, cross-border institutions are in fact necessitated not only by national political factors but by a quite separate 'economic dynamic' for a 'single island economy' (Quigley 1992). This is being advocated by business and trade union interests, North and South, to meet the new opportunities and threats posed by the establishment of the Single European Market since the early 1990s. This 'economic' dynamic is probably the most innovating element in the traditional equation of North–South relations (Anderson 1994; Bradley 1996; Hamilton 2001); and it is associated with a related but wider 'socio-cultural dynamic' which points towards an 'all-Ireland' civil society (Anderson 1998). Indeed, an 'all-Ireland' civil society is implied in the 'single island economy' – one 'economy' but two 'societies' is hardly practical – but the 'socio-cultural' dynamic is also made up of a wide range of non-economic pressures for more or closer social interactions across the border. It encompasses a variety of different groups and institutions, including cultural and sporting bodies, the extensive voluntary sector and campaigning organisations involved for instance with problems of poverty, the environment, women's equality, and gay and lesbian rights. There is a concern for a democratisation of the emerging North–South policy-making process, seen as overly dominated by business interests (Anderson and Goodman 1997). In general, the economic and social pressures mesh with the Irish nationalist dynamic, all three dynamics pointing to an island-wide institutional and political framework.

There is thus an increasing basis for cross-border co-operation which involves working through substantial *dis*agreements which cross-cut nationalist and North–South divides. They include the different class interests of capital and labour, the common interests of women, the similar problems faced by various oppressed minorities, and shared interests in protecting the environment. These and other non-national issues have the potential to unify people across and despite the national and state borders. They would give more substance to the North–South institutions set up under the Agreement; the institutions in turn would facilitate further cross-border integration in civil society; and both developments would strengthen the basis for cross-border participatory democracy.

Participatory democracy and non-national issues

As already suggested, democracy cannot be confined to a sphere of 'politics' separate from the 'economic' sphere, and it involves the prior shaping of political agendas, not simply voting for representatives at infrequent intervals. Participatory democracy can encompass a wide variety of organisations, some responsive to continuous democratic pressure and themselves vehicles for participatory democracy. It is better suited to crossing communal and territorial boundaries with its more flexible basis in non-territorial social and political movements.[21]

Some years ago it was suggested that the networks of business, trade union, community, voluntary and campaigning organisations already active, or potentially active, on the crucial North–South axis should be given their own North–South institution – an 'Island Social Forum' – to make inputs into North–South policy – (Anderson and Goodman 1996, followed by a similar idea from Percival 1996). The 'National Economic and Social Forum' in Dublin provided one possible model: a consultative body which gives marginalised groups some say in policy formulation, and includes representatives of the unemployed, the disabled, women's organisations, young people, the elderly and environmental groups as well as the corporatist 'social partners' of business, trade unions and government (NESF 1995: Annex 1–3).

A similar idea resurfaced in the Agreement where it was suggested that 'Consideration...be given to the establishment of an "independent consultative forum"' drawn from North and South and 'representative of civil society...the social partners and other members with expertise in social, cultural, economic and other issues'. However, in line with official 'common sense' which prioritises 'internal' accommodation rather than border-crossing processes, this forum was only an idea 'for consideration', unlike the similar internal forum for the North on its own which was to be 'established' not just 'considered' (*Agreement* 1998: 9, 13).

The various cross-border institutions for democracy, representative and partici-patory, which have been set up or suggested, are not simply important in and of themselves. Indeed, some may be relatively unimportant: 'civic forums', for instance, are open to accusations of being mere 'talking shops' for the powerless and excluded. But taken together, the North–South institutions could be very important as a focus and catalyst for the development of cross-border social move-ments and organisations campaigning on a variety of issues. Crucially, this would begin to consolidate a range of cross-border 'political communities' and create more political room for non-nationalist politics based on class and gender (see Bell 1998), or the many other concerns which straddle national and territorial divides.

The politics of class are particularly important, not least because the national conflict is often sharpest in working-class areas. However, the notion that the concerns of class, or of gender and other identities, are 'alternatives' to the national issue, or that they can be separated off and dealt with first (or vice versa) should be rejected. The national question cannot be simply 'side-stepped' or delayed to a later stage.[22] Conversely, non-national issues of class and gender cannot be put off to a 'promised land' of nationalist dreams (whether a united Ireland or a fully British Northern Ireland), and attempts to delay addressing them can be guaranteed to leave many workers and feminists unimpressed.

The national problem cannot be solved by simply concentrating on it to the exclusion of other major sources of identity and material interest. These other social forces could help to solve the problem, even though – or more likely because – they do not directly address it or use the language of nationalism. There are real grounds for the different 'identities' making common cause. For instance, the interests of trade unionists and women tend to be marginalised by the 'unfinished business' of national conflict, so they have a direct interest in seeing that it is 'finished'.

Tensions will always exist between the different bases for political mobilisa-tion, such as nation, gender or class. There will always be problems about the relative weighting to be given to each in particular circumstances. But these are tactical difficulties, not grounds for adopting a general strategy which fixes on any one concern to the exclusion of the others. In national struggles, whatever the leadership, it is usually working-class people, and often working-class women, who bear the brunt of the conflict.

The development of such more widely defined politics would be significantly boosted by border-crossing institutional frameworks articulating representative and participatory forms of democracy. Working-class and other movements usually have to operate to varying degrees within state-provided frameworks, and despite significant transnationalisation and 'de-territorialisation', that is likely to continue for the foreseeable future. In that sense, political movements are not alternatives to political institutions but depend on them. Cross-border/cross-community developments would stimulate various realignments of politics around other criss-crossing conflicts and disagreements – non-nationalist and non-unionist politics which escape the 'dead end' issue of national sovereignty.

Contrary to unionist attempts to minimise their remit, the more powers the cross-border institutions have, and the more they escape the straitjacket of state territoriality – moving to directly elected representatives, for instance, as did the European Parliament – the more there will be political realignments which depart from and begin to supplant traditional 'unionist versus nationalist' divides. There would be greater likelihood of developing other fissures and alliances on other social lines of class, gender, region and so forth: 'workers versus employers'; 'liberals versus conservatives' on moral or religious issues; even 'North' – including nationalists as well as unionists – versus 'South' on some issues; or 'West' versus 'East' on the disproportionate amount of investment enjoyed by eastern parts of the island, North and South.

Conclusions

National conflicts cannot be solved in nationalism's own terms which are shared not only by the immediate protagonists, but also by dominant state powers which impose 'solutions'. In Ireland, the relative weakness of the key cross-border institutions reflects collusion between different sets of nationalists: in particular, between Northern Irish unionists who wish to separate 'politics' from 'economics' in the hope of preserving their British territorial sovereignty as sacrosanct, and the British and Irish governments who favour some cross-border integration but believe it would be facilitated by avoiding the contentious 'high politics' of national sovereignty. The governments' transnationalism is weak because they share prevailing nationalist assumptions about territorial sovereignty, at least with respect to their own territories of Great Britain and the Republic of Ireland. In fact territorial sovereignty, far from being sacrosanct or avoidable, remains the nub of the conflict. Mutually exclusive conceptions of sovereignty have encouraged a 'zero-sum game' (actually 'negative-sum' with net losses all round) and these conceptions precluded any solution short of the complete but unattainable victories traditionally sought by Irish and British nationalists. Unionists had a 'winner-takes-all' form of sovereignty, but their assertion of exclusively British territoriality has been a pyrrhic victory.

The Agreement may simply bring about the replacement of the old failed policy of mainly military containment with a new political strategy of conflict management: not a resolution of the conflict, but rather – to reverse Clausewitz's dictum – 'politics as the continuation of war by other means'. That would, however, be a major advance, not only in the obvious sense of stopping the killings, but strategically in creating peaceful conditions where it becomes possible to develop *non*-nationalist politics which straddle national and territorial divides. While the cross-border institutions set up under the Agreement are very limited in their scope and powers, they offer the possibility of further development in what could be a mutually reinforcing process with its own momentum, combining national, social, cultural and economic dynamics for cross-border integration. At the same time as they further economic and various other interests, cross-border mobilisations around common agendas would begin to redefine political identities. They would create new cross-border political communities and help undercut the fixation with national territoriality.

This chapter has attempted to go beyond traditional approaches to national conflict resolution by stepping back from the clashing rhetorics of nationalism and democracy and looking at their common limitations in territoriality. It has emphasised the impossibility of democratic resolutions on the conventional basis of fixed, bounded and contiguous national territory. It has suggested that national democracy is inherently deficient even where there are no overt national conflicts.

This helps explain the prevalence of non-solutions to these conflicts. Even when not characterised by brutality or condescension, the attempted solutions tend to be at best palliatives and frequently they make matters worse. Thus the favoured and apparently 'practical' solution of 'internal consociationalism' turns out to be impractical, useful at best as a transitional mechanism to moderate overt conflict, but an obstacle to conflict resolution in the longer run. It fails theoretically to address the reproduction of ethnic and national identities; uncritically accepts the primacy and permanency of ethno-national divisions; and in practice further strengthens them. It thereby marginalises other bases of political identity and mobilisation, such as gender and class, which could lead to conflict resolution.

As we have argued, it is through border-crossing mobilisations around *non*-national issues that preoccupations with national territoriality can be challenged in practice and national conflicts resolved. Territorially based representation has to be extended across state borders and articulated with participatory forms of democracy more amenable to border crossings.

Notes

1 The Irish–British conflict features territorial partition, proposals for repartition, armed conflict, consociational or power-sharing institutions, border-crossing political institutions and non-territorial participatory democracy, the British and Irish states, the EU and the USA. The Agreement, ratified in June 1998 by 71 per cent of Northern and 94 per cent of Southern Irish voters, was to establish institutions of power-sharing between Irish nationalists and unionists in Northern Ireland, supplemented by some cross-border representative bodies drawn from the Northern and Southern parliaments (see below). However, their establishment and operations have been delayed and disrupted, primarily by 'anti-Agreement' unionists/loyalists whose capacity for 'fouling their own nest' should not be underestimated.
2 The problems of democracy and territoriality are discussed more fully in Chapter 1.

3 The frequent British complaint that 'the Irish are obsessed with history' suggests that British officialdom has strong reasons for forgetting while at least some of the Irish have even stronger reasons for remembering.

4 Chapter 1 discusses this partial separation of 'politics' and 'economics' in capitalism, reformulates it in terms of the presence/absence of democracy, and relates it to cross-border contexts and the sphere of production.

5 For example, the summer 'marching season' of the unionist Orange Order and opposition to their marching in Irish nationalist neighbourhoods, as at Drumcree. Such local 'border maintenance' events replicate or substitute for the conflict over the state border and territory at the 'national' level (Anderson and Shuttleworth 1998).

6 For example, concessions on matters of 'culture', but 'culture' kept separate from key 'political' dimensions of power. Thus the unionist Cadogan Group (1992) in Northern Ireland proposed that for Irish nationalists (but not unionists) 'culture' could be separated from 'politics' and Irish nationalism could be allowed cultural, but not political, expression. Subsequently, the Cadogan Group (1998) argued that while political sovereignty is absolute, economic cross-border co-operation could be treated as a separate 'non-political' matter. It seems there is a sacrosanct sphere of 'politics' which can and must be separated from the rest of social life!

7 Repeated failure to find a solution to the problem was neatly justified by the ideological quip that 'The problem is there is no solution.' This of course was true, and therefore plausible, within conventional nationalist, territorial terms of reference. But it was those terms which were 'the problem'.

8 Franco's harsh repression in the Basque Country, for example, galvanised the Basque nationalist opposition to Spanish centralism. In different circumstances closer to home, the Scottish National Party has the British (English?) nationalist Mrs Thatcher and her strident centralism to thank for reviving its electoral fortunes; and Irish Republicans should be grateful that her 'resolute stance' against concessions to Bobby Sands and the other hunger-striking prisoners launched Sinn Féin as a successful electoral machine. Others thank Mrs Thatcher for wrecking her own Conservative Party as an electoral machine.

9 Partition of the Indian subcontinent was accompanied by an estimated 200,000 deaths and 5 million people had to migrate across the new Pakistan–India border line; this was followed by several wars and now the threat of nuclear conflict. The partition of Palestine made three-quarters of a million Palestinians homeless refugees, and it too led to wars (Fraser 1984: 192–3), with inter-communal armed conflict and state repression now threatening the stability of the entire Middle East.

10 A further repartition of Northern Ireland was put forward by Liam Kennedy as one of the options for 'the future of Northern Ireland' (McGarry and O'Leary 1990). Not only would it produce functionally unviable (and probably discontinuous) territories, it would also encourage forced population movements of the geographically intermingled groups. Kennedy's proposal was subsequently hi-jacked by loyalist paramilitaries for their 'doomsday scenario' with threats to 'ethnically cleanse' inconveniently located Catholics.

11 Remarkably, the wave of post-Second World War decolonisations and the creation of new independent states across Africa and Asia involved very few border changes, despite the fact that colonial borders were an often highly arbitrary European imposition. Secession movements, as in Biafra, typically got little encouragement from surrounding states. 'Breakaway' Bangladesh was 'the exception which proves the rule', its success due to the intervention of Pakistan's enemy, India. The very different spate of new state creations in Eastern Europe and central Asia has been treated as the exceptional result of the defeat of Stalin's 'soviet empire' in the 'Cold War'.

12 In Northern Ireland, cross-community parties tend to be 'squeezed out'. People are forced, sometimes against their will, to declare for one or other 'camp'. Mechanisms intended to deliver 'minority rights' are (mis)used by the 'majority', thereby nullifying

their 'equalising' potential while simultaneously strengthening the divisions (in addition to the majoritarianism which negates the principle that 'majority rule' presupposes a single 'people' acting as one; see Parekh in this volume). The pressure for 'balance' can produce a phoney or distorting 'even-handedness' where the (mainly) victim minority has to be apportioned 'equal blame' in what can be a lofty 'plague on both your houses'. Irish republicanism, in principle anti-sectarian, risks being forced into the dominant sectarian mould of 'ethnic politics'; and power may be shared by socially conservative parties from each 'side', to the exclusion of more progressive forces.

13 This approach also sits well the British projection of the conflict as between 'the two Irish tribes' with Britain in the thankless but neutral position of keeping them apart, rather than the conflict being a 'divide and rule' product of the British state and the latter still an active participant.

14 McGarry's general criticisms of (unspecified) liberal/Left academia are much too sweeping (if McGarry himself is not a 'marxist', a 'post-modernist', or a 'liberal' academic, what is he?). So-called 'post-modernists' have, for instance, usefully criticised the essentialist assumptions underlying pragmatic approaches to ethnicity and nationalism. Marxists have developed various theoretical understandings superior to the 'ethno-national' empiricism of consociationalism. The Marxist theory that nationalism is reproduced by the contradictions of capitalism's 'uneven development' (Nairn 1977), far from not recognising the 'tenacity of nations', suggests that national conflicts are endemic to capitalism.

15 McGarry and O'Leary are much more 'balanced' and constructive than the one-sided, nationalistic partisanship of other academics such as Graham Gudgin of the unionist Cadogan Group (1992, 1998).

16 Since the main paramilitary ceasefires in the mid-1990s, levels of sectarian conflict in daily life in Northern Ireland have increased rather than decreased.

17 In the 1998 Agreement, Strand 1 (internal Northern Ireland issues) was much more developed and agreed than the rather vague Strand 2 (the North–South dimension), where much of the important detail had still to be decided.

18 It might be questioned just 'how pioneering?', given forerunners in the proposed Council of Ireland in 1920, and the Sunningdale Agreement of 1973. While neither was ever implemented, there are clearly similarities with current cross-border arrangements, but the latter are more worked out and actually operating.

19 Britain's electorate has never been actively involved or properly informed. The British media normally displays biased nationalism or disinterest in Northern Ireland (see O'Dowd 1998). The Southern Irish electorate, while much better informed, has been only marginally involved apart from being allowed to vote to ratify the Agreement (note 1, above).

20 They include most notably a North–South Ministerial Council, set up by the Dáil and the Northern Assembly, bringing together ministers from each, and with its own Secretariat. The Council is a condition for the Assembly acquiring powers of government and is accountable to the respective assemblies, but it can take decisions, meeting in two full plenary sessions each year. It covers at least twelve policy areas for North–South co-operation and the implementation of mutually agreed policy; and its scope and powers can be expanded by mutual agreement. To deal with matters *not* devolved to the Northern Assembly, there is a British-Irish Intergovernmental Conference, while a British-Irish Council links the parliamentary assemblies in Dublin, Belfast, Edinburgh, Cardiff, the Isle of Man and the Channel Islands. For the initial working of these institutions and the Belfast Agreement more generally, see Wilford (2001).

21 Various writers have stressed the need to encourage participatory democracy in Northern Ireland (see, for example, Percival 1996; Gallagher 1998; Wilson 1998; Bell 1998), its putative advantages including the avoidance of immutable positions, and

finding accommodation not through the formal compromise of 'splitting the difference' between extremes, but through actively searching for common ground and
interests. However, a major limitation (Percival (1996) excepted) is that (mirroring official priorities) the focus is generally restricted to the territory of Northern Ireland,
ignoring the benefits of promoting participatory democracy on a cross-border basis.

22　The mistaken strategy of 'class' before 'nation' was codified in a mechanical Stalinist
'stages theory', adopted in Ireland by 'Official Sinn Féin' in the 1960s and 1970s.
Essentially it posited two 'stages' in temporal sequence: 'stage one' – unite nationalist
and unionist workers on a purely class basis, within and accepting existing state
borders; 'stage two' – once they were united – the national question would be raised
and dealt with from a united class position. In national conflicts there is no 'pure class
basis'. The mirror-image 'stages theory' of 'nation first, class later', more typical of
nationalists, also has to be rejected.

References

Agnew, J. (1994) 'The territorial trap: the geographic assumptions of international relations theory', *Review of International Political Economy* 1(1): 53–80.

Agreement (1998) *The Belfast Agreement*, London: HMSO.

Anderson, J. (1986) 'Nationalism and geography', in J. Anderson (ed.), *The Rise of the
Modern State*, Brighton: Wheatsheaf.

—— (1994) 'Problems of interstate economic integration: Northern Ireland and the Irish
Republic in the Single European Market', *Political Geography* 13(1): 53–72.

—— (1995) 'The exaggerated death of the nation-state', in J. Anderson *et al.* (eds), *A
Global World? Re-ordering Political Space*, Oxford: Oxford University Press.

—— (1996) 'The shifting stage of politics: new medieval and postmodern territorialities?'
Society and Space 14(2): 133–53.

—— (1998) 'Integrating Europe, integrating Ireland: the socio-economic dynamics', in J.
Anderson and J. Goodman (eds), *Dis/Agreeing Ireland: Contexts, Obstacles, Hopes*, London:
Pluto Press.

Anderson, J. and Goodman, J. (1995) 'Regions, states and the European Union:
modernist reaction or postmodernist adaptation?', *Review of International Political
Economy* 2(4): 600–32; reprinted in R. Higgott and A. Payne (eds), *The New Political
Economy of Globalisation*, Cheltenham, Edward Elgar, 2001.

—— (1996) 'Border crossings', *Fortnight* 350.

—— (1997) 'Problems of North–South economic integration in Ireland: Southern
perspectives', *Irish Journal of Sociology* 7: 29–52.

—— (eds) (1998) *Dis/Agreeing Ireland: Contexts, Obstacles, Hopes*, London: Pluto Press.

Anderson J. and Shuttleworth I. (1998) 'Sectarian demography, territoriality and political
development in Northern Ireland', *Political Geography* 17(2): 187–208.

Anderson, J., Brook, C. and Cochrane, A. (eds) (1995) *A Global World? Re-ordering Political
Space*, Oxford: Oxford University Press.

Archer, R. (1995) *Economic Democracy: The Politics of Feasible Socialism*, Oxford: Clarendon.

Bell, C. (1998) 'Women, equality and political participation', in J. Anderson and J.
Goodman (eds), *Dis/Agreeing Ireland: Contexts, Obstacles, Hopes*, London: Pluto Press.

Bradley, J. (1996) *An Island Economy: Exploring the Long-Term Economic and Social Consequences of Peace and Reconciliation in the Island of Ireland*, Dublin: Forum for Peace and
Reconciliation.

Cadogan Group (1992) *Northern Limits: The Boundaries of the Attainable in Northern Ireland politics*, Belfast: Cadogan Group.

—— (1998) *Rough Trade: Negotiating a Northern Ireland Settlement*, Belfast: Cadogan Group.

Cassesse, A. (1995) *Self-Determination of Peoples: A Legal Reappraisal*, Cambridge: Cambridge University Press.

Connolly, W. (1991) 'Democracy and territoriality', *Millennium* 20(3): 463–84.

Cowling, K. and Sugden, R. (1994) *Beyond Capitalism: Towards a New World Economic Order*, London: Pinter Publishers.

Democratic Dialogue (ed.) (1998) *New Order? International Models of Peace and Reconciliation*, Report No. 9, Belfast.

Douglas, N. (1998) 'The politics of accommodation: social change and conflict resolution in Northern Ireland', *Political Geography* 17(2): 209–29.

Fraser, T.G. (1984) *Partition in Ireland, India and Palestine: Theory and Practice*, London: Macmillan.

Gallagher, T. (1998) 'Identity politics and equality', in Democratic Dialogue (ed.), *New Order? International Models of Peace and Reconciliation*, Report No. 9, Belfast.

Goodman, J. (1997) 'The EU: reconstituting democracy beyond the nation-state', in A. McGrew (ed.), *The Transformation of Democracy? Democratic Politics in the New World Order*, Cambridge: Polity Press.

Hamilton, D. (2001) 'Economic integration on the island of Ireland', *Administration* 49(2): 73–89, special issue on 'Cross-Border Co-operation', Dublin: Institute of Public Administration.

Held, D. (1993) *Models of Democracy*, Cambridge: Polity Press.

Index: on Censorship (1997) 26(6), special section on partitions.

Lijphart, A. (1983) 'Consociation: the model and its applications in divided societies', in D. Rea (ed.), *Political Co-operation in Divided Societies: Papers Relevant to the Conflict in Northern Ireland*, Dublin: Gill and Macmillan.

McGarry, J. (1998) 'Nationalism in Northern Ireland and the "politics of recognition"', Plenary Address to the American Conference of Irish Studies, Fort Lauderdale, April.

McGarry, J. and O'Leary, B. (1990) *The Future of Northern Ireland*, London: Clarendon.

—— (eds.) (1993) *The Politics of Ethnic Conflict Regulation*, London: Routledge.

McGrew, A. (1995) 'World order and political space', in J. Anderson *et al.* (eds), *A Global World? Re-ordering Political Space*, Oxford: Oxford University Press.

Miliband, R. (1994) *Socialism for a Sceptical Age*, Cambridge: Polity Press.

Nairn, T. (1977) *The Break-up of Britain: Crisis and Neo-Nationalism*, London: New Left Books.

NESF (National and Economic Social Forum) (1995) *First Periodic Report of the National Social and Economic Forum*, Dublin: DSO.

O'Dowd, L. (1998) 'Constituting division, impeding agreement: the neglected role of British nationalism in Northern Ireland', in J. Anderson and J. Goodman (eds), *Dis/Agreeing Ireland: Contexts, Obstacles, Hopes*, London: Pluto Press.

O'Leary, B. and McGarry, J. (1993) *The Politics of Antagonism: Understanding Northern Ireland*, London: Athlone Press.

Percival, R. (1996) 'Towards a grassroots peace process', *The Irish Reporter* 22.

Quigley, G. (1992) 'Ireland – an island economy', speech to the Confederation of Irish Industry, 11 February.

Ruane, J. and Todd, J. (1996) *The Dynamics of Conflict in Northern Ireland: Power, Conflict and Emancipation*, Cambridge: Cambridge University Press.

Sack, R. (1986) *Human Territoriality: Its History and Theory*, Cambridge: Cambridge University Press.

Smith, A. (1981) *The Ethnic Revival in the Modern World*, Cambridge: Cambridge University Press.

Taylor, R. (1994) 'A consociational path to peace in Northern Ireland and South Africa?', in A. Guelke (ed.), *New Perspectives on the Northern Ireland Problem*, Aldershot: Avebury.

Wilford, R. (1992) 'Inverting consociationalism? Policy, pluralism and the post-modern', in B. Hadfield (ed.), *Northern Ireland: Politics and the Constitution*, Buckingham: Open University Press.

—— (ed.) (2001) *Aspects of the Belfast Agreement*, Oxford: Oxford University Press.

Wilson, R. (1998) 'Placing Northern Ireland', in Democratic Dialogue (ed.), *New Order? International Models of Peace and Reconciliation*, Report No. 9, Belfast.

8 Democratising global institutions

Possibilities, limits and normative foundations

Anthony McGrew

In a statement to the International Monetary and Financial Committee, Lawrence Summers calls for the modernisation of the IMF, arguing that central to the achievement of this task is a more representative, transparent and accountable organisation (Summers 2000). Kofi Annan too has called for 'greater participation and accountability' in the United Nations system. Beyond the cosmocracy, the language of democracy also informs the demands of many progressive social forces, such as Charter 99, in their campaigns for more representative and responsive global governance. As the rhetoric of democracy increasingly finds expression in proposals to reinvent global institutions, most dramatically in the 'anti-globalisation' movement, the challenge of 'good governance' now confronts global governance. On the other hand, for Robert Dahl, among others, such laudable aspirations are simply utopian in that 'we should openly recognise that international decision making will not be democratic' (Dahl 1999: 23). Underlying Dahl's scepticism is a reasoned argument that, despite globalisation and the diffusion of democratic values, the necessary preconditions for democracy remain largely absent in the international public domain: a domain which lacks the normative and institutional requirements of a properly functioning polity, and one in which might still trumps right. Herein lies a curious paradox: for in an era in which democracy has increasingly become the global standard of good governance it is judged inappropriate, by many of its strongest advocates, as a principle to be applied to international governance.

Is such scepticism justified? Can global institutions be democratised? What might democracy mean in relation to structures of global governance? These key questions inform this chapter. The first of five main sections discusses how basic issues of democracy are being posed anew by contemporary globalisation, and the next two sections confront the sceptics by outlining the negative and then the positive answers to the question of whether transnational democracy is feasible or desirable. The fourth section discusses alternative normative foundations for transnational democracy in terms of democratic intergovernmentalism, republicanism and cosmopolitanism. The fifth and final section takes the World Trade Organisation (WTO) as an example and looks at attempts to democratise it and the associated discourses.[1]

Global democracy for global times?

Contemporary patterns of globalisation raise the most profound questions about how modern societies are governed and – normatively speaking – should be governed. Some argue that in an age in which many of the most serious and enduring social problems – from drug addiction to unemployment – require concerted international co-ordination and co-operation, the powers, legitimacy and role of national government is called into question (Rosenau 1997). Governments, in other words, can no longer, in an interconnected world, ensure the welfare and security of their citizens. Furthermore, as the jurisdiction and authority of international, public and private bodies, from the European Union (EU) to the International Accounting Standards Committee, expands to deal with cross-border problems, fresh concerns arise with matters of accountability and democracy, traditionally the essence of domestic politics. In short, how we are governed, by whom, in whose interests, and to what ends – the classic questions of politics – have been posed afresh by contemporary globalisation.

Until fairly recently, theories of democracy have presumed a strict separation of political life into the domestic and international realms; the 'bounded political community' and the 'anarchical society' respectively (Connolly 1991; Walker 1991). Theorists of modern democracy have tended to bracket out the anarchical society, while theorists of international relations have tended to bracket out democracy. Of course, there have been exceptions to this. Liberal internationalism in its classical version, from Woodrow Wilson's 'new world order' to the early advocates of functionalism such as Mitrany, sought to establish the normative and practical basis of a more democratic global polity (Mitrany 1975a, 1975b). Insofar as critical theory sought to provide an alternative conception of democracy, it was imbued with cosmopolitan pretensions which challenged the 'inside/outside' logic of orthodox accounts of the democratic political community (Linklater 1990; Hutchings 1999). But, for the most part, it is only in the present post-Cold War era that global governance has come to figure seriously in the writings of democratic theorists, only now that democracy has been established on the agenda of international theory (Held 1995; Clark 1999).

This theoretical convergence has been influenced by several interrelated political developments: the intensification of globalisation, the 'Third Wave' of global democratisation and the rise of transnational social movements. Economic globalisation, many argue, has exacerbated the tension between democracy, as a territoriality rooted system of rule, and the operation of global markets and transnational networks of corporate power. In a world in which even the most powerful governments appear impotent when confronted by the gyrations of global markets or the activities of transnational corporations, the efficacy of national democracy is called into question. For if, as Sandel observes, governments have lost the capacity to manage transnational forces in accordance with the expressed preferences of their citizens, the very essence of democracy, namely self-governance, is decidedly compromised (Sandel 1996). Moreover, in seeking to promote or regulate the forces of globalisation, through mechanisms of global and macro-regional governance, states have created new layers of political authority which have weak democratic credentials and stand in an ambiguous relationship to existing systems of national accountability. Under these conditions it is no longer clear, to use Dahl's classic formulation, 'who governs?'. In an era in which public and private power is manifested and exercised on a transnational, or even global scale, a serious reappraisal of the prospects for democracy is overdue.

This rethinking of democracy has also been encouraged by the global diffusion of liberal democracy as a system of political rule. In comparison with the early twentieth century, democracy – and liberal representative democracy at that – has emerged as the dominant system of national rule across the globe, at least in a formal sense (Potter *et al.* 1997). Putting aside Fukuyama's misconceived triumphalism, and whatever the causes of this 'Third Wave' (see Anderson in this volume), democracy has become an almost universal political standard. Of course, for many new democracies the aspiration and political rhetoric far exceed the realisation of effective democracy. Within the old democracies public disenchantment with elected politicians and the capacity of democratic governments to deal with many of the enduring problems – from inequality to pollution – confronted by modern societies suggest that all is not well there either. Yet despite such failings, both old and new democracies have in particular become increasingly sensitive to the weak democratic credentials of existing structures of global and regional governance, the more so as the actions of such bodies directly impinge on their citizens. As democratic states have come to constitute a majority within global institutions the pressures to make such bodies more transparent and accountable have increased (Committee on Governance 1995). Somewhat ironically, many new democracies which have been subject to strictures from the IMF and World Bank about the requirements of good governance are now campaigning for similar principles and practices to be applied in these citadels of global power. But how to combine effective international institutions with democratic practices remains, according to Keohane (1998), among the most intractable of contemporary international political problems.

One powerful response to this problem has come from the agencies of civil society. The global 'associational revolution', expressed in the enormous expansion of non-governmental organisation (NGO) activity, transnational networks of advocacy groups, and business and professional associations, among others, has created the infrastructure of a transnational civil society (Matthews 1997; Rosenau 1997; Boli and Thomas 1999). Although unrepresentative of the world's peoples, the agencies of transnational civil society have come to be instrumental in representing the concerns of citizens and organised interests in international forums (Boli *et al.* 1999). But the democratic credentials of transnational civil society are ambiguous. Whether transnational civil society is a significant force for the democratisation of world order, or simply another arena through which the privileged and powerful maintain their global hegemony, is a matter of some considerable debate (Wapner 1996; Weiss and Gordenker 1996; Burbach *et al.* 1997; Boli and Thomas 1999; and see the chapters by Van der Pijl, Hirsch and Goodman in this volume).

It is in the context of these developments that the academic discourse about transnational democracy finds a political resonance. Indeed, the rapidity with which the rhetoric, if not the idea, of democracy has acquired a certain discursive presence in current deliberations concerning the reform of global governance is quite remarkable. It is all the more so given the dogmatic dismissal of early reflections upon democracy and world order. The remainder of the chapter will offer an overview and critique of the contemporary debate about transnational democracy in relation to global institutions. Before doing so, however, the terms of the debate require some clarification and in particular the sceptical critique has to be addressed.

Transnational democracy: a feasible or desirable project ?

For communitarians and realists, the answer to the above question is an uncompromising 'no'. Whatever the intellectual merits of any particular design for transnational democracy, those of a sceptical mind question its relevance, desirability and feasibility. They do so on a number of grounds: theoretical, institutional, historical and ethical.

Communitarians take issue with the cosmopolitan premises which inform theories of transnational democracy. Democracy, argues Kymlicka (1999), is rooted in a shared history, language and political culture. These are the defining characteristics of territorial political communities and they are all more or less absent at the transnational level. Despite the way globalisation binds the fate of communities together, the reality is that 'the only forum within which genuine democracy occurs is within national boundaries' (Kymlicka 1999). Even within the EU, transnational democracy is little more than an elite phenomenon (Kymlicka 1999; and see Newman in this volume). If there is no effective moral community beyond the state there is also no demos. Advocates of transnational democracy suggest that political communities are being transformed by globalisation such that the idea of the demos as a fixed, territorially delimited unit is no longer tenable (Linklater 1998). But in problematising the demos, contest the sceptics, the critical question becomes who, or what authority, decides how the demos is to be constituted and upon what basis (see Taylor in this volume). In addressing this fundamental theoretical issue, suggest the sceptics, the advocates of transnational democracy almost uniformly fail to establish a rigorous or convincing argument (Görg and Hirsch 1998; Dahl 1999; Kymlicka 1999; Saward 2000).

For realists, the issue is that sovereignty and anarchy present the most insuperable barriers to the realisation of democracy beyond borders. Even though elements of an international society of states exist, in which there is an acceptance of the rule of law and compliance with international norms, order at the global level, suggest the realists, remains contingent rather than institutionalised. Conflict and force are ever-present and a daily reality in many regions of the world. These are not the conditions in which any substantive democratic experiment is likely to prosper, since a properly functioning democracy requires the absence of political violence and the rule of law. In relations between sovereign states, violence is always a possibility and the rule of law an instrument of *realpolitik*. Given the absence of a democratic world empire, or some form of world federation of states in which sovereignty is pooled, the conditions for the possibility of transnational democracy appear theoretically and practically unrealisable. Few sovereign democratic states are likely to trade self-governance for a more democratic world order. Furthermore, there is an irresolvable tension at the heart of theories of transnational democracy between national democracy and democracy above the state. The danger is that the latter has enormous potential to override and undermine the former, and here communitarians and realists are agreed. A case in point was the EU's recent 'democratically mandated' intervention in Austrian politics. Following the electoral success of the 'far Right', the EU threatened to withhold official recognition of any coalition government in which Mr Haider, the leader of the main 'far Right' party, played a role, and this despite the democratically expressed preferences of the Austrian electorate. Whatever the ethics of this particular case, the more general point is that transnational democracy has the potential to extinguish effective self-governance at local or national levels (Hutchings 1999: 166). Finally, the failure of theories of transnational democracy to construct a credible account of how the democratic will of the international community can be enforced against the entrenched interests of the Great Powers of the day raises fundamental questions about the limits to democracy at the international level. Without the capacity to enforce the democratic will on weak and strong states alike, transnational democracy becomes meaningless. But, paradoxically, the existence of such a capability in itself creates the real possibility of the tyranny of global democracy.

Furthermore, for many radical critics the very idea of transnational democracy is conceived as harbouring a new instrument of Western hegemony. As with the philosophy of 'good governance' promulgated by G7 governments and multilateral agencies, it is primarily a Western preoccupation and project. There are, in other words, few constituencies for transnational democracy to be found in Africa, Asia and Latin America. For most of humanity it is a distraction from the most pressing global problem, namely how to ensure that global markets and global capital work in the interests of the majority of the world's peoples and without destroying the natural environment. As the UN Development Report 1999 puts it, the most pressing issue for humankind is whether globalisation can be given a human face (UNDP 1999). In this context, transnational democracy may be an entirely inappropriate and irrelevant response, given that the critical problem is a system of global governance which promotes unfettered global capitalism (Cox 1996; Burbach *et al.* 1997). Democratising global governance is much more likely to strengthen and legitimise the hegemony of global capital than it is to challenge its grip on the levers of global power (Burbach *et al.* 1997). The historical record of advanced capitalist societies, argue the critics, illustrates how the imperatives of capitalism take precedence over the workings of democracy (Miliband 1973). Therein lies the fate of transnational democracy. Accelerating global inequality and looming environmental catastrophe will not be resolved by a dose of transnational democracy but, on the contrary, only through powerful global bodies which can override the entrenched interests of Western states and global capital by promoting the common welfare; or alternatively, by the deconstruction of global governance and the devolution of power to self-governing, sustainable local communities. Since the former would require the acquiescence of the very geopolitical and social forces it is designed to tame it is nothing but utopian. Thus the ethical and political preference of many radical critics is for forms of direct democracy not transnational democracy: true democracy in this view is therefore always local democracy (Morrison 1995; see also Goodman in this volume).

These constitute powerful arguments for questioning the relevance and desirability of a more democratic global polity. Despite their different bases, what they share is a sense that transnational democracy is neither necessarily an appropriate response to globalisation, nor an ethical possibility to be advocated. On the contrary, it is fraught with dangers. Not least among these, suggests Dahl, is the danger of popular control in respect of vital matters of economic and military security (Dahl 1999). Moreover, historically the development of democracy within most states has been a product of force and violence (see O'Dowd in this volume), and the history of national democracy illustrates how enormously difficult it is to nurture and sustain such a fragile system of rule even in the context of shared political culture (Dahl 1999). In a world of cultural diversity and growing inequality, the possibility of realising transnational democracy must therefore be judged to be negligible without its imposition either by a concert of democratic states or a benign democratic hegemon. For the sceptics, self-governance within states, whether democratic or not, is ethically preferable to the likely tyranny of nominally democratic global institutions.

Can transnational democracy be dismissed?

In response, the advocates of transnational democracy accuse the sceptics of a too hasty dismissal of the theoretical, ethical and empirical arguments which inform designs for democracy beyond borders. More specifically, they argue, by discounting the significant political transformations being brought about by intensifying globalisation and regionalisation, the sceptics seriously misread the nature of the contemporary historical conjuncture (Elkins 1995; Castells 1998; Linklater 1998; Clark 1999; Held *et al.* 1999). These transformations irrevocably alter the conditions which made sovereign, territorial, self-governing political communities possible, for in a world of global flows, the 'local' and the 'global', the 'domestic' and the 'foreign', are largely indistinguishable. To dismiss such developments is to fall prey to a timeless, essentialist conception of modern statehood and political community which disregards their historically and socially constructed nature (Devetak 1995; Linklater 1998).

Modern political communities are historical and social constructions. Their particular form, coinciding with the territorial reach of the 'imagined community' of the nation, is a product of particular conditions and forces. This form defines the metric by which the unit of modern democracy is calibrated. Historically the state has been the primary incubator of modern democratic life. But, as Linklater (1998) observes, political communities have never been static, fixed creations but have always been in the process of construction and reconstruction. As globalisation and regionalisation have intensified, modern political communities have begun to experience a significant transformation, while new forms of political community are emerging (Linklater 1998). According to Held (2000), national political communities coexist today alongside 'overlapping communities of fate' defined by the spatial reach of transnational networks, systems, allegiances and problems. These, in Walzer's terms, may be 'thin' communities, as opposed to the 'thick' communities of the locale and 'nation-state', but they nevertheless constitute necessary ethical and political conditions for the cultivation of transnational democracy. In essence, these overlapping communities of fate define the contours of new articulations of the demos.

Critics of transnational democracy, as noted, charge that at the core of such prescriptions is an indeterminate conception of the demos. This charge, however, overlooks the indeterminate and constructed nature of the modern (national) demos itself. For the constitution of the demos within the nation-state has always been the object of contestation – witness the struggle for the female vote or current controversies about citizenship – and it has evolved as a product of changing social and political conditions. Thus the contingent nature of the demos is not a problem which is specific to the idea of democracy beyond borders, as the sceptics suggest, but on the contrary is generic to democracy at all levels (Saward 1998). In the context of transnational democracy, the demos tends to be conceived not so much in universal terms – a singular global demos – but rather as a fluid and complex construction: articulated in a multiplicity of settings in relation to the plurality of sites of power and the architecture of global governance. This complexity, as indicated by the experience of the EU and federal polities, is by no means without historical precedent. In this respect the so-called problem of the demos is not as intractable as the sceptics suggest (see earlier chapters and Taylor in this volume).

In his study of globalisation, Elazar (1998) points to the growing constitutionalisation of world order. What he means by this is that the accumulation of multilateral, regional and transnational arrangements (which have evolved in the last fifty years) has created a tacit constitution for the global polity. In seeking to manage and regulate transborder issues, states have sought to codify through treaties and other arrangements their powers and authority. In so doing they have created an elaborate system of rules, rights and responsibilities for the conduct of their joint affairs. This has gone furthest in the EU, where effectively a sort of quasi-federal constitution has emerged. But in other contexts, such as the WTO, the authority of national governments is being redefined, as the management of trade disputes becomes subject to a rule of law (Shell 1995). Central to this process has been the elaboration and entrenchment of some significant democratic principles within the society of states (Crawford 1994). Thus the principles of self-determination, popular sovereignty, democratic legitimacy and the legal equality of states have become the orthodoxies of international society. As Mayall (2000) comments, there has been an 'entrenchment not just of democracy itself, but democratic values, as the standard of legitimacy within international society'. This democratisation of international society also appears to have accelerated in recent years in response to processes of globalisation, the activities of transnational civil society and the socialising dynamic of an expanding community of democratic states. Despite the unevenness and fragility of this democratisation, some argue, in contradistinction to the sceptics, that it forges the nascent conditions – the creation of 'zones of peace' and the rule of law – for the cultivation of transnational democracy (Held 1995).

Further evidence of this process of democratisation is to be found in the growing political response to economic globalisation among governments and transnational movements. This response is manifest in diverse ways, but a common theme among progressive forces is a demand for more accountable, responsive and transparent global governance. With the growing perception that power is leaking away from democratic states and electorates to unelected and effectively unaccountable global bodies, such as the WTO, has come increased political pressure on Western governments especially to bring good governance to global governance (Woods 1999). But a broader global consensus appears to be emerging on the need for such reform, drawing some political support from across the North–South divide and among diverse constituencies of transnational civil society. Of course, democracy involves more than simply transparent and accountable decision making, and it is interesting to note that the debate about reform draws significantly upon several of the discourses – of transnational democracy discussed in the next section. In the context of the WTO, for instance, the language of 'stakeholding' has been much in evidence, somewhat curiously in US proposals for its reform (Shell 1995; McGrew 1999). But whatever the immediate outcomes of the current reform process, it has lodged the problem of the democratic credentials of international governance firmly on the global agenda. In doing so it has created a global public space for continual political reflection and debate on this key structural issue.

Of course, for sceptics such as Dahl these developments do not invalidate the normative argument that international institutions cannot be truly democratic (Dahl 1999). Yet, as advocates of transnational democracy point out, there are numerous examples of international or supra-state bodies, from the EU to the International Labour Organization (ILO), whose institutional designs reflect novel combinations of traditional intergovernmental and democratic principles (Woods 1999). While the EU represents a remarkable institutionalisation of a distinctive form of democracy beyond borders (see chapters by Newman and Painter in this volume), it is by no means unique. The ILO, for instance, has institutionalised a restricted form of stakeholding through a tripartite system of representation corresponding to states, business and labour organisations respectively. Beyond this, newer international functional bodies, such as the

International Fund for Agricultural Development and the Global Environmental Facility, embody stakeholding principles as a means to ensure representative decision making (Woods 1999). Furthermore, virtually all major international institutions have opened themselves up to the formal or informal participation of the representatives of civil society (Weiss and Gordenker 1996). Even the WTO has created a civil society forum. The sceptical proposition that effective international governance is simply incompatible with democratic practices appears somewhat dogmatic in the light of the historical record of global governance. On the contrary, in certain respects democratic principles are constitutive of the contemporary global polity.

Finally, in questioning the value of democracy the sceptics raise the serious issue of whether democracy can deliver greater social justice. In this respect, suggest the critics, the historical record suggests a pessimistic conclusion. By contrast, all but the most radical theorists of transnational democracy build upon a different reading of the relationship between capitalism and democracy. This reading accepts the inevitable contradictions between the logic of capitalism and the logic of democracy. But it departs from the fatalism of the radical critique in arguing, on both theoretical and empirical grounds, that democracy can and does promote social justice: witness the significance of social democracy (Held 1995). Building upon this analysis, the argument for transnational democracy therefore also becomes an argument for global social justice. The value of transnational democracy, suggest many of its more passionate advocates, lies precisely in its capacity to provide legitimate mechanisms and grounds for the promotion and realisation of global social justice (Held 1995). The fact that existing institutions of global governance fail to do so is no surprise, since they are the captives of dominant interests. This, they argue, is not valid grounds for abandoning the project of transnational democracy but, on the contrary, is the reason to advocate it more vigorously. But what meaning(s) can be given to the idea of transnational democracy?

Transnational democracy: normative foundations

A burgeoning and diverse set of literature exists justifying and elaborating the normative principles of global or transnational democracy. Within this literature, three distinct normative accounts can be discerned: namely, *democratic intergovernmentalism*; *transnational republicanism*; and *cosmopolitanism*. Of course, this is a crude typology and it is open to challenge on a number of grounds. Not least is the danger that it may court caricature, for it is evident that individual theorists tend to draw upon a range of democratic traditions. Nevertheless, it provides a rough mapping of the intellectual field insofar as it identifies the clustering of key normative arguments. In effect, the three clusters identified constitute 'ideal types': that is, general syntheses of normative arguments and analyses which reflect a shared conception of transnational democracy. As such, this typology provides a framework for a systematic analysis of what is at stake in the debate about the democratisation of global and regional governance.

Democratic intergovernmentalism

Rooted in a broadly liberal reformist tradition, democratic intergovernmentalism embodies a primarily procedural and pragmatic conception of democracy beyond borders. It emphasises the crucial role of national governments in representing their people's interests and bringing to account the decision makers in global and regional bodies. In effect, states are considered the primary units of democratic accountability such that transnational democracy is considered synonymous with inter-national democracy, that is, a democratic order of states (rather than peoples) defined by the principles of political and legal equality. Creating more representative, responsive, transparent and accountable international institutions by widening the participation of states in key global forums and strengthening existing lines of accountability are central to this reformist vision (Committee on Governance 1995).

Of course, the agencies of transnational civil society are not excluded from this vision. Keohane, for instance, understands democracy at the international level as a form of 'voluntary pluralism under conditions of maximum transparency' (Keohane 1998: 83). A more pluralistic world order, in this view, is also a more democratic world order. Underlying this philosophy is an attachment to the principles of classical pluralism: political and civil rights, the politics of interests, the diffusion of power, the limited state and rule by consensus. It requires, in effect, the reconstruction of existing forms of liberal-pluralist democracy at the supra-state level but without the complications of electoral politics. Instead a vibrant transnational civil society channels its demands to the decision makers while in turn also making them accountable for their actions. Accordingly, 'accountability will be enhanced not only by chains of official responsibility but by the requirement of transparency. Official actions, negotiated amongst state representatives in international organisations, will be subject to scrutiny by transnational networks' (Keohane 1998: 83). International institutions thus become arenas within which the interests of states and the agencies of civil society are articulated. Furthermore, they are the main political structures through which consensus is negotiated and collective decisions legitimated. This reflects a largely procedural view of democracy as a technique for taking and legitimising public decisions.

As Falk (1995) identifies, this is a philosophy which offers a restricted and somewhat technocratic view of transnational democracy. As with liberal-pluralism more generally, it fails to acknowledge that inequalities of power tend to make democratic systems the captive of powerful vested interests. For, as Petit argues, a critical weakness of liberal-pluralism is that by making 'naked preference into the motor of social life', it exposes 'all weakly placed individuals to the naked preferences of the stronger' (Petit 1997: 205). Moreover, while transparency and accountability are necessary elements of transnational democracy, they are by no means sufficient in themselves to ensure its substantive realisation. The notion that the democratic deficit which afflicts global governance can be resolved through institutional reforms alone arises from an underlying assumption that the existing liberal world order simply requires some institutional tinkering to make it more democratic. Despite its acknowledgement of the significance of transnational civil society, the liberal-internationalist account remains singularly state-centric insofar as transnational democracy is conceived effectively in terms of enhancing the accountability of international institutions to national governments; that is, democratic intergovernmentalism.

Transnational republicanism

Advocates of a form of transnational republicanism are concerned with identifying the normative foundations of a 'new politics' which involves the empowerment of individuals and communities in the context of a globalising world (Patomaki 2000). It represents a substantive view of democracy insofar as it is concerned with the creation of 'good communities' based upon ideas of equality, active citizenship, the promotion of the public good, humane governance and harmony with the natural environment. It seeks to adapt notions of direct democracy and self-governance to fit with an epoch in which transnational and global power structures regulate the conditions of the daily existence of communities and neighbourhoods across the world.

Republicanism is essentially a 'bottom-up' theory of the democratisation of world order. Its primary agents are the multiplicity of critical social movements, such as environmental, women and peace movements, which challenge the authority of states and international structures as well as the hegemony of particular (liberal) conceptions of the 'political' (see Goodman in this volume). In 'politicising' existing global institutions and practices, not to mention challenging the conventional boundaries of the 'political' (the foreign/domestic, public/private, society/nature binary divides), critical social movements are conceived as agents of a 'new progressive politics'. Such a politics builds on the experiences of critical social movements which demonstrate that one of the 'great fallacies of political theory is the assumption that a centralised management of power...is necessary to assure political order' (Burnheim 1985: 53). Accordingly, democracy and democratic legitimacy do not have to be grounded in territorially delimited units such as national states but rather are to be located in a multiplicity of self-governing and self-organising collectivities constituted on diverse spatial scales, from the local to the global (Connolly 1991). Although the spatial reach of these collectivities is to be defined by the geographical scope of the collective problems or activities which they seek to manage, there is a strong presumption in favour of the subsidiarity principle. This is a vision of direct democracy which considers that substantive transnational democracy arises from the existence of a plurality of diverse, overlapping and spatially differentiated self-governing 'communities of fate' and multiple sites of power, without the need for 'sovereign' or centralised structures of authority of any kind. It identifies, in the political practices of critical social movements, immanent tendencies towards the transcendence of the sovereign territorial state as the fundamental unit of democracy.

Transnational republicanism is rooted in the traditions of direct democracy and participatory democracy (Held 1995). It also draws upon neo-Marxist critiques of liberal democracy. For democracy is conceived as inseparable from creating the conditions for effective participation and self-governance, including, among other things, the achievement of social and economic equality (see Newman in this volume). Furthermore, it connects to the civic republican tradition insofar as it considers the realisation of individual freedom has to be 'embedded within and sustained by a [strong] sense of political community and of the common good' (Barns 1995).

To the extent that its advocates argue that the effective conditions for the realisation of global or transnational democracy require the construction of alternative forms of global governance, transnational republicanism is subversive of the existing world. For its critics it is precisely this rejection of the existing constitution of world order that is problematic (Held 1995; Hutchings 1999: 178). In resisting the rule of law in global politics and rejecting the idea of sovereignty, the very principles of democracy, argue the critics, are decidedly compromised. Without some notion of popular sovereignty it is difficult to envisage what democracy might mean. While in the absence of the present rather imperfect liberal constitution for world order – embodying (to varying degrees) the principles of the rule of law and constraints on the exercise of force – there would seem to be no institutional foundation for constructing transnational democracy. The theoretical limitations of the radical pluralist argument are therefore to be found in its ambivalence towards the conditions – the rule of law and sovereignty – which make democracy (at whatever level) possible.

Cosmopolitan democracy

By comparison with the radical pluralist account, cosmopolitan democracy pays particular attention to the institutional and political conditions which are necessary to the conduct of effective democratic governance within, between and across states. In its most sophisticated formulation, Held develops an account of cosmopolitan democracy which, building upon the existing principles of the liberal-international order, involves the construction of a new global constitutional settlement in which democratic principles are firmly entrenched (Held 1995). Advocating a 'double democratisation' of political life, the advocates of cosmopolitan democracy seek to reinvigorate democracy within states by extending democracy to the public realm between and across states. In this respect transnational democracy and territorial democracy are conceived as mutually reinforcing rather than conflicting principles of political rule. Cosmopolitan democracy in effect seeks 'a political order of democratic associations, cities and nations as well as of regions and global networks' (Held 1995: 234).

Central to this model is the principle of democratic autonomy, namely the 'entitlement to autonomy within the constraints of community' (Held 1995: 156). This is to be assured through the requirements of a cosmopolitan democratic law, that is, law which 'allows international society, including individuals, to interfere in the internal affairs of each state in order to protect certain [democratic] rights' (Archibugi 1995). Accordingly, the principle of democratic autonomy depends upon 'the establishment of an international community of democratic states and societies committed to upholding a democratic public law both within and across their own boundaries: a cosmopolitan democratic community' (Held 1995: 229). This does not presume a requirement for a world government, nor a federal super-state, but rather the establishment of 'a global and divided authority system – a system of diverse and overlapping power centres shaped and delimited by democratic law' (Held 1995: 234). Rather than a hierarchy of political authority, from the local to the global, cosmopolitan democracy involves a heterarchical arrangement. Conceptually this lies between federalism and the much looser arrangements implied by the notion of *con*feder-alism – what some have referred to as the Philadelphian system (Deudney 1996). It requires 'the subordination of regional, national and local "sovereignties" to an overarching legal framework, but within this framework associations may be self-governing at diverse levels' (Held 1995: 234). The entrenchment of cosmopolitan democracy therefore involves a process of *reconstructing* the existing framework of global governance.

Essential to the realisation of this democratic reconstruction, it is argued, is the requirement that democratic practices be embedded more comprehensively 'within communities and civil associations by elaborating and reinforcing democracy from "outside" through a network of regional and international agencies and assemblies that cut across spatially delimited locales' (Held 1995: 237). Only through such mechanisms will those global sites and transnational networks of power which presently escape effective national democratic control be brought to account, so establishing the political conditions befitting the realisation of democratic autonomy.

Cosmopolitan democracy represents an enormously ambitious agenda for reconfiguring the constitution of global governance and world order. Its genealogy is eclectic insofar as it claims significant continuities with a variety of traditions of democratic thought. While it draws considerable inspiration from modern theories of liberal democracy, it is also influenced by critical theory, theories of participatory democracy and civic republicanism. It is distinguished from liberal-internationalism by its radical agenda and a scepticism towards state-centric and procedural notions of democracy. While accepting the important role of progressive transnational social forces, it nevertheless differentiates itself from radical pluralist democracy through its attachment to the centrality of the rule of law and constitutionalism as necessary conditions for the establishment of a more democratic world order. But the idea of cosmopolitan democracy is not without its critics.

Sandel argues that 'Despite its merits...the cosmopolitan ideal is flawed, both as a moral ideal and as a public philosophy for self-government in our time' (Sandel 1996: 342). This, he argues, is because at the core of cosmopolitanism is a liberal conception of the individual which neglects the ways in which individuals, their interests and values, are 'constructed' by the communities of which they are members. Accordingly, democracy can only thrive by first creating a democratic community with a common civic identity. While globalisation does create a sense of universal connectedness, it does not, in Brown's (1995) view, generate an equivalent sense of community based upon shared values and beliefs. Thus cosmopolitan democracy, as transnational democracy, lacks a convincing account of how the ethical resources necessary for its effective realisation are to be generated. It is also criticised for its top-down constitutionalism which fails to recognise the inherent tension between the principles of democracy and the logic of constitutional constraints upon what the demos may do (Saward 1998). Nor is it clear within an heterarchical system of governance how jurisdictional conflicts between different layers of democratic authority are to be reconciled or adjudicated by democratic means, let alone how accountability in such a system can be made effective. This raises important issues of consent and legitimacy. As Thompson argues, the problem is one of 'many majorities' such that 'no majority has an exclusive and overarching claim to democratic legitimacy' (Thompson 1999: 123). Furthermore, cosmopolitan democracy will only serve to intensify the enduring tensions between democracy and the protection of individual rights since rights claims may be pursued outside those 'local' or immediate jurisdictions whose policies or decisions have been sanctioned by a formal democratic process (Thompson 1999). Finally, some radical critiques reject cosmopolitan democracy as they consider it represents a new mode of imperialism insofar as it presumes the universal validity of Western liberal democracy, and so discounts the legitimacy of alternative or non-Western democratic cultures.

Towards democratic global governance?

For the advocates of transnational democracy there are some grounds for cautious optimism. Globalisation and regionalisation are stimulating powerful political reactions which in their more progressive manifestations have engendered a serious debate about the democratic credentials of global governance (Mittleman 2000). Furthermore, in the wake of the East Asian crisis and with the growth of the 'anti-globalisation' or 'anti-capitalism' movement since the 'Battle of Seattle' protest against the WTO, there is evidence of an emerging global consensus on the need for more effective regulation of global financial markets and global capital (UNCTAD 1998; UNDP 1999; Jones 2000). In consequence, the Washington consensus championing unfettered global capitalism no longer appears so secure or hegemonic (McGrew 2000). Regulating globalisation is now a paramount political issue and this in turn has provoked much discussion about the precise form which such regulation should take as well as the political values which might inform it. Transparency, accountability, participation and legitimacy are rapidly becoming the values associated with the reform agenda. Progressive elements of transnational civil society too are organising and mobilising to maintain the political pressure on governments and institutions to restructure and reconstruct systems of global and regional governance to accord with democratic principles. Of great significance too is the way in which different political constituencies and social forces draw upon the discourses of transnational democracy (discussed above) in their campaigns to advance global democratic change, most especially *democratic intergovernmentalism* and *republicanism*. For instance, this has been very evident in respect of the World Trade Organization.

Redressing the WTO's democratic deficit

In setting the WTO policy agenda and its institutional programmes, the legal principle of one state one vote, and the commitment to consensual modes of decision taking, do give the appearance that 'Prima facie...the decision making process is democratic' (Qureshi 1996: 6). In practice, the politics of the WTO are far from democratic in as much as decision making on strategic policy issues tends to reflect the interests of the major trading blocs, while the ideological commitment to the pursuit of a liberal trading order permeates every aspect of the trade policy agenda. Compared with many other intergovernmental organisations, the opportunities to register the concerns and interests of peoples, as opposed to member states, on the institutional agenda, let alone to give a voice to 'civil society' in policy deliberations, have been negligible. Attempts to broaden the trade agenda to include issues of the environment and labour, or to consult with NGOs, have been (and continue to be) strongly resisted.

Such resistance to the perceived 'politicisation' – *qua* democratisation – of the institution cannot simply be ascribed to an ideological commitment to a liberal trading order, nor to the actions of the most powerful member states or the pressures of global capital. The WTO has its own institutional dynamic, identity and legal personality; it would be simplistic to characterise it as purely an instrument of multinational capital or the dominant economic powers such as the USA. Indeed, the paradox is that both the USA and many leading multinationals are calling for more transparent and open decision making while many governments, especially among the emerging and newly industrialising economies, are enormously resistant both to widening the trade agenda (to include environmental or labour issues) or to giving 'civil society' a voice in the WTO's policy deliberations. But this deep resistance to any proposals to making the institution both more responsive and responsible to the 'world community' is not so much a product of an anti-democratic impulse as a result of reasonable fear that a WTO which is more open to the influence of private interests and NGOs will become even more Western dominated. A 'democratic' WTO could thereby legislate the global application of Western standards, whether in the environmental or social domain, which will erode the competitive advantages of developing economies. In this respect the struggle for the democratisation of the WTO is inseparable from the wider struggle over the distribution of global wealth and power.

Against this background the majority of member states may much prefer a WTO which is more technocratic and legalistic in the exercise of its responsibilities as opposed to more democratic. For in overseeing the efficient application of a rule-based multilateral trading order, the WTO provides an effective, regularised, predictable and juridical mechanism for negotiating and resolving trade matters between governments which moves beyond the principle of 'might is right' and towards 'a governance system based on the "rule of law"' (Shell 1995). Indeed, the shift away from the politicised mechanisms of trade dispute management of the GATT era represents, as Shell argues, a stunning victory for the technocratic and legalistic approach (Shell 1995). Rather than a 'banana republic', a more apt analogy for the WTO might be that of a classic technocracy in which the principles of efficiency and effectiveness are prized more highly than those of representation and accountability.

As a technocracy, the WTO operates to de-politicise trade issues by redefining them as legal and technical matters which are best resolved by trade experts through a process of technical deliberation and the rational application of juridical procedures. Trade governance is thus transformed into an activity in which expert knowledge and understanding are the primary credentials for participating in setting the institution's goals and policing its rules. The politics of the WTO thus reflect negotiation and consensus between trade bureaucracies in which a transnational epistemic community of trade experts (economists, lawyers, scientists, etc.) provides 'a relatively independent source of scientific evidence and authority' (Hasenclever *et al.* 1997: 149). Institutional decision making is thus legitimised more by the application and interpretation of knowledge, technical rules and expertise than it is by deference to the principles of representation and state interests. As Winner suggests, the technocratic ethic means

> the real voting will take place on a very high level of technical understanding...One may register to vote on this level only by exhibiting proper credentials as an expert. The balloting will be closed to the ignorant and to those whose knowledge is out of date or otherwise not relevant to the problem at hand. Among the disenfranchised in this arrangement are some previously formidable characters: the average citizen, the sovereign consumer...and the homegrown politician.
>
> (Winner 1977: 170–1)

The technocratic ethic thus runs completely counter to the democratic impulse since its 'premises are totally incompatible with...the idea of responsible, responsive, representative government' (Winner 1977: 146). Accordingly, those 'who are in a position to supply the desired knowledge, therefore can exert considerable influence on the choices made by policy makers' (Hasenclever *et al.* 1997: 140).

In recent years, the pressures to confront and redress the 'democratic deficit' have intensified such that, even among the technocrats of the WTO, there is a growing recognition that greater transparency and accountability is necessary. Three factors, in particular, are central to this growing concern with the institution's democratic credentials. First, as the process of trade liberalisation shifts away from tariff reductions to the removal of domestic barriers to free trade, a whole series of issue areas, from competition policy to the environment and health and labour standards, will figure increasingly on the WTO agenda. Inevitably this means that a broader range of interests will have to be consulted or brought into the decision-making process. As Renato Ruggiero, the WTO's then Director General, acknowledged in 1998, 'Whenever people talk about trade now, other issues come up immediately:...protection of the environment, social conditions, employment, public health...We have to improve our ability to respond within our own rules...to the interrelationships which undoubtedly exist' (Ruggiero 1998). Secondly, in the two years following its inception in 1995, the WTO had dealt with 120 trade disputes while by comparison, between 1948 and 1994 GATT had adjudicated only 315 cases. As the complexity, severity and number of trade disputes upon which the WTO has to adjudicate rises, so too, as is evident already, will the pressures to make these quasi-judicial proceedings more transparent, and for Panels to justify and explain their rulings to a wider political community. Thirdly, as future rounds of trade liberalisation bite deeper into the domestic economies and societies of member states, and the protectionist backlash gains momentum, the WTO will no longer be able to rely upon member governments alone to mobilise political support for the multilateral trading order. As is already the case, the WTO will be forced to seek greater legitimacy for its activities by mobilising or assuaging the many diverse constituencies of transnational civil society which, to date, it has largely ignored. Resolving this latent 'crisis of legitimacy' is unlikely to be successful without giving the representatives of civil society a voice, however muted, in the institution's deliberations.

Traces of democratic intergovernmentalism and republicanism can be detected in the discourses of politicians, diplomats, the corporate sector, labour unions and social movements, as they seek both to come to terms with a more active and powerful WTO and make it more accountable for the exercise of its inherent powers.

Democratic intergovernmentalism and the WTO

Although driven significantly by the need to assuage powerful domestic protectionist forces, the Clinton administration made reform of the WTO an inescapable aspect of future multilateral trade negotiations. As the Final Declaration of the WTO's 1998 Ministerial Conference, the organisation's executive body, concluded: 'We recognize the importance of enhancing public understanding of the benefits of the multilateral trading system...In this context we will consider how to improve the transparency of WTO operations' (WTO 1998).

Underlying official proposals is a decidedly liberal-reformist impulse (WTO 1998). The emphasis is upon transparency and accountability through existing national mechanisms. National parliaments and assemblies are invited, if not expected, to acquire a stronger role in monitoring the activities and decisions of the organisation. But such empowerment does not extend to the agencies of transnational civil society. Representation tends to fall short of actually empowering civil society actors insofar as they would be restricted to consultative status in the decision-making process and have no voting rights or rights to contest the decisions of Trade Dispute Panels.

Contemporary thinking, as reflected in US proposals for the reform of the WTO and the Commission on Global Governance, is decidedly reformist rather than radical. It is reformist in that it seeks the incremental adaptation of the institutions and practices of the organisation, as opposed to its reconstruction; and reformist also in the sense that while it gives 'peoples' a voice in global governance, it does so without challenging the primacy of states and the most powerful states in particular. Thus, the accountability and legitimacy of institutions like the WTO is ensured 'not only by chains of official responsibility but by the requirement of transparency' (Keohane 1998: 95). A more transparent and representative WTO, however, is not necessarily more democratic.

Transnational republicanism

Whereas democratic intergovernmentalism emphasises the incremental adaptation of the WTO, the republican vision proposes its reconstruction to reflect the principles of direct participation, public deliberation and the right of stakeholders to contest its decisions or actions (Shell 1995; Petit 1997: 185). As Burnheim states, 'Democracy hardly exists at the international level, and it is difficult to see how it could in the context of existing institutions and practices' (Burnheim 1985: 218). The republican vision is therefore concerned with establishing the necessary conditions which will empower those with a direct stake in, and those affected by, the activities of organisations such as the WTO. As Petit describes it, the civic republican ethic informing this vision is one in which governance is regarded as democratic 'to the extent that the people individually and collectively enjoy a permanent possibility of contesting what government decides' (Petit 1997). In this respect it is more concerned to uphold the principle of participation as opposed to representation. As Shell argues, the republican stakeholder concept 'emphasizes direct participation in trade disputes not only by states and businesses, but also by groups that are broadly representative of diverse citizen interests' (Shell 1995).

While advocates of the republican vision do not discount the importance of enhancing the transparency and consultative mechanisms of the WTO, such reforms are conceived as insufficient by themselves to deliver a more accountable and democratic system of global trade governance. What is crucial is that those with a stake in the decisions of the WTO have a voice in the governance of global trade matters 'to the degree that they are materially and directly affected by decisions in that domain' (Burnheim 1985). Moreover, having a voice means 'the active participation of people in decision making, sometimes as representatives of specific interests they themselves have, but often too as the trustees of interests that cannot speak for themselves' (Burnheim 1995). But it is not simply the capacity to participate in WTO decision making which is critical, but also the capacity to contest its decisions through formal mechanisms of rational deliberation. This is an argument also for deliberative democracy as against Keohane's liberal notion of 'voluntary pluralism under conditions of maximum transparency'. The emphasis on direct participation and the contestability of decision making means that the stakeholder vision is a much more radical challenge to the WTO as presently constituted since it is subversive of its existing technocratic ethic and practices.

As the idea of stakeholder democracy has acquired a greater resonance in the politics of democratic societies it will be more difficult for the WTO to ignore it altogether. The USA, and other states, have begun to use the stakeholder discourse in reviewing the future evolution of the WTO. In responding to the absence of any mechanism for citizens to petition the WTO's Trade Dispute Panels, the USA proposed 'that the WTO provide the opportunity for stakeholders to convey their views...to help inform the panels in their deliberations' (Clinton 1998). Of course, this a long way from suggesting that citizens and groups might have the right to contest WTO policy and rule making, but it represents the beginnings of what could be a major shift in thinking about how the WTO's democratic deficit might be redressed. In many respects the stakeholder vision reflects a normative attachment to republican notions of governance in which 'Ultimately, trade policy must come to reflect the trade-offs that citizens make among their needs as members of national communities and as consumers, workers, and investors', and as custodians of the natural environment (Shell 1995).

Despite the 'Battle for Seattle' and the 'anti-globalisation' movement, the direction taken by institutional change will not primarily be determined by the agents of civil society but by the most powerful actors within the WTO itself. In this respect the public commitment of the USA – together with other states, segments of the WTO trade technocracy (including its Director General), and the international business community – to confronting the organisation's legitimacy deficit suggests that the prospects for institutional change are not as bleak as most sceptics presume. Clearly the initial trajectory of reform will not be radical but, as the history of territorial democracy confirms, it will undoubtedly have many unintended and unforeseen consequences and acquire its own dynamic, which in many respects is why it continues to be opposed so forcefully. Given this context, the prospect of representatives of civil society acquiring some formal consultative status in future trade negotiations is probably much greater than the probability of them being granted rights to contest the decisions of the WTOs trade disputes machinery. The future evolution of the WTO is thus most likely to reflect the principles of democratic intergovernmentalism, as opposed to the more radical republican vision.

In conclusion, globalisation is generating a political debate about the necessity, desirability and possibility of transnational democracy and the democratising of global governance. According to the UNDP, the most pressing political challenge today is to 'build a more coherent and more democratic architecture for global governance in the twenty-first century' (UNDP 1999: 97). This is reinforced by Keohane's conclusion that

To be effective in the twenty-first century, modern democracy requires international institutions. In addition, to be consistent with democratic values
these institutions must be accountable to domestic civil society. Combining
global governance with effective democratic accountability will be a major
challenge for scholars and policy makers alike in the years ahead.

(Keohane 1998)

Meeting this challenge requires as a first step the re-imagining of democracy.
This chapter has made a modest contribution to that task in elaborating three
quite different normative imaginings of transnational democracy: democratic
intergovernmentalism, republicanism and cosmopolitanism. Two of these, in
varying degrees, find expression in current deliberations concerning the reform
or transformation of global and regional governance, from the EU to the IMF.
These re-imaginings necessarily warrant sceptical treatment. But idealistic or
utopian as they presently may appear, any scepticism needs to be tempered with
the caution that 'Sound political thought and sound political life will be found
only where [utopia and reality] have their place' (Carr 1981: 10).

Note

1   This chapter developed out of work for two separately published essays on transnational democracy and the WTO (McGrew 1999; McGrew 2002).

References

Archibugi, D. (1995) 'Immanuel Kant, cosmopolitan law and peace', *European Journal of
International Relations* 1(4): 429–56.
Barns, I. (1995) 'Environment, democracy and community', *Environment and Politics* 4(4):
101–33.
Boli, J. and Thomas, G.M. (1999) 'INGOs and the organization of world culture', in J.
Boli and G.M. Thomas (eds), *Constructing World Cultures*, Stanford, CA: Stanford
University Press.
Boli, J., *et al.* (1999) 'National participation in world-polity organization', in J. Boli and
G.M. Thomas (eds), *Constructing World Cultures*, Stanford, CA: Stanford University
Press.
Brown, Chris (1995) 'International political theory and the idea of world community', in K.
Booth and S. Smith, *International Relations Theory Today*, Cambridge, Polity Press: 90–109.
Burbach, R. *et al.* (1997) *Globalization and its Discontents*, London: Pluto Press.
Burnheim, J. (1985) *Is Democracy Possible?* Cambridge: Polity Press.
—— (1995) 'Power-trading and the environment', *Environmental Politics* 4(4): 49–65.
Carr, E.H. (1981) *The Twenty Years Crisis 1919–1939*, London: Papermac.
Castells, M. (1998) *End of the Millennium*, Oxford: Blackwells.
Clark, I. (1999) *Globalization and International Relations Theory*, Oxford: Oxford University Press.
Clinton, W. J. (1998) 'Statement', WTO.
Committee on Governance (1995) *Our Global Neighbourhood*, Oxford: Oxford University
Press.
Connolly, W.E. (1991) 'Democracy and territoriality', *Millenium* 20(3): 463–84.

Cox, R. (1996) 'Globalization, multilateralism and democracy', in R. Cox (ed.), *Approaches to World Order*, Cambridge: Cambridge University Press: 524–37.

Crawford, J. (1994) *Democracy in International Law*, Cambridge: Cambridge University Press.

Dahl, R.A. (1999) 'Can international organizations be democratic?', in I. Shapiro and C. Hacker-Cordon, *Democracy's Edges*, Cambridge: Cambridge University Press, 19–36.

Deudney, D. (1996) 'Binding sovereigns: authorities, structures, and geo-politics in Philadelphian systems', in T. J. Biersteker and C. Weber (eds), *State Sovereignty as Social Construct*, Cambridge: Cambridge University Press, 190–239.

Devetak, R. (1995) 'Incomplete states: theories and practices of statecraft', in J. MacMillan and A. Linklater (eds), *Boundaries in Question*, London: Frances Pinter, 19–39.

Elazar, D.J. (1998) *Constitutionalizing Globalization*, Boston: Rowman and Littlefield.

Elkins, D.J. (1995) *Beyond Sovereignty: Territory and Political Economy in the Twenty-First Century*, Toronto: University of Toronto Press.

Falk, R. (1995) 'Liberalism at the global level: the last of the independent commissions?', *Millennium* 24(3): 563–78.

Görg, C. and J. Hirsch (1998) 'Is international democracy possible?', *Review of International Political Economy 5(4): 585*–615.

Hasenclever, A. *et al.* (1997) *Theories of International Regimes*, Cambridge: Cambridge University Press.

Held, D. (1995) *Democracy and Global Order*, Cambridge: Polity Press.

—— (2000) 'The changing contours of political community', in B. Holden (ed.), *Global Democracy: Key Debates*, London: Routledge.

Held, D. *et al.* (1999) *Global Transformations: Politics, Economics and Culture*, Cambridge: Polity Press.

Hutchings, K. (1999) *International Political Theory*, London: Sage.

Jones, R.J.B. (2000) *The World Turned Upside Down?*, Manchester: Manchester University Press.

Keohane, R.O. (1998) 'International institutions: can interdependence work?', *Foreign Policy* (Spring): 82–96.

Kymlicka, W. (1999) 'Citizenship in an era of globalization', in I. Shapiro and C. Hacker-Cordon (eds), *Democracy's Edges*, Cambridge: Cambridge University Press.

Linklater, A. (1990) *Beyond Realism and Marxism*, London: Macmillan.

—— (1998) *The Transformation of Political Community*, Cambridge: Polity Press.

Matthews, J.T. (1997) 'Power shift', *Foreign Affairs* (January): 50–66.

Mayall, J. (2000) 'Democracy and international society', *International Affairs* 76(1): 61–75.

McGrew, A. (1999) 'The WTO: technocracy or banana republic?', in A. Taylor and C. Thomas (eds), *Global Trade and Global Social Issues*, London: Routledge.

—— (2000) 'Sustainable globalization?', in A. Thomas *et al.* (eds), *Poverty and Development in the New Century*, Oxford: Oxford University Press.

—— (2002) 'Transnational democracy: theories and prospects', in A. Carter and G. Stokes (eds), *Democratic Theory Today*, Cambridge: Polity Press, 269–700.

Miliband, R. (1973) *The State in Capitalist Society*, London: Routledge.

Mitrany, D. (1975a) 'A war-time submission (1941)', in P. Taylor (ed.), *A Functional Theory of Politics*, London: LSE/Martin Robertson.

—— (1975b) 'A working peace system (1943)', in P. Taylor (ed.), *A Functional Theory of Politics*, London: LSE/Martin Robertson.

Mittleman, J.H. (2000) *The Globalization Syndrome*, Princeton, NJ: Princeton University Press.

Morrison, R. (1995) *Ecological Democracy*, Boston: South End Press.

Patomaki, H. (2000) 'Republican public sphere and the governance of globalizing political economy', in M. Lensu and J.-S. Fritz (eds), *Value Pluralism, Normative Theory and International Relations*, London: Macmillan, 160–95.

Petit, P. (1997) *Republicanism – A Theory of Freedom and Government*, Oxford: Oxford University Press.

Potter, D. *et al.* (eds) (1997) *Democratization*, Cambridge: Polity Press.

Qureshi, A.H. (1996) *The WTO – Implementing International Trade Norms*, Manchester: Manchester University Press.

Rosenau, J. (1997) *Along the Domestic-Foreign Frontier*, Cambridge: Cambridge University Press.

Ruggiero, R. (1998) Address to 50th Anniversary Symposium, WTO.

Sandel, M. (1996) *Democracy's Discontent*, Cambridge, MA: Harvard University Press.

Saward, M. (1998) *The Terms of Democracy*, Cambridge: Polity Press.

—— (2000) 'A critique of Held', in B. Holden (ed.), *Global Democracy: Key Debates*, London: Routledge.

Secretary General of the United Nations (2000) *Renewing the United Nations*, New York: United Nations.

Shell, G.R. (1995) 'Trade legalism and international relations theory: an analysis of the WTO', *Duke Law Journal* 44(5): 829–927.

Summers, L. (2000) Statement to the International Monetary and Financial Committee, IMF, 16 April 2000.

Thompson, D. (1999) 'Democratic theory and global society', *The Journal of Political Philosophy* 7(2): 111–25.

UNCTAD (1998) *The Least Developed Countries 1998 Report*, Geneva: UN Conference on Trade and Development.

UNDP (1999) *Globalization with a Human Face – UN Human Development Report 1999*, Oxford: UNDP/Oxford University Press.

Walker, R.B.J. (1991) 'On the spatio-temporal conditions of democratic practice', *Alternatives* 16(2): 243–62.

Wapner, P. (1996) *Environmental Activism and World Civic Politics*, Albany, NY: State University of New York Press.

Weiss, T.G. and Gordenker, L. (eds) (1996) *NGOs, the UN, and Global Governance*, London: Lynne Reiner.

Winner, L. (1977) *Autonomous Technology – Technics out of Control as a Theme in Political Thought*, Boston: MIT Press.

Woods, N. (1999) 'Good governance in international organization', *Global Governance* 5: 39–61.

WTO (1998) Statement to the General Council, 24 April 1998.

9 Holding the middle ground in the transnationalisation process

Kees van der Pijl

This chapter approaches the question of transnational democratic development by analysing the role(s) of the new middle class of technical and managerial *cadre* in the current transnationalisation of capital and society. 'Cadre', from the French, signifies according to *Webster's Dictionary*, 'a nucleus of trained personnel capable of assuming control and of training others'. So the question focused on here is what can we expect for transnational democracy from this key salaried stratum which is developing in the process of directing the integration of the social labour processes characteristic of advanced capitalist society?

My argument is that the transnationalisation process itself, understood as the cross-border integration of bourgeois civil society and driven primarily by the internationalisation of capital, developed in response to the movements of the 1960s and early 1970s for a democratic transformation of capitalist society. These movements – including student, ethnic and gender, as well as workers' movements – despite their variety were all characterised by an attempt to roll back the discipline of capital over society, and, more generally, to reverse the subordination of society to the economy.

The conception of democracy that inspired these movements was above all one of deepening the self-determination of social forces, overcoming alienation, and achieving emancipation from ascriptive, socially encoded forms of segregation and deprivation. This built on the classical bourgeois definition of democracy, which as Görg and Hirsch (1998: 595) note, 'implies the continual contradiction between political democracy and capitalist relations of property' (see also Hirsch in this volume).

The framework in which the various segments of the 1960s/1970s democratic movements were advancing was the national state, even if the themes around which they mobilised were often international in character, such as the war in Vietnam. However, the ruling classes of the West were increasingly challenged in a national context, and transnationalisation was one aspect of redefining the political-economic terrain to their advantage. In the process, democracy, in its restricted elitist form of 'polyarchy' – the functional-institutional political complement of the capitalist social order (and the second of four meanings of 'democracy' distinguished by Görg and Hirsch (1998)) – was turned into one vector of projecting the West's power over the globe (Robinson 1996).

Intellectuals played key roles in the debates over the potential and limits of democracy. But the class struggles of the closing third of the twentieth century saw 'intellectuals' on many more fronts than simply as thinkers for, or leaders of, political movements. As I will argue below, capitalist development itself generates, under the veil of marketisation and commodification, an objective, structural interdependence of labour processes which Marx calls *Vergesellschaftung*, socialisation. This process brings into being a class of professional intermediaries who are 'intellectuals' because they are functionally necessary for the management of complex labour processes under the discipline of capital; for the provision of qualified workers capable of performing these processes; and for upholding the legitimacy of an order in which collective labour remains subordinate to private gain. These, then, are the 'trained personnel capable of assuming control and of training others', the cadre.

The presence in the social structure of this salaried cadre stratum turns the imposition of capitalist discipline into a *mediated* activity, and mediation implies a greater sensitivity to the resistance to capitalist discipline. In that sense, the cadre, and the various fractions into which they dissolve and realign, constitute a key sector in the arena where struggles over the deepening and widening of capitalist discipline are fought.

In the movements for democratic transformation of the 1960s and 1970s, which developed first as a radical quest for social autonomy and emancipation, and then, in mediated form, as a reformist drive in a statist framework, the cadres have held 'the middle ground'. They were active not only in absorbing the initial democratic thrust but also in its eventual reversal and transcendence by transnationalisation. In all these different phases, the cadre represented a modulating structure by which pressures from capital and from labour were translated into broader conceptions of the 'general interest', or 'comprehensive concepts of control', while adding the functional concern for social cohesion which is a basic characteristic of the cadre mind.

In the first section of this chapter, I describe how in the 1970s the democratic movements of the previous decade converged on two broad axes of 'reformist' social-political transformation: one seeking to deepen democracy within the national framework, the other striving for international equitability in a New International Economic Order (NIEO). Both were typically state-centric. In the second section, I analyse how the technical and managerial cadre were at first involved in this state-centric drift, but then (in a different 'line-up') became involved in the reimposition of capitalist discipline in the subsequent period which was dominated by neo-liberal transnationalism. Here I will distinguish three new 'transnational' fractions of the cadre: firstly, business services cadre such as management consultants; secondly, cadre associated with the 'internationalising of the state'; and thirdly, those operating through transnational non-governmental organisations (NGOs). Finally, in the third section, I look briefly at the prospects for transnational democracy, the factors influencing it, and the democratic potential of the new cadre, particularly as seen in terms of the 'Third Way' social democracy.

State centrality and democracy in the corporate liberal order

Western capitalist society as it evolved in the first post-war decades was structured by what I call 'corporate liberalism'. This format of capitalist discipline was upheld by a class configuration broadly committed to a productivist compromise between capital and labour, with Keynesian 'demand management' as its mode of regulation. It articulated the requirements of 'Fordist' mass production, such as the mobilisation of a semi-skilled labour force and the provision of social services to sustain its reproduction, within the hegemony of a forward-looking bloc of industrial capital and state managers.

The configuration of social forces making up the capitalist order of corporate liberalism was also held in place by the Cold War with the Soviet bloc. The Cold War worked to narrowly circumscribe the terrain of legitimate political expression, reducing democracy to its polyarchic mode; an elitist and non-participatory system. Labour militancy, whether actually or purportedly fomented by communist parties; intellectual dissent from the Cold War line, whether instigated by 'Moscow' or not; and more broadly, any failure to honour the 'limits of the possible' drawn by the corporate liberal concept of control, were all effectively discredited. This put the democratic movements in advanced capitalist society (especially the labour movement and the liberal intelligentsia) on the defensive by robbing them of their time-honoured modes of expression and organisation which often dated from the mid-nineteenth century.

The essential class compromises by which corporate liberalism was sustained oriented all the main social forces to the national state. In the 1930s, amid intense class struggles, states in the capitalist heartland had imposed controls on the circuit of money capital, which in combination with productive investment constitutes the hinge of capitalist discipline over the real economy. Banks, historically associated with transnational business activity *par excellence*, were placed under state tutelage in the New Deal in the USA and in various coutries in Europe in the same period. According to the recipe of the 'euthanasia of the *rentier*' offered by Keynes in his *General Theory*, the liberty to invest was effectively removed from the hitherto pivotal private investor/investment bank nexus. Investment became subject to counter-cyclical, 'stop-go' economic policy which tried to adjust it to the circuit of productive capital and the reproduction conditions of the labour force, such as education and welfare. Hence credit cycles, under close state monitoring, not only were 'partially independent of the industrial cycle', but were also 'national' and – until 1974–5 – 'rather de-synchronized internationally' (Mandel 1980: 12).

Another, related aspect of corporate liberal capitalism was the collective organisation of social reproduction (for example, education and the provision of social protection against unemployment, disease and old age) by welfare state arrangements. The highly varied ways in which this was achieved – by de-commodifying the sphere of social reproduction, tying it to the state or to occupational category, or leaving it to market forces – also worked to differentiate states from each other (Esping-Andersen 1990: 35, 70–1).

Within this roughly-sketched corporate liberal order, progressive leftwing forces were able to recapture their historic initiative in the course of the 1960s. This development had three aspects:

- the exhaustion of the industrial labour reserve hidden on the land and in the household, which upset the central balance of class forces in corporate liberalism in favour of the working class;
- the lessening of international tension between East and West, which defused the threat of war but also dramatically opened up new spaces of political expression outside the Cold War consensus (on both sides);
- the acceleration of de-colonisation, both from outright Western neo-colonialism as in Vietnam, and from structures of unequal exchange which had been upheld by the West through protectionism and privileged access for multinational corporations.

In each of these developments, the 'middle ground', that is, the pivotal central terrain occupied by the cadre in the capitalist heartland, was crucially affected and contested. Let us first look more closely at the processes of social tranformation that evolved under the impetus of class and international struggles from the 1960s onwards.

Socialisation of labour and democratic potential in corporate liberalism

The domestic Cold War consensus took its (narrow) definition of 'democracy' from Schumpeter, who in turn summed up the conclusions in this respect of the conservative elitist authors close to Italian fascism such as Pareto, Michels and Mosca. To Schumpeter and his predecessors, in order to speak of 'democracy' it is enough that people are offered, at regular intervals, the choice between different government alternatives (Robinson 1996: 50–1). This line of thinking, rooted in a rejection of the aspirations of the ascendant labour movement, and also in opposition to Marx, sought to radically divorce the process of popular involvement in the state from the transformation of society itself. In a sense, this assumes that such a transformation of society represents a real possibility, and is not, as is often claimed by these same conservative writers, an illusion (because of 'human nature' or other constraints such as Michels's 'iron law of oligarchy').

Marx's writings actually do contain a positive, and realistic, theory of the transformation of capitalist society which is not the theory of immiseration and collapse often referred to. Rather, along with commodification and the atomisation of market society into its separate elements, Marx observes a parallel, if still surreptitious and creeping, reintegration of parcellised labour processes which he labels socialisation, *Vergesellschaftung*. Indeed, capital as such is already a form of transcending the market. Once a particular capital has renewed itself over several cycles of accumulation, it comes to represent past and present labour under a unified direction. The totality of capitalist firms ('collective capital') represents such a unity as well, even if at this level the unity is mediated and governed by competition in markets. Therefore, collective capital is not simply the expression of society's stock of productive capacity, but represents a force distinct from the actual labour processes conducted under its control. It is a *discipline* which is imposed, increasingly, on society at large (Marx 1973: 415; for a discussion, see van der Pijl 1998: Ch. 1). The increasing scale of industrial enterprise dictates planned reintegration of divided labour directly, while at the level of collective capital, processes of unequal growth and the combination of property (with the concentration/centralisation of capital), and even socialisation of capital (for example, through the joint stock corporation), all work towards a qualitatively different relation between economy and society in which the capacity to subject the overall (re)productive process to political control gradually matures.

In the course of the socialisation of the material labour process across the economy, the workers by their common subordination to capital are welded together into what Marx in *Capital* (vol. III) calls 'the collective worker'. Both at the individual plant level and in the overall economy, the unity of technical expertise, planning functions and the actual machine/manual labour process no longer require the command of outside holders of titles to property to be able to operate. In this aspect Marx discerns the positive side of what he calls the transition to an 'associated mode of production'.

The second aspect of this transformation flows from the growth of capital creating vast financial enterprises of which the joint stock company is an example. The particular form of this type of corporation, and its dependence on the stock market and credit, fosters the separation of profit considerations from the business efficiency calculus which in an earlier age was still positively connected to them. Eventually, autonomised finance is destined to submerge in a sea of speculative piracy and swindle. This, Marx argues, is the *negative* side of the transition to the 'associated mode of production', because at some point, society through the state has to intervene to save current production from the disruptive capital flows undermining its foundations (*Marx-Engels Werke* 1956–, vol. 25: 454–6).

Elsewhere, the question of revolution is placed in a transnational perspective. Thus Marx argues, in *The Class Struggle in France (1848 to 1850)*, that the probability of the outbreak of revolution on the perimeter of advanced capitalist society is greatest because political authority there is more fragile and precarious, and the mechanisms for equilibration are weaker (*Marx-Engels Werke* 1956–, vol. 7: 97). But *if* the tremors of such a peripheral landslide reach the heartlands of developed capital, the real transformation will always depend on the maturity of the infrastructure for the associated mode of production – the 'collective worker' – while the financial crisis constitutes a critical factor in bringing society to recognise in the associated mode a viable alternative to a decadent order. With that intervention, the possibility emerges of overcoming the separation between 'politics' and 'economics' and making people citizens also in terms of economic democracy.

This scenario, then, may be seen to have come close to realisation in the late 1960s and early 1970s. Against the background of national liberation struggles in the Third World, the labour process in developed capitalism became more and more characterised by forms of work that straddled the divide between mental and manual labour on which previously shop-floor discipline had often been based. The 'new workers' as they were often termed (by authors such as Serge Mallet and Frank Deppe) also no longer seemed content with trade union representation but claimed self-determination and direct participation. In addition, the first generation of students born post-war were keenly aware of their future role as cadre. Well before the May 1968 movement would turn this into a key topic, they had begun to reflect on the notion of the 'collective worker', its elaboration by Marx, and its relevance for their own prospective function in society, including the need to transcend the historic divide between mental and manual labour (see documents in Fisera 1978). Also, a tight labour market across the entire capitalist heartland reinforced the shop-floor power of the workers. Labour militancy, in combination with the mounting movement contesting America's war in Vietnam, the black liberation struggles, student revolts, and so on, was interpreted at the time as a loss of collective self-restraint due to the erosion of market discipline. In continental Europe, where protective state intervention combined with socialisation to give a degree of de-commodification of the economy unknown in the Anglo-Saxon countries, protests were seen more particularly 'as signs of an incipient social transformation – the beginning of the transition from capitalism to socialism' (Piore and Sabel 1984: 169; see also Esping-Andersen 1990). Trade union cadres often found themselves sidelined by autonomous workplace organisation, and unions had to respond with intermediate forms such as shop stewards in order to retain their presence. Whether the crisis of the capitalist world's key currencies, the pound and the dollar, can be considered a financial crisis in the sense of Marx's analysis in *Capital* may be left aside here.

When the movements assumed more stable forms in the 1970s, this also coincided with the restoration of parliamentary, representative politics as the primary channel of democratic expression. Burying its Cold War cleavages, the traditional Left, in an attempt to accommodate, absorb and contain the demands raised in the social movements rocking the Atlantic world (as well as the most advanced state-socialist European countries such as Czechoslovakia and Yugoslavia), itself moved to the Left. The *Unidad Popular* experience in Chile played a double role here: first, because of the appeal of a parliamentary, yet overtly socialist strategy that seemed to be working; secondly, when workers' parties became more cautious after the strangling of the Allende government in 1973. Even if this did not happen everywhere as promptly as in Berlinguer's enunciation of the 'Historic Compromise' strategy of the Italian Communist Party, the element of intimidation worked on a broader front.

The social class aspect that underlay the drift towards the unity and advance of the Left in the 1970s, notably highlighted in the *Programme Commun* between socialists, communists and radicals in France, was the broadening of the actual cadre stratum by the radical students entering the job market. Certainly the metamorphosis of 'revolutionary student' to 'manager' was not always as spectacular as, for instance, in Japan. But as a consequence of the sheer size of the post-war baby boom in the demographic structure, the transformation of 1960s, 'revolutionary student' to, notably, public sector employee did have a qualitative impact across the advanced capitalist heartland. In Western Europe between 1971 and 1982, the non-profit state sector's share in salaried employment expanded from 22.6 per cent to 26.2 per cent of all wage labour (in nine EU countries; Hagelstange 1988: 366). In Denmark (where it expanded from 26 per cent to 39 per cent), the UK (28 per cent to 32 per cent), and Belgium (23 per cent to 29 per cent) the trend was even more pronounced (Hagelstange 1988: 364–5), though in Canada and the USA there was no comparable growth on this dimension.

Subject to various forms of social privilege specifically designed for the new middle classes, such as occupationally segregated welfare state arrangements (Esping-Andersen 1990: 31–2), the mental habitus of the young cadre could not but shift towards more circumscribed, managerial notions of social progress. The new Left unity phase, in contrast to the spontaneous 1960s movements, was empirically marked by a definite cadre presence – even where one would expect, as in the assault on southern European fascism or in Latin America, that the class structure would still favour a more markedly working-class movement advancing in its own right (Holman 1987–8; Eßer 1979).

Given the structural characteristics of corporate liberalism which then prevailed, and the growth of public sector employment, the offensive was emphatically undertaken in the context of national states. Thus the theme of direct self-determination by labour in the 1970s ceded pride of place to nationalisation of industry (see *Collectif* 1971, vol. 2: Ch. 10). True, the aim of nationalisation is to redress the balance between 'economy' and 'society' in favour of the latter, but the appropriation by the state of assets otherwise outside its control is done *for* society, rather than *by* social forces directly. This highlights the mediated nature of the democratic demands of the 1970s compared to those of the late 1960s which had expressly targeted alienation. This time, democracy was more narrowly defined as 'advanced democracy' (as it was called in the French case) where left-wing parties took care to inscribe themselves in the (national) democratic tradition. 'Eurocommunism' is one development which testifies to this in spite of its misleading 'Euro' label (Kriegel (1977), even speaks of the 'national-communist temptation'). The parliamentary-representative credentials of the German Social Democrats (SPD) were of course never in doubt (though its youth wing was under suspicion), but Willy Brandt's slogan 'daring more democracy' caused concern. Also, among the SPD leaders, Brandt was considered the most nation-state-oriented (Braunmühl 1973).

Even though the theme of a straight synthesis between mental and manual labour discernable in the 1960s movements was transformed into a state/cadre-mediated advance, the advance was real. For the first time since the Popular Front episodes in the 1930s, the united Left was on the offensive, this time not in an essentially defensive deployment against ascendant fascism. The Left unity or

'Historic Compromise' potential for deepening democracy was also greater than in the disparate 1960s movements *because* it aimed at the national state, which as a consequence of corporate liberal regulation had developed a vast array of levers for controlling the economy, in addition to its historical control of the means of coercion.

The statist drift on many fronts seemed close to tilting the balance against capitalist control of the world economy. As Stephen Krasner notes, the de-colonised world in its New International (NIEO) platform took what it inherited from the West – the state itself and international organisation on the basis of state sovereignty – and turned this inheritance against the former colonial or neo-colonial rulers (Krasner 1985: 124). Against the background of Cold War détente, there further emerged a pattern of long-term planning agreements between Western states and the Soviet bloc, as well as with oil producers in the OPEC cartel. Hence it would appear as if the de-commodification of socialised production and reproduction that increasingly had come to characterise the national economies of the capitalist heartland, notably in Europe, was spilling over to the international sphere. Codes of conduct for multinational corpora-tions, coming on top of actual nationalisations, further reinforced the tendency towards an expressly political world economy in which bargaining and conscious direction were challenging the sovereignty of capital (van der Pijl 1993).

It is important to see that in themselves, both détente and the drive towards a NIEO were instances of potential social democracy, and also of an actual democratisation of international relations. They certainly reverberated among segments of the cadre in the developed world which had often been closely involved in (aspects) of both détente and the various NIEO projects from the start (Cox 1979; Braunmühl 1973). The international reform movement was rooted in a consensus on the need for greater equality in the world economy, long-term stabilisation of international relations, consolidation of borders and the outlawing of war. All of these tendencies are progressive if measured on a development path towards greater democracy. Of course one may object (and the far Left at the time did object) that in the short term, repressive regimes would also profit from the benefits yielded by détente and the NIEO. But even then, with their economies bound to benefit, it is hard to imagine that, domesti-cally, repression would not be relaxed because the population would develop new aspirations, and the means for the flexible equalisation of material benefits would increase.

At this point, strong counter-forces were beginning to make themselves felt, obtaining an initial focus, and scoring their first triumph, in Chile. The paramount 'think tank' to emerge from the conservative backlash taking shape in the United States, the Heritage Foundation, in one of its first publications, launched a virulent attack on the NIEO platform (Feulner 1976). The statist framework of the NIEO drive was specifically identified as a threat to democ-racy. In the words of the US ambassador to the UN, Daniel Patrick Moynihan (quoted in Feulner 1976: 63), the NIEO rested on 'the idea of the all encom-passing state, a state which had no provision for the liberties of individuals'. In a more scholarly vein, Michel Crozier, Samuel Huntington and Joji Watanuki in their report to the Trilateral Commission entitled *The Crisis of Democracy*, argued that the demand load placed on the state exceeded its capacity to accommodate it, and they accordingly recommended its curtailment (Crozier *et al.* 1975; see also Robinson 1996: 68–9).

As two Soviet authors noted at the time, when these counter-forces were beginning to make their impact

> The movement of social protest in the 1960s contributed to the broad incul-
> cation into the consciousness of Americans of the ideological thesis
> according to which true and consistent democracy in social-political life is
> possible only as the limitation or even negation of capitalism. On the
> contrary, a number of previous [liberals] in the middle 1970s formulated the
> opposite thesis: 'true', i.e., 'rationally organized', capitalism is possible only
> as the restriction of democracy.
>
> (Zamoshkin and Melvil 1982: 225)

Cadres in the shift to transnational neo-liberalism

All management strategies of capital centre on the question of how to deal with the objective, inescapable given of the progressive socialisation of labour, *Vergesellschaftung*. How should the reality of the deepening social format of work, the ever-growing dependence of labour processes on each other, on an ever-widening scale and across the world economy, remain subordinated to private capital control? How, in other words, can the reality of social production remain encapsulated within the commodity form; how can the discipline of capital retain priority over technical equations that flow from the material process of production?

It is here that the role of the cadre assumes a particular centrality. As a separate stratum, the cadre have emerged to deal with the problem of integrating the objectively interdependent social labour processes, but, as I indicated, it does so as a class of mediators, entrusted with the imposition of the discipline of capital in specific spheres. Firstly, it mediates the actual class relation between capital and labour; and it does this as representatives of capital (management) and of labour (trade union officials). Secondly, it upholds the structure of mediation itself, that is, the public sphere, including that of politics, as a separate level of interest articulation in capitalist society. At this level, the direct clash of 'corporate' interests between different categories of economic subjects is transcended and metamorphosed into a struggle between rival conceptions of the supposed 'general interest' and comprehensive concepts of control (Holman 1996: 22–3).

The political struggle over rival concept of control presumes generic processes of alienation which involve education, the public sphere generally, and citizenship in the state. Martin Shaw even defines civil society as such, as the 'sphere of broad cultural, ideological and political *representation* of society' (Shaw 1996: 12, my emphasis), which harks back to the original Marxist interpretation of bourgeois civil society as an alienated form of human community. However, whether we use the terms 'alienation', 'mediation' or 'representation', the category of people entrusted with it – the cadre – also clearly occupies a central position in the current practice of democracy. Basically, the role of the cadres vacillates between being part of the forces imposing the discipline of capital, and being part of the 'collective worker', as mental labour. The former is their 'normal' condition, the latter a potential one – and, as I indicated above in the discussion of the 1970s, a potentially revolutionary one. This is why in capitalism there is not only the problem of continually having to renew or reproduce the subordination of socialised labour to commodification and private capital accumulation. There is also a parallel problem of having to renew the subordination to capital of the cadres themselves, as the social stratum which grows with the advance of the socialisation of labour, or *Vergesellschaftung*.

However, there is also an inherent limit to the capacity of the cadre to really become involved in a transformation of society. To the extent that alienation constitutes the structural precondition for the separation of cadre functions from the totality of the social labour process, it is hard to see how the attainment of social self-determination can be made compatible with the fact that all aspects of people's living and working together (understood in terms of processes and patterns of socialisation of labour, including the socialisation of *re*production) are handled not by themselves, but are held and managed *for them* by a separate class of specialised functionaries. Hence, the cadres functionally speaking would seem more disposed to the more limited, conservative, twentieth-century definition of democracy than to its early bourgeois interpretation which had implications of social transformation when the bourgeoise was not yet securely established as the dominant class in society. Only when the social privileges that segregate the cadre from the working class as a whole lose their meaning – as they did in the generational shift of the 1960s, or as may happen in a severe economic crisis, a war, or ecological catastrophe – can the cadre as such dissolve and merge into the collective 'proletarian' subject of a revolutionary transformation of society.

Otherwise, the cadre are a mediating stratum within the broader class configuration structured by capital and are shaped by the general conjuncture of class struggles which can push them either way. Thus the continuous dissolution and realignment of fractions, through which the unity of every social class develops under capitalist conditions, may gravitate towards a more lenient, 'progressive' configuration under the impact of a strong labour movement, as happened in the early 1970s. By drawing elements of the capitalist class and a certain segment of the cadre (notably the corporate managerial, trade union, and welfare state fractions) into a common front, the demands of the working classes could be accommodated 'economically', both in the sense of neutralising political demands and doing it piecemeal.

In the 1980s, the reorientation of the capitalist class was inspired by the ideological revanchism of Thatcher and Reagan. The transnationalisation of finance and production, placed under a new discipline after the 1979 monetarist intervention of the US Federal Reserve led by Paul Volcker, had the effect of under-mining the state-centred structures of *Vergesellschaftung* on which all democratic progress had been grafted in the preceding period. With it, the cadre which had developed in that specific context (corporate, state, international organisation and trade union bureaucracies) found that they themselves were exposed to a thorough 'rationalisation'. At the same time, however, the new structure of socialisation that was created by transnationalisation propelled forward a new configuration of cadre. The task of adjusting the transnationally distributed nodes of a wider productive structure, of managing the global debt economy, and of imposing the discipline of capital on a global scale using the former two dimensions as levers, was not undertaken only by the owners of capital in person. True, it was one of the characteristics of the neo-liberal onslaught that 'capitalists' again figured prominently and publicly in class struggles (Rupert Murdoch being an example), but the cadre, or more precisely a newly prominent fraction of it, necessarily functioned to provide cohesion to the neo-liberal project as it materialised.

Cadres and capitalist discipline

Until well into the 1970s, the growth of the salaried cadre was mostly of a bureaucratic nature. In the leading capitalist countries, cadre were usually contained within the structures of socialisation they were supposed to manage.

In the United States, the cadre component of the wage-earning workforce remained roughly constant between 1960 and 1986, while the wage-earning segment in the economically active population rose from 80 per cent to nearly 90 per cent (Esping-Andersen 1990: 213; Hagelstange 1988: 113). Within the cate-gory of cadre, the relationship between managers, professionals and technicians seems to have developed markedly in favour of the managers. In 1950, managers accounted for 5 per cent of the workforce as compared to 9.2 per cent who were specialists; but by 1986 this ratio was reversed to 11.5 per cent managers as against 9.7 per cent specialists (Semjenow 1973: 202; Esping-Andersen 1990: 205). Following Esping-Andersen, we may conclude that because the welfare state in the USA is underdeveloped, socialisation (which is an objective process) develops largely in the private sector, and therefore 'the American firm is obliged to exercise control with the aid of armies of supervisory staff' (Esping-Andersen 1990: 203). The growth of overall employment in the branches of the economy in which socialisation is organised as such (the service sector and the state sector) took place primarily in the market service sector: its share of total salaried employment in the USA rose from 39 per cent in 1961 to 50 per cent in 1982 (whereas the share of the *non*-market service sector dropped from 25 per cent to 22 per cent, while the share of total salaried employment accounted for by the state sector, which overlaps with the service sector, stayed constant at 20 per cent (Hagelstange 1988: 370)).

By contrast, in Western Europe the market service sector was also prominent but was smaller than in the USA (employing 36 per cent of the wage labour in the nine EU countries in 1982, up from 29 per cent in 1961), while the non-market service sector share actually rose from 17 per cent to 23 per cent between 1961 and 1982, and the state sector's rose from 20 per cent to 26 per cent, and both of these sectors were proportionately bigger than their US counterparts (Hagelstange 1988: 365–6, 370). Professionals and technicians outnumber managers proper within the cadre in Europe accounting, respectively, for 9.8 per cent as against 5.7 per cent of the workforce in West Germany in 1985; and in Sweden in 1984 by the even bigger margin of 13.4 per cent as against 2.4 per cent (Esping-Andersen 1990: 205).

In Japan, finally, the cadre in 1985 were composed of a segment of managers which made up 5.9 per cent of the economically active population. Professional and technical employees constituted 8.4 per cent, a pattern approximating that of Germany and Sweden, and the 1950s US pattern (Morioka 1989: 170).

But whether organised in corporate bastions or with a more pronounced state bias, and whether professional/technical or managerial cadres predominated, the corporate liberal pattern was characterised by the distribution of relatively closed units of socialised labour (private and public) across a level field. One could picture this as resembling the 'pool table' in the 'billiard ball' metaphor of international relations theory. States, intergovernmental organisations and trade unions still operated as more or less equal partners of capitalist enterprises, certainly equally 'legitimate' partners. The cadre function, broadly speaking, was that of managing/controlling their own units of socialised labour and of conducting 'foreign policy' towards other units. Because other legitimate, qualitatively different, container structures were open to them, even the technical/managerial cadre within capitalist firms were much less subject to capitalist market discipline than we would expect today. Political discipline (on all categories of cadre) is always a functional necessity for a capitalist society, but the discipline of capital for cadre was based on what we may term, using Marx's distinction in the unpublished sixth chapter of *Capital* (1976: 191–223), *formal*, as contrasted with *real*, subordination to capital.

The *formal* subordination of cadre (as of other wage labour) is the consequence of the labour contract. It was established once functions which used to be performed either by the capitalist himself, or by self-employed professionals such as lawyers, architects and engineers (who constituted the 'notables' in the old middle class), became the province of a salaried stratum of specialists. In itself, this was a change of momentous consequence, because from that moment on, manual and mental labour would be placed in the same type of relationship to capital (Sohn-Rethel 1973). As corporate liberalism matured, however, capitalist firms got bigger and management became more powerful, but the actual workings of collective capital as a force maximising and equalising profits by the competitive quest for unpaid labour was almost crowded out by bureaucratic bargaining practices between capitalist firms, the states on which they relied (and which they tried to manipulate in turn), the trade unions, and various types of intergovernmental organisations. Within their own domain, corporate managers were hardly more 'capitalistic' than state managers or trade union cadres. As late as 1987, the members of all the management boards of the 200 biggest US corporations owned a mere one-thousandth of their combined share capital (Wildenberg 1990: 58). There had been a substantial de-commodification of exchanges within sprawling corporate empires through administered prices, with self-financing bypassing the capital market, and other characteristics belonging to a common complex along with inflation, Keynesian deficit financing, and de-commodified welfare state arrangements.

This is one reason why the statist drift of the 1970s could assume such vast proportions. In 1977, a president of Atlantic Richfield advocated a planned economy in the February issue of *Fortune*, only one of many examples of what Krasner (1985: 5) calls the drift towards 'authoritative' instead of 'market alloca-tion'.

Real subordination of labour to capital occurs when labour power no longer enjoys the protection of de- or pre-commodified social reproduction, and all aspects of the reproduction of its labour power have become part of circuits of capital. For industrial labour, corporate liberalism implied, in its Fordist mode of regulation, *real* subordination to capital. In principle, all the elements entering into the reproduction of labour power were being produced under capitalist conditions. However, the bureaucratic structures of corporate liberalism retained a degree of social protection from harsh market discipline again by de-commodification. The cadres were even more exempt from this discipline.

In this perspective, the liberalisation of money capital flows and the resurrec-tion of the *rentier* active in stock and other capital markets had the effect of prying open the hitherto closed bureaucratic structures of states, of international quasi-state organisations, of trade unions, and of corporations themselves. Neo-liberalism developed as a 'revolt of capital', the (re-)establishment of the sovereignty of capital over the comprehensive process of social production and reproduction. Of course, this attack was also an attack on the actual working class with the aim of raising the rate of exploitation. But it is only if we see the neo-liberal counter-revolution as a process of reimposing the discipline of capital on the structures of socialisation and the cadre which had crystallised in them that the full meaning of globalisation will become evident.

For the cadre, as well as for all other providers of labour, the subordination to capital is now made *real*, as they are increasingly, and in principle without excep-tion, subject to capitalist discipline directly. In the case of the cadre, this implies that the 'exit option' (working for the state, or in any other de-commodified productive or reproductive structure) has been closed off in the sense that this would imply shelter from market discipline. Hence the relative independence of the cadre, like that of the '*formally* subordinated' hired craftsman who brings his own tools to the job (Marx 1976: 220), tends to disappear.

Under neo-liberalism, collective capital moves to destroy all other jurisdictions in the global political economy which hitherto limited its discipline – not unlike what the modern state did when it fully established its sovereignty over its own territory (van der Pijl 1998: 78). The transnational unification of nationally contained and state-monitored circuits of money capital turns the 'world market' from a structure *connecting* separate states and firms on a level field into a structure in which states and firms find themselves *submerged*. For the first time, the capitalist system is clearly assuming the hitherto largely theoretical configuration of 'particular capitals' operating as competitive particles of a collective, global capital.

Thus, there develops a world market for companies; that is, a market in which companies as such are bought and sold. By all kinds of new techniques such as leveraged buy-outs, a whole new kind of capitalist, the dealer in corporations, emerges (Wildenberg 1990). States, too, by giving up their capacity to organise their own national economy by redistribution and the privileging of certain forms of national accumulation, become engaged in a new sort of competition, that of trying to anchor global capital circuits to pools of labour power within their territory (Palan and Abbott 1996: 36–9).

One can imagine the huge consequences for the whole idea of management itself when Kohlberg, Kravis, Roberts & Co.(KKR), the most famous of the 'buy-out boutiques' of the 1980s, with a staff of fifty people, controlled a portfolio of nineteen companies with combined sales higher than General Electric (GE), the fifth largest US corporation (Wildenberg 1990: 89). But the strategy of the two types of business unit is radically different. Whereas GE has grown as a huge corporate-bureaucratic management empire, intimately tied to the state apparatus through its defence business and research, as well as to a web of supplier companies and house banks, and assuming huge responsibilities also in the social sphere, businesses like KKR (founded in 1976) operate by looking at corporations only as 'money-making machines', money which can be obtained by their regular operations, by asset-stripping, or taking companies apart into separate units, selling some of them, and so on. And even if states as territorial containers of human society cannot be subjected to the same draconic treatment, they too are subject to 'asset-stripping'. Thus one may certainly interpret in these terms the secession of the Czech Republic from Czechoslovakia, of Slovenia from Yugoslavia; or, in the capitalist heartlands, the underfunding of education and welfare or other forms of social protection that do not immediately support their 'competitive advantage' (M. Porter, quoted in Palan and Abbott 1996: 38).

In this sense neo-liberal globalisation/transnationalisation works to 'widen the hold of capital over the social labour process' which Marx claims is the precondition for *real* subordination. True, some of the cadre do become capitalists themselves (for example, by management buy-outs). The same happens, under drastically different conditions, in state-socialist countries, where some state managers simply appropriate state and party assets as private property. But otherwise the cadre, robbed of their capacity to secure the conditions of their reproduction as a separate stratum because of the (relative) dismantling of the above-mentioned structures of socialisation, find themselves in a situation where they either are destroyed (as happened to certain segments of the trade union cadre, to parts of the UN system prominent in the NIEO drive, and to the bureaucracies of state-socialist countries), or they are reduced in numbers and placed under a more rigid discipline (corporate management, and bureaucracies in capitalist states). (For an analysis of neo-liberalism as a counter-revolution against the managerial revolution of the 1930s–1950s , see Useem (1989).)

However, as already indicated, even in the new, comprehensive world market of neo-liberal capitalism, processes of *Vergesellschaftung* continue to operate. All talk of 'network society' is in my view little else but an expression of the fact that in spite of the rhetoric about individual entrepreneurs, advanced capital accumulation continues to presume the existence of intricate webs of division of labour which necessarily require forms of unified control, or at least some form of normative unification. Apart from information technology, which is entirely dependent on compatibility, this works in a variety of ways. Thus in some industrial sectors, standard supply agreements linking firms are in the process of changing to a competitive bidding system. New firms have sprung up which, if given the specifications of a certain item, say, a piston, can submit offers from five to ten potential suppliers of that item within half a day. Of course this can only work if the pistons on arriving conform to all standards that may apply to material, form, measurement and delivery conditions. Also, KKR can only buy and sell corporations if what they and their lawyers read in the company's books is subject to standard rules of accountancy, and so on and so forth.

New cadre fractions and transnational socialisation

As a result, several categories of cadre have come to the fore which are specifically entrusted with managing the forms of transnational socialisation that are emerging under the new, globally-enforced discipline of capital. These categories of cadre may have existed before, but only now are they becoming prominent. Their common characteristic is the condition of *real* subordination to capital: a life which is not under the discipline of capital is no longer thinkable.

I distinguish *three* fractions of cadre engaged in (aspects of) transnational *Vergesellschaftung* which are particularly prominent:

First: the broad category of functionaries who fulfill non-state mediation tasks in the new world economy. In a recent study of private international authority (Cutler *et al.* 1999: 10), these are brought together under the very significant heading of 'coordination services firms': multinational law, insurance and management consultancy firms, debt-rating agencies, stock exchanges, and financial clearing houses. This category also includes the propagandists of the neo-classical market gospel, whether they are employed as journalists, business school faculty, or otherwise engaged in upholding the structures of mediation itself, in this case, its ideological dimension. An indication of their presence in the social structure of the capitalist heartland is given by Esping-Andersen's statistics on 'post-industrial occupations' (1990: 206), which show a strong presence of cadre (managerial, professional and technical workers) in the category 'business services', albeit with marked national differences. There is one fuzzy aspect in this category of cadre in that they sometimes use the partnership form, or self-employed status, instead of the wage labour form that was included in the definition of the cadre. However, the spread of self-employment and partnership

status can also be viewed as an instance of the pervasiveness of the capital relation under real subordination, as self-employment has come to lean on a
particular, 'proletarianised' form of independence.

Second: a new category of cadres has emerged along with what Robert Cox
calls the 'internationalising of the state' (Cox 1987: 253ff.). This process involves
the creation of a transnational governance structure which turns states into
'transmission belts' of the requirements of the world market movement of
capital – requirements which are synthesised into policy prescriptions by such
institutions as the IMF, the World Bank, the WTO and so on. States, particularly
through their finance ministries, are bound to conform to these regulations
because they are not simply technical, but express hierarchical relations of power
in the global political economy. The United States, partly because of its seigno-
riage from issuing the world's reserve currency, leads this power configuration at
the state level. It has also pioneered an infrastructure for the promotion of
'polyarchy' abroad, increasingly replacing the traditional military intervention,
or rather, shifting it to the multilateral plane as 'peace keeping' and 'peace
enforcement'. This infrastructure for projecting limited or 'low-intensity' democracy abroad has been analysed by William Robinson (1996) (and see Anderson in
this volume). It is enmeshed, not only with the transnational capitalist class
networks such as the World Economic Forum (the WEF is the source of much of
the 'network society' hype, and is closely associated with the management
consultancy business), but also with the NGO sector.

Third: it is in this sector of non-governmental organisations that the third
category of transnational cadre is to be found. Distinct from class planning
networks like the WEF or Trilateral Commission, NGOs are generally humanitarian, aid and single-issue organisations. Among other developments, they have
evolved into a key channel for providing aid to, or otherwise equilibrating,
peripheral societies in the process of state collapse, often caused by asset privatisation by their own ruling strata, or by the prescriptions of some segment of the
transnational private and public authority structures referred to above. While
NGOs operate across a wide range of issues including environmental ones, those
involved in humanitarian assistance and the monitoring of human rights abroad
have received a boost from the neo-liberal transformation. By 1989, 12 per cent
of aid flows went through NGO channels. Increasingly turned into relays of
their home states, development NGOs from Canada, Germany, Italy,
Scandinavia and the Low Countries had by the end of the 1980s received more
than 70 per cent of their income from official sources, up from around 40 per
cent in 1980, and just 1.5 per cent in 1970 (Biekart 1999: 68). Committed to the
development of 'civil society' (which is usually a misnomer since most target
societies are in a pre-Hobbesian stage in terms of state/society relations), in
practice the NGO cadre are entrusted with handling the consequences of state
breakdown under neo-liberal capitalist discipline. What results from the post-
Cold War collapse of authority is usually civil *war* rather than civil society;
foreign intervention in such wars then again brings in new waves of this category
of cadre. Although not as directly subject to the discipline of capital (though

NGOs occasionally are 'retooled' by management consultancies, as Save the Children Fund was by Boston Consulting; see van der Pijl (1998: 161)), the NGO cadres may be considered, for all their variety of backgrounds, a compensatory, 'soft consultancy' sector ultimately functioning in the same historical movement and mediated normative structure (Shaw 1996: 182; and see Hirsch in this volume).

Cadres, the 'Third Way' and transnational democracy

The question whether the new transnational cadre identified above will contribute to the growth or the decline of democracy in any particular way cannot be answered categorically. As I outlined above, the cadres as mediators develop their orientation under the impact of the main antagonistic forces in the conjuncture of class and international struggles.

The French literature which has explored the cadre phenomenon (Boltanski 1982; Bihr 1989; Duménil and Lévy 1998) does identify certain collective characteristics of the cadre mind, such as a belief in meritocracy, a correspondingly negative attitude towards inherited or otherwise ascriptive privileges, and a fascination with everything supposedly 'rational/modern'. Ultimately, as I have argued elsewhere, these attitudes converge on a functional, 'systems' view of social order which can itself be a function of any particular, larger class configuration and political orientation (van der Pijl 1998: 143–8). The tendency of intellectuals to strive for the complete realisation of abstract utopias (Konrád and Szelényi 1981) in contemporary capitalist society, with its complex structures of socialisation, has practically been reduced to ideological zealotry for the hegemonic concept of control. Here neoclassical economists in neo-liberalism are a case in point (Augelli and Murphy 1997: 33).

Therefore, the political representation of the cadre has gravitated increasingly to the centre of the political spectrum, notably social democracy. The specific articulation of, on the one hand, the subordination to capital, and, on the other, representation of the reality of *Vergesellschaftung*, turns social democracy into the pivotal channel for the political expression of the cadre class position. While in practice cadres have functioned in all thinkable political currents, social democracy (and in the USA, the Democratic Party) constitutes the equivalent in politics of the cadre in society – equally multifaceted and elusive even when it comes to its true political self, but yet holding the middle ground between Left and Right (or, after the collapse of state socialism, between the Right and the non-voting lower classes). As Rudolf Bahro writes:

> Social Democracy in power is the party of the compromise between the layer of specialists susceptible to 'transcendence of the system' and the part of management oriented towards 'system reform', especially in the public sector; although always respecting the limits imposed by the long-term interests of the monopoly bourgeoisie.
>
> (Bahro 1980: 157)

The so-called 'Third Way', which has been propagated by 'New Labour' in Britain and pioneered by Clinton's 'New Democrats' in the United States, may be interpreted in this light as an expression of the transformation from *formal* to *real* subordination of the cadres. One prior moment of transition in this respect occurred in the late 1950s, when social democratic parties across Western Europe adopted new party programmes reflecting the enhanced presence of the cadre in party structures (van der Pijl 1984: 215–20, 1998: 153). The Democratic Party in the USA, already purged of its working-class activists under McCarthyism, went through a parallel transformation during the late 1950s and into the Kennedy/Johnson period (Ferguson and Rogers 1986: 51–2).

The first reorientation towards a cadre profile made it possible, most notably in the case of European social democracy, to transcend its representative role for the working class in a narrow corporative sense. As a result, in the 1970s social democratic parties (and this again holds for the US Democrats too) were much better equipped to accommodate, express and ultimately contain the working class and other social forces pressing for a more radical transformation. The development of southern European social democratic cadre parties in exile (groomed mainly by the West German SPD) in the 1970s and 1980s already heralded a further shift to a new type of party, capable of radically reversing its orientation, from corporatism to neo-liberalism (as the experience of the Spanish Socialist Party in the 1980s testifies (Holman 1996: 80)).

The triumph of neo-liberalism under Thatcher and Reagan, by afflicting historic defeats on the working class as in the British miners' strike, established the new code of normalcy which eventually resulted in the social democratic/ Democratic 'Third Way'. Across the English-speaking heartland – first in New Zealand, then in Australia, the USA and, finally, in Britain – renovated labour parties adopted neo-liberalism as a given, irrespective of the fact that among the population, the electoral potential of a more classical social democratic platform was not exhausted. Indeed in the United States, as Ferguson and Rogers show (1986: Ch. 1), the Democratic Party under the impact of the Democratic Leadership Council (interlocked with the Trilateral Commission and other elite bodies) concluded from the Reagan victory that the New Deal coalition no longer existed, although public opinion proved consistently supportive of social protection. Likewise, following the election of 'New Labour', Samuel Brittan in the *Financial Times* (3–4 May 1997) found on the basis of detailed regional data on voters' economic convictions that 'Labour could have won the election on a much more anti-capitalist platform'.

However, as the balance between capital and labour by all criteria evolved unfavourably for the working class through the 1980s and into the 1990s, the cadre veered along with the neo-liberal reimposition of capitalist discipline. The shift from *formal* to *real* subordination of the cadre is also particularly meaningful here. As John Grahl notes, Thatcher and Reagan and their entourage still considered themselves the architects of a new economic order. They proceeded on the assumption of 'politics in command', and self-consciously made a polit- ical revolution aimed at upgrading the status of capital in society. The 'Third

Way', on the other hand, in true cadre spirit, takes the sovereignty of capital as given (Grahl 1999: 908). It seeks to reorient the 'welfare state' towards a 'work-fare state' by eliminating entitlements and reversing the meaning of 'full employment' from a state guarantee to provide employment according to one's qualifications, to a generalised labour duty; the only remaining state commitment being the provision of those services that will assist 'employability'. Once everybody's participation is ensured, the *outcomes* of the capitalist economy, such as glaring (and growing) income inequalities, are no longer a matter of public concern.

The assumption that the structural characteristics of the world economy are given, which is a consequence of the real subordination of the cadre to capital, fundamentally undermines the democratic options hitherto open to national societies. In what Stephen Gill (1995) calls the 'new constitutionalism', the range of policy choices for any given state is reduced to what the discipline of capital permits. This discipline is communicated by investment behaviour, capital market credit rating, or overt recommendations by the institutions of the global governance structure and the internationalising of the state, such as the IMF and World Bank, the OECD, and so on. But in the case of the 'Third Way', this discipline is entirely internalised; which in fact gives the new constitutionalism its full meaning. For as Ryner (1998: 101) observes, 'a new constitutionalist governance structure would ideally not have to be reproduced through policy action', because the limits of the possible have effectively been naturalised by the comprehensiveness of the concept of control.

The transnationalisation of capital and the globalisation of capitalist discipline in its current thrust and ideological effects have closed off not only the early bourgeois concept of democracy, but also its conservative redefinition as polyarchy, since there are no elections beyond the national state (I will speak of the European Parliament presently). Görg and Hirsch (1998: 596) in this connection distinguish a third definition of democracy, taken from 'new models of "deliberative democracy" which are in essence a response to the state's limited scope for action'. Quoting authorities close to 'Third Way' social democrats such as Anthony Giddens, they describe this type of democracy as a culture of participation for new social actors 'deliberating' over the questions that still can be decided within the limits of the possible set by disciplinary neo-liberalism. Also, participation itself is being widened to include 'life patterns and consumption forms [which] become included in the democratic process and, in turn, are considered as a potential part of the public will-formation processes' (Görg and Hirsch 1998: 596). This, then, would be one meaning of transnational democracy – limited to single-issue concerns such as those represented by transnational NGOs, or even boiling down to intensive consumption as such.

A fourth interpretation of democracy discussed by Görg and Hirsch (1998: 596–7), which they link to concepts of 'network and governance', is also directly congruent with the 'new constitutionalism'. Here the notion of democracy is reduced to a functional concept of 'enlightened cooperation' and 'communal locational optimisation' (their qualifications). This may be considered the ultimate cadre interpretation of democracy under current conditions. The systems perspective of the cadre is well brought out in a quote from F.W. Scharpf's prescription for a neo-corporatist model of conflict resolution in which 'the underlying relations are not those of enemies but represent a form of partnership…through the recognition of basic communal interests or, at the minimum, through empathy for the actual point of view of the other party' (quoted in Görg and Hirsch 1998: 597). Thus the newer forms of democracy more closely attuned to the transnationalisation of capital and the 'new constitutionalism' it has engendered reveal a strong inner relationship with the new categories of cadre that have crystallised in this process. However, as I argued earlier, the cadre necessarily must be responsive to shifts in the overall balance of force between capital and labour.

Limits and contradictions of transnational democracy

Let me conclude this chapter by briefly sketching some events of the 1990s which illustrate how the effects of a shifting balance between capital and labour are registered in the orientations and actions of the cadre.

Paradoxically, the election of 'New Labour' in Britain occurred against the background of a popular upsurge across Europe which also catapulted left-wing coalitions into power in Germany, France and Italy. Unlike the British Labour Party, these social democrats (including the Italian ex-Communists, the PDS) had not yet completed a comparable transformation although they were subject to powerful tendencies in the same direction, notably in Germany. The exception is the Dutch Labour Party, which from 1994 to 2002 led a 'purple' coalition government committed to a neo-liberal platform (also subsequently adopted in Belgium by a comparable coalition of Social Democrats and free-market Liberals).

Blocking the attempts of the Juppé government in France to deepen capitalist discipline on society, a mass protest movement erupted in the winter of 1995–6. As in the cases of a subsequent miners' strike in Germany, popular protest against juridical corruption and moral degradation in Belgium, and continuing popular agitation in Italy over pension rights and related welfare state issues, the French mass movement revealed that the attempt to impose neo-liberal discipline by the conservative parties had reached its limits. But the new Jospin government in France (Socialist–Green–Communist), the Italian multi-party government led by PDS prime minister d'Alema, and the Socialist–Green coalition of Germany (on paper, the first left-wing-only government of Germany since the 1920s), in the face of popular expectations could not simply embark on a continuation of neo-liberalism 'by other means'.

German Finance Minister Oskar Lafontaine, grudgingly admitted into the government by the pro-business SPD Chancellor, Gerhard Schröder, did in fact propose an integral alternative to 'Third Way' neo-liberalism that unified elements already developed by the trade unions, such as the 35-hour working week and other proposals. His project of reducing working hours, creating jobs in the depressed welfare sector, and a package directed at youth (proposed by the

Jospin government at the European summit meeting on employment in Luxemburg in November 1997) was built into a broader intercontinental financial architecture, with fixed exchange rates to be agreed between the US, the EU and Japan.

The Lafontaine project sought to enhance the aspects of social protection and industrial stabilisation of the EU's Economic and Monetary Union (EMU) negotiated at the 1991 Maastricht conference. Although EMU broadly remains within the neo-liberal consensus and certainly represents an instance of 'new constitutionalism', it has the potential to keep a certain distance from an Anglo-Saxon neo-liberalism which reflects the full force of the 'revolt of the capital market' with its stress on short-term profitability and undiluted shareholder returns (see Ryner (1998) for an argument claiming a more fundamental difference).

Lafontaine indeed sought to use this margin to add a modicum of restraint to the exploitation of labour, and to redistribute job opportunities. German and French socialists were remarkably reticent, though, as Lafontaine was bashed in the financial press and subjected to all kinds of abuse and ridicule, notably in the British tabloids of the Murdoch group (who had supported Blair throughout). The *Sun* at one point dubbed Lafontaine 'the most dangerous man in Europe'. The earlier French defeat in the struggle over the presidency of the new European Central Bank is also relevant here because now Lafontaine found himself confronted with the neo-liberal Dutch bank president, Duisenberg, who refused, with barely concealed disdain, to follow Lafontaine's recommendation for lower interest rates in order to trigger new economic activity.

When Lafontaine resigned all his positions (including the SPD chairmanship) in March 1999, France soon became isolated as Chancellor Schröder turned to Britain instead, shifting the emphasis towards the 'Third Way' strategy (Wolf and Dräger 1999: 783). At the Cologne employment summit of the European Council of Heads of Government in June 1999, the 'French' orientation ('a coordinated employment strategy') was safely sandwiched between a commitment to close co-ordination between wage policies and financial and monetary policy on the one hand, and structural reforms to foster competitiveness and the operation of markets on the other (Wolf and Dräger 1999: 783–4). Four days later, Schröder co-signed a manifesto with Blair (Jospin, although invited, refused to sign) redefining the goal of European social democracy as gaining the support of the 'new Centre' for a social democracy of the 'Third Way'. Thus the social democratic cadre in their quest for the cadre vote had also come full circle in Germany.

The ensuing elections for the European Parliament were not only a crippling debacle in terms of voter turnout, but more particularly for the social democrats. As Grahl comments on this first of a longer line of electoral defeats for the 'Third Way', 'the leaders of New Labour and the SPD now got what they deserved – a Right majority in the European Parliament. National elections in the last few years had offered a real chance to give the European project a new direction. This chance was missed' (Grahl 1999: 909).

In one sense, this sums up how the democratic impulse of the 1995–6 social movements was sidelined and the possibility of finding a European focus for it foreclosed. But there was also a second important event which has contributed to this debacle and which I see as having played a key role in the reimposition of neo-liberal discipline on the EMU countries: NATO's war against Yugoslavia over Kosovo. This war, waged under the banner of human rights, falls outside the scope of this chapter. However, by allowing a key element of democracy to serve as an ideological rallying cry for what I cannot but interpret as a forward strategy of NATO towards the Black Sea and beyond, the concept of democracy itself was being perverted. With all three fractions of the new transnational cadre in place, including the 'soft consultancy' NGOs, the Kosovo adventure demonstrates how, when abstracted from the comprehensive political economy of the transnationalisation process, democracy can be turned into its opposite.

Note

This chapter was written anew for the purpose of this collection, but it was inspired by the discussions at the September 1998 Colloquium in Newcastle upon Tyne. I owe a debt in particular to Randall Germain for his stimulating chairmanship of my session, and to Otto Holman for reading the present chapter and offering important suggestions for its revision. Of course, they bear no responsibility for the result.

References

Ali, T. (1999) 'Springtime for NATO', *New Left Review* 234: 62–72.
Augelli, E. and Murphy, C.N. (1997) 'Consciousness, myth and collective action: Gramsci, Sorel and the ethical state', in S. Gill and J.H. Mittelman (eds), *Innovation and Transformation in International Studies*, Cambridge: Cambridge University Press.
Bahro, R. (1980) *Die Alternative*, Reinbek: Rowohlt.
Biekart, K. (1999) *The Politics of Civil Society Building: European Private Aid Agencies and Democratic Transitions in Central America*, Utrecht: International Books.
Bihr, A. (1989) *Entre bourgeoisie et proletariat. L'encadrement capitaliste*, Paris: L'Harmattan.
Boltanski, L. (1982) *Les cadres. La formation d'un groupe social*, Paris: Minuit.
Braunmühl, C. von (1973) *Kalter Krieg und friedliche Koexistenz. Die Aussenpolitik der SPD in der Großen Koalition*, Frankfurt: Suhrkamp.
Collectif (authors' collective from the Central Committee of the French Communist Party and the editors of *Economie et Politique*) (1971) *Le capitalisme monopoliste d'Etat*, 2 vols, Paris: Ed. Sociales.
Cox, R.W. (1979) 'Ideologies and the new international economic order: reflections on some recent literature', *International Organization* 33(2): 257–300.
—— (1987) *Production, Power and World Order. Social Forces in the Making of History*, New York: Columbia University Press.
Crozier, M., Huntington, S.P. and Watanuki, J. (1975) *The Crisis of Democracy*, New York: New York University Press.
Cutler, A.C., Haufler, V. and Porter, T. (eds) (1999) *Private Authority and International Affairs*, Albany, NY: State University of New York Press.
Duménil, G. and Lévy, D. (1998) *Au-delà du capitalisme?*, Paris: Presses Universitaires Françaises.

Esping-Andersen, G. (1990) *The Three Worlds of Welfare Capitalism*, Cambridge: Polity Press.

Eßer, K. (1979) *Lateinamerika. Industrialisierungsstrategien und Entwicklung*, Frankfurt: Suhrkamp.

Ferguson, T. and Rogers, J. (1986) *Right Turn: The Decline of the Democrats and the Future of American Politics*, New York: Hill & Wang.

Feulner, E.J., Jr (1976) *Congress and the New International Economic Order*, Washington, DC: The Heritage Foundation.

Fisera, V. (ed.) (1978) *Writing on the Wall. France, May 1968: A Documentary Anthology*, trans. by a collective directed by the editor, London: Allison & Busby.

Gill, S. (1995) 'The global panopticon? The neoliberal state, economic life, and democratic surveillance', *Alternatives* 20(1): 1–49.

Görg, C. and Hirsch, J. (1998) 'Is international democracy possible?', *Review of International Political Economy* 5(4): 585–615.

Grahl, J. (1999) 'Aufholjagd im Rückwärtsgang', *Blätter für deutsche und internationale Politik* 44(8): 907–10.

Hagelstange, T. (1988) *Die Entwicklung von Klassenstrukturen in der EG und in Nordamerika*, Frankfurt and New York: Campus.

Holman, O. (1987–8) 'Semiperipheral Fordism in southern Europe: the national and international context of socialist-led governments in Spain, Portugal and Greece in historical perspective', *International Journal of Political Economy* 17(4): 11–55.

—— (1996) *Integrating Southern Europe: EC Expansion and the Transnationalization of Spain*, London and New York: Routledge.

Konrád, G. and Szelényi, I. (1981) *Die Intelligenz auf dem Weg zur Klassenmacht*, trans. H.H. Paetzke, Frankfurt: Suhrkamp.

Krasner, S.D. (1985) *Structural Conflict: The Third World Against Global Liberalism*, Los Angeles and London: University of California Press.

Kriegel, A. (1977) *Un autre communisme?*, Paris: Hachette.

Mandel, E. (1980) *The Second Slump: A Marxist Analysis of Recession in the Seventies*, trans. J. Rothschild, London: Verso.

Marx, K. (1973) *Grundrisse*, Introduction and trans. M. Nicolaus, Harmondsworth: Penguin.

—— (1976) *Un chapitre in édit du 'Capital'*, trans. R. Dangeville, Paris: Ed. Générales.

Marx-Engels Werke (1956–), 34 vols, Berlin: Dietz; vols 23–25 are *Capital* vols 1–3.

Morioka, K. (1989) 'Japan', in T. Bottomore and R.J. Brym (eds), *The Capitalist Class: An International Study*, New York and London: Harvester Wheatsheaf.

Palan, R. and Abbott, J. (1996) *State Strategies in the Global Political Economy*, London: Pinter.

Piore, M. and Sabel, C.F. (1984) *The Second Industrial Divide: Possibilities for Prosperity*, New York: Basic Books.

Robinson, W.I. (1996) *Promoting Polyarchy: Globalization, US Intervention, and Hegemony*, Cambridge: Cambridge University Press.

Ryner, M. (1998) 'Maastricht convergence in the social and Christian democratic heartland', *International Journal of Political Economy* 28(2): 85–123.

Semjenow, W.S. (1973) *Kapitalismus und Klassen: Zur Sozialstruktur in der modernen kapitalistischen Gesellschaft*, trans. I. Alex *et al.*, Köln: Pahl-Rugenstein.

Shaw, M. (1996) *Civil Society and Media in Global Crises: Representing Distant Violence*, London and New York: Pinter.

Sohn-Rethel, A. (1973) 'Technische Intelligenz zwischen Kapitalismus und Sozialismus', in R. Vahrenkamp (ed.), *Technologie und Kapital*, Frankfurt: Suhrkamp.

Useem, M. (1989) 'Revolt of the corporate owners and the demobilization of business political action', *Critical Sociology* 16(2/3): 7–26.

van der Pijl, K. (1984) *The Making of an Atlantic Ruling Class*, London: Verso.

—— (1993) 'The sovereignty of capital impaired: social forces and codes of conduct for multinational corporations', in H. Overbeek (ed.), *Restructuring Hegemony in the Global Political Economy: The Rise of Transnational Neo-Liberalism in the 1980s*, London and New York: Routledge.

—— (1998) *Transnational Classes and International Relations*, London and New York: Routledge.

Wildenberg, I.W. (1990) *De revolte van de kapitaalmarkt*, Schoonhoven: Academic Service.

Wolf, F.O. and Dräger, K. (1999) 'Beschäftigungsglamour', *Blätter für deutsche und internationale Politik* 44(7): 782–86.

Zamoshkin, Y.A. and Melvil, A.Y. (1982) 'Between neo-liberalism and neo-conservatism', in E. D'Angelo *et al.* (eds), *Contemporary East European Marxism*, Amsterdam: Gröner.

10 The democratic potential of non-governmental organisations

Joachim Hirsch

Like the closely associated 'civil society' and 'new social movements', 'non-governmental organisations' (NGOs) have recently enjoyed increased attention from both the media and scientific communities. In many ways NGOs have been stylised as bearers of hope for emancipatory social changes, as guarantors of democratic and 'civil society' development. This discourse has become particularly relevant in the current age of globalisation, with its rise in importance of international levels where until recently it was barely possible to speak of democratic relations. Although some disillusionment has crept in, the democratic potential of NGOs is still regarded with high hopes and associated with far-reaching normative attributes and ambitious expectations. Underlying this is the fact that NGOs are well suited to the political projections and the self-legitimation strategies of social scientists who are not only in direct contact with the NGO milieu but are also close to them in socio-cultural terms. Last but not least, the increased scientific and political focus on NGOs has mirrored a fading of belief in the possibility of a more basic societal transformation, intimately connected with the dashing of perhaps inflated political hopes which had been invested in the so-called 'new social movements' (such as a now fragmenting women's movement). This situation has been spurred on by difficulties in political orientation which are traceable to the successful neo-liberal offensive, the collapse of state socialism, and the apparent historical victory of capitalism after 1989. As in the 'civil society' debates at the end of the 1980s, the focus on NGOs can in some ways be considered an expression of political resignation, a resignation to be content with a pragmatic feasibility vis-à-vis the seemingly non-transformable basic structures of existing society (Narr 1991).

As Peter Wahl (1997: 23) correctly noted, NGOs became the 'most overestimated actors in the 1990s'. This situation was rooted not only in a distorted political perspective but also in serious and closely related theoretical weaknesses. The latter centred on an inadequate theorisation of the state which led to distorted perceptions of the relations between 'state' and 'society'. In some respects, research on NGOs has been influenced by, and in turn perpetuates, the theoretical weaknesses which were already present in the 'civil society' debates of the late 1980s. Not least, there is the absence of an adequate guiding framework or a concise analysis of the current transformations of national states and the states system.

The thesis put forward in this chapter is that the 'NGO phenomenon' can only be assessed and evaluated on the basis of a properly grounded state theory and a careful consideration of the features of the neo-liberal globalisation offensive, which have acted as a stimulus for the transformations surrounding states and the states system (Hirsch 1995, 1998; Görg and Hirsch 1998). Here, two interlocking aspects are of particular importance: changes in the modes of political regulation at the national as well as international levels; and structural and functional changes in liberal democracy.

In the first of four main sections, the chapter discusses the revealing problems in defining *non-governmental* organisations. The second section outlines the main structural reasons for the increase in their numbers and prominence. This is related, in the third section, to a re-theorising of 'state' and 'civil society' in the more de-nationalised and internationalised conditions of contemporary globalisation. In the fourth section, the increased importance of NGOs is explained in terms of weaknesses in regulation and legitimation at national and international levels in the 'grey area' between states and the private economy. The chapter concludes on the implications for democratic and emancipatory politics.

What is a 'non-governmental organisation'?

The development of the 'NGO' concept is closely tied to the increase in formal 'private' organisations in the political process at national and international levels. While their existence is not new, NGOs are now found in a wide variety of forms and contexts. Indeed the term 'NGO' has become something of a 'catch-all', a confusing amalgam of 'self-definitions' and 'foreign' attributes, some of them highly charged ideologically, and with analytical and normative elements often mixed up indiscriminately. The idea of *non*-governmental organisation refers, however, to a dialectic that deserves to be treated seriously. To some extent, it signals a specific form of 'state existence' within formally private organisations, or a 'privatisation' of statal structures which are presently undergoing a socio-political transformation. The prefix 'non' points more to a contradictory determination than to a clear position in the socio-political structure, particularly with regard to state apparatuses in national and international spaces. Additionally, the term is used, not as a well-defined label, but in a very loose fashion to cover a variety of very different organisations. The resulting conceptual quagmire is evident in the wide variety of ironical acronyms such as QUANGOs (quasi-non-governmental organisations), or GONGOs (government -organised non-governmental organisations). All this irony seems a reflection of the fact that although NGOs are not often openly established by governments, they nevertheless are generally financed by governments and/or are utilised for their purposes. For example, quite frequently the purpose in establishing an NGO in dependent countries of the capitalist periphery (in more or less independent states) is to obtain and channel international financial aid. The centrality of government holds as well for the ever-growing NGOs in the capitalist metropoles, where it is very doubtful if they could continue to exist in such large numbers without a steady infusion of government subsidies. The question which arises here is, are NGOs essentially 'societal' organisations which stand in contrast to the 'state', or are they elements of a political domination and regulation complex which should be viewed in the Gramscian sense as an 'extended state' (see, for example, Gramsci 1986; Kramer 1975; Anderson 1979)?

According to Wahl (1997: 313), NGOs are often characterised as involving volunteer alliances which are independent of either state or political parties, or as 'private' organisations which do not partake in business profits and are not oriented towards fulfilling the self-interests of their members, as well as being non-exclusive in ethnic, national, religious or gender terms. In fact, however, this normative and quasi-'ideal-typical' construction rarely finds an equivalent in the real world. If we are indeed having to deal analytically with new forms of political regulation at national and international levels, then it is necessary to go beyond such idealised description and develop a more precise conception that allows us to question critically the neglected meaning of 'non-governmental'. If this is not done, 'NGO' easily becomes a meaningless label to which all sorts of attributes can be attached interchangeably. We would do better to limit our use of the term to a very specific type of organisation within a diversified arena of politically active 'private' actors, whose significance has increased as a result of the present transformation of the state apparatus and changed modes of political regulation, particularly at the international level. At any rate, this suggests that the concept will not include everything which is presently congealed in the general usage of the term 'NGO'. Leaning on Wahl's (1997) definition, 'non-governmental organisations' are understood here as formal private arrangements which operate in the political arena at both the national and international levels, and which possess the following characteristics:

- a non-profit orientation;
- a claim to represent or act as advocate on behalf of public or particular interests;
- relative organisational and financial independence vis-à-vis the state and enterprises;
- a measure of professionalism and organisational durability.

The latter characteristics are of particular interest. Because of the importance of organisational durability and self-interest, such as the safeguarding of its own income or the jobs of the individuals employed in the organisation, conflicts may arise with the claim to represent public interests, as well as with the objective of 'financial independence'. After all, NGOs as a rule are not only idealistic advocates or 'moral enterprises', however one chooses to define 'humanitarian interests'; they also have to operate with a certain amount of business-like efficiency and calculation.

These conceptual determinants allow for some (non-exhaustive) demarcations of what we mean by 'NGOs', especially in differentiating them from other 'non-government' institutions, bodies or associations which are also active in the political arena. NGOs may be fairly easily distinguished from the following: private sector enterprises (or 'hybrid' private–public consortiums); diverse types of groups and associations which represent their membership's special interests, such as trade unions and various bodies established by grass-roots initiatives; and many, more diverse or *ad hoc* forms of loosely, temporarily and weakly organised political groupings and projects. What are more difficult to delimit from NGOs, however, are the 'social movements'. They are usually defined by the fact that they do not arise from individual organisations but instead are constituted by complex networks of differentiated actors. NGOs can be, but do not necessarily have to be, part of a social movement. Occasionally they are more or less tightly associated with a movement network, or can be considered as an expression of the organisational infrastructure of a movement. They often arise from larger movements, including from their disintegration (Brand 2000); but they can also stand in opposition to social movements, particularly if these are independent from, or even in conflict with, the established institutional system which incorporates the interconnected NGO structure (see Görg and Hirsch 1998: 606ff.).

Within this conceptual framework, further distinctions are possible. For example, we can draw analytical boundaries between NGOs which are basically regional and national, and those which operate on the international level; between organised membership organisations and those without, or with only a weak, membership base; between those which posess internally more or less democratic structures, and those which do not; and finally, between those which emphasise problem definition, agenda setting and lobbying from those mainly involved in managing and implementing more practical projects, for example, emergency and developmental aid organisations. It must be underlined, however, that the boundaries between these categories are fluid in nature.

Structural reasons for the increased prominence of NGOs

NGOs have existed for quite a long time. A case in point is the Red Cross, established in 1864. What needs explaining, however, is why they have increased in numbers in the recent period, and why they have gained so much relevance, at least in terms of public attention. It may be assumed that the reasons for this are intertwined with a relative 'failure of the state' and the decline of established forms of interest support and representation, as well as a growing differentiation and institutionalisation of social movements (Messner and Nuscheler 1996; Brand and Görg 1998; Brand 2000). This can be viewed in the context of underlying economic, social and political upheaval, which amounts to the implementation of a new accumulation regime and mode of regulation. Part of the globalisation process, it involves the transformation from 'Fordism' to 'post-Fordism' and a related transformation of the system of states with the development of the 'national competition state' (Hirsch 1995; Brand 2000). From this perspective, *three* factors are particularly significant:

Firstly, there is a 'decline' of the traditional social movements, though it must be understood in a differentiated manner. This is especially important in the case of national liberation movements in the capitalist periphery, who were robbed of their material and political basis with the ending of the 'East–West' conflict and the onslaught of the neo-liberal globalisation strategy. Generally we can observe a differentiation and institutionalisation process within the emerging landscape of social movements. The loosely knit connections of social movements have transformed themselves into definitive and partly professionalised organisational forms. This has led to former movement activists searching for and creating new fields of activities and the foundations for their reproduction outside the realm of the state and private sectors. In this light, we can assume that there has been a structural change rather than a 'decline' of the movements. What usually is seen as a 'decline' is the expression of a crisis of extra-parliamentary politics in general, with a shift, for instance, from protest and active resistance to co-operative and participatory political strategies. This larger transformation finds its organisational expression in the NGO.

Secondly, there is the factor of 'globalisation', implying the implementation of new forms of internationalisation of production, based on the liberalisation of goods, services, financial and capital markets, as well as an intensification of cross-border communication, transport and information systems. Within this context, the following tendencies have arisen:

- a reduction of political spaces at the national level;
- an increase in cross-border dangers and problems, with which individual states can no longer deal adequately, or at least not on an individual basis;
- a 'hollowing-out' of liberal democracy and democratic processes, squeezed by the limited scope of individual states and global (world market) forces, leading to
- a deep-seated crisis of representation in the framework of the political institutional structures of individual states.

Thirdly, there is the development of new political content and control/steering problems (Brand 2000). With the increased scientification of politics, protest and resistance have lost some of their meaning vis-à-vis the rise in significance of expert understandings as a condition for political influence, particularly in the area of the environment. Scientifically supported problem definition has become an essential factor in political conflicts. Additionally, political implementation by state bureaucratic organisations has proved to be increasingly inadequate in many fields, for example in the area of development aid. Complex political objectives, especially with regard to systemic societal modernisation and adjustment processes, have only become realisable through co-operation with a collection of multiple state and non-state actors. Owing to the contradictory process of globalisation and regionalisation ('glocalisation'), there has been an increase in the urgency of mediation in political decision making and implementation at various political levels, from the local to the international. Finally, with the erosion of traditional representation mechanisms, political legitimation has become problematic in various ways.

State, civil society and NGOs

If the formation, meaning and effects of the developing NGO system are to be assessed properly, then a clear elaboration of the basic connections to societal and state theory is required. This is, of course, contingent on what is understood by the concepts of 'state' and '(civil) society', as well as how the actual economic, societal and political changes are to be evaluated on this conceptual foundation. Regulation theory and materialist state theory offer an analytical guide, particularly the contributions from the analysis of the state form (the so-called 'state derivation debate'), as well as from Poulantzas and Gramsci (see, for example, Poulantzas 1978; Jessop 1982; Hirsch 1995). The main concepts of these approaches will not be elaborated in detail here, only their premises relevant to the discussion at hand.

Materialist state theory defines the 'particularisation' of the state and the interrelated separation between the 'political' and 'economic', or 'state' and 'civil society', as the underlying and basic feature of bourgeois capitalist society. It is important to note however that the separation cannot be assumed as functional, but is rather a constant object of struggle. 'State' and 'society' are neither independent of each other, nor simply opposing spheres, but are an expression of a contradictory societal unity (see Anderson in this volume). The state, seen as an expression of the structure of capitalist society, is marked by the centralisation of physical coercive force and its formal separation from the societal classes. As an element of the capitalist social relations of production and a prerequisite of its reproduction, it is a class-based state. Yet, the state is not to be treated as a direct instrument of a class. In this sense, the state can neither be understood as a 'person', nor as a subject, nor as a merely rational goal-oriented organisation; it has to be seen rather as a materialisation of social power relations which possesses its own institutional form and dynamic, a 'relative autonomy'. This definition implies that the 'state' embodies a multitude of apparatuses which often operate against each other with different and partly conflictual social and class relations.

Unlike the state as a coercive apparatus, 'civil society' embodies an area of (in relative terms) freely constituted and independent social and political organisations, such as interest associations, political groups, newspapers, radio stations, churches, scientific establishments and research institutes, intellectual circles, and 'think tanks'. Within this organisational network, political concepts and interests are articulated and confronted in the public sphere. This is not to be understood as a domination-free sphere but instead one which is interlaced with economic and political power and structures of dependency. Hence, following Gramsci, the relation between the two spheres is to be understood as a contradictory unity. 'Civil society' is the space where, via public discussion and debates, the dominance of the state becomes legitimised and hegemony produced ('consensus'); while, at the same time, it is the object of statal interventions ('coercive force'). As a political-ideological battlefield, however, it is simultaneously an arena in which alternative hegemonic concepts of societal order and development can be generated. Taken together, 'state' and 'society' create a complex dominant interconnection which is supported by coercion and consensus, a 'hegemonic bloc'. Within this contradiction, civil society may be seen as a part of the 'extended state'.

The existing plurality of the states system – the existence of a multiplicity of national states – is not a random occurrence; rather, it is a basic component of capitalist social relations of production. The divisions within social classes brought about by state borders, and particularly the division of subordinate classes into their 'national' subdivisions, are an essential precondition for the regulation of social relations: they allow the establishment of overarching class compromises within the framework of national states and enable classes and class fractions to be played off against one another. In a sense, the state form reproduces itself vis-à-vis societal structures as a relative autonomous complex of heterogeneous and contradictory apparatuses which extend to the international level (see, for example, Hirsch 1995: 31ff.).

Following Jessop (1997a; see also Görg and Hirsch 1998: 558ff.; Zürn 1998), we can identify three essential tendencies in the contemporary transformation of the state and the states system:

Firstly, there exists a tendency towards a *de-nationalisation of the state*. This does not imply the disappearance of the national state form as such, but rather a loosening of the relations between states and 'nationally' identified societies. It has been brought about by, on the one hand, progressive social heterogeneity caused by marginalisation and fracturing processes, migration and refugee movements, and, on the other hand, by dispersed economic regionalisation processes which have cut across state borders and are associated with a decline in the capacity of states to steer economic development within their own borders.

Secondly, there is a tendency towards a *de-statification of politics*, which is reflected in the increased importance of 'governance', in contrast to 'government', as a political steering mode. Political regulation networks emerge in which the state prefers to act as 'first among equals', as a moderator and co-ordinator of various societal actors, such as transnational corporations, interest groups, and scientific and research establishments, as well as NGOs (Rosenau 1992; Messner and Nuscheler 1996; Messner 1995; Kommission für Weltordnungspolitik 1995; Kenis and Schneider 1997). As an alternative to bureaucratic-legislative steering, informally negotiated procedures have become increasingly important, though they are still based on the existing physical coercive potential of the state. In a sense, the new term 'negotiation state', as currently used in political science (Scharpf 1996), is rather misleading, since these types of political processes are in no way new. But the basis for their increased importance is to be found in the contemporary processes of globalisation, particularly in the reduction of the political possibilities of the state, the greater prominence of powerful 'private' actors, especially transnational corporations, and the necessity, in the context of intensificated competition between states and societies, of mobilising complex societal knowledge and power resources to strengthen 'national competitive capabilities'.

Thirdly, there has been a tendency for an *internationalisation of policy regimes*, resulting from the increasing need for international regulation of the global accumulation processes and their consequences, as well as the increasing region-alisation of global capital, as in the EU. This tendency expresses itself in the growing significance of international and supranational organisations and inter-national regimes (for regime theory see Mayer *et al.* 1993). At the same time, internationalisation also involves an increased relevance of sub-state regional and local political levels ('glocalisation') and wider interconnected co-ordination and negotiation requirements in both a horizontal and vertical sense.

It would, however, be an analytical error to interpret these processes as pointing to an abolition of the difference between 'state' and 'society', or as a general 'weakening' of states (for example, a general 'hollowing out' process) (see Messner 1997). In actuality, what is occurring is a transformation of states and the states system, including a reorganisation of the relations between 'state' and 'society', and a transformation of social and class relations which are institution-alised by the state. The assumption of a 'loss of state sovereignty' emerges from theories within political science which use a limited legal-organisational concept of the state. In doing so, these approaches neglect the fact that the bourgeois state is an expression of social power relations, and thus, in reality, never was nor could be 'sovereign'. Now as before, the state remains the main agent of social cohesion and of redistribution process (Jessop 1997b). The transition to 'network steering' and 'negotiation' strategies can even serve to enlarge the ability of states to mobilise societal resources as 'national competition states'. In some respects, the state may actually increase its significance in the processes of organising society with these strategies (Jessop 1997b). It should also be taken into account that, within these networks, the 'partners' – states, transnational corporations, NGOs and so forth – exhibit extremely unequal relationships in terms of their power and resources.

The basis of this transformation of states and the states system is the transition to a 'post-Fordist' accumulation regime in global terms, and the inter-connected undermining of traditional forms of political regulation by horizontal and vertical fragmentation processes. States react to this situation with a quasi-defensive strategy of self-transformation, with the consequence that they are less able to embody a long-term and coherent concept of 'society' (Bonder *et al* 1993: 339). This includes a progressive loss of democracy in national, international and supranational regulation. As traditional liberal democratic agenda formation and decision-making processes are being replaced and undermined through more or less formalised 'negotiation systems', their democratic meaning is systematically weakened. Seen from this angle, the conditions of accumulation increasingly collide with the state's democratic political legitimation (Taylor 1994: 122ff.). More specifically, the internationalisation of policy regimes often serves to unhinge internal democratic agenda formation and decision-making processes, inducing the 'internalisation' of self-created international constraints (see Streek 1996; Grinspun and Kreklewich 1994).

NGOs have been widely stylised as 'organisations of a global orientated international civil society that possess a vision of a world-citizenry', albeit weakly developed (Messner and Nuschler 1996: 2; see also Habermas 1998). However, the absence of a state theory in the research surrounding NGOs becomes evident here, particularly in the way in which the concepts 'international society' or 'world society' have been construed and applied. The above outline of the transformation processes of the state and states system suggests that there have been considerable consequences for the relationship between 'state' and 'society' both at national and international levels. In terms of international space, there is evidence of an intensification of economic relations (the creation of a real 'world market') as well as the rapid improvement of transportation and communication systems and growth of interconnected technical and cultural homogenisation processes. At the same time, this development is marked by a 'world society' that has become extremely heterogeneous, segmented and fragmented as well as being characterised by highly unequal relations of power, dominance and dependency (see Bonder *et al.* 1993; Görg and Hirsch 1998: 593; Slater 1998). If the notion of 'civil society' is to be grasped as meaning more than a collection of people, organisations and institutions but instead as a formation that is interrelated with the reproduction of a delimited economic system, basic value patterns and a relatively coherent political institutional system, then this definition of society can hardly be applied to the international arena. Following Gramsci's conceptualisation, 'civil society', strictly speaking, can only be understood vis-à-vis coherent political dominance and institutional structures, all of which together create the contradictory unity which Gramsci terms the 'extended state'.

A decisive factor is that the 'state' as proprietor of a relative monopoly of violence cannot exist on an international level under the conditions of capitalist social relations. Therefore, a basic contradiction within current global development has been *the progressive break-up of economic-technical, societal and politico-institutional processes*. Economic globalisation, and all of its effects listed here, has not been accompanied by a corresponding and coherent political structure; rather, it remains determined by the existence of particularised individual states (Görg and Hirsch 1998: 593). Seen from this perspective, it is so far very difficult to apply the term 'world civil society' as analogous to a corresponding concept at the national level. The fact that a corresponding political structure (such as a 'world state') cannot be implemented within (economic) globalisation implies that political decisions tend to be shifted towards opaque negotiation systems with changing actors and levels. The effects of this are a strengthening of exclusionary and marginalisation processes, in the form, for example, of the economic-political disassociation of entire world regions.

In Gramsci, as well as in the classical bourgeois theory of 'civil society' (see Keane 1988), the creation of consensus and hegemony arises within the framework of free organisations in the public arena, which in effect creates the basis of institutionalised political agenda formation and decision-making processes. This presupposes the existence of a centralised state through which decisions may be made within a formally institutionalised system and implemented by the adherence to codified rules. In this way, hegemonic projects become materialised and consolidated. The state transformation processes within economic globalisation have greatly changed the conditions of consensus and hegemony-building as well as political legitimation. This is particularly true at the international level, where various authors, instead of speaking in terms of a 'world civil society', have with good reason opted for the terms 'neo-feudalism' or simply 'structural anarchy' (Görg and Hirsch 1998: 600ff.).

Sometimes, the concept of a 'world civil society' has been closely associated with the gradual emergence of an internationalised strata of capitalists and managers (see van der Pijl in this volume). This (cadre) strata comprises enterprise functionaries, scientists, the personnel of international organisations and parts of state bureaucracies, as well as the manifold 'private' political actors which include NGOs (Cox 1993; Sklair 1997; Demirovic 1997: 257ff.; see also Görg and Hirsch 1998: 591). The assumption here is that this strata essentially contributes to the transformation of the states system through the development of 'a particular form of self-steering technique' and being in a position to implement 'a particular global consensus and state project' (Demirovic 1997: 247). Clearly these types of tendencies do exist. At the same time, however, it must be borne in mind that this group of international managerial elites also remains dependent on and connected with the wider context of state regulations and intensifying competition. Its inner structure remains determined by the economic and social fragmentation processes of globalised capitalism. If, within this context, there exists the possibility of the emergence of a 'world state project', it would first be necessary to explain the conception of the state on which this notion rests. It needs to be stressed that this conception would have very little to do with what is traditionally understood by a bourgeois-capitalist national state. In sum, it is highly problematic to use the concepts of 'state' and 'civil society' at the international level.

NGOs and the weakness of international regulation

The contemporary functions and meaning of NGOs cannot be understood simply by referring to individual organisations and their respective structures and objectives. They can only be understood in the larger context of the 'post-Fordist' restructuring of international regulations. An important starting point for explaining the increased prominence of NGOs is the weaknesses surrounding the processes of regulation and legitimation of the states system which are apparent both at national and international levels.

NGOs mobilise expertise and (scientific) knowledge which the bureaucratic state apparatuses cannot manage; they have a decisive influence on the larger symbolic construction and definition of societal problems and issues; and they thus play a crucial agenda-setting role in political negotiation and decision-making processes. NGOs represent interests which are either neglected or do not find expression within the established institutions (for example, on lobbying, see Brand and Görg 1998: 102; Princen and Finger 1994: 34). They also serve a supervisory function vis-à-vis international negotiation processes (for example, on monitoring, see Brand and Görg 1998: 101). In this sense, NGOs represent a reaction to the crisis of representation which is closely intertwined with the larger 'post-Fordist' transformation of the states system. NGOs take part in a considerable amount of problem and interest mediation between various political levels, such as the local, regional and international, and are thus confronted with manifold actors, including international organisations, states, local initiatives and other NGOs (Brand and Görg 1998: 101; see also Princen and Finger 1994: 38ff.; Brunnengräber and Walk 1997: 71ff.). Last, but not least, NGOs undertake practical work, especially in development, catastrophe and emergency areas, which is not done by state apparatuses because the states are simply not in the position to implement such programmes or tend to 'outsource' them for reasons of legitimation.

In the absence of the possibility of formalised co-operation in political decision-making processes and their usually uncertain and limited financial basis (i.e., their dependency on donations and monetary contributions), *knowledge and publicity* become the NGO's basic resources of power. Knowledge implies scientific-technical expertise as well as familiarity with sectoral and local structures and problems. On this basis, their relations with governments and international organisations are marked by co-operative as well as conflictual relationships in the processes of problem definition, decision making and administrative implementation. However, the decisive power resource of NGOs remains their ability to mobilise the public, which is a precondition for their entrance into the political arena. As such, the struggle for and establishment of publicity constitutes the central terrain of NGO politics (Wapner 1995; Brunnengräber and Walk 1997; Wahl 1997; Brand 2000). In light of the relative weakness of NGOs' material resources, they are dependent on the co-operation of a powerful media industry, which forces them to subjugate their means and objectives to the media's functional mechanisms. In contrast to media-marketed catastrophes, which win over not only a substantial amount of public attention but also large financial contributions, it is very difficult for NGOs to maintain public attention on a long-term basis for unspectacular projects such as development aid. In effect, this issue influences the priority-setting of NGO work, which is visible in the expansion of international NGO 'rescue activities' of recent years. As the example of Greenpeace makes clear, predominately media-oriented 'NGO transnationals' can gain considerable influence over governments and enterprises, but not without paying the price of allowing their objectives to be tactically set by the criteria of media interests.

The diversity and heterogeneity of NGOs has made them an essential factor in compromise and consensus formation, especially at the international level. To a certain extent, this contributes not only to the expansion of interest considerations, but also to the rationalisation of political decisions. All in all, it may be assumed that a new and independent actor has entered the political stage

(Princen and Finger 1994: 41ff; Wapner 1995; Brand 2000), an actor which stands in stark differentiation from other traditional 'civil society' organisations such as political parties and associations, as well as contributing substantially to the 'post-Fordist' transformation of the relations between 'state' and 'society'. What is more, the question of whether NGOs should be seen as a 'civil societal' counterpart of state institutions, or as a component of the 'extended state', can no longer be answered adequately using these traditional concepts. The relationship between NGOs and the state is decisively determined by the fact that NGOs as professional organisations working on a long-term basis are continually dependent on a steady inflow of financial resources, especially in the case of extensive projects which cannot be carried through on the basis of mere donations. Hence, NGOs are dependent on states, statal associations (for example, the European Union), international organisations, and occasionally interest associations and private enterprises. Even if they do not establish and guide NGOs, states as well as international organisations can also take advantage of this dependence through instrumentally using NGOs for their own ends.

Not least, NGOs play a significant role in conflicts and disputes within and between national government apparatuses as well as international organisations. For example, they are used by metropole states as a means of gaining access to the governmental affairs of peripheral countries, and they are positioned by national governments against international organisations, or vice versa (Bruckmaier 1994; Walk 1997; Wahl 1997; Görg and Hirsch 1998: 602ff.). The structural 'state fixation' of NGOs arises not only from financial dependence, but also from the fact that the realisation of their goals is basically dependent on the legislative and executive potential of states (not to mention the goodwill of private enterprises) (Brand 2000). Broadly speaking, their effectiveness depends on the willingness of states to co-operate with them. Thus the possibility of being used for the latter's purposes increases. This is apparent in the fact that the formation of NGOs is strongly tied to 'demand dependency', which suggests it is easier where there are already statal interests in co-operation in the form of information, legitimation or regulation needs (Görg and Hirsch 1998: 602ff.). To this extent, it may be more fruitful to understand NGOs simply as statal 'foreground organisations'. However, this is only one aspect of their role, for NGOs can only fulfill their functions – of interest organisation and interest articulation, of legitimation and knowledge transmission – if they do not become fully part of the state apparatus but instead maintain a certain measure of financial, organisational and political independence.

From this perspective, the function and meaning of NGOs cannot be evaluated within the usual pattern of traditional state–society relations at the national level, or on the basis of traditional 'civil society' concepts. Equally, because an integral state does not exist at the international level, the Gramscian concept of the 'extended state' may only be used in a restricted manner. NGOs are components of a complex international 'governance' system and their effectiveness essentially stems from the 'internationalisation of the state' (Hirsch 2000). It is the heterogeneity, conflict and contradiction of the ensuing international regulation system which represent the 'gateway for strategic invasion' by NGO politics (Brand 2000; see also Wapner 1995; Brand and Görg 1998). This results not least from the conflicts within and between the national states, as well as between the states and international organisations, which in any event can also be utilised by the NGOs (see Gebauer 1998).

In some respects, the personnel of internationally active NGOs can be understood as part of a globally acting functionary and managerial class, which basically share the same fields of work and common behavioural modes, cultural orientations and language codes (see the cadre discussed by van der Pijl in this volume). This commonality becomes a precondition for access to informal as well as formal negotiation and decision-making processes. In this vein, there exists a truly complex web of co-operative and conflictual relations. Thus, it may be assumed that in the attempts to implement their conflictual interests vis-à-vis bureaucracies as well as multinational enterprises, the personnel of international organisations, in like manner, lean upon the NGOs, as do conflicting individual state apparatuses. The upshot of this is the emergence of an 'international ruling class', to use a term of Poulantzas, albeit a ruling class without a central state to which it may refer. This suggests that the internal fragmentation that arises from differing social references, interest orientations and connections with national states can only be weakly smoothed over institutionally. While this complex of internationalised, highly fragmented and heterogeneous governing cadre is emerging, there is the absence of an institutional precondition for the implementation of a coherent political project.

Both in scientific literature and political discussion, there is a basic expectation that NGOs will contribute to civilising and democratising international politics (see, for example, Habermas 1998). An analysis which is rooted in actual emerging structures and processes, however, may come closer to the supposition that while NGOs have indeed become, or at least are beginning to become, an essential component of an international regulatory system, their democratic effects remain highly questionable. Here the decisive question is whether NGOs are mere functional components of the wider regulatory complex, or are they actors with the potential for democratic self-determination and design? If one simply equates 'democracy' with system functionality and the rationality of political process and decision making, as is often done in current theoretical discussions (see Görg and Hirsch 1998: 594ff.), then they are without doubt 'democratic' organisations in this limited sense. Obviously, NGOs do contribute to several broader interest considerations as well as to a rationalisation of problem definition and decision making. This position also remains valid if one understands 'democracy' in the pluralist sense as a system of 'checks and balances' with limited participatory elements. Within such a conceptual framework of democracy, NGOs may be seen as part of an 'international democratic civil society', albeit only when this is narrowly conceived.

However, in contrast to the above understanding, if we see 'democracy' in more far-reaching terms as the realisation of freedom and self-determination, then the case becomes more complicated. NGOs are structurally dependent on bureaucratic state apparatuses at national as well as international levels, and are essentially state-oriented in their political bearings (Wahl 1997; Brand 2000). This considerably limits their ability to develop and follow projects of extensive social change. Furthermore, because of the absence of a corresponding institutional mechanism, their democratic traits of representation and legitimation remain questionable, even though they demonstrate a certain internal organisational democracy and 'basic nearness'. In addition, their role as agents representing subordinate or oppressed interests remains essentially precarious because of the massive organisational self-interest running counter to the needs of those who are afflicted. Nor should it be forgotten that NGOs are quite capable of bringing democratically illegitimate or one-sided partial interests into the political realm. Another point that should be considered here is that up to now the activities of NGOs have generally been restricted to areas of 'soft politics', such as the environment, social security, development and human rights. Largely due to the lack of co-operative interest by states, NGOs have played a rather marginal role with regard to 'hard politics' in such policy areas as economics, technology, security and the military (apart from the remarkable exception of the international landmine campaign; see Gebauer (1998)). It should also be kept in mind that their political possibilities regarding resources, negotiation potential and scope are extraordinarily varied, and especially in the differences between NGOs from the 'North' and the 'South' (Bruckmaier 1994; Demirovic 1997). Within the NGO system there also exists a hierarchy of power in which the majority of the more powerful, usually metropole-based, 'NGO transnationals' have procured considerably more advantages compared with smaller and weaker organisations at local or regional levels (Wahl 1997; Walk 1997). In a sense, the NGO system mirrors the unequal division of power which exists between national states.

Up to now, a narrowly defined thematic specialisation has been an important facet underlying success in international NGO work. However, this condition can also lead to the neglect of overarching problems and interests; and it can result in fragmenting resistance and protest (Demirovic 1997: 256; Wahl 1997). The fact remains that NGOs which operate at the international level are essentially tied to interest mediation and negotiation processes which lack formalised democratic procedures with regard to representation criteria and decision-making rules. While NGOs do indeed provide a venue for the expression of ignored interests and repressed political perspectives, nevertheless this occurs within the framework of a structurally opaque and highly empowered negotiation system, which lacks accountable and transparent decision-making processes and in some ways has become an institutionalised anarchical system of 'sub-politics'. Seen from this angle, NGOs represent a basic element in the 're-feudalisation' of international politics. In essence, NGOs can best be understood as a type of 'catalytic converter for a certain democratisation in the international system' (Wahl 1997: 311). Seen from the wider perspective of the tendency to fragmentation in 'world society', NGOs are something of a 'necessary compensation for democracy' (Görg and Hirsch 1998: 605).

By and large, the increased prominence of NGOs in national and international spaces can best be understood as resulting from 'post-Fordist' neo-liberal restructuring which has led to a substantial transformation of the state and states system, a wide-reaching 'privatisation' of political decision-making and implementation processes, and a fundamental change of the relations between 'state' and 'society'. Related to this is a change in the character of liberal democracy at national state level. There is a growing 'hollowing out' of democratic processes within the national framework, while at the international level, democratic structures are developed either in very weak form, or do not find any institutionalised expression at all. The swelling presence of NGOs may be regarded as an expression of the crisis of the 'Fordist state' and its mode of regulation. In this respect, it is accurate to observe that the increased numbers of NGOs, as well as their strengthened scientific and political perceptions, are aspects of the larger dominant neo-liberal paradigm (Brand and Görg 1998; Wahl 1997). The significance of NGOs and particularly their democratising potential should not be overestimated in the context of present economic and political structures, increased economic and societal fragmentation, and, not least, the still decisive relevance of national states. Nevertheless, NGOs can be viewed as an increasingly important element of the newly emerging system of international regulation. To be sure, they are something more than organisations which are simply situated on 'the margins of globalisation' (Wahl 1997: 295).

Conclusions

When their empirical reality and the context of their political-economic functions are taken into account, it is only in a very restricted sense that NGOs can be seen as elements of a newly emerging democratic system. In a broader perspective, we can view the international NGO scene as a field of activity of professional political managers who derive their political justification from the claim to represent interests and provide material assistance. This is structurally situated in a politically diffuse 'grey area' which lies between states and the private economy. Equally, their roles of representation and legitimation remain necessarily as vague and uncontrollable as their responsibility to members, financial contributors and the general public. Basically, interests committed to the continuance and expansion of the professional organisation generate a dependence on state subsidies and media-mobilised financial donations, and this entails a strong inclination towards political and societal behaviour which is adaptive or accommodating. The existence of an 'NGO transnational', such as Greenpeace, depends on the continuity of environmental 'dangers' and their media exploitation. Because their political mobilisation and organisational potential is rather weak and remains largely within the realm of media mediation, NGOs are primarily dependent on co-operative relations with statal organisations and private enterprises, and this severely limits their scope for action. Seen from this viewpoint, their potential for radical political democratisation and societal change must be assessed sceptically (Wahl 1997; Walk 1997; Demirovic 1997: 256ff.; Brand 2000).

Ultimately, however, the democratic quality of NGOs in general does not depend so much on the goals and functioning of the individual organisations, nor on their internal democratic structures, as on the position and function of the NGO system within the overarching system of international political regulation (Wahl 1997: 313; Görg and Hirsch 1998: 602). Viewed through the lenses of democratic theory, NGOs are merely one set of actors among many; and a set marked by heterogeneity and contradiction. In principle, however, NGOs could play a larger role in the democratic process, but only on condition that they safeguard their material and political autonomy vis-à-vis the states, international organisations and private enterprises. Granted, this is by no means an easy feat. It presupposes that the organisational and functional kernels of NGOs remain independent from financial contributions from states, while at the same time they at least limit their dependence on the media and private industries by mobilising private donations. In concrete terms, this means that there is an imperative for NGOs to lean upon a politically specific and active environment of political movements and initiatives. Political autonomy cannot be achieved by direct mailing and television benefit shows. Rather, it can be accomplished only through informed, wide-ranging and self-critical discussion about the work of NGOs – about, for example, the conditions in which they operate, their difficulties and the reasons for their failures. Only on such a basis could NGOs win some measure of political relevance as a 'countervailing power' which is more than merely symbolic vis-à-vis state apparatuses and private enterprises. Indeed, such a basis is a precondition for developing political perspectives and content which are capable of going beyond the dimensions and forces of the existing system of domination and regulation (Görg and Hirsch 1998). Equally, it is a precondition for entering into the realm of 'hard' politics and thus becoming active within the decisive political areas of the international socio-political order, where co-operative offers and assistance from statal institutions do not exist. With regard to a strategy of emancipatory societal change, there needs to be a fundamental widening of the concept of the 'political' in the sense of emphasising themes such as forms of production, consumption patterns, and gender relations, all of which should be related to the political activation of social learning and the transforming of the dominant consciousness. This requires political orientations and behavioural modes which cannot be reduced to lobbying within established negotiation systems (Princen and Finger 1994: 35; Wapner 1995).

The dependence both on states and international organisations becomes relativised when success occurs in establishing independent co-operative and practical contexts at the NGO level (Princen and Finger 1994: 36; Wapner 1995; Wahl 1997: 313; an important example of this is again the international land-mine campaign, see Gebauer (1998)). This takes place when there is an attempt to make transparent the complex and opaque negotiations occurring within the international system of 'sub-politics' (Princen and Finger 1994: 35). The democratic quality of NGOs is basically shaped by the way relationships are forged with the groups whose interests they claim to articulate and represent. Interests can be formulated and represented and practical help given in such a way that the recipients simply become more dependent and their possibilities for political self-organisation are thoroughly distorted. This is apparent in numerous development and emergency projects. However, NGO work can also explicitly aim to promote self-organisation structures, albeit less sensational in terms of the media industry and, as a rule, highly conflictual in relation to dominant state apparatuses. But even so, such work still remains in a contradictory situation: it is generally questionable whether outside intervention will lead to practical self-determination, and the interrelated risk remains that the NGO may be instrumentally used in conflicts between governments or, more specifically, in the undermining of weaker states by stronger ones. The democratic effect of NGOs is essentially dependent on the degree to which they are in the position to empower decentralised political structures (Wapner 1995: 334), both local and regional (see Görg and Hirsch 1998: 609ff.). Insofar as NGOs are, and remain, components of an 'extended state', it would be a serious mistake to regard them simply as 'counter-statal' political actors (Wapner 1995). At best, what may be achieved at the NGO level is a political strategy 'in and against the state' (Brand and Görg 1998; see also Walk 1997). However, this is quite difficult as well as risky and highly conflictual.

To accept NGOs as a 'substitute for radical political action' is extremely misleading. Even in the 'best case' scenario, they are only part of a larger complex which also involves social movements. If we are to think in terms of the abolition of the worldwide relations of domination, exploitation and dependency, then there surely cannot be a substitute for radical political action. Direct and extra-institutional confrontation with the dominant political agendas and consensus, and the struggle against the ramified complex of apparatuses of domination at both national and international levels, cannot be substituted, at least not in the form of negotiations within diplomatic circles and 'round tables'. Given their structural and functional conditions of existence, NGOs possess a limited capacity for this type of action. At most, it can be anticipated that they will try to express the results of 'radical political action' and through this strengthen the position of countervailing power vis-à-vis international negotiation processes and in confrontational encounters with governments and international organisations (examples of which can be seen in the so-called 'anti-globalisation' protest mobilisations around the World Bank, IMF, WTO and G7 meetings which started in Seattle 1999 and Prague 2000). This assumes, of course, that there exists the will and capacity on the part of the NGOs to undertake even this action, and it is in fact often unlikely given the nature of their internal structures. Radical political and social movements which do not allow their resistance and protest potential to become institutionalised remain a fundamental precondition for democratic development (see Goodman in this volume). From this perspective, a paradox emerges: the democratic character of the NGO system only becomes effective when it enters into permanent dispute and conflict and allies itself with radical political discussions and movements (Brand 2000). Here the argument that the growing prominence of NGOs has been a reaction to the decline of radical political movements may be regarded as a highly sceptical understanding of their democratic potential.

What has been broadly understood by the term NGO relates to an extensive and heterogeneous reality, even when the concept, as presented here, is analytically narrowed and more precisely defined than usual. Greenpeace, Oxfam or Doctors without Borders are only comparable in a limited sense, although they have basically similar functions and organisational principles. Moreover, this chapter has been silent on virtually pure business enterprises such as World Vision. The democratic quality of the NGO system is not least influenced by the fact that these differences themselves become objects of political debate within the NGO scene. As materialist social and state theory has pointed out, 'civil society' represents a very heterogeneous political terrain on which the formulation of hegemonic concepts of society and their implementation are fought out. In this context, NGOs co-operate with one another in a thoroughly conflictual manner. Their democratic potential does not rest so much on their 'co-operative' activities within international negotiation systems as on their ability to criticise dominant politics, despite the fact that they are an aspect of these politics – a 'critique in mêlée', so to speak. If this situation were to arise, we could speak a little more seriously of the NGO system in terms of a 'democratic civil society'. The dissolution of the 'NGO myth', perpetuated both in scientific and public realms, together with the highly undifferentiated normative attributes attached to these organisations, becomes therefore a basic prerequisite for democratic and emancipatory politics.

References

Anderson, P. (1979) *Antonio Gramsci. Eine kritische Würdigung*, Berlin: Olle & Wolter.

Bonder, M., Röttger, B. and Ziebura, G. (1993) 'Vereinheitlichung und Fraktionierung in der Weltgesellschaft. Kritik des neuen Institutionalismus', *Prokla* 91: 327–41.

Brand, U. (2000) *Nichtregierungsorganisationen Staat und ökologische Krise*, Münster: Westfälisches Dampfboot.

Brand, U. and Görg, C. (1998) 'Nichtregierungsorganisationen und neue Staatlichkeit', in J. Callies (ed.), *Barfuß auf diplomatischem Parkett. Die Nichtregierungsorganisationen in der Weltpolitik*, Loccumer Protokolle 9/97, Loccum: Evangelische Akademie.

Bruckmaier, K. (1994) 'Nichtstaatliche Umweltorganisationen und die Diskussion über eine neue Weltordnung', *Prokla* 95: 227–41.

Brunnengräber, A. and Walk, H. (1997) 'Die Erweiterung der Netzwerktheorien: Nicht-Regierungsorganisationen verquickt mit Markt und Staat', in E. Altvater *et al.* (eds), *Vernetzt und verstrickt. Nicht-Regierungsorganisationen als gesellschaftliche Produktivkraft*, Münster: Westfälisches Dampfboot, 65–84.

Cox, R.W. (1993) 'Gramsci, hegemony and international relations', in S. Gill (ed.), *Gramsci, Historical Materialism and International Relations*, Cambridge: Cambridge University Press, 49–95.

Demirovic, A. (1997) *Demokratie und Herrschaft*, Münster: Westfälisches Dampfboot

Gebauer, T. (1998) 'Die NGOs und die Perspektiven internationaler Solidarität', in C. Görg and R. Roth (eds.), *Kein Staat zu machen. Zur Kritik der Sozialwissenschaften*, Münster: Westfälisches Dampfboot, 484–502.

Görg, C. and Hirsch, J. (1998) 'Is international democracy possible?', *Review of International Political Economy* 5(4): 585–615.

Gramsci, A. (1986) *Selections from Prison Notebooks*, ed. Q. Hoare and G.N. Smith, London: Lawrence and Wishart.

Grinspun, R. and Kreklewich, R. (1994) 'Consolidating neoliberal reforms: "free trade" as a conditioning framework', *Studies in Political Economy* 43: 33–61.

Habermas, J. (1998) 'Jenseits des Nationalstaats? Bemerkungen zu Folgeproblemen der wirtschaftlichen Globalisierung', in U. Beck (ed.), *Politik der Globalisierung*, Frankfurt/Main: Suhrkamp.

Hirsch, J. (1995) *Der nationale Wettbewerbsstaat*, Amsterdam-Berlin: Edition ID-Archiv.

—— (1998) *Vom Sicherheitsstaat zum nationalen Wettbewerbsstaat*, Berlin: ID-Verlag.

—— (2000) 'Die Internationalisierung des Staates. Anmerkungen zu einigen aktuellen Fragen der Staatstheorie', *Das Argument* 42(236): 325–39.

Jessop, B. (1982) *The Capitalist State: Marxist Theories and Methods*, Oxford: Martin Robertson.

—— (1997a) 'Capitalism and its future: remarks on regulation, government and governance', *Review of International Political Economy* 4(3): 561–81.

—— (1997b) 'The regulation approach: implications for political theory', *Journal of Political Philosophy* 5(3): 287–326.

Keane, J. (ed.) (1988) *Civil Society and the State*, London: Verso.

Kenis, P. and Schneider, V. (1997) 'Policy networks and policy analysis', in B. Marin and R. Mayntz (eds), *Policy Networks*, Frankfurt: Campus.

Kommission für Weltordnungspolitik (1995) *Nachbarn in einer Welt, Bericht, hg.v.d. Stiftung Entwicklung und Frieden*, Bonn.

Kramer, A. (1975) 'Gramscis Interpretation des Marxismus', in *Gesellschaft. Beiträge zur Marx'schen Theorie* 4, Frankfurt/Main: Suhrkamp, 65–118.

Mayer, P., Rittberger, V. and Zürn, M. (1993) 'Regime theory: state of the art and perspectives', in V. Rittberger (ed.), *Regime Theory and International Relations*, Oxford: Clarendon Press, 391–430.

Messner, D. (1995) *Die Netzwerkgesellschaft. Wirtschaftliche Entwicklung und internationale Wettbewerbsfähigkeit als Probleme gesellschaftlicher Steuerung*, Köln: Weltforum.

—— (1997) 'Netzwerktheorien: Die Suche nach Ursachen und Auswegen aus der Krise staatlicher Steuerungsfähigkeit', in E. Altvater *et al.* (eds), *Vernetzt und verstrickt. Nicht-Regierungsorganisationen als gesellschaftliche Produktivkraft*, Münster: Westfälisches Dampfboot, 27–63.

Messner, D. and Nuscheler, F. (1996) 'Global governance', *Herausforderungen an die deutsche Politik an der Schwelle zum 21. Jahrhundert*, Bonn: Stiftung Entwicklung und Frieden, Policy Paper No. 2.

Narr, W.-D. (1991) 'Vom Liberalismus der Erschöpften', *Blätter für deutsche und internationale Politik* 2: 216–27.

Poulantzas, N. (1978) *Staatstheorie*, Berlin: VSA.

Princen, T. and Finger, M. (1994) *Environmental NGOs in World Politics: Linking the Local and the Global*, London/New York: Routledge.

Rosenau, J.H. (1992) 'Governance, order, and change in world politics', in J.N. Rosenau and E.O. Czempiel (eds), *Governance Without Government: Order and Change in World Politics*, Cambridge: Cambridge University Press, 1–29.

Scharpf, F.W. (1996) 'Versuch über Demokratie im verhandelnden Staat', in R. Czada and M.G. Schmitt (eds), *Verhandlungsdemokratie, Interessenvermittlung, Regierbarkeit. Festschrift für Gerhard Lehmbruch*, Opladen: Westdeutscher Verlag 1996, 25–50.

Sklair, L. (1997) 'Social movements for global capitalism: the transnational capitalist class in action', *Review of International Political Economy* 4(3): 514–38.

Slater, D. (1998) 'Post-colonial questions for global times', *Review of International Political Economy* 5(4): 647–78.

Streek, W. (1996) 'Public power beyond the nation-state: the case of the European Community', in R. Boyer and D. Drache (eds), *States Against Markets: The Limits of Globalization*, London/New York: Routledge.

Taylor, P. J. (1994) 'States in world-system analysis: massaging a creative tension', in R.A. Palan and B. Gills (eds), *Transcending the State-Global Divide*, Boulder/London: Lynne Rienner, 107–24.

Wahl, P. (1997) 'Mythos und Realität internationaler Zivilgesellschaft. Zu den Perspektiven globaler Vernetzung von Nicht-Regierungsorganisationen', in E. Altvater *et al.* (eds), *Vernetzt und verstrickt. Nicht-Regierungsorganisationen als gesellschaftliche Produktivkraft*, Münster: Westfälisches Dampfbott, 293–314.

Walk, H. (1997) 'Ein bißchen bi schadet nie: Die Doppelstrategie von NGO-Netzwerken', in E. Altvater *et al.* (eds), *Vernetzt und verstrickt. Nicht-Regierungsorganisationen als gesellschaftliche Produktivkraft*, Münster: Westfälisches Dampfboot, 195–221.

Wapner, P. (1995) 'Politics beyond the state: environmental activism and world civic politics', *World Politics* 47: 11–340.

Zürn, M. (1998) *Regieren jenseits des Nationalstaates*: Frankfurt/Main: Surhrkamp.

11 Contesting corporate globalism
Sources of power, channels for democratisation

James Goodman

Neo-liberal globalism is creating a series of power-shifts and sharp democratic and legitimacy 'deficits' in global politics. Economic power is increasingly exercised through cross-national corporate institutions, whether in finance, production or distribution. Political power is increasingly vested in intergovernmental institutions or geared to the demands of private transnational agencies. Socio-cultural power is increasingly expressed in a globalised consumerism and carried through transnational media empires. However, this strengthening of transnational power sources lays the foundations for new forms of contestation and emancipation as well as domination. As sources of power shift out of the national regulatory framework, 'social movements' are developing new strategies. In doing so they are opening up new channels and prospects for democracy. Reflecting the uneven impacts and different experiences of corporate globalism, a range of responses are emerging, and in this respect 'the idioms of regulation and emancipation are inextricably linked together' (Sousa-Santos 1995: 456). This chapter explores the emerging channels for social movement politics and their potential for transnational democracy.

There are powerful indications that the strengthening of transnational power sources 'short-circuits' liberal democracy and necessitates an extensive re-democratisation of the emerging 'hybrid' political system. Various models have been promoted for achieving this. Some argue for an institutional transformation towards 'cosmopolitan democracy', through for instance democratised transnational agencies and cross-country referenda which would allow the processes of governance to escape the confines of national states (Held 1995). Such institutional cosmopolitanism hinges on a normative transformation and reorientation in the legal regimes that underpin citizenship rights. In this vein, some argue for a 'cosmopolitan citizenship…to counterbalance the increased opportunities for elite dominance which accompany the decline of the modern territorial state' (Linklater 1998: 193). But the required changes in political culture will only emerge as a result of political mobilisation and here, for many observers, hopes are often vested in an array of 'old' and 'new' social movements. The World Order Models Project, for example, argues that this 'globalisation from below…gives promise to the vision of cosmopolitan democracy' (Falk 1995: 254; Falk 1999). As Sousa-Santos argues, social movements are emerging as 'a global transformative audience, in charge of the agendas of cosmopolitanism', and in doing so 'constitute the backbone of transnational agency' (Sousa-Santos 1995: 267; see also Lipschutz 1992; Keck and Sikkink 1998; Smith *et al.* 1998; Sakamoto 1996; Walker 1994).

But what types of mobilisation are emerging, and with what forms of democratisation are they associated? Here debates about the politics of globalisation centre on conflicting interpretations of the dominant sources of power in globalising late modern society, as represented by three main macro-theoretical traditions: liberal-internationalism, post-Marxism, and Marxism or neo-Marxism. They see the key power sources as, respectively, institutional, cultural and material. Their contrasting conceptions of globalised power then generate three distinctive perspectives about the most likely or feasable forms of contestation and democratisation. These are characterised here as *globalist adaptation, localist confrontation* and *transnational resistance*. In the following three sections of this chapter, each of the three models and their theoretical underpinnings are analysed. The differences between them are highlighted in each case by focusing on their contrasting responses to the main or dominant configurations of global power: transnational corporations, intergovernmental institutions and global norms. The concluding section summarises the main features of the three models; assesses their implications for democracy; and questions how the different forms of democracy which they imply might conflict or complement one another.

Global governance and globalist adaptation

The liberal-internationalist or 'globalist adaptation' perspective sees social movements as taking a broadly reformist approach, seeking to reorient existing globalising institutions and practices. The demand is typically for greater institutional accountability and the formulation of goals that address popular priorities rather than elite interests (see McGrew in this volume). This often involves a focus on weakly legitimated intergovernmentalism, with social movements exploiting emerging political opportunities to widen participation and reorient institutional goals. This approach is popularised most enthusiastically by relatively dominant international non-governmental organisations (NGOs) which are based in the global 'North', and which integrate cosmopolitan values with a relatively privileged worldview, allowing for a critical accommodation with dominant sources of institutional power. International NGOs assert their legitimacy as key components of an emerging 'global civil society', counterposing their own cosmopolitanism to localist or nationalist alternatives. In this reformist approach, contestation is confined within relatively bounded 'epistemic communities' which have shared understandings of the political process as a matter of 'rational' and 'informed' debate (O'Brien *et al.* 2000). The process of consensus formation sees NGO elites recruited into the existing institutional and policy framework, enabling the development and elaboration of modes of globalist regulation (van der Pijl 1998; see also chapters by van der Pijl and Hirsch in this volume). Critical engagement communicates policy failings to policy elites and engenders policy adaptation, but it also legitimises institutional power and normalises neo-liberal discourses. Confrontation between globalising elites and subordinated peoples is then displaced into a series of intra-movement conflicts between relatively 'co-opted' and relatively 'autonomous' NGOs (Waterman 1998).

Arguments that 'global governance' can and should be democratised reflect a broadly cosmopolitan set of assumptions, and have their origins in the liberal-internationalist tradition of international relations. Liberal-internationalists argue that greater inter-societal interdependence, whether economic, cultural or environmental, requires the creation of inter-state and supra-state institutions to manage interdependency (Rosenau 1980). The emphasis is on the emergence of state-like institutions which span nationally centred civil societies. This shapes the concurrent need for cross-national vehicles for democratic participation which are capable of mirroring the newly empowered global institutions. These vehicles are frequently named as international NGOs, are orientated to cosmopolitan goals, and are founded on (potentially) global mobilisation. In some liberal-internationalist accounts (for example, Held 1995), social movements are downplayed in favour of inter-state elites as the architects of 'cosmopolitan democracy'. Others see the latter as 'part of the problem': these more radical versions see social movement globalism 'from below' as the necessary corollary to, and the primary means of, contesting the new forms of inter-state institutional power (for example, Falk 1995). The hoped-for result is a deepening of global governance, leading to the emergence of a 'global civil society' (Walzer 1995). In general terms, though, the approach is founded on a contractarian understanding of the political process. When national sources of institutional power – despotic states – emerged in the early modern period, a range of social movements emerged to contest their power. These movements secured rights to political participation in state affairs through liberal democracy, with the national state contracted to uphold the interests of 'its' people, an assumption expressed in the concept of popular sovereignty (Held 1995; Linklater 1998). But now, as state power becomes increasingly supplemented by inter-state institutions, it is to be expected that new cross-national democratic agendas will emerge, carried by new transnational social movements (Falk 1999; Markoff 1996).

These assumptions are echoed in internationalised versions of the 'political process' strand of social movement theory. Here the assumption is that the primary purpose of social movements is to extend participation in the processes of public decision making. To this end, movements are described as mobilising political resources and exploiting political opportunities at the national level; an example being the labour movement in the struggle to achieve and extend social democracy (Kreisi 1995; McCarthy and Zald 1995). Social movements have a broad repertoire of mobilising resources – from the cultural to the physical – and in this respect they can be distinguished from political parties, though in the final analysis the formal political process shapes social movements, and if that process changes so will they (Tarrow 1994).

As some of the political structures and sources of institutional power shift beyond the state, new cross-national political opportunities begin to open up and new transnational mobilising resources begin to become available for social movements (McCarthy 1998; Keck and Sikkink 1998). Like their counterparts in the early days of state formation, social movements exploit these opportunities and resources to contest institutional power. In the process they open up new realms for democratisation and for widened participation, and are themselves transformed from national to transnational social movements (Smith *et al.* 1998). The inter-state and corporate institutions face sharp legitimacy deficits, and respond in varying degrees of defensiveness and flexibility, in a transnationally defined democratisation process (Sakamoto 1996). Hence, much like nationally centred social movements, transnational movements are seen as encouraging the emergence of accountable and 'transparent' institutions in the inter-state context. Democratic participation, for instance in 'global regions' such as the European Union, is interpreted as one indicator of progress along the road to a healthy pluralist democracy at the transnational level (Goodman 1997). The assumption is that mobilisation is primarily geared to the political process and is invariably programmatic, a social means to a political end. The purpose of social movements is to broaden political participation, and hence under globalisation the primary modes of contestation are politically centred and orientated to globalist or cosmopolitan aspirations. While movements may sometimes confront the political process, they are primarily geared to participating in it and their actions are shaped by it. This constitutive role of political institutions is then reflected in dilemmas over whether to critique or to advise agents of globalisation, such as transnational corporations.

An expanding constituency of international NGOs takes this approach in targeting transnational corporations, inter-state institutions and global norms. Transnational corporations are often encouraged to listen to their non-financial 'stakeholders', to act 'responsibly' and promote concepts of 'corporate citizenship'. NGOs have developed 'triple bottom line' accounting methods, where the social and environmental impacts of corporate activity are monitored and assessed along with assessments of financial return. In response, several high-profile corporations have introduced a variety of schemes designed to demonstrate their capacity to self-regulate, and have sought to engage NGOs in consensus-forming monitoring groups, out of the glare of publicity. Mining companies, for instance, are constructing new ways of managing NGO 'outrage', including the creation of a 'Global Mining Initiative' to rehabilitate the industry's image (Phillips 2002; Evans *et al.* 2002). Manufacturing and retail corporations can face similar pressures, largely from boycott activities in their Northern markets, and produce similar responses; examples here include campaigns around Nike, Walmart, Monsanto and Nestlé (Klein 2000; Sklair 1995).

A similar set of arguments have been developed to critique intergovernmental agencies. Instead of seeking to limit the power of these institutions, international NGOs have focused on encouraging institutional elites to become more accountable and to develop policies that serve popular rather than dominant interests (O'Brien *et al.* 2000). Rather than limiting the extent of institutional power, NGOs attempt to change the way it is exercised. At the very least this involves persuading negotiators to incorporate some compensatory 'side agreements' into the policy framework. Rather than arguing that the institutions are irredeemably anti-democratic, NGO representatives generally call for meaningful consultative structures and lobby for greater 'transparency': institutional elites often respond to criticism by adapting their structures in order to legitimise their policies. An example is the campaign by the International Confederation of Free Trade Unions (ICFTU) for minimum labour rights to be incorporated into the international trading regime overseen by the World Trade Organisation (WTO) (ICFTU 1998). This draws on an earlier initiative by North American trade unions for a labour clause to be included in the North American Free Trade Agreement (NAFTA), which was successful, but has proved to be signally inneffective (Cohen 1997).

International NGOs are also engaged in constructing and institutionalising global norms. Prevailing norms are contested as inadequate and alternatives are presented in order to reframe existing practices. For instance, NGOs have become key players in the development of norms for the regulation of the environment, the workplace, the status of women and the administration of justice (Dickenson 1997). The emphasis is on articulating universal norms as a necessary foundation for globalisation. Such universalism often relies on abstract and legalist measures of formal equality, drawn from individualised conceptions of rights and obligations, that may fail to address substantive power differentials. The US-based Womens Environment and Development Organisation (WEDO), for instance, found that the status of women had deteriorated after the 1995 UN Conference on Women in Beijing: many states had implemented the Beijing Platform for Action, but at the same time had been implementing 'structural adjustment' programmes, which generally have the most negative impacts on women (WEDO 1998). Hence the process of adapting global norms can leave dominant practices untouched and can even be complicit with those practices. The norm of possessive individualism, for instance, disseminated through globalised consumerism and perhaps the most engrained manifestation of corporate globalisation, may then be shored up rather than challenged (Johnston 2002).

In arguing for an adaptation of corporate practices, intergovernmental institutions and global norms, international NGOs seek a deepened globalism. Cosmopolitan affiliations are asserted over nationalism or localism, civil society is legitimised against state power, and inter-state governance is privileged over state government. This ideological logic of adaptive globalism is increasingly appropriated by global elites (see Fine 1999). As other political options are marginalised or forced off the agenda, international NGOs based in the global 'North' can in general be characterised as elitist and as agents of globalist domination, rather than as vehicles for emancipation from it (see also Hirsch in this volume).

Globalised culture and localist confrontation

In contrast to the cosmopolitanism of international NGOs, some social movements react to the emergence of transnational power sources by marking-out and constructing local communal or national autonomies. These forms of collective action are driven by a logic of 'localist confrontation' that contrasts dramatically with 'globalist adaptation'. These movements do not engage with or accommodate themselves to neo-liberal globalist rhetoric – they reject it. The approach, indeed, may be explicitly defined against international NGOs and involves a critique of 'ngoism' and elite cosmopolitanism (Petras 1997). Linkages with 'the global' are severed and alternative foundations for political legitimacy, mobilisation and participation are constructed. Forms of autonomy, including self-determination and self-government, are defined as ends in themselves, not as means to broader goals.

This assertion of local legitimacy is especially prevalent in the global 'South' where corporate globalism compounds pre-existing subordination under neo-colonialism, and where movements for self-determination have a strong recent history. In these regions especially, globalist regulation is permanently confronted and disrupted by a multiplicity of localist political projects. Economic autonomy is asserted against transnationalised corporate power; political structures are created and defended against inter-state 'governance'; cultural practices are asserted against consumerist norms. There are numerous attempts at managing and marginalising these as 'irrational' reactions to the globalist project, and by international NGOs as well as by neo-liberal institutions, but in many respects localist responses continue to pose the most powerful challenge to the integrative logic of corporate globalism.

This logic of localist confrontation can be seen as reflecting an overarching dynamic of cultural domination under neo-liberal globalism. The structures of global governance pattern the political processes of globalisation, but may also give rise to fundamental cultural developments that prefigure and define the boundaries of political contestation. The frameworks of globalised cultural domination, as manifested for instance in the liberal state and possessive individualism, can be seen as establishing the foundations for neo-liberal hegemony. The only cosmopolitanism that is encouraged is the cosmopolitanism of dominant elites, a form of ideology that legitimises the dominant script and suffocates other alternatives including locally based ones (Zolo 1997). But a focus on the fragmented nature of cultural identification and localist responses in many ways echoes, perhaps surprisingly, the conservative, state-centred 'realist' tradition in international relations theory. This approach emphasises the necessary fragmentation of the international political community into state-centred societies, mirror-imaging the cosmopolitanism of the liberal-internationalist model (Walker 1994). For 'realists' the states system resolves the problem of cultural difference by enabling the expression of distinct identifications through the system of 'nation-states'. If state power is weakened, societies are seen as necessarily lapsing into inter-communal conflict (Buzan 1996).

These expectations mesh with a second strand in the sociology of social movements, one that stresses the role of culture and identity in the logic of collective action. This 'new social movements' approach is most clearly articulated by 'post-Marxist' sociologists who claim that capitalist industrial society and its class-driven dynamic is passing into history (Cohen 1985). Instead of being shaped by class conflict over material resources, 'advanced' societies are allegedly shaped by conflicts over informational resources and over the power to programme and process social practices. In these societies, material conflicts subside and are replaced by cultural conflicts. Instead of class domination being contested in conflicts over the distribution of material resources, information domination is fought out in conflicts over autonomy and recognition (Fraser 1997).

In this context, demands for cultural democracy quickly begin to replace demands for social democracy (Touraine 1995, 1977). The cultural logic of late modern society thus gives rise to a new type of social movement; one that is not simply a vehicle for a programme, but itself embodies the movement's demands and aspirations. Instead of being a social means to a political end, movements become ends in themselves. By their existence they mark out realms of autonomous collective action and assert the right to different social roles and identities from those imposed by the disciplinary logic of informational or programmed society. They carve out alternative social spaces by constructing and mobilising around cultural identities – in effect, cultural categories – that produce practices defined against the dominant 'master codes' (Melucci 1996). These movements for autonomy are seen as presenting a profound and potentially incommensurable challenge to the modern social system. Significantly, their success is primarily measured by the degree to which they are able to construct cultural categories and defend cultural boundaries; their ability to secure wider social and political transformation becomes an incidental, perhaps irrelevant, consideration.

It is a short step from arguing that cultural movements for autonomy are the primary agents of resistance in late modern society to suggesting that they will also become the primary foundations for resistance to a globalised information society (see Castells 1997). Globalised information networks – and their elites – create new forms of subordination and are increasingly confronted by communities of resistance, in which localised collective action and locally constructed identities are marshalled in the name of autonomy. As the state is progressively disempowered – willfully or otherwise – cultural communities are increasingly exposed to transnational pressures. The role of the state in mediating between local practices and global pressures is undermined, and sharp discontinuities open up between the logic of power in the global context and the logic of everyday association and representation in societies. This gulf creates a profound revalorisation of the local, generating a powerful impulse to embrace and mobilise communal cultural identities in the name of 'community'. The resulting social movements are aimed at securing a radical break with dominant ideologies, with liberalism as well as with neo-liberalism. The hollowing-out of state power, the weakening of state structures of representation, and the declining cultural legitimacy of the national unit all contribute to a growing vulnerability to globalised informational power. Here the dystopias constructed by realists to underpin their advocacy of the states system are invoked as the necessary consequence of globalising forces that strengthen the power of informational elites.

The identities of resistance are likely to be highly defensive and reactive, although it is conceivable that they may develop more proactive 'project' identities geared to broader social transformation (Castells 1997). An historical parallel might be the interaction between anti-colonial nationalism (a resistance identity) and anti-imperialism (a project identity) in the emergence and development of anti-colonial movements and post-colonial states. But from the 'new social movement' perspective, project identities can only be built on resistance identities. This raises the difficult question of how to articulate movements that have as their guiding rationale the continued assertion of cultural identity and the defence of autonomy. If the assertion of cultural autonomy is the foundation stone of the movement, then any cross-cultural agendas and alliances geared to broader aspirations cannot be allowed to impinge on that autonomy. Any common ground that emerges will inevitably be contingent, secondary and always subject to renegotiation. This contrasts, of course, with the relatively unified common purpose of the power elites that drive globalised networks. The relatively strong network of dominant groups is confronted – if that is the right word – by a range of groups whose priority is to maximise their autonomy, and whose power is thus necessarily fragmented. The result can be a process of endless skirmishing on the fringes of globalised power.

That this channel for social movement politics is defined against 'globalist adaptation' should come as no surprise. Meaningful participation in 'global civil society' may be available to some representatives of elite NGO opinion, but for large sections of the population, globalisation is experienced as an external threat, not as an opportunity, much less an opportunity for participation. It is therefore to be expected that many social movements will respond to globalising pressures by forging defensible enclaves. In contrast with those seeking to adapt global structures, whose legitimacy rests on cosmopolitan claims, movements for localist resistance base their legitimacy on local claims against globalist domination.

Transnational corporate power is thus confronted by campaigns for local self-determination. Rather than lobbying corporations to change their practices, localist movements assert the right of veto over the exercise of corporate power. Rather than seeking, for instance, to convince a corporation to respect environmental values or to promote local development, such movements may refuse to permit the opening of facilities, such as mines or hydro-electric dams (Connell *et al.* 1996). Examples include the Bougainville Revolutionary Army, which fought a successful war to close what was at the time the world's largest copper mine, and which then continued asserting rights to self-determination against the government of Papua New Guinea and its regional allies. Another example is the Ogoni people's campaign for self-determination against the the Nigerian government and the oil company Shell (Obi 1997; Gedicks 1993).

Just as corporations are confronted, so are intergovernmental agencies. Rather than persuading intergovernmental institutions to adapt themselves to broader public pressures, localist confrontation movements argue that the institutions should be dismantled. Attempts at increasing the transparency and accountability of institutions, or reforming their policy agendas, are discarded.

Instead, movements assert the right of local control or sovereignty against inter-state decision making. An example here is the Philippine 'Peoples Power' movement, the 'BAYAN' New Patriotic Alliance, which in 1996 organised a 'Peoples Conference Against Imperialist Globalisation' targeted at the Manila meeting of the Asia-Pacific Economic Community (APEC). BAYAN has become a central element in a global anti-imperialist alliance, which in the Philippine context is focused on realising genuine national popular sovereignty as reflected in BAYAN's first guiding principle, that 'True national sovereignty lies in asserting our nation's independence from imperialist domination' (BAYAN 1996). The paramount legitimacy of communal, local or national frameworks for autonomy is asserted as the foundation for collective action. Rather than adapting global norms, the emphasis is on mobilising local norms and cultural practices against transnationalised consumer ideology. An impulse to de-link from globalised consumerism is combined with the assertion of self-reliance and production for needs rather than for wants, in relatively self-contained communities that then become carriers for counter-culture.

One example, that has been celebrated as a beacon of hope for a more inclusive localism orientated to internationalist norms, is the Zapatista indigenous peoples movement in Mexico. Here local norms governing social organisation, in relation for instance to issues of social hierarchy, have been mobilised to affirm community solidarity and to contest both the global neo-liberal agenda and the centralist institutions imposed by the Mexican state (Cleaver 1999; Reinke 2002). In sharp contrast, many other localist movements are much less internationalist and less inclusive, and some are extremely reactionary. The Taliban militants in Afghanistan and associated religious 'fundamentalists' are prime examples, though Islam has no monopoly on 'fundamentalism' and other examples include millennialist religious sects in the United States and Japan. Localist confrontation is also a dominant characteristic of various other far-right groups in the 'Global North', such as US survivalists, Australian One Nationists and Austrian Nazi-revivalists. And, in a very different context, localism characterises the 'Shining Path' insurgents in Peru.

Movements for autonomy are thus very diverse, but they generally tend to be nostalgic and divisive. They may be founded on myths of the past, of a lost golden age, when globalising pressures were more distant or less oppressive. They may also valorise local authenticity as a mark of community membership and mobilise this against inauthentic 'outsiders'. In practice, also, they may be weakened by the assumption that there are no sources of power or political leverage for counter-movements beyond the immediately local or 'communal' context. Internationalised forms of new social movement theory can offer a powerful explanation of the emergence of some localist movements – especially ethno-nationalist or racist ones – but they may have difficulty in explaining movements that are more inclusive and cosmopolitan, such as the Zapatistas. Movements often articulate demands for autonomy with universal norms, and pursue these demands through transnational partnerships, for instance as part of a wider anti-imperialist movement, as well as through the defence of local autonomy. Indeed, many social movements have found localist reactions to be excessively defensive and disempowering. A wide range of movements – including environmental, womens and indigenous peoples movements, which are often described as fitting the 'new social movements' model – have created and exploited sources of transnational political leverage, and in the process they have constructed powerful transnational affiliations and loyalties.

Global hegemony, transnational resistance

Movements that reject the counterposed 'globalist' and 'localist' positions are developing transnational resistance strategies to defend and enhance autonomy from domination by globalised fluxes and flows. Here, autonomy and transnationalism are not seen as contradictory but as complementary, at least potentially. This may reflect the logic of mobilisation: movements founded on everyday participation are rarely able to leap straight into the global realm, but they often recognise that to retreat defensively into local or national enclaves would be disempowering. Such movements build on 'grass-roots' inter-personal legitimacy but assert their legitimacy through emerging channels for transnational mobilisation (James 2002). The emphasis is on bridging 'levels' of solidarity and contestation, in a range of balancing acts across the 'domestic–foreign' divide.

Movements of this sort are focused on the difficult task of bringing together relatively autonomous constituencies into 'coalitions of the dispossessed'. They may be simply geared to exploiting tactical advantage and hence may be conjunctural and contingent, in effect 'rainbow' alliances, generating a 'thin' solidarity resting simply on a common perception of the source of domination. Alternatively, they may be grounded in a common alignment of shared socio-economic or politico-cultural exclusions. Such coalitions have at least the potential to create a counter-hegemonic bloc, capable of generating a more durable 'thick' solidarity (Held *et al.* 1999).

These 'transnational resistance' movements may reflect broader structural transformations as globalising pressures strengthen the common foundations for action and thereby encourage the emergence of shared aspirations and guiding principles. The interaction between social stratification and spatial division that produces counter-hegemonic movements in global politics has been explored by many Marxists and neo-Marxists, especially World System theorists. Here, in contrast with post-Marxist perspectives, the emphasis is on material power not informational power: late modern societies remain class-divided and their historical development is still primarily driven by class conflict. While there may have been a transition into a new mode or epoch of capital accumulation, in which information becomes a centrally important commodity, the logic of class domination remains in place (Arrighi 1994). Here, states are seen as agents for hegemonic domination by ruling classes and inextricably part of the world capitalist system.

The interaction between a still fragmented states system and a more unified world economy – between the logic of geo-politics and the logic of transnationalism – is particularly emphasised by World System theorists. While liberal-internationalists emphasise the shift away from state-bound society to global society, and 'realists' repeat the mirror-image argument that societies are necessarily contained by states, Marxists and neo-Marxists focus on how state power and social power interact to constitute global capitalism. The focus is on the historical development of the states system and world capitalism: phases of hegemony are periodised and spatialised, and the coalitions, spheres of influence and associated institutional practices of successive hegemonic 'world orders' are highlighted and debated (Hopkins and Wallerstein 1996; Wallerstein 2000).

Changes from one 'world order' to the next are driven by the contradictions and conflicts created by particular modes of accumulation. This dialectical reading sees the world capitalist system locked into a constant battle with a range of anti-systemic movements, with specific modes of resistance shaping the capacity to accumulate and the direction of change. Neo-Gramscian theorists adapt this framework, emphasising its cultural and political aspects in a process of contestation between 'hegemonic' and 'anti-hegemonic' forces (Cox 1987). Others stress the ideological role of the states system in defining the boundaries of 'the political' and creating a de-politicised realm for dominant economic interests, a 'non-political' economic imperialism legitimated by 'political' sovereign equality (Rosenberg 1994).

Thus, in contrast to 'new' social movement theorists, Marxist perspectives assert that there is a common underlying class dynamic that drives and shapes resistance. Whether the source of domination is local or global, this provides the possibility for counter-hegemonic forces to coalesce in common cause. How this is realised depends on the specific logic of accumulation and on the resulting responses. Forms of domination can vary, sometimes dramatically, and so too can the resulting resistance. The dynamics of class struggle can be very different across different modes of accumulation, and here three are outlined (the argument drawing heavily on van der Pijl (1998); see also van der Pijl in this volume).

Firstly, 'original' capitalist accumulation breaks apart pre-existing, pre-capitalist social structures in an often violent process of establishing the priority of commodity exchange over non-commodified practice. Here the resistance is to the discipline of capital being imposed over use value, as expressed for example in contemporary indigenous claims to ancestral lands.

Secondly, in the contrasting case of 'industrial' accumulation the main resistance is to the disciplines of capital being imposed over labour. Here resistance is primarily expressed in struggles over the distribution of the economic surplus, whether manifested in industrial militancy or in pressures to increase state welfarism.

Thirdly, with more intensive modes of accumulation, capitalism begins to exhaust the social and environmental 'substratum' on which accumulation depends. Here resistance is typically expressed as a series of struggles over the means of reproduction, in effect struggles for survival, whether planetary, environmental, cultural or social.

All three forms of accumulation/resistance can exist concurrently, and there is clearly a potential for tension between the respective types of movements, not least between workplace-centred and survival-centred approaches, where the former may be locked into a productivist logic, while the latter are defined against it. Yet all three forms share a common logic of contesting accumulation, as expressed in a shared class dynamic. There are underlying foundations for strategy and action arising from this dynamic which can be exploited, particularly in the context of sharpening rivalries between sectorally or regionally centred factions of dominant classes.

This raises directly the question of consciousness and mobilisation. In analysing the current dynamics of hegemony and counter-hegemony, Marxist and neo-Marxist perspectives generally stand somewhere between 'globalism' and 'localism', asserting that counter-hegemonic strategy must be transnational in scope. For some, capitalist globalisation is driven by the interests of an emerging transnational capitalist class: a newly empowered formation that exercises economic power through transnational corporations, political power through intergovernmental institutions, and cultural power through ideologies of neo-liberalism and consumerism (Sklair 1995). This analysis suggests the necessity for movements with the capacity to range across the 'levels' of international politics, flowing through local and national to global contexts to match the transnational scope of material domination. As transnational class power crystalises in the form of global corporations, institutions and norms, a range of common targets may begin to emerge. A shared experience of the processes and causes of exclusion may provide a powerful basis for a common response across otherwise unrelated and autonomous movements (as is beginning to happen in the 'anti-globalisation/anti-capitalism' movement). In the process, movements may become more closely articulated, to constitute a counter-hegemonic bloc with the capacity to generate the necessary 'paradigmatic transition' into a new global order (Sousa-Santos 1995; Arrighi *et al.* 1989).

Yet, even if it is accepted that the structural preconditions are in place, there are still powerful pressures against the emergence of transnational counter-hegemonic configurations. The logic of corporate globalisation may integrate societies and lead to the emergence of cross-national norms and institutions, carried by emerging transnational classes, but its impact is also felt in the form of sharpened divides between localities and peoples. Transnational social divides may be emerging, but they overlay and reproduce diverging modes of accumulation and have the effect of sharpening pre-existing spatial divides between geographic cores and geographic peripheries (Chossudovsky 1998). Global capitalist unity may be emerging, but this does not necessarily or automatically generate a global anti-capitalist response. On the contrary, as happened in other phases in the development of the world system, various 'core–periphery' divisions provide manifold opportunities for 'divide and rule' strategies, leading to recurrent inter-national conflicts. Hopes vested simply in the emergence of anti-capitalist cosmopolitanism will surely be dashed, as they have been in the past (see Waterman 1998). Clearly a more grounded response is required, one which recognises and expresses the spatial unevenness as well as the social logic of transnational class formation. Local confrontation to defend and extend autonomy is very often an immediate objective necessity, a precondition for survival. Yet, by the same token, we have seen that local movements for autonomy are necessarily impoverished in the face of globalising power sources: they must in some way be correlated and linked to contest transnational forces beyond the ambit of the local.

While there is a plethora of international NGOs engaged in the political processes of globalisation, and many examples of movements that seek to mark out autonomy against globalising pressures, movements which employ strategies of transnational resistance are harder to find. This may reflect limitations on the potential of NGOs to resist the dominant sources of power (see Hirsch in this volume). More generally, it may reflect the nature of the category 'transnational': given the traditionally powerful divide between 'domestic' and 'foreign' domains, it can be particularly difficult to construct movements that bridge the two. There can be a very deep divide between cosmopolitan globalism and defensive localism. Nonetheless, transnational movements able to bring together locally based demands for veto powers and transnationally defined norms and forms of organisation can reap substantial rewards.

For example, corporate power can be particularly vulnerable to coalitions that mobilise across First World–Third World divides to politicise the economic activities of transnational corporations. Corporate exposure and vulnerability to small shifts of perception in globalised finance and product markets are consciously being exploited by transnational coalitions which challenge the corporate 'license to operate'. Resource-based corporations, such as mining companies, become vulnerable not only to local opposition but also to shareholder-focused opposition that targets reputational capital and seeks to undermine shareholder confidence. An example is the campaign against Rio Tinto, which is co-ordinated by the international mineworkers confederation, and hailed as the first global trade union campaign to focus on a transnational corporation (Goodman 2001).

In other sectors, corporations are also vulnerable but through their customers rather than through their shareholders. Transnational corporations in manufacturing and services sectors are constantly required to construct cross-national consumer wants, and these can be highly unstable and vulnerable to transnational campaigns that exploit the gulf between corporate claims and actual practices. Consumerism may be emerging as a new weak link in the circuit of capital, and consumer campaigns increasingly draw common strength from sources of opposition centred on the production process. New modes of transnational social-movement unionism are emerging that bridge production and consumption, as labour movements recognise the limits of national mobilisation and also the necessity for counter-hegemonic coalition-building, crossing both national boundaries and boundaries between movements (Munck and Waterman 1999; Moody 1997). Examples include the Northern-centred sweatshop campaigns in the garment industry, which often link consumers and producers across gobal development divides, for instance in the case of the Nike campaign (Diller 1999; Community Aid Abroad 1996).

In a similar vein, a wide range of movements have coalesced to confront intergovernmental institutions. A particularly effective strategy has been to construct alternative forums that doggedly 'shadow' the meetings of these institutions. These forums have been particularly important in politicising neo-liberal constitutionalism, and also in articulating movement objectives. They highlight the lack of accountability in decision making in the intergovernmental context, and critique the neo-liberal models that are pursued. For example, a series of peoples' Assemblies were mounted against the 'Asia-Pacific Economic Cooperation' meetings of state leaders, first in Okinawa in 1996, then Manila 1996, Vancouver 1997, Kuala Lumpur 1998 and Auckland 1999. These played a key role in developing Asia-Pacific co-operation between social movements, and assisted in the more effective promotion of alternatives to neo-liberal globalism.

From 1998 there has been a dramatic shift beyond these contingent and relatively loose forms of opposition into much more dense forms of transnational alliance building. With this, groups campaigning against neo-liberal globalism have begun to take the initiative, to the extent of forcing issues off the intergovernmental negotiating agenda. One example is the campaign against the Multilateral Agreement on Investment (MAI), the first campaign to successfully derail a neo-liberal intergovernmental agreement. The MAI was designed to institutionalise market 'disciplines' as against government regulation of international capital flows. Working on the NAFTA model, it would have granted corporations rights to sue governments for breach of the Agreement, and would have led to a winding back of 'protections' for public sector provision as well as for national or indigenous private-sector businesses. The MAI was an OECD agreement, but was directed against 'protections' in the non-OECD world. Significantly, though, opposition to the MAI was centred on the OECD, as a campaign in defence of national democratic institutions. A direct common interest emerged across the North–South divide. This began to put unbearable pressure on the negotiators, and within a year the MAI had been shelved (Goodman and Ranald 2000).

One crucial consequence of the MAI campaign was increased confidence on the part of those contesting and politicising neo-liberal intergovernmentalism, and this was expressed in the 1999 campaign against a Millennium Round of WTO liberalisation. Such a spillover from campaigns targeting the MAI into the WTO arena had been anticipated by the Secretary-General of the UNCTAD, Rubens Ricupero, who predicted a growing clash with NGOs which could impede trade liberalisation and damage the credibility of the WTO itself.

This proved surprisingly accurate as the politicisation process culminated in the December mobilisation of NGOs against the WTO Ministerial in Seattle. Displays of public opposition, by mostly Northern-based NGOs, were mirrored by a strengthened unity among non-OECD governments, seventy of which then voted as a bloc against the proposal for a renewed round of 'liberalisation', forcing it off the WTO agenda (Raghaven 2000; Gill 2000).

Finally, in confronting globalised consumerism and neo-liberal 'norms', some movements have constructed powerful linkages between alternative global norms and local claims. Perhaps the clearest examples are from transnational indigenous peoples campaigns, where conceptions of continuing indigenous sovereignty directly confront hegemonic conceptions of state power, property ownership and commodification (Maguashca 1996). The political demand is invariably for greater self-government, but this cannot be confined to the granting of limited autonomy from the central state, nor can it be simply dismissed as a demand for secession. Since 1974, when the term 'Fourth World' was coined to describe a world of stateless peoples denied self-determination, indigenous groups have constructed a series of international associations demanding the recognition of indigenous self-determination as a global norm. A mutually reinforcing relationship has emerged between locally based claims to prior sovereignty, often defined against the commercialisation of natural resources, and transnational campaigns for the recognition of indigenous self-determination. As Mick Dodson, former Aboriginal Social Justice Commissioner in Australia, stated in 1998:

> The feeling that we are not alone has transformed the way many of us approach the whole struggle. We now see that it is a global struggle, not just between a single indigenous people and a government, but between the world's indigenous peoples and the world's colonial governments.
>
> (Dodson 1999: 62)

In the process, indigenous campaigns have established norms that cannot easily be contained within the existing states system (Sousa-Santos 1995).

Whether it is corporations, inter-state institutions or global norms that are targetted, the key issue is the ability to articulate contending movement objectives across the local–global axis. This difficult process of managing potentially conflicting perspectives is rendered less problematic by the logic of transnational class formation and domination. The various dimensions of transnationalised class power in the 'global age' have different impacts in different locations, but often they share the same source, and frameworks for action are increasingly defined in social rather than spatial terms, with many 'Third Worlds' within the 'First', and vice versa (Hoogvelt 1997; Hettne 1995). Neo-liberal globalism threatens 'post-colonial' states with a form of recolonisation and it also undermines popular democracy in post-imperial and other 'First World' contexts. This common disempowerment, under a new wave of transnational imperialism, may create the foundations for common consciousness and common action. The compounding revolt against globalised neo-liberalism in the global 'North' thus very effectively dovetails with ongoing opposition from the global 'South'. This creates what might be seen as a counter-hegemonic movement against the institutionalisation of the power of transnational capitalist classes. Certainly, the balance has shifted towards transnational coalition building, and these coalitions are becoming more grounded in a sense of common purpose.

The limitations of this perspective stem largely from the problems of trans-lating presumed structural contradictions into effective social movement strategy. One or other of the twin 'magnetic poles' of elite cosmopolitanism and defensive localism may prove too strong to resist. Despite the clear emer-gence of common power sources and the experience of common subordination, cross-movement divisions may be too strong to overcome. Similarly, despite an objective necessity to confront sources of power, rather than accommodate them, the option of adaptation in the context of appar-ently monolithic neo-liberal ideology may prove to be the much more attractive and apparently realistic strategy. Nonetheless, transnational resistance has the potential to open up more possibilities than it closes down – especially in terms of redefining the boundaries of the possible, both in local and global contexts.

Conclusions

Social movements can be thought of as contesting globalisation along three pathways, characterised here as *globalist adaptation, localist confrontation* and *transna-tional resistance*. Each of these models reflects a particular experience and interpretation of the dominant sources of power under globalisation, and each implies a particular understanding of the appropriate 'level' and most effective form of contestation. We have seen that the three models privilege particular organisational vehicles and political tools. These are summarised in Table 11.1, which also highlights their implications for democracy.

The 'globalist adaptation' model of contestation clearly implies a cosmopolitan form of democracy in which national representative liberal democracy is extended into cross-national contexts through, for instance, democratised intergovernmental organisations grounded in transnational norms. Here, democratisation is promoted by international NGOs (INGOs). These politicise transnational power sources and force the creation of new forms of accountability and levels of representation beyond the state, thus extending the national level of democracy 'upwards'. 'Localist confrontation', by contrast, defines democratisation not in terms of constructing cross-national levels, but rather in terms of strengthening existing locally centred

Table 11.1 Social movements under globalisation: three models of contestation and democratisation

Models	Source of power	'Levels' of contestation	Modes of contestation	Vehicles and tools	Forms of democracy
'Globalist adaptation'	institutional	global	critical accommodation	INGOs critique	cosmopolitan
'Localist confrontation'	info-cultural	local or national	reactive grass-roots	autonomous veto	local republican
'Transnational resistance'	material	transnational	proactive coalitions	transnational movements	transnational participatory

institutions that are grounded in day-to-day practices. The local focus is often subnational and expresses a growing frustration with increasingly constrained state-centred democratic structures.

Conflicts between 'globalist adaptation' and 'localist confrontation' can be read as conflicts over the appropriate territorial levels for democracy in the 'global age'. The 'transnational resistance' model contrasts with both these approaches in emphasising cross-national vehicles for local autonomy. It thereby grounds democratisation in transnational participation. This form of democracy is still tenuous and certainly relatively uninstitutionalised. But this may express its strength – as a source of inspiration and mobilisation, rather than as a mechanism of channelling and perhaps containing the democratic impulse. In this respect, it promises much, although as yet it has delivered relatively little.

Going beyond a comparison of the three models, the central question becomes how they interrelate. In what ways might they come into conflict, and in what ways might they complement each other? As highlighted in Table 11.1, they are certainly founded on very different assumptions about the primary sources of power under corporate globalisation. Reflecting this, they also embody different interpretations of the most effective levels and modes of contestation, and very different vehicles for mobilisation. As a result, the main or dominant configurations of power that are strengthened by globalising pressures – transnational corporations, intergovernmental institutions and global norms – are contested in very different ways in the three models. This may lead to conflict between the three approaches, and a weakening of the prospects for contestation as dominant elites face contradictory demands and are able to play one off against the other.

As summarised in Table 11.2, transnational corporations may be pressured into acknowledging their status as 'corporate citizens', while at the same time facing local vetos and transnational campaigns which challenge their 'licence to operate'. In some contexts these strategies may be mutually reinforcing, with international NGOs relying on locally based confrontation to legitimise their demands that corporate practices be reformed. In other contexts, though, the approaches may be locked into conflict, with, for example, some international

Table 11.2 Contesting the dominant configurations of global power

Models of contestation	Transnational corporations (TNCs)	Inter-state institutions	Global norms
'Globalist adaptation'	Promote global 'corporate citizenship'	Lobby for transparency, consultation and 'side agreements'	Reform norms, develop conscientious consumerism
'Local confrontation'	Assert right to local veto of corporate practices	Define right to subsidiarity or local sovereignty	Mobilise local norms and cultural practices
'Transnational resistance'	Construct cross-national alliances focused on TNCs	Create alternative transnational forums	Define alternative universal norms linked to local claims

NGOs helping multinational corporations to shore-up their legitimacy in the face of local confrontation or transnational resistance. Likewise, intergovernmental institutions may face pressures for greater accountability, or for the reform of existing practices, but these pressures may directly conflict with demands that such institutions be dismantled, or that alternative structures be constructed. In other contexts, though, campaigns that pose a fundamental challenge to the legitimacy of intergovernmental organisations, and put forward arguments for alternative organisations, can strengthen the pressure for reform. Finally, in relation to the formation of norms, arguments for strengthening universal norms, defined and monitored through intergovernmental institutions, may stigmatise local practices as particularisms which must be brought into conformity with cosmopolitan values. Alternatively, global norms may express locally based aspirations and strengthen the legitimacy of local demands for autonomy, framed, for instance, as rights to development or rights to self-determination.

Clearly the scope for consistency across the three perspectives depends on the ways in which power is exercised, as well as the ways in which resistance is constructed. Reflecting this, it may be argued that one perspective can and should be privileged over the other two: that the three are founded on incommensurable assumptions about the sources of power under globalisation. Indeed, it may be the case that one source of power – be it institutional, info-cultural or material – plays the main constitutive role in global politics. The task, then, would be to identify the logic of resistance in this context and seek to define the 'correct' model, and defend it against the alternatives.

In practice, though, each model responds to a particular dimension of power under corporate globalisation, and all three forms of contestation may have a role to play in reshaping global politics. Each approach has its built-in limitations, and this could be an argument for exploiting all channels to the full. This assumes that some consistency can be constructed across the differing perspectives. A key factor in challenging corporate globalism may well be the ability to concertise contestation so that the various channels and prospects for transnational democracy become mutually reinforcing rather than mutually excluding. This is still an inadequate response, with faith perhaps (mis)placed in the possibility of a solidarity that is likely to be a relatively weak or qualified form of pluralist acceptance. But it can be speculated that more grounded forms of solidarity will emerge, as movements begin to realise the potential leverage that can be gained from transnational resistance. The logic of contestation certainly seems to point in this direction.

Note

I would like to thank students who participated in the undergraduate course on 'Social Movements and Globalisation' at University of Technology Sydney: many of the ideas outlined here were first developed and clarified through seminar discussions on that course. Comments welcome, to James Goodman UTS, email james.goodman@uts.edu.au

References

Arrighi, G. (1994) *The Long Twentieth Century*, London: Verso.

Arrighi, G., Hopkins, T. and Wallerstein, I. (1989) *Anti-Systemic Movements*, London: Verso.

BAYAN (1996) *Peoples Conference Against Imperialist Globalisation: Strengthen International Solidarity and Advance the Peoples Struggle Against Imperialism*, conference statement, Bagong Alyansang Makabayan, Manila, November.

Buzan, B. (1996) *People, States and Fear*, London: Harvester Wheatsheaf.

Castells, M. (1997) *The Power of Identity*, Oxford: Blackwell.

Chossudovsky, M. (1998) *The Globalisation of Poverty: Impacts of IMF and WB Reforms*, Sydney: Pluto Press.

Cleaver, H. (1999) 'The Chiapas uprising and the future of class struggle in the New World Order', *Common Sense* 15: 5–62.

Cohen, J. (1985) 'Strategy or identity: new theoretical paradigms and contemporary social movements', *Social Research* 52(4): 663–716.

Cohen, M. (1997) *What to do About Globalization*, Vancouver: Canadian Centre for Policy Alternatives.

Community Aid Abroad (1996) *Sweating for Nike*, Report for CAA Nike campaign, Sydney: CAA.

Connell, J., Hirsch, P. and Howitt, R. (eds) (1996) *Resources, Nations and Indigenous Peoples*, Melbourne: Oxford University Press.

Cox, R. (1987) *Production, Power, and World Order: Social Forces in the Making of History*, New York: Colombia University Press.

Dickenson, D. (1997) 'Counting women in: globalisation, democratisation and the women's movement', in A. McGrew (ed.), *The Transformation of Democracy?*, Cambridge: Polity Press.

Diller, J. (1999) 'A social conscience in the global marketplace? Labour dimensions of codes of conduct, social labelling and investor initiatives', *International Labour Review* 138(2): 99–129.

Dodson, M. (1998) 'Comment: Mick Dodson', in S. Pritchard (ed.), *Indigenous Peoples, the United Nations and Human Rights*, Sydney: Zed Books and Federation Press.

Evans, G., Goodman, J. and Lansbury, N. (eds) (2002) *Moving Mountains: Communities Confront Mining and Globalisation*, London: Zed.

Falk, R. (1995) *On Humane Governance: Towards a New Global Politics*, Cambridge: Polity Press.

—— (1999) *Predatory Globalization: A Critique*, Cambridge: Polity Press.

Fine, B. (1999) 'The developmental state is dead – long live social capital?', *Development and Change* 30(1): 1–19.

Fraser, N. (1997) *Justice Interruptus: Critical Reflections on the 'Post Socialist' condition*, London: Routledge.

Gedicks, A. (1993) *The New Resource Wars: Native and Environmental Struggles Against Multinational Corporations*, Boston: South End Press.

Gill, S. (2000) 'Toward a postmodern prince? The battle in Seattle as a moment in the new politics of globalisation', *Millennium* 29(1): 131–40.

Goodman, J. (1997) 'The EU: reconstituting democracy beyond the "nation-state"', in a. McGrew (ed.), *The Transformation of Democracy?*, Cambridge: Polity Press.

—— (2001) 'Targeting Rio Tinto: cross-national social movement unionism, Australia and beyond', in R. Munck (ed.), *Labour and Globalisation: Results and Prospects*, Liverpool: Liverpool University Press.

Goodman, J. and Ranald, P. (2000) *Stopping a Juggernaut: Public Interests versus the Multilateral Agreement on Investment*, Sydney: Pluto Press.

Held, D. (1995) *Democracy and the Global Order*, Cambridge: Polity Press.

Held, D., McGrew, A., Goldblatt, D. and Perraton, J. (1999) *Global Transformations: Politics, Economics, Culture*, Cambridge: Polity Press.

Hettne, B. (1995) *Development Theory and the Three Worlds: Towards an International Political Economy of Development*, London: Longman.

Hoogvelt, A. (1997) *Globalisation and the Postcolonial World: The New Political Economy of Development*, Basingstoke: Macmillan.

Hopkins, T. and Wallerstein, I. (eds) (1996) *The Age of Transition: Trajectory of the World System 1945–2025*, London: Zed Press.

ICFTU (1998) *The WTO in the Next Century: A Trade Union Perspective on the Development of the Multilateral Trade Regime*, Submission for the Second Ministerial Meeting of the World Trade Organisation, May 1998, International Confederation of Free Trade Unions, Geneva.

James, P. (2002) 'Principles of solidarity: beyond a postnational imaginary', in J. Goodman (ed.), *Protest and Globalisation: Prospects for Transnational Solidarity*, Sydney: Pluto Press.

Johnston, J. (2002) 'Consuming global justice: fair trade shopping and the search for alternative development strategies', in J. Goodman (ed.), *Protest and Globalisation: Prospects for Transnational Solidarity*, Sydney: Pluto Press.

Keck, M. and Sikkink, K. (1998) *Activists Beyond Borders*, Ithaca, NY: Cornell University Press.

Klein, N. (2000) *No Logo: Taking Aim at the Brand Bullies*, New York: Picador.

Kreisi, H. (1995) 'The political opportunity structure of new social movements: its impact on their mobilisation', in J. Jenkins and B. Klandermans (eds), *The Politics of Social Protest: Comparative Responses on States and Social Movements*, London: UCL Press.

Linklater, A. (1998) *The Transformation of Political Community*, Cambridge: Polity Press.

Lipschutz R. (1992) 'Reconstructing world politics: the emergence of global civil society', *Millennium* 21(3): 389–420.

Maguashca, B. (1996) 'The transnational indigenous movement in the changing world order', in Y. Sakamoto (ed.) *Global Transformations: Challenges to the State System*, Tokyo: UN University Press.

Markoff, J. (1996) *Waves of Democracy: Social Movements and Political Change*, Los Angeles: Pine Forge Press.

McCarthy, J. (1998) 'The globalisation of social movement theory', in J. Smith *et al.* (eds), *Transnational Social Movements and Global Politics: Solidarity Beyond the State*, Syracuse, NY: Syracuse University Press.

McCarthy, J. and Zald, M. (1995) 'Resource mobilisation and social movements: a partial theory', in J. McCarthy and M. Zald (eds), *Social Movements in Organisational Society*, New Brunswick, NJ: Transaction.

Melucci, A. (1996) *Challenging Codes: Collective Action in the Information Age*, Cambridge: Cambridge University Press.

Moody, R. (1997) *Workers in a Lean World: Unions in the Era of Globalisation*, London: Verso.

Munck, R. and Waterman, P. (1999) *Labour Worldwide in the Era of Globalisation*, London: Macmillan.

Obi, C. (1997) 'Globalisation and resistance: the case of Ogoni versus Shell', *New Political Economy* 2(1): 137–47.

O'Brien, R., Goetz, A., Scholte, J. and Williams, M. (2000) *Contesting Global Governance: Multilateral Economic Institutions and Global Social Movements*, Cambridge: Cambridge University Press.

Petras, J. (1997) 'Imperialism and NGOs in Latin America', *Monthly Review* 49(7): 10–27.

Phillips, R. (2002) 'Confrontation to partnership: corporations and NGOs', in J. Goodman (ed.), *Protest and Globalisation: Prospects for Transnational Solidarity*, Sydney: Pluto Press.

Raghaven, C. (2000) 'After Seattle, world trade system faces an uncertain future', *Review of International Political Economy* 7(3): 495–504.

Reinke, L. (2002) 'Utopia in Chiapas? Questioning disembodied politics', in J. Goodman (ed.), *Protest and Globalisation: Prospects for Transnational Solidarity*, Sydney: Pluto Press.

Rosenau, J. (1980) *The Study of Global Interdependence: Essays on the Transnationalisation of World Affairs*, New York: Nichols Press.

Rosenberg, J. (1994) *The Empire of Civil Society*, London: Verso.

Sakamoto, Y. (1996) 'Democratisation, social movements and world order', in R. Cox *et al.* (eds), *International Political Economy: Understanding Global Disorder*, London: Zed Books.

Sklair, L. (1995) *Sociology of the Global System*, London: Harvester Wheatsheaf.

Smith, J., Chatfield, C. and Pagnucco, R. (1998) *Transnational Social Movements and Global Politics: Solidarity Beyond the State*, Syracuse, NY: Syracuse University Press.

Sousa-Santos, B. (1995) *Towards a New Common Sense: Law, Science and Politics in the Paradigmatic Transition*, New York: Routledge.

Tarrow, S. (1994) *Power in Movement*, Cambridge: Cambridge University Press.

Touraine, A. (1977) *The Voice and the Eye: An Analysis of Social Movements*, Cambridge: Cambridge University Press.

—— (1995) 'Democracy: from a politics of redistribution to a politics of recognition', in L. Maheu (ed.), *Social Movements and Social Classes: The Future of Collective Action*, London: Sage.

van der Pijl, K. (1998) *Transnational Classes and International Relations*, London: Routledge.

Walker, R. (1994) 'Social movements/world politics', *Millennium*, special issue on social movements and world politics, 23(3): 669–700.

Wallerstein, I. (2000) 'Globalisation or the age of transition? A long term view of the trajectory of the world-system', *International Sociology* 15(2): 249–65.

Walzer, M. (ed.) (1995) *Toward a Global Civil Society*, Providence, RI: Berghahn Books.

Waterman, P. (1998) *Globalisation, Social Movements and the New Internationalism*, London: Cassell.

WEDO (1998) *Mapping Progress: Assessing the Implementation of the Beijing Platform for Action*, New York: Womens Environment and Development Organisation.

Zolo, D. (1997) *Cosmopolis: Prospects for World Government*, Cambridge: Polity Press.

12 Relocating the demos?

Peter J. Taylor

> Today, the major dynamics at work in the global economy carry the capacity to undo the particular form of the intersection of sovereignty and territory embedded in the modern state and the modern state system.
>
> (Sassen 1996: 5)

> ...the rise of civil society has toppled entrenched regimes and has changed political geographies in ways that were unthinkable only a decade ago.
>
> (Douglass and Freidmann 1998: 2)

States, as we have known them, are under threat. The above quotations encapsulate two major strands in the argument on the nature of the threat: externally from a newly virulent globalisation, and internally from newly assertive peoples. The political implications of this are, of course, profound, perhaps more so than is often appreciated. Certainly traditional political theories will have little to offer if a stage should be reached where states are no longer the prime political communities. Already this is reflected in a contradiction at the heart of current democratic theory and practice: just as representative democracy has spread to more countries than ever before, its supporters have massive new doubts as to its effectiveness in defending the interests of electorates. This contemporary 'democratic paradox', to use Giddens's (1999: 71–2) phrase, is a prime concern underlying the arguments of much of this volume. Clearly defined and accountable *government* seems to be giving way to a nebulous *governance*: who ever voted for a governance?

The fundamental problem seems to be that there is serious erosion of the idea that franchised peoples are also communities of fate (Held *et al.* 1999: 30–1). The contemporary state has been legitimated as 'nation-state' where the 'nation' is an imagined community, and this state-model claims to provide a designated 'people' with a common past upon which to build a common future. It is this combining of roots with fate that has made democracy a plausible collective enterprise. Taking the future of a people out of its own hands is the basic political threat of globalisation: 'rule by the people' is meaningless if elected leaders are deprived of the 'levers of power'. To avoid this outcome it is necessary that we rethink the 'demos'. There is surprisingly little past literature to draw on for such a task which is why our theme of transnational democracy is so important. Ever since franchise reforms produced universal suffrage in Western countries, concern for democratic change has generally focused upon procedural matters (electoral reform, PR or not PR, and so on) with the demos usually playing the role of a taken-for-granted given (but see Taylor 1996, 1999: 69–72). My purpose in this discussion is to open up the question of demos to further scrutiny under conditions of contemporary globalisation. In the analysis attempted here, it is assumed that an effective and legitimate demos will need to reintegrate community of fate and imagined community.

This concluding chapter is written in the spirit that, at this time of acute social change, questions are more important than answers. Hence the argument is developed through four simple questions starting with basics and ending with practices. First, I open up the question of democracy's building block: who actually constitute a demos? Second, I tackle the common idea of 'multiple demos-es' at different scales: can people be part of several different demos(es) simultaneously? Third, I search out alternative spaces for the demos: what are the options for creating new demos-es? Fourth, I consider the question of how new building blocks for democracy might be created: who are the agents who might relocate the demos? All four questions bring up very large issues and I only scratch at the surface in my attempts at answers. To bring this ambitious agenda to a manageable order, I focus on one alternative demos, the city. Seen as combining a territorial *space of places* with a network *space of flows*, cities are plausible candidates in a possible transnational democratic trajectory. As Anderson (in this volume) argues, conventional territorial democracy is put in question by globalisation, and, despite being problematic, territoriality in various forms is likely to be an important element of democracy for the foreseeable future.

Who are the demos?

This is the simplest yet most fundamental question of all. In the social world of embedded statism, the answer is equally simple: the citizens of a democratic state are its demos. This is a product of the territorial congruence at the heart of the modern state. It is assumed that national society, national politics and the national economy coincide precisely in a particular, specific space, the state's sovereign territory. Thus democracy is bounded like the society it reflects, the politics it controls and the economy it directs. The imagined community of the nation is also the community of fate in politics and economics. In this way territory is the absolute category through which democracy operates in an ideal world of representation and policy making.[1]

Of course, operationalising absolutisms always creates practical difficulties (Taylor 1996). In the case of the modern state, the spatial congruence was rarely achieved so that the demos has always had the potential to be problematic. Certainly democracy has been notoriously found wanting in dealing with multi-ethnic conflicts in states where elections can be reduced to little more than ethnic head counts.[2] As Parekh clearly shows, where there are different 'national communities' within the bounds of one state, the demos is called into question even before transnational (in the sense of trans-state) issues are raised (see Parekh in this volume). In such states there appears to be more than one demos and important issues arise around 'minority rights'; while in national conflicts where borders are disputed, cross-border democratisation provides one avenue towards a resolution (see Anderson and Hamilton in this volume). With contemporary globalisation, this endemic failure of imagined communities has now been joined by doubts about whether they can still be communities of fate. It is the latter which particuarly threatens the many Western states which have a largely unitary demos, the states which produced the successful liberal democratic regimes that dominated the world economy and its politics for most of the twentieth century. It was in these countries that the democratic-representative ideal came closest to realisation: voters belonged to the same imagined community which they equated with their community of fate. It is this equation which is now being eroded.

If boundaries count for less and less in the world economy (or at the very least are becoming selectively more porous; see O'Dowd in this volume), whither bounded democracy? And where is the demos? The latter only makes sense to the degree that the members understand that collectively they can have a voice in the things that matter to them. As 'extra-territorial' powers – economic, political and cultural – grow, democracy may still reflect its territorial society but it loses its levers of political control and economic direction. In such circumstances it is hard to predict anything other than a waning of the traditional demos: globalisation will be associated with less popular involvement in electoral politics as currently organised. Assuming the liberal democratic ideals of formal (transparent) popular inputs into politics are deemed important, it might be time to begin thinking about how to reinvent the demos.

Can there be multiple demos-es?

Apart from the various resurgent nationalists, there seems to be agreement that fundamental political reform needs to produce a more flexible organisation; territorial absolutism is out. Typically, the multiple identities of individuals are emphasised leading to different 'layers' of representation being proposed. This is a core feature of Held's (1995) influential 'cosmopolitan democracy' and features prominently in several of the chapters of this volume. The celebrated case is the European Union (starting with Bull 1977: 255–6; see also Giddens 1999: 79–80,and the Painter and Newman chapters in this volume) where the 'state level' competes with the 'European level' for power and influence, and with the recent promotion of the 'regional-level' suggesting a future triple pattern of 'governance'. This is supposed to reflect the individual's multiple identities, which in territorial terms might for instance be 'Bavarian and German and European'. But what of the demos? Such a relatively complex layered democracy attempts to directly address issues of identity by enabling multiple imagined communities to be formed while assuming the largest scale to be the new community of fate – beyond the 'nation-state' – in a globalising world.

Does this new relation of communities of the imagination within a larger community of fate make for a viable demos or demos-es? In the traditional liberal democratic model, functional political parties (largely class-based as opposed to territorial-cultural; see Rokkan (1970)) had the key role of periodically accepting the position of 'loyal opposition', opposers of the government but supporters of the state. In other words, the losing parties at an election, and their supporters, remained firmly part of the demos; hence the political stability of liberal democratic regimes. But in a multi-layered politics it is unclear how such stability could be replicated. By splintering the imagined community through multiple identities, is the depth of allegiance – the essence of the concept – lost? With solid community attachments replaced by shallower, multiple attachments, is this a cacophony politics of lowest common denominators? In short, does the effective operation of a demos assume a dominant scale or focus of allegiance? The historical evidence suggests this to be the case.

Currently, this depth (shallowness?) of imagination is broadly measured by electoral turnout; for instance, in the UK it is low both for European and local elections, but relatively high for general (i.e. national) elections. Will genuinely equal multi-level elections lead to low turnouts across the board? On the other hand, multiple elections provide opportunities for losers at one level to compensate at another as in all federal systems. Such smaller-scale victories may satisfy single-issue supporters with real depth to their politics and keep them in the demos: abortion illegal here, available there; cars controlled here, freedom to drive there; and so on. But the downside is a political world of multiple oppositions at many different levels (see also Agnew in this volume). This is a recipe for political immobility or incoherence. To be reproduced as an effective and legitimate politics, new political institutions will need to be invented with a cross-issue orientation (Falk 2000: 379). This was the integrative role of the political party in liberal democracy – but it was difficult enough with just a single demos and it is not clear that an equivalent institution is possible for a seriously multi-level democratic politics. The real winners in this political confusion will be political elites who, with the necessary economic input (advertising, media ownership, etc.), will be able to chose the appropriate demos to obtain the right decisions on matters of critical concern to them and their backers.

But is this the only alternative to the 'nation-state'? Notice that the multi-layered model remains very territorialist in nature. The single sovereign territory may be eclipsed but only by other (larger and/or smaller) territories, and the thinking still equates politics only with territories. In the terms of Castell's (1996) 'network society', politics remains condemned to a *space of places* leaving the *space of flows* to other activities. But in a globalising world it might well prove impossible to equate imagined community with community of fate simply through a territorial (re)organisation of politics. Can the demos be non-territorial?

What are the alternative spaces for the demos?

As will have been adjudged, I am sceptical of the possibility of a 'transnational democracy' where political reforms remain territory-based or are seen only in terms of different places: the necessary reintegration of imagination and fate, of past and future, in any new territorial community-building is highly problematic. But this does not mean that politics can simply be flipped over to a network model: I am equally sceptical of the possibilities of creating a simple 'network demos'. Certainly there is the technological potential for an electronic democracy but this individualises political activity. This may work for single-issue politics, but it is not at all clear how a sense of community could be developed, no matter how sophisticated virtual alternatives to real face-to-face communication may become. Such an 'on-line democracy' in a virtual space would have difficulties in building allegiances and defining communities of fate. This is democracy without demos, better termed 'ego-ocracy'.

Transnational democracy may take many different forms based upon a variety of different building blocks. As well as 'cross-border regions' which retain a territorial definition (O'Dowd in this volume), there are two non-territorial institutions which have become prominent in discussions of 'global governance': non-governmental organisations (NGOs) and social movements (see the chapters by Hirsch and Goodman). However, while interesting for the promotion of participation in political decision making, and contesting the 'democratic deficit' of global institutions like the World Trade Organisation (see McGrew in this volume), both NGOs and social movements have 'democratic deficits' themselves (Princen and Finger 1994: 12). In losing territorial constraints, these entities seem often to have lost any community attachment: who do they represent beyond their own network of members? At least bounded democracy has provided representation for, and allowed participation by, all within its territory.

One alternative approach is to think in terms of both *places* and *flows* simultaneously. The argument is straightforward: the *space of places* is necessary for building an imagined community while the *space of flows* is necessary for any meaningful depiction of a community of fate. Cities (or city-regions) together with their networks are the obvious geographical candidates that fit both needs. On the one hand, cities (and their immediate surroundings) are places, or territories, yet, on the other hand, they are territories of a particular type defined by their position as nodes within urban networks. Cities are places with long histories of being distinctive communities; indeed, most cities are older than the states which govern them, yet under contemporary conditions of globalisation, world cities have created the basic spatial architecture through which key global activities are organised. In short, they define an alternative world meta-geography – in the sense of the basic spatial structures and networks used to order the world (Lewis and Wigen 1997: ix) – an alternative to the familiar world political map mosaic (Beaverstock *et al.* 2000a). There are of course a myriad of urban networks, linking different segments of the urban hierarchy, depending on which urban functions and processes are considered. But the key point is that cities as the crossroads of society are inherently anti-state-territorialism (Taylor 2000b).[3] Contemporary globalisation is in the process of further 'unbounding' them, revealing the full network potential of cities beyond the 'nation-state'.

Replacing 'homeland' by 'hometown' is particularly relevant today when for the first time in human history urban dwellers are a majority of humanity. In a fluid world of increasing migration, cities are now the goals of migrants, for the days of mass agricultural settlement are long gone. Hence the peasant/ landscape core of nation as imagined community is being eroded by the ever-increasing importance of ever-growing cosmopolitan city communities. Of course, ideas of citizenship and democracy originated in cities and the question being asked is whether they can be reconstituted there (Douglas and Friedmann 1998).[4] Cities already constitute 'communities', so that constructing them as critical political units of imagination is feasible, but what of their possible role as communities of fate? This can take the form of new city leagues where republicans eschew their modern penchant for mimicking territorial kingdoms and return to city networks. For instance, Manchester and Lyons may come to see that they have more in common with each other than they have with their respective capital cities, London and Paris. For both of these 'second' cities, the experience of being in the shadow of a major global city might provide a basis for identifying a community of fate with other cities similarly afflicted.

Such leagues are currently rare in our boundary-obsessed world, but there is one example that is instructive because it contrasts directly with nation-state organisation. In the north-west Mediterranean there are two rival cross-border political alliances: a 'Euroregion' combining Catalonia, Languedoc-Roussillion and Midi-Pyrenees, and the 'C6 network' consisting of Barcelona, Montpellier, Palma de Mallorca, Toulouse, Valencia and Zaragoza (Morata 1997). Modest in scale, nevertheless these two opposing organisations represent different worlds – territorial and network – with different potentials for transnational democracy under conditions of increasing globalisation.

Who will be the agents for relocating the demos?

We cannot know what form(s) transnational democracy will take in the future. We can speculate on which contemporary trends might lead to a particular cross-border, non-territorial or network organisation of democracy. Put crudely: who will do the deed, who are the putative agents for creating transnational democratic forms? The story of producing national democratic forms in the West is the story of a reluctant bourgeoisie being forced to concede more and more radical demands until universal suffrage was achieved. In the process the original (pre-democratic) cadre parties coached the new radical mobilising parties into being 'good party citizens' on the promise that their turn in government would come (Taylor 1999: 82–4). The resulting integral states, each with its own demos, are what globalisation is challenging. It seems highly unlikely in the future that this particular configuration of political forces can be replicated outside state confines to produce a transnational democracy.

The changing nature of what were the cadres of the system is a major obstacle to such replication. Traditionally located between capital and labour (see van der Pijl in this volume), these 'brain workers', notably in the 'professions', took leadership roles in pressing for political reform. In the information age, however, we have to come to terms with the fact that the leading new knowledge workers are being transmuted into something that looks very much like 'knowledge capitalists'. For instance, large share options have become the norm for key workers in some sectors (such as in finance), whereas in other sectors practitioners are 'partners' in what are in reality multinational firms (such as in global law). Always in an ambiguous position as 'professionals', they are managed through codes of service to clients in their respective sectors, while at the same time operating as profit-making firms and partnerships in the marketplace. The key point is that globalisation's network society is changing the balance between service and profit, to the detriment of the former. In the world economy today, advanced producer services are at the cutting edge of innovation in the production of new instruments of service (Sassen 1991). As is typical of such innovations, the result is to create new high profit margins. This has induced a change in location strategies. Instead of their initial reactive behaviour of following clients to service them as they globalise, producer-service firms now have their own global strategies for selling their products in a world service market.[5] Products, in their design and implementation, are embodied in the knowledge of these professionals who are among the most successful group of 'capitalists' in the world today. They are the prime creators of the world city network which is their global workplace (Taylor 2000b).

These 'ex-cadres', now 'knowledge capitalists', are politically interesting for two reasons. First, their global interests will clash with national interests and when this happens they can be mobilised against the state. Their interests coincide with London, not the UK, with New York and not the USA, and so on. Second, because they are located in all the major cities they cannot be mobilised in practices of inter-city competition. They are emphatically not local capitalists, they are 'network capitalists'; it is in their interests to see London *and* Frankfurt prosper. Competition between cities will be important to them – it is something they can take advantage of to enhance profits – but they will have no inherent reason to take sides. Service city 'capitalists' should be major supporters of co-operation between cities – promoters, perhaps, of city leagues.

Of course, like the national bourgeoisies of the past, this new network bourgeoisie will have no direct interest in promoting democratic politics. It will constitute a global plutocracy, directly reflected in world cities through their high levels of economic polarisation. It is an understatement to say that this is not good raw material for creating a new demos.[6] But the twenty-first-century city network is not necessarily worse than the nineteenth-century 'nation-state' as a demos nursery. The latter requires Falk's (2000) 'globalization from below' to create a new progressive politics. This will have to involve a range of processes, including NGOs and social movements as mentioned previously. What cities provide is an alternative community-grounding for such a politics, for instance in the role of strong city mayors mediating between the global and the local. To be effective the latter has to be radicalised, not just in one city, but as part of a new global wave of radicalisation. Given the current global hegemony of neo-liberal market ideology this does not seem likely in the near future. But alliances between local city political parties and networked NGOs and social movements can change things around – historically radicalism has certainly been very cyclical in nature (Silver 1995). And we are always being told how globalisation speeds things up! Radicalism is facing a false dusk (as opposed to numerous past 'false dawns'). When this becomes self-evident it will be time to reassess the investment of radical political effort which goes into territorial states, time to release some of this energy for experimenting with building new civic demos-es with network potentials.

Notes

1   This is neatly encapsulated in a diagram by Held (1995: 224) where 'citizen-voters' are 'the people in a bounded territory' serviced by 'decision-makers'.
2   For instance, in the case of Bosnia the Serbs made a sensible decision in 1992 to boycott the referendum on setting up an independent state: as a minority in Bosnia, voting would have only confirmed their democratic impotence.
3   Of course, cities as places have traditionally been 'bounded' – by pre-modern walls and more recent administrative boundaries – but their *raison d'être* is always nodal as a centre for flows.
4   Although Held (1995) builds his concept of cosmopolitan democracy on the existence of states he does leave room for cities (1995: 234), though not as networks.
5   The particular case of this process operating in global law is described in Beaverstock *et al.* (2000b).
6   It is for this reason that cities have featured in recent dystopias: see, in particular, Petrella (1995). Giddens (1998: 129) interprets 'a world of a thousand city-states' as a recipe for chaos.

References

Beaverstock, J.V., Smith, R.G. and Taylor, P. J. (1999) 'A roster of world cities', *Cities* 16: 445–58.

—— (2000a) 'World city network: a new metageography?', *Annals, Association of American Geographers* 90: 123–34.

—— (2000b) 'Geographies of globalization: United States law firms in world cities', *Urban Geography* 21: 95–120.

Bull, H. (1977) *The Anarchical Society*, London: Macmillan.

Castells, M. (1996) *The Rise of the Network Society*, Oxford: Blackwell.

Douglas, M. and Friedmann, J. (eds) (1998) *Cities for Citizens*, New York: Wiley.

Falk, R. (2000) 'The quest for humane governance in an era of globalization', in D. Kalb, M. van der Land, R. Staring, B. van Steenbergen and N. Wilterdink (eds), *The Ends of Globalization*, Lanham, MD: Rowman and Littlefield, 369–82.

Giddens, A. (1998) *The Third Way*, Cambridge: Polity Press.

—— (1999) *Runaway World*, Cambridge: Polity Press.

Held, D. (1995) *Democracy and the Global Order*, Cambridge: Polity Press.

Held, D., McGrew, A., Goldblatt, D. and Perraton, J. (1999) *Global Transformations*, Cambridge: Polity Press.

Lewis, M.W. and Wigen, K.E. (1997) *The Myth of Continents*, Berkeley, CA: University of California Press.

Morata, F. (1997) 'The Euro-region and the C-6 network: the new politics of sub-national co-operation in the western Mediterranean area', in M. Keating and J. Loughlin (eds), *The Political Economy of Regionalism*, London: Frank Cass, 292–305.

Petrella, R. (1995) 'A global agora versus gated city-regions', *New Perspectives Quarterly* Winter: 21–22.

Princen, T. and Finger, M. (1994) *Environmental NGOs in World Politics*, London: Routledge.

Rokkan, S. (1970) *Citizens, Elections, Parties*, New York: McKay.

Sassen, S. (1991) *The Global City*, Princeton, NJ: Princeton University Press.

—— (1996) *Losing Control?*, New York: Columbia University Press.

Silver, B.J. (1995) 'World-scale patterns of labor-capital conflict', *Review* (Fernand Braudel Center) 18: 155–92.

Taylor, P.J. (1996) 'Territorial absolutism and its evasions', *Geography Research Forum* 16: 1–12.

—— (1999) *Modernities: A Geohistorical Interpretation*, Cambridge: Polity Press.

—— (2000a) 'Is there a Europe of cities? World cities and the limitations of geographical scale analyses', in R. McMaster and R. Shepherd (eds), *Scale and Geographic Inquiry* (in press).

—— (2000b) 'Specification of the world city network', *Geographical Analysis* 33:181–94.

Taylor, P.J. and Hoyler, M. (2000) 'The spatial order of European cities under conditions of contemporary globalisation', *Tijdschrift voor Economische en Sociale Geografie* 91: 176–89.

Index